R

6ω

DICTIONARY
OF
ANCIENT
HISTORY

DICTIONARY
OF
ANCIENT
HISTORY

by

P. G. WOODCOCK

PHILOSOPHICAL LIBRARY
New York

PREFACE

The purpose of this work is to make available, in one concise
and comprehensive volume, information on most of the important people and events of classical antiquity. In order to reflect
as complete a picture as possible of those cultures which are our
special heritage, emphasis has been placed upon Greek and
Roman history. However, many entries pertaining to other early
civilizations are included, particularly from the Judaic, Egyptian
and Persian cultures.

The period covered is, roughly, from the beginning of recorded
history in the Mediterranean world, to the fall of the Roman
Empire, with the greater number of references applying to the
Greek and Roman civilizations at the peak of their flowering.
This means, of course, the exclusion of most Christian writers,
except the very earliest church figures.

Limitations of space naturally necessitated the omission of
some terms that might otherwise have been included. Generally
speaking, the items included are those which occur most frequently in classical writings. In the case of less important data,
the author has exercised personal judgment and discrimination
in choosing or rejecting a given entry.

The categories of knowledge covered may be divided, for purposes of classification, into those of biography, history, geography, mythology, literature and the arts, philosophy and
science, and miscellaneous data (such as law, politics, dress,
manners, etc.) which can be lumped under the general heading
of antiquities.

Under biography may be found the names of those who were
important in many fields of human endeavor—military, political,
philosophic, artistic, and so on. The historical entries cover the

most significant political events of Greek and Roman history. In many cases, of course, entries overlap, and important historical information will often be found under place names and bibliographical sketches. The geographical entries include the names of those towns, cities, provinces, states, countries and other places that occur most frequently in classical writings. These are usually listed under the name they bore in antiquity. The length of an entry is less likely to correspond to the size of the place than it is to the historical importance of the events which occurred there.

Mythological entries include those personages whose names appear in Greek and Roman—and to a somewhat lesser extent, in Jewish and Egyptian—stories. The great writers of antiquity are dealt with as fully as space permits. The same may be said of the outstanding philosophers, scientists and religious leaders. Coverage of the affairs of everyday life—such as dress, food, manners and customs, etc.—had to be sacrificed to more important historical events; but much information on these matters may be found under other headings.

The information in this book has been gleaned from many sources, and has been carefully checked. But, since to err is only human, indulgence is begged for any mistakes which have been allowed to creep in, unnoticed by author or publisher.

P. G. W.

DICTIONARY
OF
ANCIENT
HISTORY

A

AAHHOTEP, name of two Egyptian queens. The coffin of Aahhotep I, mother of Aahmes I (c. 1580 B.C.), was found at Thebes in 1859 by A. Mariette, containing her mummy, with a collection of fine jewelry.

AAHMES, name of two Egyptian kings called Amasis by the Greeks. Aahmes I (c. 1580 B.C.) expelled the Hyksos from Memphis, and founded the XVIIIth dynasty. Aahmes II (died 526 B.C.), revolted against the Pharaoh-hophra and seized the throne. He opened Naucratis to Greek traders.

ABACUS, (a) an instrument employed by the ancients for arithmetical calculations, consisting of a frame traversed by stiff wires, on which beads or counters were strung so as to move easily. The beads on the first right hand row were units, those on the next tens, and so on. Until recently the Chinese used a similar instrument, known as a Swan-Pan, for teaching the rudiments of arithmetic in elementary schools.
(b) In architecture, a level tablet on the capital of a column supporting the entablature.

ABAE, town in ancient Greece in the E. of Phocis, famous for the oracle and temple of Apollo. The temple was plundered and burnt by the Persians in 480 B.C. and later by the Boeotians in 346 B.C., Hadrian restoring it on a smaller scale. Its remains near Exarkho may still be traced.

ABANO, town of N. Italy, S. W. of Padua having thermal springs. Known to the early Romans as *Aponi Fons*, also Aquae Patavinae.

ABANTES, the early people of Euboea who partly colonized a number of Ionic cities of Asia Minor. Thracian in origin, they settled on Phocis, founding Abae, afterwards crossing to Euboea.

ABDERA, (a) maritime town of Thrace in *Ancient Geography,*

E. of the estuary of the Nestus, supposedly founded by Hercules but actually, according to Herodotus, first colonized by Timesias of Clazomenae, whom later the Thracians expelled. It was recolonized in 541 B.C. by the people of Seos, becoming of some importance. It was reduced by Thrasybulus the Athenian in 408 B.C., and its prosperity was impaired by its war with Triballi in 376 B.C., after which little is heard of it. Its inhabitants were remarkable for lack of wit and judgment, but a number of eminent persons were born there, including Protagoras, Democritus, Anaxarchus, Hecataeus, and Nicaenetus.

(b) town in Hispania Boetica founded by the Carthaginians, situated between Malaca and Prom. Charidemi, on the S. coast.

ABERICUS, *see* EPITAPH of

ABILA, city of ancient Syria, capital of the tetrarchy of Abilene: its site is indicated by inscriptions, and ruins on the banks of the Barada between Baalbek and Damascus.

ABORIGINES, originally the proper name of a people of ancient Latium who appear to have been an Oscan or Opican tribe, descending from the Apennines into Latium, uniting with some Pelasgic tribe to form the Latins. The stories of Aeneas's landing in Italy represent the Aborigines as at first opposing, and later joining with, the Trojans, and state that the united peoples became the Latins, (from Latinus, their king). These traditions indicate that the Latins were a mixed race, which is proved by their language, in which are many words connected with Greek, but many more of a different origin, the non-Greek words being mostly related to Optican dialects. Today the word aborigines has an extended signification, indicating inhabitants found in a country at its discovery.

ABYDOS, (a) In *Ancient Geography*, a city of Mysia, in Asia Minor, on the Hellespont, famed for the story of Hero and Leander. Probably originally a Thracian town it became colonized by Milesians. Across the Hellespont stood Sestos; here it was that Xerxes crossed the strait on his famous bridge of boats when invading Greece. Abydos offered vigorous resistance when besieged by Philip II of Macedon.

(b) In *Ancient Geography*, a town of Upper Egypt, to the W. of the Nile, between Ptolemais and Dispolis Parva, famous for the palace of Memnon, and the temple of Osiris.

ACADEMY, a northern suburb of Athens, part of the Ceramicus, a mile beyond the Dypilum gate, said to have belonged to the hero Academus. Hipparchus enclosed it with a wall, and Cimon, son of Miltiades, added to its splendor and at his death bequeathed it to the citizens for a pleasure-ground. Plato resorted to the Academy, where he taught for nearly fifty years until his death in 348 B.C., his school receiving the name of The Academics in contradistinction to the Peripatetics. Later Cicero gave the same name to his country-residence near Puteoli, where he composed his famous dialogue, *The Academic Questions*.

ACAMAS, (a) one of the bravest of the Trojans, son of Antenor and Theano. (b) A leader of the Thracians in the Trojan War. (c) Son of Theseus and Phaedra, who went to Troy with Diomedes to recapture Helen.

ACARNANIA, province of ancient Greece, bounded on the N. by the Ambracian gulf, on the N.E. by Amphilochia, on the W. and S.W. by the Ionian Sea, and on the E. by Aetolia. It consisted of broken country with many lakes and some rich tracts of pasture having its hills capped with thick woods. The Acarnanians, though allowed to enter the Pan-Hellenic games as Greeks, were more akin to their barbarian neighbors of Epirus. Before the time of the Peloponnesian war they are mentioned only as a race of rude shepherds. They were distinguished from their Aetolian neighbors by their fidelity, and were excellent soldiers famed for their use of the sling. Acarnania produced a renowned breed of horses.

ACCIUS or ATTIUS, LUCIUS, Latin tragic poet, son of a freedman, born in Rome. He became known by a dramatic piece before the death of Pacuvius, which he staged the same year as one put on by Pacuvius. He wrote from celebrated Greek stories but composed at least one wholly Roman piece called *Brutus* dealing with the expulsion of the Tarquins. Only fragments of his works are extant. In addition to dramatic writings he left other productions, notably his *Annals,* mentioned by Macrobius, Priscian, Festus, and Nonius Marcellus. He was criticized for harshness of style but esteemed as a great poet. Cicero speaks of having conversed with him in his youth.

ACERRA, (a) *in Antiquity,* a container for incense and perfumes to be burned on the altars of the gods and before the dead. The name was also applied to a Roman altar erected near the bed of a newly deceased person, upon which incense was offered daily until burial. The Chinese have a similar custom. (b) Town in Italy N.E. of Naples: the ancient Acerrae, whose inhabitants were allowed the privileges of Roman citizenship as early as 332 B.C. It was plundered and burnt by Hannibal in the second Punic war.

ACHAEANS and **ACHAEAN LEAGUE,** the early inhabitants of Achaia were known as Achaeans, the name also being given to tribes occupying E. Peloponnesus, and later, the people of Achaia Propria took the name. The republic though small was noted for heroic virtues. The government was democratic and liberty was maintained until the time of Philip and Alexander, when they became subjected to the Macedonians and tyrants. The Achaean commonwealth contained 12 towns in Peloponnesus. About 280 B.C. the republic recovered its old institutions and cohesion, and the foundation was laid for the famous Achaean League, having for its object substantial political union. Dating from 280 B.C. its importance was due to its connection with Aratus of Sicyon, some 30 years later, being strengthened by the ability of Philopoemen. So it became the greatest of the states of Greece in the closing days of its national independence. The people of Petrae and Dyme were the first proclaimers of ancient liberty, tyrants were banished and towns again unified. Public councils were held and their transactions recorded. The council had two presidents nominated alternately by two towns; later they elected only one president. Adjoining towns admiring the League were incorporated and allowed full privileges. The League was the perfect example in antiquity of federal government, and allowing for differences of time and place, its resemblance to the U.S.A.

government is very remarkable.

ACHAIA, in *Ancient Geography,* differently applied at different periods. First applied to a small district in S. Thessaly, the first settlement of the Achaeans. The name was later applied to a narrow tract in the N. of the Peloponnesus, stretching 65 miles along the Gulf of Corinth; its capital was Patrae. Still later the name was applied to the states that joined the Achaean League. When the Romans had subdued Greece, the name was given to the most southerly of the provinces into which they divided the country.

ACHATES, in *Roman Legend,* the friend and faithful companion of Aeneas the Trojan hero: he is always distinguished by the epithet *fidus* (faithful), and his name has become proverbial.

ACHELOUS, the longest river of Greece (130 miles) rising in Mt. Pindus, and dividing Aetolia from Acarnania before emptying into the Ionian Sea. The river brings quantities of fine mud down from the mountains, depositing it upon its banks and at its mouth, forming a number of small islands there. It was formerly known as Throas from its impetuosity at its source; Homer named it the "King of Rivers." The epithet *Acheloius* is used for *aqueus* (Virgil), the ancients calling all water Achelous, according to Ephorus.

ACHILLES, one of the most celebrated characters of the mythic age of Greece—the hero of the Iliad. He is of the intermediate period between truth and fiction. In Homer's account of his life there is scarcely anything impossible, but beyond his account everything is fabulous. According to legend Achilles was son of Peleus and Thetis, and third in descent from Zeus. As king of the Myrmidons he fought at Troy. By his mother he was made invulnerable, the most popular version being that she did this by dipping him in the river Styx. In so doing she held him by the heel; this being untouched by the water remained vulnerable, hence originated the proverbial phrase about the heel of Achilles. After he reached Troy he performed redoubtable deeds against his foes, carrying confusion into the Trojan ranks. His death is variously described, but Homer tells how his remains were buried on the shores of the Hellespont.

ACINACES, an ancient Persian sword worn on the *right* side. Among the nobility it was frequently made of gold, being worn as a mark of distinction. According to Herodotus this sword was an object of worship with the Sythians and others.

ACIS, in *Ancient Mythology,* son of Faunus and the nymph Smaethis, was a beautiful shepherd of Sicily. He was beloved of Galatea which angered Polyphemus so much that he crushed his rival with a rock. Acis's blood flowing from beneath the rock was metamorphosed into the river bearing his name. This river more modernly known as *Fiume di Jaci,* or *Aque Grandi* rises under the lava bed on the E. base of Etna.

ACQUI, *Aquae Statiellae* of the Romans; a town of N. Italy, 18 miles S.S.W. of Alessandria, on the left bank of the Bormida; it is of great antiquity, well-known for its hot sulphur baths.

ACRE, AKKA, or ST. JEAN D'ACRE, in ancient times this town was a celebrated seaport and city of Syria; probably Accho of the Bible. It was known among the ancients as *Ace,* but it is only from the time that Ptolemy Soter, king of Egypt, was in possession of it that history gives any real account of it, under the name which he gave it, *viz.,* Ptolemais. When the Roman Empire began to extend over Asia, Ptolemais came into Roman possession. Strabo mentions it as a city of great importance and grandeur.

ACROCERAUNIA, in *Ancient Geography,* a headland in the N.W. of Epirus, terminating the Montes Ceraunii range; is supposed to have derived its name from being frequently struck by lightning.

ACROLITH, statues of a transitional period of plastic art, the trunks of the figures were of wood, and the head, hands, and feet of marble. The wood was concealed by gilding or drapery. Pausanias frequently mentions acrolith; the best known specimen is the Minerva Areia of the Plataeans.

ACROPOLIS, the upper town, or chief place of a city; a citadel: such buildings were common in Greek cities and are found elsewhere, such as the Capitol at Rome and the Antonia of Jerusalem. The most famous was at Athens; it was enclosed by walls, having nine gates, the principal one of Pentelican marble, in Doric style, and known as Propylaea.

ACTA DIURNA, ('proceedings of the day'), the title of a gazette, drawn up and published daily in Rome both under the empire and republic, with abstracts of proceedings of public assemblies, the law courts, the punishment of offenders, with an account of public works in progress and births, deaths, marriages and divorces.

ACTA SENATUS, minutes and decisions of the Roman Senate, also known as *Commentarii Senatus*. Before the days of Julius Caesar minutes were sometimes kept and published unofficially but under him they were ordered to be kept and published officially: minutes were also kept under Augustus but publication was forbidden. A prominent Senator was usually responsible for the *Acta*.

ACTIAN GAMES, in *Roman Antiquity*, solemn games instituted by Augustus in memory of his victory over Antony at Actium.

ACTIUM, in *Ancient Geography*, headland in the N. of Acarnania, at the mouth of the Sinus Ambracius, opposite Nicopolis. An ancient temple of Apollo was built on this promontory which was enlarged by Augustus. The place is famous on account of Augustus' victory over Antony, 31 B.C. A small town on the headland was also called Actium.

ADDA, the ancient *Addua*, a river of N. Italy, flowing into Lake Como.

ADDUA, Roman name for a river of Lombardy, rising in the Rhaetian Alps, and passing through the Valteline, it enters the Lake of Como, from the S.E. branch of which it issues below Lecco; crossing the plain of Lombardy it falls into the Po 8 miles above Cremona. Before the fall of Venice it divided the territory of that republic and the Duchy of Milan. It is now known as the *Adda*.

ADHERBAL, *see* JUGURTHA

ADMON, one of the most celebrated engravers of gems of Greece. No date is known in connection with him, but the many excellent works of his that are known, point to the best period of art.

ADRASTUS, in *Legendary History,* King of Argos and Sicyon: with six other chiefs he organized the expedition of the Seven against Thebes to restore the fugitives Tydeus and Polynices, in which all the leaders perished except himself. Ten years later he led the sons of the fallen leaders, known as Epigoni, or descendants, in a second expedition in which Thebes was destroyed.

ADRIAN, PUBLIUS AELIUS, Roman Emperor; *see* under Hadrian.

ADRIANUS, *see* HADRIANUS

ADRIATIC SEA, the *Adriaticum Mare* of the ancients; an arm of the Mediterranean extending N.W. between Italy and Yugoslavia. Its length is 470 miles, mean breadth 110 miles, and area (including islands) 52,000 sq. miles. The W. shore is comparatively low, having few inlets: the E. is steep and rocky and fringed with islands. The Dalmatian and Albanian coasts are picturesque, while near Cattaro high mountains dip down to the sea. Its chief ports are Venice, Ancona, Bari, and Brindisi on the W., and on the E., Trieste, Pola, Fiume, Ragsura, Cattaro, Durazzo, and Avlona.

ADULTERY, (from Latin *adulterium*) is sexual intercourse of a married person with another than the offender's husband or wife. With the Greeks, and in the earlier period of Roman Law, it was not adultery unless a married woman was the offender. *Lex Julia de adulteriis* was the basis of later Roman Law regarding adultery, which was passed by Augustus in 17 B.C.

ADYTUM, the most sacred part of ancient temples, officiating priests only being allowed to enter. The Most Holy Place of the Jewish Temple approximated the pagan adytum, none but the high-priest entering it, and that only once a year.

AEACUS, in *Greek Mythology,* son of Jupiter by Aegina, and King of the island named after her. He was father of Telamon and Peleus; was renowned for integrity and justice, and after death, with Minos and Rhadamanthus, was made one of the judges of the underworld by Pluto.

AEDILE, in *Roman Antiquity,* a magistrate whose chief responsibility was the care of public buildings, bridges, aqueducts etc. Aediles also supervised the police, public games and archives. First instituted 494 B.C. they were two in number, both plebeians; in 336 B.C. two more were added, named "curules" because they sat in a curule chair. In 45 B.C. Caesar appointed a new kind, called *aediles cereales,* to manage the corn supply. These, like the curules were patricians. Mention is also made of *aedilis alimentarius* who seem to have provided the food for those maintained at the public charge. Also, *aedilis castrorum,* aediles of the camp, is found in one ancient inscription.

AEDUI, a Celtic tribe, settled between the Loire and the Saone; the first Gallic people to join the Romans. Caesar favored them, and defended them from external foes. Their capital was Bibracte, later Augustodunum (Autun).

AEETES, in *Greek Legend,* King of Colchis in Asia Minor, possessor of the Golden Fleece. His daughter Medea assisted Jason and his Argonauts in their quest for it.

AEGADES, or AEGATES, group of three islands off the west coast of Sicily, betwen Trapani and Marsala, called Maretimo, Levanzo, and Favignana; the scene of the great naval victory by the Romans over the Carthaginians in 241 B.C., which brought the first Punic war to a close.

AEGEAN CIVILIZATION, name of pre-Hellenic civilization, known also as Minoan and Mycenaean, its chief cities being Troy in Asia Minor, Mycenae and Tiryrns in Greece, and Cnossus and Phaestus in Crete. Excavations have shown that such a civilization existed in 1500 B.C. About 3000 B.C. Crete emerged from the stone to the bronze age and was peopled by those whose civilization, anterior to those of Greece and Mycenae, reached its height about 2000 B.C. —The term Minoan, though less comprehensive than Aegean or Mediterranean suggests Crete under a great ruler of the Minoan dynasty as the center of this civilization. Its successive phases have been divided into Early, Middle, and Late Minoan, the periods covered dating from 3000 to 1100 B.C. The first palaces of Cnossus and Phaestus were built about 2000 B.C. being destroyed about 1750 B.C. They were rebuilt and modified. 15-1400 B.C. may be termed the golden age of Crete, but towards the end of the period the island was invaded and the palace destroyed. The Minoan civilization declined in the 14th cent. B.C. and collapsed in the 11th B.C.

AEGEAN SEA or GREEK ARCHIPELAGO, a part of the Mediterranean lying between Greece and Asia Minor, in length from N. to S. 400 miles, with a greatest breadth of 170 miles. Navigation is difficult: fish and sponges abound. The most important islands are Euboea, Mitylene, Thasos, Samothrace, Imbros, Lemnos, Chios, Cos, Samos and the Sporades and Cyclades. Various derivations of the name Aegean are given by ancient grammarians—one from the town Aegae, another from Aegea, queen of the Amazons, who was drowned in this sea, and a third from Aegeus, father of Theseus, who threw himself into it.

AEGEUS, in *Legendary History,* King of Athens and father of Theseus. On returning from Crete, where he had gone to deliver Athens from the tribute to the Minotaur, Theseus forgot to change his black sails for white, the agreed signal of success. Aegeus, when he saw the sails, threw himself into the sea.

AEGINA, in *Legendary History,* daughter of Asopus, King of Boeotia, beloved of Jupiter, who carried her from Epidaurus to a desert island called *Oenone,* or *Oenopia,* which was later called by her name.

AEGINA, EGINA or ENGIA, an island in the Saronic Gulf, 20 miles from Piraeus, formerly vying with Athens in naval power, and at Salamis disputing the palm of victory with the Athenians. In fact the victory was in a great measure due to the thirty ships of Aegina; grateful Greece recognizing this, awarded her warriors the prize of valour. The rivalry of Athens again clouded the prosperity of the islanders and Aegina sank under the enormity of a relentless commercial rival that banished her people, filling their places with Attic colonists. After the Peloponnesian war Lysander restored the banished ones, but Aegina was never to recover her ancient prosperity.

AEGIS, in *Classical Mythology*, name given to the shield of Jupiter. Amalthaea, the goat who suckled the god, being dead, he used her skin to cover his buckler, hence *aegis*, (G. for goat). Later Jupiter restored the animal to life and placed it among the gods. Apollo and Minerva are also frequently represented with the *aegis*.

AEGISTHUS, in *Ancient History*, son of Thyestes by Pelopia, his own daughter, who, to hide her shame, concealed her son in the woods, where some say he was found by a shepherd, and suckled by a goat, whence his name. When grown up his father recognized him, and upon the king's death he succeeded to the throne of Mycenae. After the departure of the Trojan expedition, he seduced Clytemnestra, wife of Agamemnon, living with her during the siege of Troy. Later, with her assistance, he killed her husband, reigning in Mycenae 7 years. Later they were both killed by Orestes.

AEGOSPOTAMI, in *Ancient Geography*, a small river in the Thracian Chersonesus, running into the Hellespont, N. of Sestos, having a town of the same name at its estuary, where the Athenians, under Conon, were defeated by the Lacedemonians under Lysander c. 405 B. C., involving the fall of Athens and ending the Peloponnesian war.

AEGYPTUS, (Egypt), country in *Ancient Geography*, forming the N. E. of Africa, bounded N. by the Mediterranean, on the E. by Palestine, Arabia Petraea, and the Red Sea, on the S. by Ethiopia, and on the W. by the Libyan Desert. Probably for some centuries before the first dynasty of Egypt a fresh race had been permeating the country. Of a higher civilization they brought with them the elements of writing, artistic skill, and organization. Eventually Memphis became the capital of the 1st dynasty under Menes and his successors (about 5600-5300 B.C.) Altogether there were XXX dynasties, the last terminating in 342 B.C., followed by the golden age of Alexander's conquest. The transition from Alexander to the rule of the old general Ptolemy Soter was slow. The earlier family were able men backed by powerful queens. From 300-200 B.C. Egypt was more peaceful and prosperous than it had been for some centuries. — The Roman Age lasted from 30 B.C.–A.D. 640. The end of Egyptian independence was a death-stroke to the country which became the milch-cow of the Roman Emperor.

AELIANUS, CLAUDIUS, a native of Praeneste in Italy, who taught rhetoric at Rome under Alexander Severus, (according to Perizonius), but more likely under Hadrian. He was called "Honey-tongued" on account of the beauty of his Greek: he was also known as the "Sophist." Although a Roman he preferred the writings of the Greeks and used their language for his works.

AEMILIA, wife of Scipio Africanus I, and grandmother of the Gracchi. The celebrated Cornelia was her daughter.

AENEAS, in *Legendary History*, Trojan hero, who, according to Virgil, escaped after the fall of Troy with his father Anchises, and his son Ascanius or Iulus. After many wanderings he was driven by storm to Carthage where he won the love of Dido, its queen, who being abandoned by him killed herself. He afterwards went to Latium, where Latinus, the King, promised him his daughter Lavinia in marriage. Having killed his rival, Turnus, he married Lavinia, and became ancestor of the Romans. He was killed fighting against the Rutulians. After death he received divine honours.

AENEAS SILVIUS, son of Silvius, third in the list of the mythical kings of Alba.

AENIANES, ancient Greek race in S. Thessaly, between Oeta and Othrys, who had originally settled near Ossa.

AEOLIS, or AEOLIA, in *Ancient Geography*, a country of Asia Minor, peopled by colonies of Aeolian Greeks. In its widest acceptation it included Troas and the coasts of the Hellespont to the Propontis.

AEOLUS, (a) in *Pagan Mythology*, god and father of the winds represented as the son of Hippotes, or of Neptune by a daughter of Hippotes, or of Jupiter. He is referred to in the *Odyssey* as King of the Aeolian isle to whom Jupiter gave the superintendence of the winds. Strabo and others consider that he was a real person and connect the fable with his skill in meteorology. (b) son of Helen, ruler of Thessaly and founder of the Aeolic branch of the Greek nation.

AEPYTUS, son of Heraclid Cresphontes, King of Messenia, and of Merope, daughter of Cypselus, King of Arcadia. His father and brothers being killed in an insurrection Aepytus and his grandfather alone escaped. When he grew up he returned to his kingdom putting the usurper Polyphontes to death.

AEQUI, ancient, warlike people of Italy living in the upper valley of the Anio, who with the Volsci carried on a series of hostilities with the early Romans; they were finally subdued in 302 B.C.

AERARIANS, a class of citizens in ancient Rome who suffered the severest degradation the censors could inflict. They were heavily taxed but did not enjoy the rights of citizenship beyond their liberty and general state protection. They had no vote and could not serve in the army, and were excluded from all posts of honour and profit.

AERARIUM, public treasury of ancient Rome, containing monies and accounts of state, the legion standards, public laws, etched on brass, decrees of the Senate, together with other papers and registers. From the establishment of the republic, the temple of Saturn was used for this purpose. There was also a reserve treasury, housed in the same temple, called *aerarium sanctum,* or *sanctius* maintained by a 5 p.c. tax on the value of manumitted slaves, which was to remain untouched except in extreme necessity. Under the emperors the Senate had the nominal charge of the *aerarium,* while the emperor had a separate exchequer called the *fiscus.* Later emperors had an *aerarium privatum,* for their own use, distinct from the *fiscus* they administered for the state.

AESCHINES, Athenian orator and statesman, 389–314 B.C., leader of the party which urged futility of resistance to Macedon. Demosthenes accused him of corrupt motives. After the Macedonian victory at Chaeronea in 338 B.C., Ctesiphon proposed that the golden crown should go to Demosthenes for service to the state. In 330 B.C., Aeschines prosecuted Ctesiphon on technical grounds. Demosthenes' speech of the defense was a masterpiece and Aeschines was exiled.

AESCHYLUS, father of Greek tragic drama, born at Eleusis in 525 B.C. He fought with distinction at the battles of Marathon and Salamis. He first entered for the prize for the best tragedy in 499 B.C. but did not obtain first place until in 484 B.C. Most of his later years were spent away from Athens. He made two or three visits to Sicily, where he died at Gela in 456 B.C. Seventy tragedies are attributed to him of which seven survive. The most outstanding are the Persians, Prometheus Bound, and the great trilogy, Agamemnon, Choephori, and Eumenides. The Agamemnon is one of the world's masterpieces of dramatic literature.

AESCULAPIUS or ASCLEPIUS, in *Classical Mythology,* god of medicine; son of Apollo and the nymph Coronis. Chiron the centaur educated him and taught him the healing art. Jupiter, angered at his restoring Hippolytus to life, killed him with a thunderbolt. Cicero mentions three deities of this name; one who invented the probe and bandages; the second, a brother of Mercury, who was killed by lightning; and a third who first taught dentistry and purging. Aesculapius' statue of gold and ivory, showing him with a long beard, a knotty stick in one hand and the other entwined by a serpent, was to be seen at Epidaurus. The Romans crowned him with laurel, to show his descent from Apollo, while the Phliasians represented him beardless. The cock, raven, and goat were sacred to him. His chief temples were at Pergamos, Smyrna, Tricca, and the isle of Coos, but his most famous shrine was at Epidaurus, where every five years games were held in his honour.

AESOP, Greek historian, whose life of Alexander the Great is preserved in a Latin translation by Julius Valerius, and is abounding in errors.

AESOPUS (AESOP), the fabulist, thought to have been born in 620 B.C., either at Samos, Sardis, Mesembria, or Cotiaeum. As a boy he was brought to Athens as a slave, eventually he was released by Iadmon the Samian. He visited Croesus, king of Lydia, at whose court, says Plutarch, he reproved Solon for discourtesy to the king. Returning to Athens he wrote the fable *Jupiter and the Frogs* for the instruction of the citizens. Croesus employed him on important missions, one of these being to Delphi; where he gave offence to the Delphinians who threw him over a precipice in 564 B.C. He is represented as being very ugly but very witty.

AETHALIA or AETHALIS, known to the Romans as *Ilva,* an island in the Tuscan Sea, famous for its iron ore.

AETION, Greek painter whose picture of the marriage of Roxana and Alexander was exhibited at the Olympic Games, gaining him so much reputation that the president gave him his daughter in marriage. Lucian describes the picture in detail.

AETOLIA, a division of ancient Greece, bordered on the N. by Epirus and Thessaly, on the E. by Doris and Locris, on the S. by the Gulf of Corinth, and on the W. by the river Achelous. The Aetolians were a restless people, regarded by other Greek states as outlaws and robbers, but bold in war and jealous defenders of their liberties. They opposed the ambitious designs of the Macedonian princes who were forced to grant them peace on honourable terms. The basis of the Aetolian league was similar to that of the Achaeans. The Cleomenic and Social wars were kindled by the Aetolians with a view to humbling the Achaeans.

AFRANIUS, LUCIUS, (a) Latin poet of about 100 B.C., who wrote comedies in the style of Menander, being commended by Cicero and Quintilian for genius and fluency. Fragments of his work are extant. (b) Companion and friend of Pompey. He served with distinction in the Sertorian and Mithridatic wars. He was raised to the consulship in 60 B.C. While governor of Cisalpine Gaul he was honoured with a Triumph. On the allotment of Spain to Pompey in 55 B.C. Afranius and Petreius were charged with its government. In 49 B.C. they were defeated by Caesar. Afranius joined Pompey, at the battle of Pharsalia in 48 B.C. and at the battle of Thrapsus in 46 B.C. He was made prisoner by the troops of Sittius, delivered to Caesar and put to death.

AFRICA, the continent's ancient history is confined to the northern part; the primitive population consisting of pigmies and immigrants from Arabia and Asia. The first settlements were Phoenician, Egyptian and Greek. (For detailed information see under appropriate heading).

AFRICANUS, surname of the Scipios.

AGAMEDES, and Trophonius his brother were famous architects, building a temple of Apollo at Delphi, and a treasury for Hyrieus, King of Hyria in Boeotia, which they so constructed as to be of easy access to them for the purpose of robbery. The King set a trap, catching Agamedes. Trophonius cut off his head to avert discovery, but was immediately swallowed by the earth in the grove of Lebadea, where he was worshipped as a hero.

AGAMEMNON, in *Greek Legend,* King of Mycenae in Argos, leader of the Greeks in the Trojan war. Helena, his brother's wife, had been abducted by Paris, this being the cause of the war. The Greek fleet was ready at Aulis but becalmed by the act of Artemis, who was offended because Agamemnon had killed a stag sacred to her. To appease her Agamemnon agreed to sacrifice his daughter Iphigenia, but at the moment of sacrifice Artemis carried her away. When Agamemnon returned after the war he was murdered with the Trojan princess Cassandra by his wife Clytaemnestra and her lover Aegisthus. The story forms the subject of the trilogy, Agamemnon, Choephori, and Eumenides, by Aeschylus.

AGASIAS, Greek artist who painted the "Borghese Gladiator," now in the Louvre: he flourished in the 1st Century B.C.

AGATHARCHIDES, celebrated Greek grammarian and geographer, born at Cnidos, flourishing about 140 B.C. His works have perished except some quotations by Diodorus Siculus and others.

AGATHARCHUS of SAMOS, a Greek painter who first applied the laws of perspective to architectural painting, which led to further investigation by Anaxagoras and Democritus. He painted scenery for Aeschylus and decorated the house of Alcibiades. He flourished about 480 B.C.

AGATHON, tragic poet of Athens, disciple of Prodicus and Socrates; he was praised by Plato in his *Protagoras* for virtue and beauty. He obtained the prize in the fourth year of the 90th Olympiad, being crowned in the presence of 30,000, when just over 30 years old.

AGELADAS, a notable statuary of Argos, teacher of the eminent sculptors, Phidias, Polycletus, and Myron. His period of activity is uncertain.

AGENOR, (a) Son of Antenor and Theano, and one of the bravest of the Trojans. (b) Son of Poseidon, King of Tyre, and father of Cadmus and Europa. Virgil describes Carthage as the city of Agenor, since Dido was descended from him.

AGESILAUS, King of Sparta about 442-360 B.C., and an outstanding general. At the instigation of the Greeks of Asia Minor he made war against Persia. After a victory on the Pactolus in 396 B.C. he had to return to protect Sparta against a federation of Athens, Thebes, Argos, and Corinth: these he overcame at Coronea, in Boeotia, in 394 B.C., but Thebes increased in power, and in 371 B.C., Sparta was defeated at the battle of Leuctra and might have been destroyed but for the aid of Agesilaus. In 361 B.C. he led an army into Egypt as ally to King Tachos against the Persians.

AGONOTHETA or AGONOTHETES, in *Grecian Antiquity*, the president of the sacred games. In earliest times the agonothetes was the person who instituted, and defrayed the expenses of, the games, but in the Olympic and Pythian games these presidents were representatives of different states.

AGORA, first used in connexion with the assembly of persons summoned by the Kings of ancient Greece, the term came to mean a meeting place, usually the central square of a city, corresponding to the Roman forum.

AGORACRITUS, Greek sculptor: The head of his statue "Nemesis" is in the British Museum. Phidias was his master.

AGORANOMOI, magistrates of the republics of Greece, similar to the aediles of Rome. In Athens there were ten, chosen annually by lot, five having charge of the city, and five the harbour.

AGRARIAN LAWS, when used in the most extended signification, were laws for regulation and distribution of property in land, but the expression was more commonly used with reference to the enactments among the Romans for management of public domains.

AGRIGENTUM, called AKRAGAS, by the Greeks, in *Ancient Geography,* city on the S. coast of Sicily, founded by immigrants from Gela c. 581 B.C. It soon acquired wealth, territory, and, at one time, a population of 200,000. It had numerous pretentious temples, that of Jupiter being the finest. The city was destroyed by the Carthaginians in 405 B.C., but it was rebuilt by Timoleon in 340 B.C. During the first Punic war it was sacked, and again in 210 B.C., but it remained a center for trade for some centuries. Birthplace of Empedocles, its ancient remains may still be seen.

AGRIONIA, annual festivals of the Boeotians in honor of Dionysus.

AGRIPPA, name of two Idumean rulers of Judea under the Romans. Agrippa I, grandson of Herod the Great, killed James and cast Peter into prison. His reign was pompous, but his death at Caesarea, described by Josephus, was of a horrible character. — Agrippa II, his son, together with his sister Berenice, heard S. Paul's statement before Festus, being "almost persuaded to become a Christian." At the fall of Jerusalem he returned to Rome, dying 100 A.D., aged 70.

AGRIPPA, MARCUS VIPSANIUS, Roman general and statesman, born of humble parents in 63 B.C. He was friend of Octavian who became the Emperor Augustus. During the civil wars, after Caesar's death, he was successful in Gaul, checking the menace of Sextus Pompeius by a naval victory at Naulochus in 36 B.C.; he also led the fleet at Actium in 31 B.C. After Augustus assumed the purple he conducted other successful campaigns. He was also responsible for public works in Rome, and patronized art and letters. He married, as his third wife, Julia, the emperor's daughter. He died in 12 B.C.

AGRIPPINA, (a) daughter of M. Vipsanius and Julia; she

married Germanicus; she had nine children, including Caligula the emperor and Agrippina, the mother of Nero (b) daughter of Germanicus and Agrippina (c) mother of Nero, born at Oppidum Ubiorum. She was beautiful but licentious and cruel. She married Cn. Domitius Ahenobarbus by whom she had a son, afterwards to become the emperor Nero: later she married Crispus Passienus, then the emperor Claudius, whom she prevailed upon to adopt her son to the prejudice of Britannicus his own son; in order to secure succession for her son she poisoned the emperor in 54 A.D. The young emperor, resenting his mother's authority, caused her to be killed in A.D. 59.

AGROTERAS THUSIA, annual festivals in honour of Artemis and Diana, held at Athens.

AGYRIUM, town in Sicily, N. W. of Centuripae, birthplace of Diodorus Siculus.

AHALA, noble Roman family of the gens Servilia, producing many famous men, the most celebrated being C. Servilius Structus Ahala, master of the horse to Cincinnatus, 439 B.C., who slew the popular agitator Sp. Maelius in the forum for refusing to appear before the dictator on a charge of conspiracy. Ahala was brought to trial, but to save himself from condemnation retired into exile.

AHENOBARBUS, name of a Roman family of plebeians of the gens Domitia, which later rose to distinction. They were so named from the red beard and hair by which many of them were distinguished: Nero was of this family.

AJAX, in *Greek Legend,* the name of two heroes who fought for the Greeks at Troy. One, son of Telamon, was accounted, next to Hercules, the mightiest warrior in the host. He committed suicide after the award of Achilles' armour to his rival claimant Odysseus. The other Ajax was son of Oileus; he was small of stature but fleet of foot and a skillful warrior. He profaned the temple of Athena at the fall of Troy, on which account he was shipwrecked on his way home, but found refuge on a rock. Further defiance of the gods led Poseidon to shatter the rock, Ajax being drowned.

ALA, a "wing" in battle. This term was applied to each of two contingents of *socii* on a legion's flanks, before 90 B.C., after that date it denoted a unit, numbering, under Augustus, 1,000 or 500 men, divided into *turmae* or squadrons.

ALABASTRON, perfume jar with a narrow neck.

ALBA LONGA, most ancient city of Latium, 15 m. S.E. of Rome, on a ridge overlooking the Alban Lake. Mother city of Rome; legend ascribes its foundation to Aeneas, about 300 years before the foundation of Rome.

ALBANIA, in *Ancient Geography,* country of Asia, bounded on the W. by Iberia, on the E. by the Caspian, on the N. by Sarmatia, on the S. by Armenia and the R. Cyrus; it was extremely fertile on account of the alluvial deposits from the Cyrus. The Albanians were tall and graceful and of nomadic habit, becoming known to the Romans during Pompey's expedition in pursuit of Mithridates in 65 B.C. The Albanians opposed Pompey with a force of 60,000 foot, and 22,000 horse. He extracted their nominal submission but they continued practically independent.

ALBINUS or ALBUS, POSTUMIUS, Roman family of patricians whose members held high offices of state under the republic. The founder of the family was dictator in 498 B.C., when he overcame the Latins in the battle near Lake Regillus.

ALBION, ancient name for the British Isles, first used about 525 B.C. by a Massiliote explorer: the name Britannia was used by Pytheas c. 300 B.C. The Romans used Albion to denote the chalk cliffs at Dover because of the word's likeness to Latin *albus* - white.

ALBUM, in *Ancient Rome,* a tablet on which decrees, edicts, and public notices were inscribed; so called because the tablet was made of whitened material. (Some writers suggest that it was the inscriptions that were in white characters). The annals of Pontifex Maximus, were written by him on an album. The word was later used in a more restricted way for lists of official names, e.g. *Album Judicum, Album Senatorum,* etc.

ALCAEUS, great lyric poet of Greece, born at Mitylene in

Lesbos, flourishing c. 600 B.C. On more than one occasion he fought for the oligarchy to which he belonged, which resulted in his banishment to Egypt. Returning, he opposed the tyrant Pittacus, being taken prisoner he was generously pardoned. Extant fragments of his political poems are passionate and manly, while his love and drinking songs are sensuous. He is said to have been first to use the Alcaic metre.

ALCAMENES, famous Athenian sculptor, pupil of Phidias, celebrated for skill in art by Cicero, Pliny, Pausanias, Lucan, etc: flourished c. 448 - 400 B.C. being one of the great triumvirate, Phidias, Alcamenes, and Polycletes. He competed with Phidias to produce a statue of Minerva, his style was excellent in finish, but he overlooked that it was designed for a high column and would not bear comparison with the work of his master. His masterpiece was the statue of Venus Urania at Athens.

ALCESTIS or ALCESTE, in *Greek Legend,* daughter of Pelias and Anaxibia, wife of Admetus, king of Pherae in Thessaly; at the request of Apollo, the fates had granted immortality to her husband on condition that he procured one to die in his stead. Alcestis nobly accepted death. One version says she was brought back to her husband from the underworld by Hercules. The story is the subject of Euripides' *Alcestis.*

ALCIBIADES, son of Clinias; he was born at Athens c. 450 B.C., during the ascendency of his kinsman Pericles. He was of the companions of Socrates but not an imitator of him. Socrates saved his life at the battle of Potidaea in 432 B.C., he in return, saved Socrates at the battle of Delium in 424 B.C. Shortly after Alcibiades turned to politics, stirring up the Athenians to attack Syracuse in 415 B.C., when the war between Athens and Sparta suspended. He procured his own appointment to command, with two other generals, but was accused of sacrilege and recalled. He fled to Sparta intriguing for a renewal of the war against Athens. Later he quarrelled with the Spartans and in 412 B.C., went to the court of the Persian Satrap Tissaphernes, deflecting the latter's alliance from Sparta to Athens, thus bringing about his own reinstatement in favour of his countrymen. Military and naval victories brought him popularity, but following two defeats he was again exiled. He was assassinated in Phrygia in 404 B.C.

ALCINOUS, in *Greek Legend*, king of the Phaeacians living on the island of Scheria (possibly Corfu). Odysseus and his companions, being shipwrecked there, were hospitably received and sped on their homeward way. Alcinus was regarded as a good prince: his subjects were skilled seamen.

ALCIPHRON, most famous of Greek epistolary writers, contemporary with Lucian. 116 of his letters have been published, written in the purest Attic dialect, and models of style. The supposed authors are country people, fisherwomen, courtesans, etc. who express themselves in elegant terms without apparent inconsistency. The letters are valuable as picturing private life at this period.

ALCMAEONIDAE, noble Athenian family, descendants of Alcmaeon, an immigrant from Pylos. Megacles, a member of the family, having committed sacrilege, the family was banished c. 630 B.C., and did not settle again in Athens until 509 B.C., when the head of the family, Cleisthenes, introduced a more democratic institution in that city.

ALCMAN or ALCMAEON, one of the most ancient and distinguished of Greek lyric poets, said by some to have been born at Lydia. He lived at Sparta from an early age, flourishing c. 670 - 630 B.C., and may be considered father of Greek lyric poetry. He wrote in vigorous, broad Dorian dialect; only small fragments of his works are known to us.

ALERIA or ALALIA, a chief city of Corsica, founded by the Phocaeans in 564 B.C.; it was made a Roman colony by Sulla.

ALEXANDER, (a) King of Epirus, son of Neoptolemus and brother of Olympias, the mother of Alexander the great: he was made king of Epirus by Philip in 342 B.C. In 332 he crossed into Italy to aid the Tarentines against the Lucanians and Bruttii. He was overcome and slain in battle near Pandesia in 330 B.C.

ALEXANDER, (b) King of Epirus, son of Pyrrhus and Ianassa, who succeeded his father in 272 B.C.

ALEXANDER BALA, (c) King of Syria, of humble origin, pretending to be son of Antiochus IV Epiphanes: he reigned 150 — 145 B.C., being defeated and dethroned by Demetrius II Nicator.

ALEXANDER THE GREAT, (d) King of Macedonia, son of Philip II, whom he succeeded in 336 B.C., being the third of five kings of Macedonia to bear this name. This remarkable conqueror was educated by Aristotle, being richly endowed with natural abilities, strength, energy, and ambition. His father being dead, he quelled revolt among the Illyrians and Greeks and early in 334 crossed the Hellespont with an army to carry out Philip's projected conquest of the Persian empire which, under Darius, included all western Asia and Egypt. He shattered a great Persian force at the river Granicus, later marching against the army of Darius, completely overthrowing it at Issus in 333 B.C. Darius escaped leaving great spoils in the victor's hands. Having subdued Syria and Phoenicia, Alexander marched into Egypt, founding Alexandria. In 331 B.C. he again routed Darius at Arbela sweeping on to Babylon, and thence to Susa and Persepolis, the Persian capital. His next great undertaking was to lead his army to India in 326 B.C. where he conquered the Punjab, but was forced to return to Persia as his troops refused to go farther. In 323 B.C. he intended to round off his Asiatic dominion by the subjugation of Arabia, and was about to start when he was stricken with fever at Babylon and died in his 32nd year. There being no provision for a successor the inevitable result was the disintegration of the empire, which was divided among the most powerful of his military leaders. He had married Roxana, daughter of the Bactrian chief Oxyartes, of whom he obtained possession on the conquest of a mountain fortress. He owned the famous horse Bucephalus, founding the town Bucephala in honour of his steed which died there. Aegus, his son by Roxana was born after Alexander's death, and was acknowledged in 323 B.C. as partner of Philip Arrhidaeus, under the guardianship of Perdiccas, Antipater, and Polysperchon. Alexander, with his mother Roxana, was imprisoned by Cassander, when he took Macedonia in 316 B.C., being put to death by Cassander in 311 B.C.

ALEXANDER ZEBINA or ZABINAS, (e) King of Syria, son of a merchant. He was set up as a pretender to the throne by Ptolemy Physcon in 128 B.C. He was defeated and slain by Antiochus Grypus in 122 B.C.

ALEXIS, Greek writer of the middle Attic Comedy, 4th cent. B.C., and uncle to Menander, is said to have written 245 plays, of which 130 titles are known.

ALFENUS VARUS, distinguished pupil of the jurist Servius Sulpicius, the friend of Cicero. Pomponius states he became consul in A.D. 2. Horace and Catullus mention him under the name of Suffenus. Originally he was a shoemaker or barber.

ALIMENTUS, L. CINCIUS, (a) senator and annalist of Rome: was praetor in Sicily in 209 B.C. He wrote the history of Rome to his own times in Greek containing a good account of the second Punic War. (b), Antiquary and jurist who wrote in the days of Augustus.

ALLOBROGES, powerful people of Gaul, living between the Rhone and the Isère, as far as Lake Geneva. Their capital was Vienna on the Rhone. Q. Fabius Maximus Allobrogicus subdued them in 121 B.C. making them subject to Rome, but they were always inclined to rebellion. In imperial times they were known as Viennenses.

ALPHEUS, a chief river of Peloponnesus, rising in Arcadia, flowing through Elis, past Olympia to the sea, receiving in its course the rivers Hellison, Ladon, Erymanthus, Cladeus and a number of smaller streams, and falling into the Ionian Sea. Near its source the Alpheus is joined by a stream and sinks underground rising close to the fountain of Eurotas. After flowing a short distance the streams are again swallowed up and reappear. The statement of Pausanias is to some extent confirmed in the story that the river passed through the sea, retaining its freshness, rising again as a fountain.

ALSIUM, ancient Etruscan town near Caere, on the coast, which became a Roman colony after the first Punic War.

ALTIS, sacred grove, near Olympia, where the games were

celebrated.

ALYATTES, king of Lydia, father of Croesus: after a reign of 57 years he died c. 562 B.C. A huge mound of earth was raised to his memory, near Lake Gygaea. Herodotus says that its base circuit was 3800 Greek feet and the width of the base 2600.

ALYPIUS, one of the seven Greek writers on music, the time in which he flourished is not known precisely, but he is said to have written before Euclid and Ptolemy. Cassiodorus places his work *"Introduction to Music"* between those of Nicomachus and Gaudentius.

AMASTRIS, (a) wife of Xerxes, and mother of Artaxerxes. (b) Niece of Darius, last king of Persia: she was also known as Amastrine.

AMATHUS, ancient town on the S. coast of Cyprus, nearby the copper-mines. There was a famous temple of Aphrodite here.

AMAZONS, AMAZONES, AMAZONIDES, (*breastless*), in *Greek Legend,* race of warlike women whose kingdom lay on the S. shores of the Black Sea. Headed by their queens, they fought against Greece and other States, extending their kingdom as far as the Caspian Sea. No men were allowed within their borders; when they wished to have children they visited other tribes. Their female children had their right breasts cut off that they might draw the bow more easily, the males being killed or disabled. Of their legendary queens, Penthesilea led her hosts against the Greeks in the Trojan War, and, dying at the hand of Achilles, drew tears of pity from her slayer.

AMBIORIX, a leader of the Eburones in Gaul, who cut to pieces the troops of Sabinus and Cotta in 54 B.C.

AMBITUS, the canvassing for public office in republican Rome, open to many abuses, leading to the word being used of any appointment obtained by illegal means.

AMBRACIA or AMPRACIA, in *Ancient Geography,* important city of Epirus, on E. bank of the Arachthus 7 miles from the Ambracian Gulf. Tradition says it was originally a Thesprotian town founded by Ambrax, or Ambracia, daughter of Augeas. The Corinthians colonized it about 635 B.C., or later, so it became a Greek city. Pyrrhus made it his capital, adorning it with fine buildings as statues. It joined the Aetolian League in 229 B.C. It was taken by the Romans in 189 B.C. and became a free city. Part of the population was transported to Nicopolis.

AMBRACICUS SINUS, in *Ancient Geography,* gulf of the Ionian Sea between Epirus and Acarnania.

AMBRONES, a Celtic people who supported the Cimbri and Teutoni in the invading of Roman dominions, being defeated by Marius near Aquae Sextiae in 102 B.C.

AMEIPSIAS, comic writer of Athens, a contemporary of Aristophanes. In 414 B.C. he defeated his famous rival with the *Revellers* which was considered superior to the *Birds,* and again in 423 B.C. when his *Clouds* was placed third, while Ameipsias' work *Connus* was judged second to Cratinus' *Pytine.*

AMISUS, coastal city of Pontus, founded by Phocaea in the 6th cent. B.C. and enlarged by Mithridates.

AMITERNUM, ancient Sabbinic town, birthplace of Sallust the historian.

AMMONIUS, (a) scholar of Alexandria of the 2nd. Cent. B.C., pupil of Aristarchus. He wrote commentaries on Aristophanes, Pindar and Homer. (b) one of the founders of Neoplatonism: he was born of a Christian family but became a pagan. He had as pupils, Origen, Longinus and Plotinus.

AMORGUS, Grecian island, a place of banishment under the Roman emperors; birthplace of Semonides.

AMORICA, (*Celtic*—land by the sea), ancient name for Brittany, which was at one time inhabited by the Amorici.

AMPHIARAUS, in *Greek Legend,* brother-in-law of Adrastus, prime mover in the Argive expedition against Thebes. Amphiaraus, possessing the prophetic gift, wished to take no part in it, knowing that he would perish. He went into hiding but his wife Eriphyle, bribed by Polynices, disclosed his whereabouts. During the flight of the Argive chiefs from Thebes, Amphiaraus and his chariot were swallowed by the earth. He was later deified.

AMPHICTYONIC COUNCIL (LEAGUE), A representative council in ancient Greece of neighboring states united in worship at a common temple. Such a council met at Delos as early as the 7th cent. B.C.; the council enforced interstate rights and organized the Pythian games, meeting twice yearly at Delphi and Thermopylae, in turn; each member state having two votes.

AMPHILOCHUS, son of Amphiaraus and Eriphyle, and brother of Alcmaeon. He joined the expedition of the Epigoni against Thebes; assisted his brother in the murder of Eriphyle, and fought against Troy. He was slain by Mopsus. Amphilochus inherited his father's gift of prophecy.

AMPHION, in *Greek Legend*, son of Zeus by Antiope, divorced wife of Lycus, king of Boeotia. Amphion and his twin Zethus were placed on Mt. Cithaeron at birth, being discovered and reared by shepherds. When grown up they avenged the cruelty of Lycus to their mother, killing him and his new wife Dirce. Obtaining possession of Thebes, of which Lycus had been king, they raised fortifications, the stones of which moved to their places when Amphion played the lyre, an accomplishment learned from Hermes. Niobe later became wife of Amphion.

AMPHIPOLIS, in *Ancient Geography*, town of Macedonia. After several attempts the Athenians overcame the original Thracian inhabitants and founded a colony in 437 B.C. In 424 B.C., it was taken by the Spartan Brasidas, being recovered by Philip of Macedon in 358 B.C., remaining Macedonian until 168 B.C. when it fell into the hands of the Romans, who made it capital of one of their four Macedonian provinces.

AMPHISCII, in *Ancient Astrology*, a Greek term, (literally 'shadowed on both sides'), applied to inhabitants of the torrid zone, where the sun passes the meridian at noon, sometimes on the N., sometimes on the S. of the zenith. The people's shadows therefore are turned to the S. during one part of the year, at noon, and to the N. for the remainder.

AMPHISSA, in *Ancient Geography*, a chief town of Ozolian Locris on the borders of Phocis 7 m. from Delphi. The Amphictyons declared a Sacred War against Amphissa, the town being destroyed by Philip in 338 B.C. It was afterwards rebuilt.

AMPHITHEATRE, slightly elliptical structure, designed for gladiatorial exhibitions of the ancient Roman world, being built round an open space reserved for the combatants. This area was separated from the spectators by a wall sufficiently high to protect them from wild beasts introduced into the arena. At each extremity were doors through which the gladiators and beasts emerged. The seating rose in tiers, divided into sections by concentric gangways, and there were openings, at intervals, in the back wall for entrance and exit. The most notable was the Colosseum. q.v.

AMPHITRYON or AMPHITRUO, in *Greek Legend,* son of Alcaeus and Hipponome, and husband of Alcmene, who was mother of Heracles (Hercules); Zeus (Jupiter) having visited her in the form of her husband. He fell in a war against Erginus, king of Minyae.

AMPYCUS, father of Mopsus the seer.

AMYCLAE, (a) Ancient town of Laconia, abode of Tyndareus, and of Castor and Pollux. After Peloponnesus had been conquered by the Dorians, the Achaeans maintained themselves at Amyclae, but at last it was taken by Lacedaemonians under Teleclus. Amyclae continued to be well-known on account of the yearly festival of Hyacinthia, and of the colossal statue of Apollo. (b) An ancient town of Latium: the people are said to have deserted it on account of a plague of serpents.

AMYNTAS, (a) King of Macedonia, c. 540-500 B.C. (b) King of Macedonia, son of Philip, c. 393 - 369 B.C. He won the crown by the murder of the usurper Pausanias: his policy was friendly relations with the Athenians. By his wife Eurydice he had three sons, Alexander, Perdiccas, and the renowned Philip. (c) Greek epigrammatist c. 350 B.C.

ANACHARSIS, Scythian philosopher c. 600 B.C. His father was one of the chiefs of his nation, having a Greek wife, who instructed Anacharsis in that language. He prevailed upon the King to entrust him with an embassy to Athens. On his arrival he met Solon, from whom he rapidly acquired learning and wisdom. After living several years at Athens, he travelled in search of knowledge, returning home with a desire to instruct his countrymen in the laws and religion of Greece. Herodotus says he was killed by his brother Saulius while sacrificing to Cybele. His simple and forceful mode of expression gave birth to the expression "Scythian eloquence."

ANACREON, Greek lyric poet, born at Teos in Ionia. He fled to Abdera in Thrace before the invading Persians. Later he lived at the court of Polycrates, tyrant of Samos, until 525 B.C., then under Peisistratidae at Athens, and perhaps lastly at Thessaly. He wrote in Ionic dialect in simple terms on themes of love, wine, dancing and enjoyment. Only a few fragments of his work have survived (*Anacreontica*, composed later, is spurious). He died in his 85th year.

ANAGNIA, (now *Anagni*), capital of the Hernici in Latium, subsequently a Roman colony. Cirero's estate Anagnium was in this vicinity.

ANAS, a chief river of Spain, dividing Lusitania and Baetica: it was spanned at Emerita Augusta by a bridge of 64 arches built by Trajan.

ANAXAGORAS, Greek philosopher, born at Clazomenae, in Asia Minor, and settling in Athens, where Pericles became his patron. Anaxagoras held that the universe was composed of an infinite number of seeds of different kinds of matter, which in the beginning were in chaos, but with the advent of intelligence, a rotary impulse was given to the mass. The result being that all cognate seeds drew together to form different substances. He was condemned as atheistic for his suggestion that the sun and moon were not divinities, being forced to leave the city. He died 428 B.C. at Lampsacus, aged 72.

ANAXANDRIDES, King of Sparta c. 560 B.C. to 520 B.C. His wife was barren, and on his refusing to divorce her the ephors made him take with her a second, by whom he was father of Cleomenes.

ANAXARCHUS, philosopher of Abdera, of the school of Democritus. He went to Asia with Alexander in 334 B.C. After

Alexander's death in 323 B.C. he was shipwrecked, coming into the power of Nicocreon, King of Cyprus, to whom he had given offence: Nicocreon pounded him to death in a stone mortar.

ANAXIMANDER, Greek philosopher, born at Miletus, in Asia Minor, was friend of Thales, living many years at the court of Polycrates of Samos. He held that the material substances of the universe derived from the element, *apeiron*, which contained and governed all things, being immortal and imperishable. He is credited with the invention of the sundial and celestial globe, etc.

ANAXIMENES, Greek philosopher born at Miletus in Asia Minor, c. 500 B.C. who held that all substances of the material universe were derived from one natural element, air, as a result of rarefaction and condensation.

ANCAEUS, (a), Son of Lycurgus, and father of Agapenor; was one of the argonauts, being killed by the Calydonian boar. (b), Son of Poseidon and Astypalaea; was another of the argonauts, helmsman of the ship after Tiphys died.

ANCHISES, in *Greek Legend*, son of Capys and Themis, the daughter of Ilus, and King of Dardanus on Mt. Ida. By his beauty he attracted Aphrodite, who became by him mother of the Trojan hero Aeneas. In the story of Virgil's *Aeneid* the aged Anchises was carried off from the burning city at the fall of Troy. He died in Sicily, being buried on Mt. Eryx.

ANCONA or ANCON, (Greek - elbow), founded by the Greeks of Syracuse c 385 B.C.; a town and harbour of Picenum on the Adriatic, lying in an "elbow" between two promontories. It was a Roman naval station in the Illyrian War in 178 B.C. Caesar took it on his famous march north; Trajan enlarged it.

ANCUS MARCIUS, Fourth legendary king of Rome, 640 to 616 B.C., reputed grandson of King Numa; he is credited with the founding of the port of Ostia, and the fortification of Janiculum which he connected with the city by a wooden bridge, Pons Sublicius.

ANCYRA, (now Ankara), city of Galatia, whose citizens had a copy made of Augustus' record of the chief events of his life on bronze tablets at Rome. The copy was cut on marble blocks and placed in a temple of Augustus at Ancyra. This inscription, called *Monumentum Ancyranum,* is extant, having been discovered in 1555 A.D. It gives in Augustus' own words, what is almost the dying statement of the founder of the Roman republic. The record has four divisions: 1. summary of 'deeds done' 44 B.C. to 28 B.C. (mostly of a military character); 2. domestic administration and constitutional changes, and public "acts," triumphs, honours etc.; 3. financial matters; 4. political and diplomatic. Augustus wrote it in his 77th year and we learn from it that he had been pontifex maximus, was princeps senatus for 40 years, built temples of Apollo, Minerva, Juno, and Jupiter; completed the Forum of Julius, built bridges and roads, extended his frontiers, made expeditions, established many colonies, etc.

ANDOCIDES, one of the ten Attic orators, born at Athens in 440 B.C. In 415 he was forced to leave Athens under suspicion of being concerned, with Alcibiades, in the mutilation of the statues of Hermes. After two unsuccessful attempts he cleared himself in 399 B.C. The most important of his three surviving speeches was delivered in 390 B.C. in which he advocated peace with Sparta.

ANDROGEOS, son of Minos and Pasiphae, who conquered all his rivals in the games of the Panathenaea at Athens, and was slain at the instigation of Aegeus. His father made war on the Athenians to avenge his death.

ANDROMACHE, in *Greek Legend,* wife of Hector. Homer's description of Hector's parting with his wife and son, Astyanax, before his fatal meeting with Achilles is one of the finest passages in literature. After the taking of Troy, Andromache became the captive of Neoptolemus, son of Achilles, who took her to Epirus. She later married Helenus, brother of Hector.

ANDRONICUS LIVIUS, *See* Livius

ANDRONICUS RHODIUS, leader of the peripatetic school after 40 B.C. He edited Aristotle's works, which Sulla had brought to Rome in 86 B.C.

ANTALCIDAS, Spartan diplomatist, and naval commander. He was sent with a dispatch to Persia from Athens in 393 B.C. which he accomplished successfully. This agreement, and the blockading of their fleet by Antalcidas compelled the Athenians to accept the terms known as the *Peace of Antalcidas* in 387 B.C. By this the Greek towns in Asia Minor were to remain under Persia, all others being declared independent. Athens was to retain the islands of Imbros, Lemnos, and Scyros.

ANTENOR, (a) son of Aesyetes and Cleomestra, and husband of Theano, and one of the wisest elders of Troy. When Menelaus and Ulysses came to Troy as ambassadors he received them into his house; he advised his fellow citizens to restore Helen to Menelaus. When Troy was captured Antenor was spared. Later he is thought to have gone with the Heneti to the w. coast of the Adriatic, where he founded Patavium. His descendants were known as Antenoridae. (b) Athenian sculptor of 6th cent. B.C.

ANTESSIODORUM, (now *Auxerre*), town of Gallia Lugdunensis.

ANTHESTERIA, *See* Greek Festivals

ANTHOLOGY, THE GREEK, the oldest collection known, containing selections from 300 Greek poets. Its present form was reached by degrees. In the earliest days the Greeks used to carve sentences in verse upon tombs and monuments; these were later collected. The inception of the Anthology as we know it was due to Meleager. Others followed, and so the Anthology grew.

ANTICYRA, in *Ancient Geography*, name of two towns, one in Thessaly on the Malian Gulf, the other was in Phocis, on the Corinthian Gulf. Both were renowned for Hellebore, a supposed remedy for lunacy; hence a person suspected of lunacy was told to sail to Anticyra.

ANTIGONUS or ANTIGONIA, (a) Town of Syria, founded by Antigonus as capital of his empire in 306 B.C. (b) Town in Epirus near a pass in the Acroceraunian mountains.

ANTIGONUS, (a) King of Asia, son of Philip of Elymiotis, and surnamed the One-eyed. He was father of Poliorcetes by Stratonice. He was one of Alexander The Great's generals, and in the division of the empire in 323 B.C. he received Greater Phrygia, Pamphylia, and Lycia. On the death of Antipater in 319 B.C. he aspired to the rule of Asia. He defeated Eumenes in 316 B.C., putting him to death. He later waged war with Seleucus, Ptolemy, Cassander, and Lysimachus with varying success. After the defeat of Ptolemy's fleet in 306 B.C., he assumed the title of King. Antigonus and his son Demetrius were later defeated by Lysimachus at the decisive battle of Ipsus in 301 B.C. Antigonus was killed in battle in his 81st year. (b) Antigonus Gonatas, King of Macedonia 276-239 B.C., grandson of the above.

ANTILOCHUS, in *Greek Legend,* son of the venerable Nestor. He went with his father to the siege of Troy where he met his death at the hand of Memnon or Hector.

ANTIMACHUS, Greek epic poet, flourishing at the end of the Peloponnesian War. His principal work was *Thebais*: only fragments of his work remain.

ANTINOOPOLIS, city built by Hadrian on the E. bank of the Nile.

ANTINOUS, favorite of the Emperor Hadrian; born at Claudiopolis in Bithynia; he was drowned in the Nile 122 A.D. The emperor's grief was unbounded. He enrolled Antinous among the gods, erecting a temple to him at Mantinea and founded the city of Antinoopolis in his honour.

ANTIOCH, (Antiochia and -ea,), (a) Capital of the Greek Kingdom of Syria, stood on the left bank of the Orontes, 60 m. W. of Aleppo. It was built by Seleucus Nicator, c. 300 B.C., who named it in honour of his father Antiochus, peopling it from the neighboring city of Antigonea. It played a leading part in the early days of Christianity, and it was here that Christ's followers were first called Christians. (b) A city of Caria, on the Maeander, built by Antiochus I Soter. (c) A city on the borders of Phrygia and Pisidia: it was made a colony under Augustus, and named Caesarea.

ANTIOCHUS, *Kings of Syria.* 1. ANTIOCHUS I SOTER, 280 —261 B.C., son of Seleucus I, founder of Syrian Kingdom of the Seleucidae; married Stratonice his stepmother; slain in battle against Gauls, 261 B.C. 2. ANTIOCHUS II THEOS, 261-247 B.C., son and successor of above; went to war with Ptolemy Philadelphus, King of Egypt; ended this war by discarding his wife Laodice, and marrying Ptolemy's daughter Berenice. At death of Ptolemy he recalled Laodice, but in revenge she caused Antiochus and Berenice to be murdered; was succeeded by son Seleucus Callinicus: younger son A. Hierax also assumed crown, carrying on war with his brother. *See* SELEUCUS II. 3. ANTIOCHUS III the GREAT, 223 - 187 B.C., son and successor of S. Callinicus. Warred with Ptolemy Philopator, King of Egypt to win Coele-Syria, Phoenicia, and Palestine, being defeated at Raphia, 217 B.C. Attempted for 7 years (212-206 B.C.) to regain E. provinces of Asia, which had revolted under Antiochus II, with some success but could not subjugate Parthians and Bactrians, but concluded peace with them. Conquered Palestine and Coele-Syria, 198 B.C., giving them as dowry with daughter Cleopatra, on her marriage with Ptolemy Epiphanes. Later involved with Romans; was urged by Hannibal to invade Italy; advice rejected. Crossed to Greece, 192 B.C.; defeated by Romans at Thermopylae, 191 B.C.; returned to Asia. Again defeated by Romans under L. Scipio, at Mt. Sipylus, 190 B.C.; sued for peace which was granted 188 B.C. on condition of ceding all dominions E. of Mt. Taurus, and paying idemnity. To raise money raided temple in Elymais; was killed by people of this place, 187 B.C. Succeeded by son S. Philopator. 4. ANTIOCHUS IV EPIPHANES 215 - 163 B.C., son of Antiochus III, succeeded brother S. Philopator, 175 B.C. Warred with Egypt, 171-168 B.C. with success; prepared to encircle Alexandria, 168 B.C. when Romans compelled him to retire. Endeavoured to expunge Jewish Religion and introduce Greek pagan worship which led to Jewish revolt under Mattathias and his sons the Maccabees, which Antiochus could not quell. Attempted to plunder temple in Elymais, 164 B.C., was repulsed, dying shortly after while raving mad, which Jews and Greeks attributed to sacrilege. 5. ANTIOCHUS V EUPATOR, 173-162 B.C., son and successor of Epiphanes, 9 years old at father's death, was dethroned by Demetrius Soter, son of S. Philopater, and put to death. 6. ANTIOCHUS VI THEOS, son of Alexander Balas, was brought forward as claimant, 144 B.C., against D. Nicator by Tryphon, but was murdered by latter, who took throne, 142 B.C. 7. ANTIOCHUS VII SIDETES, 159-129 B.C., succeeded Tryphon; was defeated and slain in battle by Parthians, 129 B.C. 8. ANTIOCHUS VIII GRYPUS, 125-96 B.C., second son of D. Nicator and Cleopatra; warred with half-brother, Antiochus IX.; in 112 B.C. brothers agreed to share Kingdom. Grypus assassinated 96 B.C. 9. ANTIOCHUS IX CYZICENUS, brother of A. VIII reigned over Coele-Syria and Phoenicia, 112-96, fell in battle, 95 B.C. against S. Epiphanes, son of A. VIII. 10. ANTIOCHUS X EUSEBES, son of CYZICENUS, defeated S. Epiphanes and maintained throne. Succeeded father in 95 B.C. 11. ANTIOCHUS XI EPIPHANES, son of Grypus, and brother of S. Epiphanes, warred against Eusebes, was defeated, and drowned in the Orontes. 12. ANTIOCHUS XII DIONYSUS, brother of A. XI, reigned short time, fell in battle against Aretas, King of Arabians. Syrians worn by civil broils with the Seleucidae, offered the Kingdom to Tigranes, King of Armenia, who united it with his own in 83 B.C., holding it until defeated by Romans, 69 B.C. 13. ANTIOCHUS XIII ASIATICUS, son of Eusebes, succeeded 69 B.C., being deprived by Pompey, 65 B.C., who made Syria a Roman province. This ended the Seleucidea dynasty.

ANTIOCHUS, *Kings of Commagene* 1. Mithridates I made alliance with Romans, c. 64 B.C.; assisted Ptolemy in 49 B.C.; was attacked by Antony 38 B.C.; was succeeded by Mithridates II c. 31 B.C. 2. Succeeded Mithridates I; was put to death at Rome by Augustus, 29 B.C. 3. Succeeded Mithridates II, dying A.D. 17. Commagene now became a Roman province, remaining so until 38 A.D. 4. EPIPHANES, A.D. 38, received back dominion from Caligula, assisted Romans against Parthians and Jews: was deprived of his Kingdom for alleged conspiracy, retired to Rome for remainder of his life.

ANTIOCHUS of ASCALON, founder of the fifth Academy, was a friend of Lucullus and teacher of Cicero at Athens, 79 B.C.

ANTIPATER, Macedonian general who acted as regent for Alexander while on his Persian campaigns. After Alexander's death Antipater shared the government of Macedonia with Craterus. The Greeks hoped to regain their freedom under the new regime, but were defeated at Crannon in 322 B.C. After the murder of Perdiccas in 321 B.C. Antipater was declared regent of the empire.

ANTIPATER, L. CAELIUS, Roman historian c. 123 B.C., wrote *Annales*, including a good account of the second Punic War. He was contemporary with C. Gracchus.

ANTIPHANES, writer of Greek comedy, who with Alexis, was most important author of the Attic middle comedy.

ANTIPHILUS, Greek painter, born in Egypt, flourishing c. 330 B.C., painted portraits of Philip and Alexander. He was rival of Apelles.

ANTIPHON, most ancient of ten Attic orators, born 480 B.C. at Rhamnus. He participated in the forming of the government of the Four Hundred; after its overthrow he was arraigned, condemned, and put to death in 411 B.C. He conducted a school of rhetoric which Thucydides attended. His only public oration was his defense when brought to trial. Of his written orations (for others) 15 remain.

ANTISTHENES, founder of the Cynic school of Greek philosophy; was born at Athens in 440 B.C. He became pupil of Gorgias, and a follower of Socrates, after whose death he founded a school. He devoted himself to the ethical side of his master's teaching, holding virtue to consist in doing without all but the barest necessities and the avoidance of evil. Diogenes was his most famous pupil. He died 370 B.C.

ANTIUM, one of the oldest cities and ports of Latium, 33 m. S.E. of Rome, was a stronghold of the Volscians and the haunt of pirates until conquered by Rome in 338 B.C. It became a famous watering place. Caligula and Nero were born there. Antium had temples of Fortune and Neptune.

ANTONIA, MAJOR, oldest daughter of M. Antonius, triumvir, by Octavia, half-sister of Augustus, born 39 B.C. Her daughter

Domitia Lepida, was mother of Messalina, who married the emperor Claudius; her son, Cn. Domitius, married Agrippina, and became father of Nero.

ANTONIA, MINOR, sister of Antonia Major, who married Drusus Nero, brother of Tiberius, by whom she became mother of (a) Germanicus, (b) Livia, who was first married to Caius Caesar, and after his death to Drusus, son of Tiberius; (c) of the emperor Claudius. She was celebrated for beauty and chastity.

ANTONIA TURRIS, tower on the rock at the N.W. corner of the Temple of Jerusalem, commanding the city and the temple.

ANTONINUS, M. AURELIUS, *See* Aurelius.

ANTONINES, AGE OF THE, Period of Roman Empire covered by rule of the emperors Antoninus Pius and Marcus Aurelius: a golden age.

ANTONINE'S WALL, Roman rampart, 36 m. long, between the Forth and Clyde, built by Lollius Urbicus A.D. 140-1, during reign of Antoninus Pius: northernmost outpost of Roman Britain.

ANTONINUS PIUS, Roman Emperor, born near Lanuvium, A.D. 86. Had held administrative posts with credit; was a friend of Hadrian, who adopted him and named him as his successor. During his reign military operations were carried out in Britain, reforms made in the Roman system of law, and the code dealing with relations between freemen and slaves. The provinces were well governed, arts encouraged, and Christian persecution checked. He died A.D. 161, in his 75th year.

ANTONIUS, MARCUS, orator, son of C. Antonius, born 142 B.C. Was colleague of A. Postumius Albinus in the consulship, 99 B.C. In 98 B.C. he defended M. Aquilius on a charge of extortion during the servile war in Sicily. He was censor in 97 B.C. He fell victim to Marius and Cinna when they entered Rome 87 B.C.

ANTONIUS, MARCUS, (MARK ANTONY), grandson of Antonius the orator and son of A. Creticus, born c. 83 B.C. Early lost his father, being brought up by Lentulus, whom his mother had married. In 58 B.C. he went to Greece to escape his creditors. He later fought with Gabinius in Palestine, and in support of

Auletes in Egypt. In 54 B.C. he visited Caesar in Gaul, by whose influence he was raised to quaestor, augur, and tribune of the Plebs. He was bold in his patron's cause in opposition to the oligarchical party, who at length expelled him from the curia. Political contest became civil war. The Rubicon was crossed, Caesar successful, with Antony sharing his triumph. Antony became inferior in power to none save the dictator. In 46 B.C. he took offence at Caesar, but not for long, for we find him meeting the dictator at Narbo the following year. In 44 B.C. he was consul with Caesar, seconding his ambition by the famous offer of the crown on Feb 15th, so, unconsciously preparing the way for the tragedy of the 15th of March. By his eloquence he stirred the populace against the assassins and drove them from the city, made peace with the senate and almost succeeded to the power of his unlucky patron. But Octavius, whom Caesar had adopted, claimed his "father's" inheritance: war ensued. The senate supported Octavius, and the veterans of the dictator flocked to his standard.   Antony was denounced as a public enemy; his cause lost ground, and his army was defeated at Mutina, 43 B.C. Escaping to Cisalpine Gaul he joined Lepidus, and they marched to Rome with 17 legions and 10,000 horse. Octavius betrayed his party, and made terms with Antony and Lepidus; the three adopting the title *Triumviri reipublicae constituendae,* and sharing the power and provinces. Gaul went to Antony, Spain to Lepidus, Africa, Sardinia, and Sicily to Octavius. In the following year Antony and Octavius proceeded against the conspirators Cassius and Brutus, in Macedonia; and in the battles of Philippi stamped out the embers of republican Rome. Octavius returned to Italy, Antony went to Greece and thence to Asia Minor to recruit funds. On passing through Cilicia in 41 B.C. he was visited by Cleopatra, who sailed up the Cydnus in a gorgeous bark and equipage, bringing all her charm to bear on the voluptuous Roman who was captivated and led by her to Alexandria. He was later aroused by the Parthian invasion of Syria, and reported outbreak between Fulvia, his wife, and Lucius, his brother, on the one hand, and Octavius on the other. On going to Italy he found the war over, with Octavius victor. A reconciliation was effected between the triumvirs, and a new division of the Roman world agreed on, Lepidus receiving Africa, Octavius the West, and Antony the East. Returning to his province, Antony was for a time successful in conquest. After another visit to Italy, during which the triumvirate was extended for 5 years, Antony sent away his wife yielding himself wholly to Cleopatra. An expedition against the Parthians failed but success against the King of Armenia compensated. At this time Octavius determined to get rid of Antony, bringing charges against him. After some delay, in 31 B.C. Antony's fate was decided by the battle of Actium. Defeated he sought consolation of Cleopatra but was followed by his relentless rival. He made an effort to defend himself, but convinced of the hopelessness of his position, and assured of the suicide of his mistress, he followed the example which he was falsely informed she had given (30 B.C.).

ANYTUS, the most formidable accuser of Socrates, 339 B.C. He was a leader of the democratic party who took part in the overthrow of the Thirty Tyrants.

AONES, ancient people of Boeotia.

APAMEA ad ORONTEM, city of Syria, in strategic position on the Orentes, on the site of the more ancient Pella, built by Seleucus Nicator, and named after his wife Apama.

APAMEA ad MAEANDRUM, city built by Antiochus I Soter, in Phrygia, on the Maeander, named after his mother Apama.

APELLES, Greek painter, flourishing during latter half of the 4th Cent. B.C., probably born at Colophon in Ionia. He was the contemporary of Alexander, and the only person whom A. would allow to make a portrait of him. He painted on panels, and not on walls. His portrait of Alexander, and Venus rising from the Sea, were two of the most famous pictures of antiquity.

APELLICON, Peripatetic philosopher, had a valuable library at Athens, with autographs of Aristotle's works: it was taken to Rome in 84 B.C.

APER, ARRIUS, Son-in-law of the Emperor Numerian, a

praetorian prefect. He is said to have murdered his father-in-law: he was put to death by Diocletian A.D. 284.

APHRODITE, in *Greek Mythology,* goddess of love and fruitfulness of nature; she was counterpart of the Roman Venus. According to some she was daughter of Zeus, others say she rose from the foam of the sea, near Cyprus, hence the name; (Greek, aphros — sea-foam). Aphrodisias was the name of several places famous for her worship.

APHYTIS, town on the peninsula of Pallene in Macedonia, with temple and oracle of Zeus Ammon.

APICIUS, name of three famous epicures (a) lived in the days of Sulla. (b) M. Gabius Apicius, in time of Tiberius, spent his time and fortune inventing and eating new dishes; his money being all gone he hanged himself. (c) Contemporary of Trajan to whom he sent fresh oysters (preserved by his own method) when in Parthia.

APIS, Sacred bull worshipped at Memphis throughout dynastic Egypt. Symbolizing the second life of Ptah, he bore a white forehead mark upon a black hide. At death he became one with Osiris, his embalmed remains being enshrined in a huge sarcophagus. There are 24 Apis tombs in the Sakkara mausoleum.

APOLLO, a greater deity of ancient Greece, son of Zeus and Leda (Latona), born in the island of Delos. In Homer's writings, Apollo is not identified with the sun, but in later mythology became sun god. Aesculapius, god of medicine, was represented as his son. The foreknowledge of Apollo was developed in an eminent degree, and there were many oracular shrines of Apollo, notably at Delphi. He was patron of colonies, no colony being founded without consultation with his oracle. He is represented as a tall, handsome, beardless youth, holding a bow or a lyre: he was also patron of athletes. Apollo was also worshipped at Rome. The famous statue, known as the Apollo Belvedere, in the Vatican, does not represent the Greek conception in the strictly classical age.

APOLLODOROS, (a) Greek poet of New Comedy born at Carystus. (b) Greek historian of 2nd cent. B.C. (c) Greek painter, c 430 B.C. first to introduce light and shade in pictures. (d) Architect of Trajan's Forum, and Hadrian's temple of Venus.

APOLLONIA, in *Ancient Geography,* name of several cities. One in Illyria near the mouth of the Aous, was founded by emigrants from Corinth and Corcyra. Another, founded by the Milesians in Thrace, was famous for its temple and statue of Apollo by Calamis. A third town was the harbour of Cyrene, in N. Africa.

APOLLONIUS, (a) OF ALABANDA, taught rhetoric at Rome c. 100 B.C. (b) OF ALABANDA, taught rhetoric at Rhodes. In 81 B.C.: he came to Rome as ambassador of the Rhodians, being received by Cicero, who also received instruction from him. (c) PERGAEUS, from Perga in Pamphylia, one of the greatest ancient mathematicans. He was educated at Alexandria under Euclid's successors. (d) RHODIUS, poet and grammarian, born at Alexandria, flourishing 222 - 181 B.C. He became chief librarian at Alexandria, succeeding Zenodotus (q.v.). (e) TYANENSIS, a Neo-Pythagorean philosopher, born a few years before the Christian era. He pretended to miraculous powers, but was a quack. Philostratus wrote his life.

APPIAN, Roman historian born at Alexandria, flourishing mid-2nd cent. A.D. His Roman history, written in Greek is in 24 books of which 11 survive in entirety. The account of the civil wars of Rome are based on authorities no longer available.

APPIAN WAY, (APPIA VIA), Highway of Ancient Rome, separating the 12th from the 2nd and 1st districts; was begun by the censor Appius Claudius, in 312 B.C. Through the Appian Gate it led to the port of Brundusium, 234 miles distant.

APPIANUS, Rome historian, born at Alexandria, living at Rome during days of Trajan, Hadrian, and Antoninus Pius. He wrote in Greek, in clear style, but has few merits as an historian.

APULANI, Ligurian people on the Macra, subdued by the Romans after long resistance and sent to Samnium 180 B.C.

APULIA, included S.E. Italy from the Frento to the headland Iapygium. Originally civilized by Greek colonists, Apulia submitted to Rome in 317 B.C. suffering severely in the Punic Wars, and social war of 90-88 B.C., after which it never recovered its ancient prosperity.

AQUEDUCTS, ROMAN, are amongst the finest structures of the ancient world. Many conveyed water long distances, in stone channels, on high arcades. The oldest, Aqua Appia, was built in 312 B.C. Four are still in use. The best preserved are at Tarragona and Segovia in Spain. The finest is *Pont du Gard* in S. France with its lowest arches 65 ft. above the water's-edge, the second row is 65 ft. higher, and the top row 28 ft. higher still. (158 ft. high). The water channel being at the top.

AQUILEIA, town at the head of the Adriatic in Gallia Transpadana; founded by the Romans in 181 B.C. as a check to the northern barbarians. It became flourishing and, in imperial times, a center of Mithraic worship. It was destroyed by Attila in A.D. 452.

AQUILLIUS, or AQUILIUS, (a) Consul, 129 B.C., who ended the war with Aristonicus. (b) Consul 101 B.C., ended the Servile war in Sicily. He was put to death by Mithridates, in 88 B.C., by pouring molten gold down his throat.

AQUINUM, Juvenal's birthplace in Latium.

AQUITAINE, name given 2000 years ago to a district between the Pyrenees and the river Garumma (*Garonne*). The name spread N. and, under the Romans, was known as AQUITANIA. After the fall of the West it fell into the hands of the Franks.

ARABIA, great peninsula forming the S. W. part of Asia, having on its W. border Arabicus Sinus, on its S. and S. E. the Erythraeum Mare, and N. E. Persicus Sinus. Its N. Boundaries were ill defined, but it included the desert between Egypt and Syria, on one side, and the banks of the Euphrates on the other. Arabia had three divisions. 1. ARABIA PETRAEA, made up of the triangular land between the two heads of the Red Sea, and adjacent country to the N. and N. E., being named from its capital, Petra. 2. ARABIA DESERTA, being the Syrian desert and part of the interior land of the Peninsula. 3. ARABIA FELIX, including the remaining country. On the W. there is a belt of fertile land which caused the ancients to apply the epithet *Felix* to the whole peninsula. The people of Arabia were Semitic and nearly related to the Israelites. Arabia Petraea was the home of tribes constantly referred to in Jewish history, Amelekites, Edomites, etc., whom the Greeks and Romans called Nabataei. The inhabitants of Arabia Deserta were known as Arabes Scenitae and Arabes Nomades, from their habit of tent dwelling and mode of life. From the earliest times the people of the north trafficked by means of caravans, while the people of the S. trafficked by sea, chiefly in spices, gums, and precious stones. Arabia Petraea was the only part of Arabia ever conquered, which became a Roman province under Trajan.

ARACHOSIA, an eastern province of the Persian empire, bordered on the E. by the Indus, on the N. by the Paropamisadae, on the W. by Drangiana, and S. by Gedrosia. Afterward became part of the Parthian empire.

ARATUS of SICYON, Greek general and statesman. From 245 B.C. he generalled the Achaean League for many years. He alienated Sparta, also sought alliance with the Macedonians, depriving the League of its distinctive character as champion of Greek freedom. Aratus was poisoned by Philip's order in 213 B.C.

ARAXES, (*Aras*) (a) Armenian river rising in Mt. Alba, joining the Cyrus, and emptying into the Caspian. (b) branch of the Euphrates (also ABORRHAS). (c) Persian river on which Persepolis stood.

ARBELA, ancient city of Assyria, known also as Arbailu, 40 m. S. E. of Mosul. It gave its name to the battle in which Alexander defeated Darius, in 331 B.C.

ARCADIA, country of ancient Greece, occupying the center of Peloponnesus, its mountainous nature helped the inhabitants to preserve a semblance of independence. Its chief towns were Mantinea, Tegea, and Orchomenus. Traditionally its inhabitants were racially the oldest in Greece. They were pastoral people and worshippers of Pan: they were also great music lovers. The Lacedaemonians endeavoured to take parts of Arcadia, but were prevented by the battle of Leuctra in 371 B.C. To prevent further aggression the Arcadians built the city of Megalopolis. They later joined the Achaean League, finally becoming subject to Rome.

ARCADIUS, First Roman Emperor of the East, elder son of Theodosius I. On the division of the empire on his father's death in 395 A.D. he received the eastern part, and his brother Honorius the western. Arcadius reigned until 408 A.D.

ARCESILAUS, Greek philosopher, born at Pitane; he succeeded Crates c. 266 B.C. in the Academic Chair at Athens, becoming founder of the middle Academy. He is said to have died during a drinking bout in his 76th year.

ARCHELAUS, King of Egypt, of the Ptolemaic dynasty; son of the Cappadocian Archelaus, one of Mithridates' generals. He married Berenice, d. of Ptolemy Auletes, in 56 B.C. She had been raised to the throne instead of her father; at the end of six months, both were slain during an invasion by Aulus Gabinius, who restored Ptolemy.

ARCHIDAMUS, name of 5 kings of Sparta from the 7th-3rd centuries B.C. The second was the most famous: he invaded Attica with 100,000 men in 431 B.C.

ARCHILOCHUS, Greek lyric poet, born Paros, in Ionia c. 700 B.C. He went to Thrasos when still young, there writing verses satirising the family of Neobule, whose father Lycambes had forbidden her to marry Archilochus after having given his consent. Fragments of his work remain. Although not its inventor, he was first to use perfect iambic verse.

ARCHIMEDES, most famous of ancient mathematicians, born at Syracuse in 287 B.C. He wrote on nearly all the known mathematical subjects of his period: his theory of the lever, supported the science of statistics until the time of Stevinus, A.D. 1586. His theory of hydrostatics was nearly as long lived: his geometrical discoveries of the quadrature of a parabolic area, and a spherical surface as well as the volume of a sphere, were notable achievements. The Archimedean screw for water-raising was attributed to him. When Syracuse was taken in 212 B.C. he was killed by the Roman soldiers, being intent on a mathematical problem at the time.

ARCHON, name of the chief magistrate in many Greek towns, especially the nine chief magistrates of Athens. When royalty was abolished, one Archon was appointed for life, subsequently limited to ten years, and finally to one, when a board of 9 was instituted in 683 B.C. As democratic power increased their functions became mainly judicial and religious.

ARCHYTAS, born at Tarentum c. 400 B.C.: philosopher, general and statesman; contemporary with Plato, whose life he saved by his influence with Dionysius. He was drowned in the Adriatic.

ARDEA, chief town of Rutuli in Latium, one of the most ancient Italian places, and capital of Turnus. It was taken and colonized by the Romans in 442 B.C. The imperial elephants were housed here.

ARDYS, son of Gyges, king of Lydia, 678-629 B.C.

ARELATE, ARELAS, or ARELATUM, (*Arles*), city of Gallia Narbonensis, on the Rhone, and a Roman colony, with important remains.

AREOPAGUS, (*Greek—Hill of Ares*). Rocky promontory W. of the Acropolis in Athens on which the temple of Ares stood; meeting-place of the famous council of the Areopagus, an assembly of elders drawn exclusively from the noble classes. Originally a governing body, its powers were limited by the constitution of Solon, later by Cleisthenes, and further reduced by Ephialtes in 462 B.C.

ARETAS, name of several kings of Arabia Petraea.

ARGILETUM, Roman district, reaching from the south of the Quirinal to the Capitoline and Forum, inhabited by booksellers, shoemakers and mechanics.

ARGINUSAE, three islands off Aeolis, famous for the naval victory of the Athenians over the Lacedaemonians under Callicratidas in 406 B.C.

ARGOS, in *Ancient Geography*, city of Greece, in Argolis, 3 m. inland from the head of the Gulf of Nauplia, said to be the oldest city of Greece, becoming nucleus of a kingdom with Mycenae as capital. It came under Spartan influence in the 7 cent. B.C., but remained independent until taken by the Romans in 146 B.C. Remains include those of the temple of Hera. Argos was famous for sculptors in brass, and musicians.

ARGYRIPA, See ARPI.

ARIA, most important of the eastern provinces of the Ancient Persian empire, bordered on E. by the Paropamisadae, on the N. by Margiana and Hyrcania, on the W. by Parthia, and S. by the desert of Carmania.

ARIARATHES, name of several kings of Cappadocia (a) Son of Ariamnes I., defeated by Perdiccas, crucified in 322 B.C. (b) Son of Holophernes. (c) Son of Ariamnes II, married Stratonice. (d) Son of Ariamnes III, reigned 220-162 B.C. (e) Son of (d), surnamed Philopator, reigned 163-130. (f) Son of (e) reigned 130-96 B.C., was slain by Mithridates. (g) Son of (f), also killed by Mithridates who became king. (h) Second son of (f).

ARICIA, in *Ancient Geography*, town of Latium on the Appian Way, 16 m. from Rome: was subdued by Romans in 338 B.C. receiving Roman franchise. Diana was worshipped here, her priest always being a runaway slave, who obtained office by slaying his predecessor in combat.

ARIMINUM, (*Rimini*), town in Umbria on the Adriatic, with important harbour and splendid Augustan remains.

ARIOBARZANES, A. *Kings of Pontus* (a) Betrayed by son Mithridates c. 400 B.C. (b) Son of Mithridates I., reigned 363-337, founder of Pontus. (c) Son of M. III, reigned 266-250, was succeeded by M. IV. B. *Kings of Cappadocia.* (a) Ariobarzanes I, reigned 93-63 B.C. (b) Ariobarzanes II, named Philopator, succeeded in 63 B.C. (c) A. III named Eusebes, son of (b) whom he succeeded c. 51. He fought with Pompey against Caesar. He was slain by Cassius in 42 B.C.

ARION, lyric poet, native of Lesbos, inventor of dithyrambus; a great musician, was contemporary with Periander of Corinth, and Alyattes, king of Lydia, he travelled to Southern Italy, acquiring wealth by his professional skill. He lived about 625 B.C. His adventure with a dolphin is told by Herodotus.

ARISTAGORAS, Son-in-law of Histiaeus, who left him to govern Miletus, while he was away at the Persian court. He failed in an attempt upon Naxos on behalf of the Persians in 499 B.C., fearing the result he induced the Ionian cities to revolt from Persia. He sought assistance from Sparta and Athens, which was not forthcoming from the former, but the latter sent some ships and troops. His army captured and burnt Sardis in 497 B.C., but was finally driven to the coast. The Athenians left him, the Persians then capturing most of the Ionian cities. Aristagoras fled to Thrace, where he was killed by the Edonians.

ARISTARCHUS of SAMOTHRACE,   Alexandrian grammarian and critic; pupil of Aristophanes, at Alexandria where he founded a critical and grammatical school and took charge of the education of Ptolemy VI Philometor's children. When his pupil, Ptolemy Physcon, who had usurped the throne, began to persecute men of learning, Aristarchus fled to Cyprus, where he is said to have starved himself to death, because he was suffering from incurable dropsy: he was 72 when he died c. 145 B.C.

ARISTIDES or ARISTEIDES,   Athenian general and statesman, surnamed the Just. After the first Persian War, in which he distinguished himself at Marathon, he opposed the naval policy of Themistocles, and in 483 B.C. ostracism was resorted to, Aristides having to go into exile. But in the second Persian War he did good service, with a force raised by himself, and in 478 B.C. commanded the Athenians at the battle of Plataea. Aristides was chosen to organize the Delian League, and determine the contribution of each state. He further democratized the Athenian state. Three others of this name figure in history. Aristides, Greek painter, flourished 360-330 B.C. Aristides, a Greek writer, 1st cent. B.C. Also Publius Aelius Aristides, c. 129-189 A.D., a rhetorician, who rebuilt Smyrna after an earthquake.

ARISTIPPUS, Greek philosopher, born at Cyrene c. 430 B.C., founder of the Cyrenaic school. He taught that happiness was to be found in the enjoyment of the present, neglecting past or future. He was one of the pupils of Socrates, and was the first to seek payment for his teaching.

ARISTOBULUS, (a) Name of several princes of Judaea. (b)

of ALEXANDRIA, a Jew of 2nd cent. B.C., who wrote a commentary on the Pentateuch. (c) of CASSANDRIA, served under Alexander in Asia and wrote his history.

ARISTOGITON, *See* HARMODIUS.

ARISTOMENES, THE MESSENIAN, belongs more to legend than to history; hero of the second war with Sparta. Born at Andania, of the royal line of Aepytus. Tired of the Spartan yoke he began war in 685 B.C. After defeat in the third year of war he retreated to the fortress of Ira, and there carried on war for eleven years, ravaging Laconia. The Spartans overpowered him, taking him and fifty others to Sparta, casting them into a pit, but Aristomenes, favourite of the gods, escaped, an eagle bearing him on its wings as he fell, a fox guiding him the third day from the cavern. Ira fell into the Spartans' hands, and they became masters of Messenia 668 B.C. A. settled in Ialysus, where he married his daughter to Damagetus, king of Ialysus.

ARISTONICUS, natural son of Eumenes II of Pergamos. When his brother Attalus III died in 133 B.C. he left his kingdom to the Romans, but Aristonicus claimed the crown. He defeated P. Licinius Crassus in 131 B.C., but he was defeated in 130 B.C. being taken prisoner by M. Perperna and executed in Rome 128 B.C.

ARISTOPHANES, Athenian comic dramatist, writing in all 54 comedies, 11 of which survive. The first, *The Banqueters,* was produced in 427 B.C. His earlier comedies contain violent attacks upon those, who in his eyes, stood for democratic tendencies. The Demagogue Cleon, and philosopher Socrates, whom he unjustly identified with the Sophists, were particularly obnoxious to him. He appears to have later learned caution, for his plays during the next period were less outspoken. In his last plays personal satire almost disappeared. He was born about 444 B.C., dying about 380 B.C.

ARISTOTLE (ARISTOTELES), the philosopher, born at Stagira, in Macedonia in 384 B.C. He went to Athens in 367 B.C. spending 17 years in association with Plato. Several years of adventure in Mysia followed: in 343 B.C. he was called by Philip to Macedonia, to educate his son. When Alexander passed into

Asia in 334 B.C. "to subdue the world," Aristotle returned to
Athens, founded his Peripatetic school at the Lyceum; supported
by gifts from his royal friend he lived 12 years, lecturing and
absorbed in scientific research. In 322 B.C. he went to Euboea to
spend the last months of his life in peace, where he died the
same year, aged 63.

ARSACES, founder of the Parthian empire, his successors being known as Arsacidae: he was of obscure origin, but persuaded
the Parthians to revolt against Antiochus II, king of Syria; becoming first monarch of the Parthians c. 250 B.C.

ARSINOE, name of several Egyptian princesses. (a) Daughter
of Ptolemy Lagus, wife of Lysimachus, King of Thrace, and,
after his death, of Ptolemy Philadelphus. (b) Daughter of Lysimachus, and wife of Ptolemy Philadelphus. Convicted of conspiring against her husband, and banished. (c) Daughter of
Ptolemy Auletes, and queen of Egypt in 47 B.C.; put to death at
Miletus by Mark Antony. Arsinoe is also the name of cities in
Egypt and Cyprus, founded in honour of the above princesses.

ARTAVASDES or ARTABAZES,   (a) King of Armenia Major,
who betrayed Antony in his campaign against the Parthians in
36 B.C. Antony invaded Armenia in 34 B.C., took the king prisoner,
carrying him to Alexandria. After Actium he was killed at Cleopatra's order. (b) King of Armenia, put on the throne by Augustus, but deposed by the Armenians. (c) King of Media
Atropatene: died c. 20 B.C.

ARTAXATA, capital of Armenia Major, built by Artaxias, at
the instigation of Hannibal. After being burnt by the Romans
under Corbulo in 58 B.C., it was rebuilt by Tiridates, and named
Neroniana.

ARTAXERXES, name of three Persian kings: (a) LONGI-
MANUS (long-handed), third son of Xerxes I: reigned 464-425
B.C. He was a successful ruler; carried on war with the Egyptians;
generally thought to be the Ahasuerus of the Bible. (b) MNE-
MON, son of Darius II Nothus. The revolt of his brother Cyrus,
who was defeated and slain at Cunaxa in 401 B.C. is described
by Xenophon, who took part in it. MNEMON'S life is recorded

by Plutarch: he reigned 404-358 B.C. (c) OCHUS, son of Mnemon, was a weak and cruel despot, under the bad influence of the Egyptian eunuch Bagoas, by whom he was put to death in Egypt: he reigned 356-338 B.C. (Another ARTAXERXES was founder of the Sassanidae q.v.).

ARTAXIAS, name of three kings of Armenia. (a) The founder of the kingdom; a general of Antiochus the Great, who revolted, becoming an independent sovereign, at whose court Hannibal sought refuge. He was conquered by Antiochus IV Epiphanes, and taken prisoner c. 165 B.C. (b) Son of Artavasdes, who was slain by his subjects in 20 B.C. Tigranes was then put on the throne by Augustus. (c) Son of Polemon, King of Pontus, proclaimed king by Germanicus 18 A.D. (These Kings sometimes went by the name of Artaxes).

ARTEMIDORUS of EPHESUS, wrote a treatise on general geography, in eleven books, in the last cent. B.C.

ARTEMISIA, (a) queen of Halicarnassus, who accompanied Alexander in his Greek invasion, and at Salamis, in 480 B.C., distinguished herself by prudence and courage. (b) ARTEMISIA II, wife of Mausolus, king of Caria, whose sorrow for the death of her husband was so great that she mixed his ashes with what she drank. The Mausoleum she erected at Halicarnassus to his memory was one of the seven wonders of the ancient world. She died 350 B.C.

ARTEMISIUM, headland on N. coast of Euboea; the Greeks defeated Xerxes off this coast.

ARVERNI, Gallic people in Aquitania who at one time were the most powerful people in S. Gaul; they were overcome by Domitius Ahenobarbus and Fabius Maximus in 121 B.C. Their capital was Gergovia, afterwards moved by Caesar to Vercingetorix in 52 B.C.

ASANDER, (a) one of Alexander's generals, son of Philotas, brother of Parmenion. After Alexander's death in 323 B.C. he was given charge of Caria. (b) A general of Pharnaces II, king of Bosphorus.

ASCLEPIADES, Greek poet contemporary with Theocritus.

ASCULUM, (a) capital of Picenum, a Roman municipium, destroyed by the Romans in the Social War in 89 B.C., being later rebuilt. (b) town of Apulia, near which the Romans were defeated by Pyrrhus in 279 B.C.

ASELLIO, P. SEMPRONIUS, tribune under P. Scipio Africanus 133 B.C., who wrote a Roman history of the Punic wars.

ASIA, one of the three great divisions of the ancient world. The name was first used by the Greeks for the W. part of Asia Minor. The S. part of the continent was supposed to extend further E. than it does, and too small an area was assigned to the N. and N. E. On the European side the border was formed by the river Tanais (Don), the Sea of Azov, the Black Sea, Sea of Marmora and the Aegaean. Its general division was into two parts, known by different names. To the earliest Greek colonists the river Halys, formed a natural division between Upper and Lower Asia; afterward the Euphrates was the boundary. Another division was made by Taurus, the part of Asia N. and N. W. of the Taurus, and all the rest of the continent. The ultimate division in the 4th cent. A.D. was Asia Major, and Asia Minor. ASIA MAJOR, was the part E. of Tanais, the Euxine, a line drawn from the Euxine at Trebizond to the Gulf of Issus, and the Mediterranean: this area included Sarmatia Asiatica, with all the Scythian tribes to the E. and Colchis, Iberia, Albania, Armenia, Syria, Arabia, Babylonia, Mesopotamia, Assyria, Media, Susiana, Persis, Ariana, Hyreania, Margiana, Bactriana, Sogdiana, India and the land of Sinae, and Serica, q.v. ASIA MINOR, was the peninsula on the extreme W. of Asia, bordered by the Euxine, Aegaean, Mediterranean on the N. W. and S.; and on the E. by the mountains to the W. of the upper course of the Euphrates: this comprehended Mysia, Lydia, and Caria, on the W., Lycia, Pamphylia, and Cilicia, on the S.; Bithynia, Paphlagonia, and Pontus on the E.; and Phrygia, Pisidia, Galatia, and Cappadocia, in the centre. There was also ASIA PROPRIA, the Roman province, formed out of the kingdom of Pergamus, bequeathed to the Romans by Attallus III in 133 B.C., and the Greek cities on the W. coast, with Rhodes.

ASINIUS GALLUS, *See* GALLUS SALONINUS

ASINIUS POLLIO, *See* POLLIO

ASSESEUS, Ionian town, near Miletus, with temple of Athena.

ASSUS, city in the Troad, opposite Lesbos, birthplace of Cleanthes the stoic; an important stronghold.

ASSYRIA, ancient empire of Mesopotamia. The Assyrian homeland was an arid, treeless upland region above the alluvial plain of Babylonia to the S., being bounded on the N. by the Armenian highlands, on the E. by the Zagrus ranges, and on the W. by the middle Tigris. Originally Assyria included no more than the city of Asshur. It was long a dependency of Babylonia, but under Tiglath-Pileser I, c. 1120 B.C., the position was reversed. Vast territories were acquired by the usurping general Tiglath-Pileser IV, 745-727 B.C., with Nineveh the center of government. More was added by Sargon II, 722-705 B.C., his son Sennacherib keeping the empire intact. Under his son Esarhaddon, 681-668 B.C., Egypt was added, the Assyrian empire attaining its greatest extent and power. At Esarhaddon's death the empire was divided between his two sons. At this time Medes and other enemies were gathering on the borders, Egypt was lost, and other parts of the empire were tottering. A Chaldaean prince became king of Babylon and added continually to his gains. In 606 B.C. the Medes and Babylonians made a united attack on Assyria when Nineveh was taken and destroyed and the Assyrian empire came to an end.

ASTACUS, Bithynian city, on the Sinus Astacenus, where was a colony from Megara, later joined by colonists from Athens who named the place Olbia. Lysimachus destroyed it, but it was rebuilt near by, by Nicomedes I, who named it Nicomedia. q.v.

ASTURICA AUGUSTA, capital of the Astures, founded by Caesar.

ASTYAGES, last king of Media, 594-559 B.C., was deposed by Cyrus.

ASTYNOMI, Greek officials who had the care of the streets, and, in some cases, harbours and markets. Ten were chosen annually at Athens by lots.

ATHENA, or ATHENE, major deity in ancient Greece, identified by the Romans with Minerva. A daughter of Zeus, she is represented as having sprung fully armed from the head of her father. She was goddess of wisdom and war, a master of strategy and tactics, patron of useful arts, and protectress of Athens. The Parthenon was erected in her honour on the Acropolis. In the Trojan war she espoused the cause of the Greeks. She was regarded as the maiden goddess, and in art represented as of somewhat masculine appearance, wearing helmet and shield.

ATHENAE, (ATHENS),   capital city of Attica, lying 3 m. from the coast, and built around the Acropolis which was a Mycenaean palace-fort, which until classical times was called "the City," but in the more extended sense, Athens included the lower city and the port of Piraeus, the latter being connected with the city by the famous 'long walls' of Pericles. Athens was surrounded on three sides by the Attic plain, with Mt. Hymettus on the E. and Pentelicus on the N. E., and Parnes on the N. The Agora, q.v., was N. of the entrance to the Acropolis, and was bounded on the S. by a great colonnade, and on the E. by another, and on the W. was the smaller Stoa of Zeus. Outside the walls were suburbs, gardens, and cemeteries. The Ceramicus (N. W. suburb) had a road bordered by tombs of illustrious dead, which led to the Academy. To the E. of the Acropolis was the Odeum (Hall of Song), and to the S. E. the great stone theatre (holding, 25,000 spectators) dating from c. 330 B.C. A. was an Aegaean city state in the 2nd millennium. Traditionally ancient Athens (the Acropolis) was founded by the mythical Cecrops, while Theseus is credited with the formation of the city by union of 12 independent states of Attica. The city grew in importance between 800-600 B.C., and the story of Theseus probably represents the work of a real statesman of the 8th cent. The rulers were kings who acted as chief-priest, and who later, about 650 B.C., lost their kingly power. A polemarch, military ruler, took his place, and an archon, or civil ruler. Semi-mythical Dracon established the first code of laws, but Solon (q.v.) is the first historical name; his archonship was followed by the tyranny of Pisistratus, who further established the power of the city without destroying the democracy of Solon. Further democratic reforms came with Clisthenes q.v., and were strengthened by the guidance of Themistocles (q.v.). Xerxes burnt the city in 480 B.C. but Themistocles and Cimon soon rebuilt it, it being completed by Pericles on a grand scale. Athens came into conflict with Sparta, and Cimon, who believed in co-operation with Sparta, was exiled in 461 B.C. This date marks the rise of Pericles (q.v.) and the commencement of the greatest period of Athenian history, which ended with war against Sparta in 431 B.C. and the death of Pericles. The Peloponnesian War ended in the final surrender of Athens in 404 B.C. The walls were dismantled, and Lysander, the Spartan commander, set up an oligarchy, carried on by Critias and the Thirty Tyrants, which was overthrown by Thrasybulus (q.v.) in 403 B.C. but the restored democracy did not recover its supremacy. Athens owed its beauty to its public buildings. Private houses and streets were insignificant and badly planned. There were 10,000 houses towards the end of the Peloponnesian War, with a population of about 120,000. Athens continued to flourish under the Romans. It suffered on its capture by Sulla, in 86 B.C. It was a chief seat of learning in the early centuries of the Christian era. Hadrian frequently resided in the city, adorning it with new buildings, also Herodes Atticus in the reign of M. Aurelius.

ATLANTIS, in ancient tradition, a great island to the W. of the Pillars of Hercules, opposite Mt. Atlas; its rulers invaded Africa, but were defeated by the Athenians and their allies. The people of the island became impious, so that it was swallowed by the ocean. The legend is said to have been told to Solon by Egyptian priests.

ATOSSA, daughter of Cyrus, and mother of Xerxes by Darius Hystaspis.

ATROPATENE, N. W. division of Media, adjoining Armenia; it was long an independent kingdom, having been founded by Atropates, who had been appointed its governor by Alexander.

ATTALUS, *Kings of Pergamus.* (a) Son of Attalus, succeeded Eumenes I; reigned 241-197 B.C. (b) Attalus Philadelphus, second son of Attalus; reigned 159-138, he supported the Romans.

(c) Attalus Philometer, succeeded Attalus II; reigned 138-133; his kingdom was claimed by Aristonicus.

ATTICA, district of ancient Greece, bounded by Boeotia on the N:, Megara on the N. W., and the Aegaean on the E., and S. W., consisting of plain and mountains, among the latter being Hymettus, Pentelicus, and Cithaeron. The language of Athens and Attica represented the highest standard of literary Greek and correct diction.

ATTIC ORATORS, the Ten Greater Orators of Athens, viz. Antiphon, Andocides, Lysias, Isocrates, Isaeus, Lycurgus, Aeschines, Demosthenes, Hyperides, and Dinarchus.

ATTICUS, TITUS POMPONIUS, Roman eques, born 109 B.C., literary man and publisher. His close friend was Cicero, whose letters to Atticus are a model of familiar correspondence. Atticus was an Epicurean, of great wealth, possessing a large library. He wrote a chronicle of Roman history, and an account of Cicero's consulship in Greek. He died 32 B.C.

AUFIDIUS BASSUS, Roman historian, 1st cent. A.D. He wrote *Bellum Germanicum,* and a history of the period following Caesar's death to c. 50 A.D.

AUGUSTULUS ROMULUS, last emperor of the West, deposed by Odoacer, A.D. 476.

AUGUSTUS, GAIUS OCTAVIUS, first Roman emperor, born Sept. 23rd, 63 B.C., son of another Gaius Octavius, by a niece of Caesar. In the years between the murder of Julius, March 15th, 44 B.C., and his ascending the throne, he is generally known as Octavian. The murder of Caesar threw Rome into chaos. The young Octavian was absent from Italy but returned at once with his friend and counsellor Agrippa, to claim inheritance. Caesar's partisans were already in arms under Antony, who imagined Octavian could be disregarded. The veterans gave allegiance to Caesar's adopted son and an alliance was soon made between him and Antony. In 42 B.C. Octavian and Antony, who with Marcus Lepidus had been recently chosen triumvirs, took their armies to the Balkan Peninsula to fight the chiefs of the republican party, Brutus and Cassius. The victory of Philippi, in 42

B.C., made the Caesarians all powerful. Octavian and Antony in effect divided the Roman empire between them. Meanwhile Octavian was organizing his supremacy in the West. In 31 B.C. the arrogance of Cleopatra of Egypt, provided the excuse for an attack, which was in effect an attack on Antony. Agrippa won a decisive victory at Actium, Sept. 2nd, 31 B.C., and when Octavian advanced against Egypt, the year following, Antony and Cleopatra committed suicide, and Octavian stood without rival. He returned to Rome, and the Senate conferred titles which in themselves did not imply power.

Within the empire Augustus established *Pax Romana,* the Roman Peace, and the provinces were well governed.

AULIS, seaport of ancient Greece, in Boeotia, standing on the Epirus. Here the Greek fleet assembled before setting out for Troy.

AURELIANUS, Roman emperor born c. A.D. 213, son of a Pannonian peasant. He became one of the chief officers of his predecessor Claudius, upon whose death he was proclaimed emperor by the soldiers. He first attacked the barbarians in Italy defeating them A.D. 271. After quelling rebellion in Rome he turned his attention to Zenobia, queen of Palmyra, a brilliant campaign ending in the destruction of Palmyra and capture of Zenobia. The defeat of Tetricus, the rival emperor of Gaul, brought the whole empire again under Aurelian's rule. The title *Restitutor Orbis* (Restorer of the World) was conferred upon him, and his triumph in 274 was the most splendid ever staged at Rome. He reigned A.D. 270-275.

AUXILIA, auxiliary Roman army formed by Augustus. The force was recruited from unenfranchised provincials, the men being attached to individual legions, and also employed as provincial garrisons. The auxiliaries were paid less than the men of the legions, but granted franchise at the end of their service.

B

BAALBEK, "City of the Sun," in Coele Syria. *See* Heliopolis.

BABYLON, ancient city of Asia, on the Euphrates in a spacious fertile plain 60 m. S. of modern Bagdad; was capital of the Babylonian and then of the Assyrian empire. Belus (*Baal*) is credited with its foundation, and Ninus with its extension and embellishment. The period of its greatest glory was 1800-539 B.C., with a short break about 689 B.C. when part of the city was destroyed by Sennacherib. The city was built on both banks of the river, and had palaces, temples and fine streets. Its ruins spread over 50 sq. m. Among other things, excavations have brought to light the Ishtar Gate which Nebuchadrezzar built at the N. E. corner of the southern citadel for an approach to the processional road leading to the temple of Marduk, Nebuchadrezzar's fortress palace with its hanging gardens, and the temple of Esagila. Many tribes dwelt on the rich plains of lower Mesopotamia, and about 2300 B.C. Babylon became their acknowledged capital. That city endured for more than 16 centuries, and after Sennacherib's destruction was rebuilt, becoming one of the world's greatest cities under Nabopolassar and Nebuchadrezzar, who in his turn was followed by Belshazzar followed by Cyrus in 538 B.C., when Babylon passed to the Persians, who in their turn gave way to Alexander, who died there. From that time the city decayed, until it became ruins, covered under huge mounds of sand. See *Ancient History: the Near East*, 11th edition (pub. 1950).

BABYLONIA, ancient empire of Mesopotamia. It lay between the Tigris and Euphrates, low-lying country, formed of alluvial mud. Assyria bounded it on the north, Chaldaea, (Kaldu) on the S., the mountains of Elam on the E., and the Syrian and Arabian deserts on the W. The earliest inhabitants were the

Sumerians, who lived in the S., spoke a Turnanian language, having features and costume wholly Semitic: Akkadians, a Semitic race from Arabia, settled in the N. The earliest Babylonian culture was Sumerian, but Semites in the N. took over the cuneiform script, their culture, and religious ideas. Early Babylonia was made up of a large number of independent city states. The first dynasty commenced 2,300 B.C., and from then there is a continuous history down to 539 B.C. when supremacy in the East passed to Persia. The sixth king, Hammurabi or Khammurapi c. 2100 B.C. is the only ruler of importance belonging to this dynasty: he brought all Babylonia under his sway, became suzerain of Assyria, and added territory in Elam, etc. He promulgated the famous legal code, which was engraved on stone, and set up at various centres, one stone is to be seen in the Louvre. —The Kashite dynasty ran from about 1750-1169 B.C. and under it the empire declined. Nebuchadrezzar revived it, handing to his successor a larger Babylonia.—Under Tiglath-Pileser, c. 1100, B.C. Babylonia became a dependency of Assyria but when Nabopolassar became king an age of prosperity set in for what has been called Neo Babylonia.—Nebuchadrezzar II, 604-562 B.C., raised the empire to its highest pitch of power. In 606 B.C. he conquered Jerusalem, firing the city in 586 B.C., taking most of the people to his own country.—Under his successors the empire gradually collapsed. The last king Nabonidus, 555-539 B.C. was absorbed in his own pursuits when his country was invaded by Cyrus of Persia, who entered Babylon unopposed. In 539 B.C. Babylon fell, never to rise again.

BACCHYLIDES, one of the nine great lyric poets of Greece, born at Iulis in Ceos. c. 467 B.C.; was nephew of Simonides. Only about 100 lines of his poems were known until 1896, when a papyrus containing 20 odes was discovered in Egypt. (For a translation see A. S. Way's book.)

BACTRIA, or BACTRIANA, in *Ancient Geography*, stretch of land comprising the N. slope of the Hindu Kush as far as the river Oxus (*Amu Daria*). Alexander over-ran it in 328 B.C., establishing Greek garrisons. Following a short Seleucid domination, the Greek satrap Diodotus, rebelled, founding the Greco-Bactrian Kingdom about 250 B.C.

BAGOAS, a eunuch who poisoned Artaxerxes III (Ochus) in 338 B.C. after having been a trusted servant. He was put to death in 336 B.C. by Darius III, after an attempt to poison the king. The name recurs in Persian history, Latin writers making it synonymous with eunuch.

BAIAE, ancient town of Italy, in Campania, on a bay 10 m. W. of Naples. Its pleasant situation and hot sulphur springs made it a favourite resort of the emperors, and the rich; Julius Caesar, Marius, Nero, and Alexander Severus, built villas there. Tiberius and Hadrian died there.

BALBINUS, DECIMUS CAELIUS,   Roman emperor, one of the two chosen by the Senate in April, 238 B.C. as rivals to Maximinus: the other being Clodius Pupienus Maximus.

BALBUS, L. CORNELIUS,   was granted Roman citizenship by Pompey, after having served under him against Sertorius in Spain. Returning to Rome he lived on intimate terms with Pompey and Caesar. In the civil war he had charge of Caesar's affairs at Rome. After Caesar's death, Octavian made him consul in 40 B.C., he being the first alien to hold the office.

BALEARES, (BALEARIC ISLES),   called also by the Greeks, Gymnesiae; group of four large and eleven small islands in the Mediterranean, off the east coast of Spain. Colonised by Phoenicians and Carthaginians, the islands were conquered by the Romans in 123 B.C.

BALLISTA, weapon for hurling stones, used by the Romans in sieges. Strong strands, placed vertically, were twisted with a windlass: on being released they discharged the stone with tremendous force.

BARBARI, to the Greeks, all foreigners whose language was not Greek; to the Romans, all who spoke neither Latin nor Greek.

BARCA, *See* HAMILCAR.

BARCA, ancient city in Cyrenaica, between Cyrene and Hesperides, 11 m. inland, on top of rising ground overlooking the Syrtes. It was founded c. 554 B.C. by a colony from Cyrene, fleeing from the ill-treatment of Arcesilaus II, assisted by some Libyans. Pheretima, mother of Arcesilaus II, revenged her son 44 years after the foundation, when the place was captured and pillaged by the Persians, on whom she had called for aid. In the times of the Ptolemies the founding of Ptolemais drew from the older site most of the population, but Barca continued to exist, and rose to some importance under the Arabs.

BARSINE, (a) wife of Alexander the Great, mother of Heracles and daughter of Artabazus. She was put to death with her son by Polysperchon in 309 B.C. (b) Elder daughter of Darius III, also called Statira, who married Alexander at Susa in 324 B.C. She was murdered by Roxana after Alexander's death.

BASILICA, in the Hellenistic age, a large building accommodating many people gathered for business or for the sitting of a court of justice. The Romans adapted the Hellenistic basilica to many uses. With Constantine's conversion to Christianity, the basilica suggested a model for the Christian Church: the one known as Constantine's Basilica, in the Forum Romanum was started by Maxentius and finished by Constantine in A.D. 312; having an area of 19,500 sq. ft. The best preserved early Christian basilicas are in Ravenna.

BATTIADAE, eight kings of Cyrene; 1. Battus I, at the command of the Delphic oracle, led a colony to Africa and founded Cyrene, c. 631 B.C. 2. Arcesilaus I, 590-574 B.C. 3. Battus II, called "the Happy", 574-c. 560. 4. Arcesilaus II, called "the Oppressive", c. 560-550 B.C.; his brothers founded Barca. 5. Battus III, "the Lame", c. 550-530 B.C.; introduced a new constitution. 6. Arcesilaus III, c. 530-510. 7. Battus IV. 8. Arcesilaus IV; a popular form of government was introduced at his death in c. 450 B.C.

BAUCIS, *See* PHILEMON.

BELGAE, a tribe of German-Celtic origin living in N. E. Gaul, their land being bounded by the Rhine on the N., by the Sequana (*Seine*) on the S., and by the Treviri on the E. They were a warlike people whom Caesar subdued after they had shown marked resistance. In 75 B.C. and again about 50 B.C. part of the Belgae migrated to Britain.

BELLEROPHON, in *Greek Legend,* hero falsely accused by Anteia, who was sent by her husband Proetus, king of Argolis, to her father, Iobates, king of Lycia, with a letter requesting him to arrange the death of Bellerophon. With this end in view he was sent to kill the fire-breathing Chimaera. With the aid of Athena, Bellerophon caught and bridled the winged horse Pegasus, on which he rose above the monster, slaying it with arrows. After other exploits Iobates gave him his daughter, and made him his successor, but Bellerophon, having drawn upon himself the hatred of the gods, fled and lived a wanderer.

BELUS, Phoenician river, whose bed was of fine sand, which probably led to the Phoenicians' invention of glass.

BELUS, father of Aegyptus and Danaus, wrongly credited with the founding of Babylon.

BEMA, the tribune or rostrum from which Athenian orators made their speeches; hence the apse or chancel of a basilica (from Greek *bema,*—a step).

BENEVENTUM, city in Samnium, on the Appia Via, on a hill, between the rivers Sabato and Calore, 31 m. N. E. of Naples, formerly known as Malventum. One of the most ancient places in Italy, probably founded by Diomedes. It was conquered by the Romans in the Samnite wars, who colonised it in 268 B.C.

BERENICE, or PHERENICE, city of ancient Egypt, situated on a bay of the Red Sea, mentioned by Strabo. At one period it was chief center of commerce between India and Arabia. Ptolemy II Philadelphus, founded it, naming it after his mother.

BERENICE, name of several Jewish and Egyptian princesses. The best known of the former is the daughter of Herod Agrippa I, king of Judaea. An earlier Berenice, was daughter of Salome and mother of H. Agrippa I. The Egyptian princesses include the wife of Plotemy Soter; a daughter of Magas, king of Cyrene, who became wife of Ptolemy Euergetes; the sister of Cleopatra, who was put to death by the Romans in 55 B.C.

BEROEA, (a) Ancient town of Macedonia, S. W. of Pella. (b) Town near Antioch in Syria, enlarged by Seleucus Nicator. It is mentioned in Ezekiel xxvii. 18 under the name of Helbon.

BEROSUS, wrote a history of Babylonia in Greek. He was priest of Belus at Babylon, in the reign of Antiochus I, 324-261 B.C. Fragments of his writings are preserved by Josephus, Eusebius, and the Early Fathers.

BERYTUS, (BEYRUT), ancient port of Phoenicia, mid-way between Byblus and Sidon, destroyed by Tryphon, king of Syria in 140 B.C. It was restored by Agrippa under Augustus, and became a center of learning.

BESSUS, satrap under Darius III who murdered the king, and fled to Bactria, where he assumed the royal style. He was betrayed to Alexander by followers, and put to death c. 333 B.C.

BIAS, one of the Seven Sages of Greece, flourishing about 550 B.C. He was born at Priene in Ionia.

BIBRACTE, a Gaulish settlement on Mont-Beuvray, controlling the route from Marseilles into the Loire and Seine basins; the Aedui made the hill-top their capital. Excavations have brought to light many finds of great interest. Caesar wintered there in 52 B.C.

BIBULUS, M. CALPURNIUS, became curule aedile 65 B.C., praetor in 62 B.C., and consul in 59 B.C. His colleague was C. Julius Caesar. In his consulship he was unable to resist the powerful three, Caesar, Pompey, and Crassus, and so he retired. During the civil war he commanded Pompey's fleet in the Adriatic, dying in 48 B.C., while still in charge of this fleet.

BION of SMYRNA, Greek Bucolic poet, flourishing about 100 B.C., he spent the latter part of his life in Sicily, where he was poisoned by a jealous rival. His most famous poem is "Lament for Adonis."

BITHYNIA, ancient division of Asia Minor, bounded on the W. by the Sea of Marmora (the Propontis), on the N. by the Black Sea, on the S. by Phrygia, and on the E. by Paphlagonia. It belonged to Lydia in the 7th cent. B.C., but was captured by the Persians in 546 B.C. Later its princes became independent under Nicomedes I, their kingdom maintaining until Nicomedes III who bequeathed it to the Romans in 74 B.C. The Romans united it with Pontus.

BITURIGES, a powerful people in Gallia Aquitanica of Celtic origin, who early held supremacy over other Celts in Gaul.

BOCCHUS, father-in-law of Jugurtha: he was king of Mauretania: at first with Jugurtha he made war against the Romans, but he later delivered up his father-in-law to Sulla, the quaestor of Marius, in 106 B.C.

BOEOTHIUS, ANICIUS MANLIUS SEVERINUS, was born about 476 B.C. He was a Roman philosopher and statesman notable for his knowledge of Greek philosophy. He married Rusticiana, daughter of Symmachus, and became consul in 510 B.C. Theodoric the Great, made him head of the civil administration at Rome, his integrity in office preventing the spoliation of the Italians, but raising enemies. He was accused of supporting the Senate against Theodoric, deprived of office, imprisoned at Padua, and finally executed in 524 B.C. His most important writings were produced in captivity, the most outstanding being, *De Consolatione Philosophiae,* in five books.

BOEOTIA, district of ancient Greece, bounded on the E. by the Euripus, on the N. and W. by Locris and Phocis, and on the S. by Attica, Magaris, and the Corinthian Gulf, the whole covering an area of 1,000 sq. m. It had a damp and oppressive climate, which is said to have accounted for the proverbial dullness of the inhabitants. But Boeotia produced some brilliant men, such as Pindar, Epaminondas, and Pelopidas. The capital was Thebes, all cities were united in a league with Thebes at its head. The chief magistrates, Boeotarchs, were elected annually.

BOII, a powerful Celtic race originally of Transalpina, Gaul. Quite early they migrated in two bodies, one crossing the Alps c. 400 B.C. Settling between the Po and the Apennines with their chief city at Felsina; the other crossing the Rhine settled in Boihemum in Germany, between the Danube and the Tyrol. Boii were also found in Gaul. Those in Italy carried on a fierce struggle with the Romans, but were overcome by the Consul P. Scipio, in 191 B.C. The Boii in Germany retained power longer, but finally were exterminated by Burebistas the Dacian, about 50 B.C.

BOMILCAR, a Numidian confidant of Jugurtha, who arranged the assassination of Massiva for him at Rome in 109 B.C., but in 107 he himself plotted against Jugurtha.

BONONIA, the ancient town known as Felsina in Gallia Cispadana, the capital of N. Etruria. It was captured by the Boii, q.v., but was colonized by the Romans, after defeating the Boii, in 191 B.C. when the name was changed.

BOSPORUS, name applied by the Greeks to a number of straits but particularly to two. 1. THE THRACIAN BOSPORUS, uniting the Propontis and Euxine Seas. At the entrance to this were the famous Symplegades, q.v. When Darius invaded Scythia he built a bridge across the Bosporus. 2. THE CIMMERIAN BOSPORUS, uniting the Palus Maeotis with the Euxine Sea. With the river Tanais (Don) it was the division between Asia and Europe.

BOSTRA, (BOZRAH of the Bible), Hadrian made this city of Arabia Nabataea capital of the province. It was situated in an oasis of the Syrian desert.
East. Rome colonized it in 245 B.C. Virgil died here in 19 B.C.: the poet Pacuvius was born here.

BOTTIAEA, a division of Macedonia which reached as far as Pieria on the W. in the days of Thucydides. The Bottiaeai were of Thracian extraction.

BOUDICCA, popularly but erroneously known as Boadicea; British queen, wife of Prasutagus, king of the Iceni, a people of E. Britain. To ensure the safety of his kingdom he had bequeathed it jointly to his daughters and the emperor Nero, but the Romans seized his lands at his death, his widow was scourged and his daughters ravished. Boudicca with her host burnt Camalodunum (Colchester) and some other towns, but being eventually overcome poisoned herself, in A.D. 61.

BOULE, the Athenian Senate, traditionally established by Solon, which consisted of 500 members, divided into sections of 50. The *prytaneis* (members) were of one tribe, and acted as presidents of the councils and assemblies during 36 or 37 days, in order to complete the lunar year of 354 days. Each tribe functioned in turn, the period of office being known as a *prytany*.

The Boule discussed and prepared measures for consideration of the Ecclesia, q.v.

BRANCHIDAE, ancient town of Asia Minor, on the W. coast, 60 m. S. of Smyrna, famed for its temple and oracle of Didymeia, which gave it its other name, DIDYMA. The temple was destroyed by the Persians in 494 B.C., and rebuilt a century later, and was the largest in the Greek world.

BRASIDAS, one of the most famous of the Spartan leaders in the early stages of the Peloponnesian War; relieved Methone, when besieged by the Athenians in 431 B.C. Assisted Cnemus in unsuccessful attack on Piraeus in 429 B.C.; accompanied Alcides to Corcyra; was severely wounded in assault on Pylos in 425 B.C.; in 424 B.C., he relieved Megara; he assisted Perdiccas against Arrabaeus, and succeeded in gaining Acanthus, Stagira, Amphipolis, and Torone; gained a brilliant victory over Cleon in 422 B.C. Cleon was slain and Brasidas mortally wounded; he was buried at Amphipolis, the inhabitants making him founder of their city and instituting games in his honor.

BRENNUS, historical name of two chiefs of the Celtic Gauls. The first crossed the Apennines with 70,000 Gauls and ravaged Etruria in 391 B.C. A Roman army of 40,000 went to meet them taking up a position on the banks of the Allia. Brennus defeated them with great slaughter, took Rome, besieged the capitol for six months then quit the city, receiving 1000 lbs. of gold as ransom for the Capitol. The second was leader of the Gauls who invaded Macedonia and Greece in 279 B.C.

BRITANNIA (BRITAIN), country inhabited by the Britons, and used for England and Scotland before the advent of Teutonic invaders. Briton is the name of the tribes who made up the 2nd and 3rd (Brythonic and Belgic) waves of Celtic invaders which, previous to Roman civilization coming into contact with them, subjugated all of what is now England, Wales, and the Lowlands of Scotland. The Belgic wave was not earlier than 150 B.C., and the Brythonic not later than 400 B.C. There was early intercourse between the Phoenicians, and Britain was first brought within the orbit of civilization by Julius Caesar. His first military reconnaissance was in 55 B.C.; he returned the following year with a greater force, but retired without effecting a conquest or establishing a garrison. His account of the native fair-haired warriors with their blue war-paint, wicker coracles, primitive huts, loose tribal organization, human sacrifices, and priesthood of Druids is familiar. Aulus Plautius led the Roman army of conquest to Britain in A.D. 43. Agricola established the Roman rule as far as the Tyne in A.D. 78-84, carrying his arms as far as the Forth, tracing a fortified wall across the neck of Scotland to hold back the Gaels (Caledonians, Picts) of the north. The Romans remained in Britain until 407 A.D. Then the tribes of the north surged in, and by the middle of the century the English tide began to flood Britain and submerge the British people.

BRITANNICUS, son of the emperor Claudius and Messalina, born A.D. 41 or 42, was originally called Claudius Tiberius Germanicus, receiving the name Britannicus on account of conquests in Britain about the time of his mother's execution in A.D. 48, but Claudius' new wife, Agrippina, persuaded him to adopt her son of a previous marriage, Lucius Domitius, later known as Nero. Britannicus was poisoned, at Nero's instigation, A.D. 55.

BRIXELLUM, town in Gallia Cisalpina, on the river Po, where the emperor Otho killed himself, A.D. 69.

BRUNDISIUM, (BRINDISI), town on a bay in the Adriatic, in Calabria, with a safe harbour. Brundisium was the terminus of the Appia Via, and the usual starting place for Greece and the East.

BRUTUS, name of a distinguished plebeian family at Rome, first borne by Lucius Junius Brutus, one of the first two consuls, 509 B.C., his mother being sister of Tarquinius Superbus, last of the kings of Rome. His elder brother was murdered by Tarquinius, Lucius escaping by pretending lunacy, hence the name Brutus. After Lucretia had stabbed herself Brutus incited the Romans to expel the Tarquins; this accomplished he was elected first consul with Collatinus. Brutus' two sons being implicated in a conspiracy to restore the banished dynasty, were executed by their father's order and in his presence.—Many of the family rose to eminence, and are found, ranged on the popular side, the most distinguished being Decius Junius B., consul, 325 B.C.—Later MARCUS JUNIUS B. appears as a jurist of high authority and one of the founders of Roman civil law.—His son, of the same name, made a great reputation at the Roman bar as a prosecutor, becoming known as "the Accuser."—DECIUS JUNIUS BRUTUS first served under Caesar in Gaul, and later commanded the fleet, being held in high esteem, but he joined in a conspiracy against his patron, becoming one of his assassins. He was put to death by order of Antony in 43 B.C.—MARCUS JUNIUS BRUTUS, son of a father of the same name, and Servilia, sister of Cato and Utica, is best known of all. At his father's death he was eight years old. In early life he was an advocate: he at first supported the cause of Pompey against Caesar, but was pardoned by the latter, and appointed governor of Cisalpine Gaul. Influenced by Cassius he joined the conspiracy against the dictator, becoming one of the foremost in his assassination. He held Macedonia against Antony's forces and was joined by Cassius. At Philippi they were defeated by Anthony and Octavianus Caesar: rather than be taken prisoner he fell on his sword, in 42 B.C. He wrote treatises and poetry of which nothing has survived. Curiously he was also a money-lender, having Cicero and King Ariobarzanes among his clients.

BRYAXIS, Greek sculptor, contemporary with Scopas and Praxiteles, whom he assisted in the production of sculptures in the mausoleum at Halicarnassus c. 345 B.C. He produced five colossal figures of gods at Rhodes, and a number of other statues.

BULLA, a Roman term for any boss or stud, but applied more particularly to an ornament, worn suspended from the neck by children of noble birth, until they assumed the *toga vicilis,* when it was hung up and dedicated to the household gods.

BURSA, *See* PLANCUS (b)

BUTHROTUM, flourishing port of Epirus, on a peninsula facing Corcyra.

BUXENTUM, town on the W. coast of Lucania, originally known as Pyxus; founded by Micythus, tyrant of Messana, in 471 B.C., later becoming a Roman colony.

BYBLUS, ancient city of Phoenicia, chief seat of Adonis worship.

BYRSA, the citadel of Carthage.

BYZANTIUM, a Doric colony, founded by Megarian colonists under Byzas c. 660 B.C., on the Golden Horn. It was devastated by the Persians under Darius Hystaspes, being raised by the Spartan leader Pausanias to an important maritime city. For over 100 years after the Persian war it was alternately hostile and friendly to Athens, until it became independent in 355 B.C. In the 1st cent. A.D. Byzantium was included with Thrace in the Roman Empire. Constantine enlarged it and made it a new capital of the empire under the name Constantinopolis, later Constantinople.

C

CABIRI, 'The Great Gods' of the Greeks, being fertility gods of Phrygian origin. They varied in number, and were later identified with the Corybantes and Curetes. At Thebes they were represented as an elder and a child. Strabo says that the rites of their cult were akin to those of the Thracian Bendis. Their sanctuary at Samothrace dates from the 6th cent. B.C.

CADMUS, in *Greek Legend*, son of Agenor, King of Phoenicia. His sister Europa was abducted by Zeus, Cadmus being sent by his father to search for her. After consulting the oracle at Delphi, Cadmus built Thebes. He married Harmonia, daughter of Aphrodite, the pair being changed into serpents by Zeus, who placed them in Elysium. Cadmus is credited with the introduction of the Phoenician alphabet into Greece.

CADYTIS, mentioned by Herodotus as a city of the Syrians not much less in size to Sardis. It was captured by Necho, king of Egypt, after he had defeated the Syrians at Magdolus.

CAECILIA, (a) daughter of T. Pomponius Atticus, who married M. Vipsanius Agrippa. (b) Roman name of Tanaquil, wife of Tarquinius Priscus. (c) Wife of the dictator Sulla.

CAECILIUS, (a) The Roman who adopted Atticus, leaving him a fortune of 10 million sesterces. (b) A Roman comic poet who preceded Terence; he was born in Milan, and as a slave bore the servile appellation of STATIUS. He died in 168 B.C. Some forty of his play titles are known.

CAECINA, Etruscan family of Volaterrae. (a) Was defended by Cicero in a law suit, in 69 B.C. (b) Son of (a) who published libellous matter referring to Caesar, being exiled in 48 B.C. (c) A quaestor in Spain when Nero died, who joined Galba's party.

CAECUBUS AGER, low-lying district of Latium, near Fundi, famous for a wine called *Caecubum.*

CAELIUS, MARCUS C. RUFUS, a Roman orator, some of whose letters to Cicero are extant.

CAELIUS or COELIUS MONS, See ROMA.

CAENI or CAENICI, a people of Thracia, inhabiting the land between the Black Sea, and the Panysus.

CAEPIO, Q. SERVILIUS, Roman consul sent to oppose the Cimbri, by whom he was defeated in 105 B.C., with the loss of 80,000 soldiers and 40,000 camp followers. In 95 B.C. he was brought to trial by the tribune C. Norbanus, for misconducting this war: he was condemned and imprisoned.

CAERE, called *Agylla* by the Greeks, a city of S. Etruria, near the Tyrrhenian Sea, about 32 m. from Rome. In Virgil Caere appears as the seat of the Etruscan King Mezentius, but the earliest historical fact is its participating in an attack on the city of Alalia in Corsica. Caere gave refuge to the Tarquins on their expulsion from Rome, and it was used by the Romans as a secure hiding-place for their treasures during the Gallic occupation. Interesting finds from excavations are to be seen in the Vatican and Villa Julia museums at Rome.

CAESAR, cognomen of the great Julian family in Rome, tracing its mythical descent from Iulus, son of Aeneas. Gaius Julius Caesar was its most important representative. The family name was borne by the emperor Augustus, as the adopted son of the dictator, and by later emperors belonging to the family, the last being Nero. Their successors used the name as a title during their reign.

CAESAR, L. JULIUS, consul in 90 B.C. Fought against the Socii; introduced legislation giving citizenship to the Latins and Socii who had remained faithful to Rome; was censor in 89 B.C.; was put to death by Marius in 87 B.C.—CAESAR STRABO VOPISCUS, brother of the foregoing, was curule aedile in 90 B.C., and a candidate for the consulship in 88 B.C. He was a notable orator and poet. He and his brother were slain by Marius in 87 B.C.—L. JULIUS CAESAR, son of Strabo Vopiscus, and uncle of M. Antony. He was consul in 64 B.C.; he was of the aristocratical party but seems to have changed his views; he appears in Gaul in 52 B.C. as a legate of C. Caesar. After the death of Caesar in 44 B.C. he sided with the Senate against Antony, being proscribed by the latter in 43 B.C. but was pardoned by the good offices of Julia.—L. JULIUS CAESAR, son of the foregoing; he joined Pompey at the outbreak of civil war in 49 B.C., being sent to Caesar with peace proposals.—C. JULIUS CAESAR, the dictator. Born at Rome July 12th, 102 B.C. (traditional date 100). He was nephew of the great democratic leader Marius, which influenced his support of the popular party. He saw military service in Asia in 81 B.C. After another term of service with Mithradates, Caesar returned to Rome, plunging into politics as a supporter of popular measures. He became quaestor in Spain in 68 B.C., and curule aedile in 65 B.C. His first wife died in 68 B.C., and in 67 Caesar married Pompeia, Pompey's cousin. In 59 B.C. he held the consulship, and making common cause with Pompey, formed with him and Marcus Crassus the First Triumvirate. He then desired great military command, the province of Gaul being allotted to him for five years, which was extended for five years more. At the end of nine years he had subjugated the whole of Transalpine Gaul. He invaded Britain in 55-54 B.C. His success aroused animosity, and Pompey, now thoroughly jealous, stood as his rival. His demands having been refused Caesar crossed the Rubicon, the dividing line between Italy and the provinces, thus bringing about civil war. He was elected consul for 48 B.C., routing Pompey at Pharsalus, and becoming mixed up in a war in Egypt. He now fell victim to the charms of Cleopatra, who is said to have borne him a son, Caesarion. Further victories over Pompey in Asia Minor, Africa, and Spain preceded a period of power in Rome, where he became dictator for ten years, and then for life. He introduced many reforms, including that of the calendar. Now a conspiracy was formed, under Cassius, against Caesar on the ground that he was aiming at a tyranny, many honestly believing the accusation, notably Marcus Brutus, a friend of Caesar. The conspirators surrounded their victim in the senate house on the Ides (15th) of March, 44 B.C. and stabbed him to death.

CAESAREA, name given to several cities of the Roman empire in honour of one of the Caesars. (a) CAESAREA AD AR-GAEUM, earlier known as Mazaca, also as Eusebia; one of the most ancient cities of Asia Minor, built on Mt. Argaeus, in Cappadocia. It was named Caesarea in A.D. 17 when the country was made a province by Tiberius: it was later destroyed by an earthquake. (b) CAESAREA PHILIPPI, city of Palestine, near the source of Jordan; built in 3 B.C., by Philip the tetrarch. (c) CAESAREA PALAESTINAE, important coastal city of Palestine, near the boundary of Samaria and Galilee. Herod built a harbour here and surrounded it with a wall. It became capital of Palestine under the Romans.

CAESARION, son of C. Julius Caesar by Cleopatra, known also as Ptolemaeus; after his mother's death he was executed by order of Augustus. He was born in 47 B.C.

CALAMIS, embosser and statuary of Athens who flourished about 480-450 B.C. His colossal statue of Apollonia Pontica stood 30 cubits high.

CALATINUS, A. ATILIUS, Roman consul in 258 B.C. who became dictator in 249 B.C. and as such the first to command an army outside Italy.

CALAUREA, island off the coast of Argolis to which Demosthenes fled from Antipater, later taking poison there in 322 B.C. The temple of Poseidon here was regarded as an inviolable sanctuary for refugees.

CALCHAS, son of Thestor; he was the famous soothsayer who accompanied the Greeks during the Trojan war. He foretold the wrath of Apollo, and from the number of a flight of sparrows the length of the war. He is associated by a later legend with the wooden horse. He died of grief on being proved inferior as a soothsayer to Mopsus, Son of Apollo.

CALEDONIA, Roman name for Britain N. of the firths of Forth and Clyde.

CALENDS, Roman name for the first day of the month. To undertake to settle a debt at the Greek Calends indicated the intention not to pay at all, the Greeks having no Calends.

CALENUS, Q. FUFIUS, tribune of the plebs in 61 B.C.; he saved P. Clodius from condemnation for violating the mysteries of the Bona Dea. He was praetor in 59 B.C. and active in support of Caesar. After the death of Caesar he joined M. Antony, commanding the legions in N. Italy.

CALIGULA, Roman emperor, A.D. 37-41; Son of Germanicus and Agrippina, his real name being C. Caesar. His name Caligula came from *Caligae,* soldier's boots which he wore as a boy with the army in Germany. His reign promised well, but a serious illness left him a changed man, and he became extravagant, cruel and capricious. The Roman world growing tired of the mad tyrant he was murdered on the 24th Jan. 41. His wife and daughter were also put to death.

CALLIAS and HIPPONICUS, belonged to a noble family of Athens, possessing great wealth; they were hereditary torch-bearers at the Eleusinian mysteries. Callias fought at Marathon in 490 B.C.; was ambassador from Athens to Artaxerxes, negotiating peace with Persia in 449 B.C. Returning to Athens he was accused of having accepted bribes, being fined fifty talents. His son Hipponicus was killed at Delium in 424 B.C. Pericles married his divorced wife.—The scene of Xenophon's *Banquet,* and Plato's *Protagoras,* is laid in the house of Callias, son of Hipponicus.

CALLIMACHUS, Greek grammarian, poet, and critic, born at Cyrene. Most of his life was spent at Alexandria where Ptolemy Philadelphus made him superintendent of the library, which position he held until his death. He is credited with more than 800 works of prose and verse. Among his pupils were Eratosthenes, Aristophanes of Byzantium, and Apollonius Rhodius.

CALLINUS, OF EPHESUS, earliest of the Greek elegiac poets, about 700 B.C. Only one of his elegies survives.

CALLIPPUS OF CYZICUS, renowned Greek astronomer and friend of Aristotle; lived c. 370-300 B.C.

CALLIRRHOE, the most celebrated well in Athens, in the S. E. of the city, afterwards called Enneacrounos, or the "Nine Springs", because its water was distributed by nine pipes.

CALLISTHENES, nephew and pupil of Aristotle, who accom-

panied Alexander to Asia. He was accused of conniving a plot by
Hermolaus to assassinate Alexander, was in chains for seven
months and then put to death. (Some say he died of disease).
Fragments of his work remain.

CALLISTRATUS, Greek rhetorician, who wrote fourteen descriptions of statues by famous artists in the third century B.C.

CALPURNIA, the last wife of Julius Caesar; is said to have had
an ominous dream the night before the fatal Ides of March, and
to have urged her husband not to take part in the celebrations.
She was daughter of L. Capurnius, the consul.

CAMARINA, coastal town of S. Sicily, founded by Syracuse in
599 B.C. In the first Punic War it was taken by the Romans.

CAMBYSES, (a) father of Cyrus the Great, q.v., (b) King of
Persia, 529-521 B.C., son of Cyrus the Great; he captured Egypt
in 525 B.C., but conducted an unsuccessful campaign against
Ethiopia. Suspecting his brother Smerdis of designs on the throne,
he arranged his assassination. A false Smerdis named Gaumata,
claiming to be brother of the king, obtained some following in
Persia. Cambyses had to leave Egypt to crush this threatened
insurrection, but died in Syria on his way, of an accidentally self-
inflicted wound.

CAMERINUM, a town in Umbria, on the border of Picenum,
which became a Roman colony.

CAMERINUS, Roman poet who versified Hercules' capture of
Troy. He lived in the days of Ovid.

CAMICUS, in *Ancient Geography,* coast of S. Sicily occupying
the site of the citadel of Agrigentum.

CAMILLA, in *Roman Legend,* daughter of the Volscian King
Metabus, was brought up by her father as a handmaid of Diana;
she was famed for fleetness of foot. She assisted Turnus against
Aeneas, slew many Trojans, being at last slain by Aruns.

CAMILLUS, MARCUS FURIUS, hero of the early Roman Republic; is said to have been dictator five times, and to have held
other magistracies. He took the city of Veii after a ten years'
siege; being accused of unjust distribution of the booty he went
into exile. In 390 B.C., when the Gauls under Brennus occupied

all Rome, except the Capitol, and the Romans were about to buy off the invaders, Camillus, reappeared and drove the Gauls from Rome. He died 365 B.C.

CAMPANIA, district of Italy, divided from Latium by the Liris; in the time of Augustus it went no further S. than the promontory of Minerva. It was known as Campania Felix on account of its scenery and climate, and was a favourite summer retreat of Roman nobles.

CAMPI RAUDII, scene of the defeat of the Cimbri by Marius and Catulus in 101 B.C. It was a plain of N. Italy near Vercellae.

CAMPUS MARTIUS, (Field of Mars), part of ancient Rome, named from an altar of Mars erected there: it was formerly surrounded by magnificent buildings. Hadrian or Aurelian enclosed it within the walls of Rome.

CAMALODUNUM, (Colchester), the Trinobantes capital in Britain, and the first Roman colony in that country, founded by Claudius in A.D. 43. Remains are extant including a Mithraeum.

CANDACE, name common to the Ethiopian queens. In 25 B.C. one invaded Egypt, being defeated by Petronius, Roman governor of Egypt.

CANDAULES, last king of Lydia, also known as Myrsilus.

CANEPHORI, Athenian maidens of high birth, who carried the sacred baskets at the Panathenaic festival.

CANIDIA, a courtesan beloved by Horace; when she deserted him he ridiculed her in public as an old sorceress. Her real name was Gratidia.

CANNAE, scene of the defeat of the Romans by Hannibal in 216 B.C., situated on the Aufidus, in Apulia.

CANOPUS, ancient town of Lower Egypt, giving its name to the Canopic branch of the Nile; was prosperous in trade until superseded by Alexandria. The Canopus stele, discovered at Tanis in 1866, (now at Cairo), is a slab of limestone, inscribed in hieroglyphic, demotic, and Greek, recording a priestly decree in honour of Ptolemy III. There was a renowned temple of Serapis here.

CANTABRI, a people of N. Spain of warlike proclivity, whom Augustus subdued between 25-19 B.C.

CANTIUM, a district of Britain roughly covering the same area as *Kent*, but including Londinium (London).

CANUSIUM, a Greek colony in Apulia, on the Aufidus, founded by Diomedes, celebrated for mules and woollen goods.

CAPENA, an early Etruscan town which eventually became a Roman municipium: it was founded by Veii. Here was the renowned grove and temple of Feronia.

CAPHEREUS, headland to the S. E. of Euboea; scene of the wreck of the Greek fleet on its return from Troy.

CAPITO, C. ATEIUS, a Roman jurist, who, by flattery, was favoured by Augustus and Tiberius. With his contemporary Labeo he was reckoned on the highest level of experts on legal points.

CAPITO, C. FONTEIUS, went with Maecenas to Brundisium in 38 B.C. to arrange a reconciliation between Octavianus and Antony.

CAPITOLINUS MONS, *See* CAPITOLIUM.

CAPITOLIUM, (CAPITOL), general name for the Capitoline Hill (MONS CAPITOLINUS), one of the seven hills of Rome. Its southern extremity ended in the Tarpeian Rock, over which criminals were thrown. The Capitol, or temple of Jupiter, founded by Tarquinius Priscus, was completed by T. Superbus. It was burnt in 83 B.C. and in A.D. 69 and 80. Domitian restored it as the chief temple of Rome. On Mons Capitolinus were many other temples and statues.

CAPPADOCIA, district of Asia Minor; rough hilly country, bounded in Roman times by Pontus on the N., Armenia on the E., the Taurus Mts. on the S., and by Lycaonia and Galatia on the W. After forming part of the Persian and Greek empires, it became independent for a time, but by A.D. 17 had become a Roman province. At one time it had included Pontus. Its capital was Mazaca, afterwards Caesarea.

CAPREAE, (*Capri*), small island at the entrance of the Gulf of Puteoli, celebrated in Roman times. Augustus and Tiberius resided here, the latter building twelve villas: Roman remains are still extant.

CAPSA, ancient fortified city of Byzacena, N. Africa, destroyed by Marius in the war with Jugurtha, being later rebuilt.

CAPUA, Capital of Campania, founded by the Etruscans 856 B.C. The Samnites made many attacks on it, and in 343 B.C. Capua put itself under the protection of Rome. The city became second only to Rome in commerce and wealth, but luxury led to degeneracy. It revolted to Hannibal in 216 B.C., being taken by the Romans in 211 B.C. There are remains of antiquity, notably the amphitheatre and baths.

CARACALLA, emperor of Rome, reigned A.D. 211-217; was born at Lyons A.D. 188, son of Septimus Severus. His original name was Bassianus, afterward changed to Marcus Aurelius Antoninus. He was nicknamed Caracalla from the long Gallic cloak of that name, which he usually affected. Severus died at York during a punitive expedition against the northern tribes. Caracalla, who was suspected of having poisoned him, was proclaimed joint emperor with his brother, Geta, whom he later assassinated, together with many of his leading adherents. The remainder of Caracalla's reign was extravagant and cruel. He was murdered at Edessa at the instigation of Macrinus, who succeeded him.

CARACTACUS, king of the Silures in Britain, c. A.D. 51; son of Cunobelin. After long and determined resistance he was defeated by the Romans, fleeing for protection to Cartismandua, queen of the Brigantes, who betrayed him to the Romans. He was taken to Rome, and figured in a procession before Claudius, who freed him.

CARANUS, descendant of Hercules, said to have settled, with an Argive colony at Edessa, in Macedonia, about 750 B.C., becoming founder of a dynasty of Macedonian Kings.

CARIA, maritime province of Asia Minor, forming the S. E. angle of the whole peninsula. It was not merely a territorial division, but an ethnographical district; the Carians are spoken of, by ancient writers, as a distinct nation from their neighbours, the

Lydians, Phrygians, and Lycians. Their origin and early history is uncertain, but tradition says they were originally Leleges from the island of the Aegean, where they were subject to Minos, King of Crete.

CARINUS, MARCUS AURELIUS, Roman emperor, A.D. 283-285; cruel and dissolute, he was an able soldier, fighting with success against the Britains and Alamanni. He put down the revolt of Julian in Pannonia, and defeated Diocletian, who had been declared emperor by the soldiers at Chalcedon.

CARMANIA, a province of the Persian empire.

CARNEADES, Greek philosopher, founder of the Third, or New Academy, born at Cyrene, c. 213 B.C. Little is known of his life; he died in 128 B.C.

CARNUTES, a powerful people of Gaul, living between the Liger and Sequana, with their chief city at Genabum, (*Orleans*).

CARPETANI, people of Hispania Tarraconensis.

CARPI or CARPIANI, a German people living between the Carpathians and the Danube.

CARTHAGE, (MAGNA CARTHAGO), famous ancient city on N. W. coast of Africa, on a peninsula, near the modern Tunis: founded by Phoenician settlers under Dido. The most ancient part of the city was called Byrsa, (citadel). There were two harbours, the city was protected on the land side by a triple wall. The Carthaginians had reached the height of their power before the first Punic War in 264 B.C. Their empire extended in the 4th cent. B.C., from the altars of the Philaeni, near Syrtis, on the E., to the Pillars of Hercules (Gibralter) on the W. They held Sardinia, Corsica, and Malta; the navigator Hanno, founded colonies on the W. coast of Africa. The Carthaginians' importance as traders is shown by the fact that as early as 509 B.C. they concluded a commercial treaty with Rome. The Carthaginians were defeated by Gelon, the tyrant of Syracuse in 480 B.C. but would probably have succeeded in subduing Sicily but for the intervention of the Romans. The three Punic wars ended in the triumph of the Roman arms. The demand of Cato, *delenda est Carthago,* (Carthage must be destroyed), was carried out to the letter. After being besieged for three years the city was taken by storm by the younger Scipio, who destroyed it; the territory then became the Roman province of Africa. In Augustinian days Carthage began to revive, and in the first two centuries of the Christian era was the next city in importance to Rome and Alexandria, becoming the home of what was known as African Latinity. Also it became a stronghold of Christianity, several councils and synods being held there, and it had its own bishop from the end of the 2nd century. Augustine, Cyprian, and Tertullian were natives of N. Africa.—The vandals under Geiseric made themselves masters of the Roman dominions in 439, and Carthage the capital of their kingdom. The city was reconquered by Belisarius in 533, being re-united to the eastern empire under the name of Justinianopolis. It was burned by the Arabs in A.D. 698.

CARTHAGO NOVA, town on the E. coast of Hispania Tarraconensis, founded in 228 B.C. by Hasdrubal, and later colonized by the Romans.

CARUS, MARCUS AURELIUS, Roman emperor A.D. 282-283; was prefect of the praetorian guard under Probus, after whose murder he was declared emperor by the military: he in his turn was assassinated by the soldiers.

CARYAE, Laconian town near the boundary of Arcadia.

CARYATIDES, sculptured figures of women used instead of columns in ancient architecture. The name probably refers to the attitude of the dancers at the festival of Artemis at Caryae.

CASCA, PUBLIUS SERVILIUS, Roman noble of the reactionary party; one of the conspirators against Julius Caesar, who was said to have struck the first blow. He was tribune of the Plebs in 43 B.C.

CASILINUM, town in Campania, famous for its stand against Hannibal in 216 B.C.

CASMENA, ancient town in Sicily, founded by Syracuse about 643 B.C.

CASPIAE PORTAE (CASPIAN GATES), name given to mountain passes around the Caspian Sea, the best known being near the ancient Rhagae, from which distances were measured owing to its central position.

CASPIUM MARE (CASPIAN SEA), also known as Hyrcanium, Albanum, and Scythicum; from names of people living on its shores. It is really a great salt-water lake.

CASSANDER, son of Antipater, whose dying father appointed Polysperchon regent, leaving his son with only secondary dignity of chiliarch. Cassander made war on Polysperchon, forming an alliance with Ptolemy and Antigonus. Later he joined Seleucus, Ptolemy, and Lysimachus in their war against Antigonus, which was, on the whole, unfavourable to Cassander. In 306 he styled himself king: in 301 B.C. the battle of Ipsus put Cassander in possession of Macedonia and Greece. He died in 297 B.C.

CASSIODORUS, MAGNUS AURELIUS, a celebrated statesman, and one of the few men of learning at the downfall of the West: he was born A.D. 487 and died 583.

CASSITERIDES, (TIN ISLANDS), ancient names for Britain and adjacent islands, possibly including Ireland.

CASSIUS, name of one of the most important of the Roman gentes. (a) C. CASS. LONGINUS, murderer of Caesar; was quaestor of Crassus in 53 B.C. and during his campaign against the Parthians gained an important victory in 52 B.C., and another in 51 B.C. He became tribune of the plebs in 49 B.C., supported the aristocratical party in the civil war, fleeing with Pompey from Rome. After Pharsalia he surrendered to Caesar, who pardoned him, and made him praetor in 44 B.C. In spite of this he was still Caesar's enemy, and it was he who formed the conspiracy against his life. At the death of Caesar Cassius went to Syria, which he claimed as his province, although it had been allotted to Dolabella. He defeated Dolabella, who committed suicide. After plundering Syria and Asia he went to Greece with Brutus in 42 B.C., to oppose Octavian and Antony. At the battle of Philippi, Cassius was defeated by Antony, while Brutus succeeded in routing Octavian. Cassius ignorant of his success commanded his freedman to put an end to his (Cassius') life. (b) C. CASS. LONGINUS, famous jurist, governor of Syria in 45 A.D.; was banished by Nero in A.D. 65 for having among his images a

statue of Cassius who had murdered Caesar. He was recalled by
Vespasian. (c) CASS. PARMENSIS, born at Parma, was one of
Caesar's assassins; after Actium he was put to death by Octavian,
in 30 B.C. (d) L. CASS. LONGINUS, tribune 137 B.C. (e) CASS.
AVIDUS, born in Syria, one of M. Aurelius' generals; in A.D. 175
he proclaimed himself emperor. He was slain by the soldiers.

CASSIVELAUNUS, British prince, chief of the Catuvelauni
tribe, N. of the Thames, about 54 B.C. He led the resistance to
Caesar's second invasion in 54 B.C.

CASTRA, Roman camp; it was arranged in a square, with a
ditch outside it, and a wall. It had four chief gates and two main
roads. It housed headquarters, the general's tent, an altar, and a
platform from which the general addressed his men.

CASTULO, town in Hispania Tarraconensis, of importance to
the Romans on account of the adjacent silver and lead mines.

CATANA or CATINA, town founded by Naxos in 729 B.C.,
situated in Sicily, at the base of Mt. Aetna. It was captured by
Hiero I in 476 B.C., who transferred its people to Leontini, settling Syracusans and Peloponnesians in their place. After the
death of Hiero the former inhabitants regained the town. It was
the Athenian base for the Syracusan expedition in 415 B.C. Catana
came under Roman rule in the first Punic War.

CATILINA, L. SERGIUS (CATILINE), Roman politician and
conspirator who was an unsuccessful candidate for the consulship in 66 B.C. This led him to organize his first conspiracy in
65 B.C. Failing in this he organized another seeking support
among bankrupt nobles. This attempt was foiled in 63 B.C. by
Cicero, who accused him in the Senate. After an attempt to just-
ify himself he escaped from the city.

CATO, name of a famous family of the Porcia gens. (a) MAR-
CUS PORCIUS CATO, Roman statesman and writer, known as
Cato the Censor. He became consul in 195 B.C. with Valerius
Flaccus. He gained military successes in Spain, and against
Antiochus the Great in Greece. Cato was a stern moralist in a
decadent age, who set himself to check the younger generation.
He was censor in 189 B.C., his tenure of office being marked by

legislation against luxury, and by the expulsion from the Senate of unworthy members. During the year before his death he was one of the leading instigators of the third Punic War. He died in 149 B.C. aged 85. He wrote several books, his *De Re Rustica* (On Agriculture) is the only one to survive. (Translation by "F. H." in "Roman Farm Management," published in New York, in 1913) (b) MARCUS PORCIUS CATO, great-grandson of the Censor, born 95 B.C.; a Roman statesman who served with distinction in the Spatacist insurrection, and became one of the leaders of the senatorial and aristocratical party. He was always opposed to Caesar; when civil war broke out he joined Pompey's party, after whose defeat at Pharsalus in 48 B.C., he went to Africa joining forces with Quintus Metellus Scipio, but was defeated at Thrapsus in 46 B.C. He took refuge at Utica, but finding the position hopeless, he took his own life.

CATTI or CHATTI, important people of Germany, first mentioned, wrongly, by Caesar as Suevi. The Romans never completely subdued them.

CATULLUS, VALERIUS, greatest of the Roman lyric poets; born at or near Verona in 84 B.C., he came to Rome early in life, being only about thirty when he died. He wrote 116 short pieces, many being addressed to a lady named Lesbia, thought to be the notorious Clodia, sister of Clodius. He also excelled in satire. Of the longer poems the best known are *Lock of Berenice,* in imitation of Callimachus, *Epithalamia,* the *Wedding of Peleus and Thetis,* and *Attis.* Catullus wrote in a variety of metres.

CATULUS, a distinguished family of the Lutatia gens. (a) C. LUTATIUS CATULUS, was consul in 242 B.C. Brought the first Punic War to an end by defeating the Carthaginian fleet off the Aegates islands in 241 B.C. (b) Q. LUTATIUS CATULUS, consul with C. Marius IV in 102 B.C. The next year these two gained the victory over the Cimbri near Vercellae. C. belonged to the aristocratical party; he supported Sulla; was proscribed by Marius in 87 B.C.; ended his life by suffocation. (c) Q. LUTATIUS CATULUS, son of the above, and a leader among the aristocracy, winning respect by uprightness of character. He was made consul in 75 B.C. and censor in 65.

CAUCASUS, CAUCASSII MONTES, chain of Asian mountains, running from the E. shore of the Black Sea, to the W. shore of the Caspian. There were two principal passes, one called Albaniae, the other Caucasiae Pylae. In very early times these mountains were already known to the Greeks.

CAUDIUM, town in Samnium: it was near here that the Roman army surrendered to the Samnites in 321 B.C.

CAYSTER, river of Lydia, whose valley is called "the Asian Meadow" in Homer.

CEBES, (a) of Thebes, pupil of Socrates, who was present at the sage's death. (b) Writer of an allegorical picture of human life called *Pinax.*

CELAENAE, important city of Phrygia, at the sources of the river Maeander and Marsyas. It had a citadel built by Xerxes. Its inhabitants were transported by Seleucus Nicator to Apamea.

CELSUS, A. CORNELIUS, Roman writer on scientific subjects. His book *De Medicina* in 8 volumes, is extant. He probably lived in the days of Augustus and Tiberius.

CELT, name used by classical writers to describe the tall, fair-haired, blue or grey-eyed peoples N. of the Alps. They originally lived on both banks of the upper Danube whence they invaded Italy, founding important settlements there. About 300 B.C. the subjugated Teutonic tribes of the German lands taken by early Celtic conquests rose against their oppressors, driving them westward. At the same time the Celts invaded Macedonia, later founding the province of Galatia, in Asia Minor. Now they lost Spain and were driven from N. Italy by the Romans, who then, under Caesar (Julius), invaded Gaul, which was then the chief seat of Celtic power. It seems there were Celts in Britain before the end of the Bronze Age.

CELTIBERI, powerful people in Spain who proved formidable enemies to the Romans. They submitted to Scipio Africanus in the second Punic War, but later rebelled. They were reduced to submission by the capture of Numantia by Scipio Africanus The Younger in 133 B.C. They took to arms once more under Sertorius, but after his death in 72 B.C. they began to adopt Roman customs and language.

CENCHREAE, the E. harbour of Corinth, important for its Eastern trade.

CENSOR, chief magistrate of ancient Rome. The censors, two in number, were first appointed in 443 B.C. Their chief duty was to take a census of persons and property; they had power to disfranchise; issued regulations to curb extravagance, to secure morality, and were charged with maintenance of public buildings. They also administered finances. The censorship of the elder Cato in 184 B.C. was notable for its severity.

CENTUMVIRI, the civil jury of Rome.

CEOS, island in the Aegaean; its chief town Iulis was birthplace of Semonides.

CEPHALLENIA, largest of the Ionian islands, separated from Ithaca by a narrow strait.

CEPHEUS, (a) King of Ethiopia, son of Belus, husband of Cassiopea, and father of Andromeda. (b) Son of Aleus, one of the Argonauts, was King of Tegea in Arcadia.

CERASUS, colony of Sinope, noted as the place from which Europe obtained both the cherry and its name. Lucullus is supposed to have brought back the plants to Rome.

CERAUNII MONTES, mountains along the coast of Epirus dangerous to shipping: also called Acroceraunia.

CERCINA and CERCINITIS, two alluvial islands in the mouth of the Lesser Syrtis, joined by a bridge, and possessing a good harbour.

CHABRIAS, Athenian general who in 378 B.C. commanded the forces sent to the assistance of Thebes against Agesilaus.

CHAEREA, C. CASSIUS, tribune of the praetorian cohorts responsible for the conspiracy by which Caligula was murdered in A.D. 41. He was put to death by Claudius.

CHAERONEA, town of Boeotia where the Athenians and Boeotians were defeated by Philip in 338 B.C.; also the scene of Sulla's victory over Mithridates in 86. Plutarch was born here.

CHALCEDON, city of ancient Bithynia on the E. shore of the Sea of Marmora, founded by Greek colonists from Megara, in 684 B.C.; became a free Roman city under the empire. The 4th Council of the Church was held there in 451 A.D.

CHALDAEA, the term used in its widest sense included the whole of Babylonia. Xenophon mentions Chaldaeans in the mountains N. of Mesopotamia.

CHAONES, one of three tribes inhabiting Epirus, q.v.

CHRYSIPPUS, born at Soli in Cilicia in 280 B.C.; he became a Stoic philosopher, had studied at Athens, first at the Academy under Arcesilaus, then under Cleanthes, whom he succeeded. He died, aged 73 in 207 B.C.

CHRYSOSTOMUS, JOANNES, (ST. CHRYSOSTOM), Father of the Church; born at Antioch, brought up as a Christian by his mother Anthusa. For six years he lived as a hermit, then returned to Antioch, being ordained priest in 386 A.D. He was appointed to the archbishopric of Constantinople in 398 by Eutropius, minister of the emperor Arcadius. His zeal for reforms made him many enemies, and he was banished in 403, recalled in 404, and again banished. He died A.D. 407. A prayer in the English liturgy is attributed to him. He enjoyed the love and respect of the common people, and was generous in almsgiving.

CICERO, MARCUS TULLIUS, Roman orator, statesman, and man of letters, born at Arpinum in 106 B.C.; his father was of the equestrian order. Cicero visited Greece and the East in 79 and 78 B.C., to study oratory, beginning his public career in 77 B.C., joining the aristocratical party, but was not a consistent supporter, often criticising some of its members. His oratorical powers were first evinced in the law courts where he was a pleader. He became consul in 63 B.C. and during his term of office resolutely crushed the Catiline conspiracy to overthrow the republic. In 58 B.C. his enemy Clodius introduced a measure bringing Cicero to book for illegalities in putting the Catilinarian conspirators to death without trial. Cicero left Italy, but was recalled in 57 B.C. Cicero joined the Pompeians during the Civil War, and after the murder of Caesar in 44 B.C., in which he had taken no part, he reappeared in public life, delivering violent speeches against Antony. He was killed by Antony's emissaries in 43 B.C. It is as a man of letters that Cicero is best known. There are 60 speeches extant and he wrote books on oratory, philosophy, law, and politics. Many of his letters have come down to us.

CILICIA, district of S. E. Asia Minor, noted for flax and grapes. The earliest inhabitants seem to have been a Syrian race. The country was independent until the time of the Persian empire, under which it became a satrapy. Alexander subdued it. After the division of his empire it became part of the kingdom of the Seleucidae: Greeks settled in the plains, the original inhabitants being driven to the mountains, where they remained more or less independent being devoted to piracy until Pompey drove them from the seas. Cilicia became a Roman province 67-66 B.C. so far as the flat country was concerned. The mountain country became a Roman province in the days of Vespasian.

CILICIAE PYLAE or PORTAE, mountain pass between Cilicia and Cappadocia on the way from Tyana to Tarsus.

CIMBRI, a Celtic people of the Chersonesus Cimbrica (now *Jutland*). Together with the Teutoni and Ambrones, they moved south at the end of the second century B.C. They several times defeated the Romans, and in 105 B.C. defeated the united armies of the consul Cn. Mallius and the proconsul Servilius Caepio. Fortunately for Rome the Cimbri, instead of crossing the Alps, marched into Spain and remained there some time. Meanwhile the Romans prepared to resist these foes. They returned to Gaul in 102 B.C., when the Teutoni were cut to pieces by Marius, near Aquae Sextiae. In 101 B.C. the Cimbri were finally routed in the battle of Campi Raudii, in N. Italy.

CIMON, Athenian general and statesman, son of Miltiades. His distinguished service at the battle of Plataea in 479 B.C. was followed by a double victory over the Persians, by land and sea. After the death of Aristides, Cimon led the aristocratical party at Athens; he was responsible in 450 B.C. for the truce between Athens and Sparta.

CINCINNATUS, hero of the early Roman republic. He was consul in 460 B.C. and in 458 was appointed dictator when the country was invaded by the Aequians. The deputation found him ploughing his own fields. He defeated the Aequians in 16 days, resigned his dictatorship and returned to his plough.

CINEAS, the most eloquent man of his day, was a Thessalian, and the friend of Pyrrhus, King of Epirus. He went as ambassador to Rome with peace proposals from Pyrrhus after the battle of Heraclea in 280 B.C.

CINNA, (a) L. CORNELIUS CINNA, leader of the popular party during Sulla's absence in the east. In 87 B.C. he became consul with Cn. Octavius, Sulla making the condition that he take an oath not to change the constitution. However, he soon tried to overpower the senate, and recall Marius and his followers. He was defeated by his colleague in the Forum and was deposed. He soon returned and aided by Marius, took possession of Rome, killing Sulla's friends. He was consul 86, 85, 84 B.C. In 84 Sulla prepared to return from Greece; Cinna was slain by his own soldiers. (b) L. CORNELIUS CINNA, son of the above, who joined M. Lepidus in an attempt to overthrow Sulla, in 78 B.C. (c) C. HELVIUS CINNA, Roman poet and friend of Catullus. He was tribune of the plebs in 44 B.C. and killed while in office, the mob mistaking him for his namesake.

CIRCUS, place in Rome specially built for holding chariot and horse races, games, and, later, athletic and wild beast contests. In form it was a long rectangle with a semicircle at one end. The most notable was the Circus Maximus 1,875 ft. long by 625 ft. broad. Its capacity was enlarged from time to time, and by the fourth century could seat 385,000.

CIRTA, city of the Massylii, in Numidia; the capital of Syphax and Masinissa and their successors. It held an impregnable position, surrounded by the river Ampsaga. Constantine the Great restored the city, its name then being changed to Constantina.

CITIUM, town in Cyprus; birthplace of Zeno. Another Citium was in Macedonia, N. W. of Beroea.

CIUS, ancient city of Bithynia colonized by the Milesians; was destroyed by Phillip III of Macedonia, but rebuilt by Prusias, King of Bithynia, after whom it was named Prusias.

CLAUDIA, QUINTA, a Roman matron who had been charged with incontinency, but vindicated her innocence when a vessel carrying the image of Cybele grounded at the mouth of the Tiber. Soothsayers announced that only a chaste woman could release it. Claudia took the rope, the vessel following her at once in 204 B.C.

CLAUDIANUS, more often called CLAUDIAN; last of the Latin classic poets. Born at Alexandria he came to Rome about A.D. 395. His largest work is an unfinished epic *On the Rape of Proserpine*. He wrote panegyrics on Stilicho and Honorius. He died about A.D. 408.

CLAUDIUS I, Roman emperor, son of Drusus, and nephew of Tiberius, born at Lugdunum, 10 B.C: he was of weak intellect; when 50 years of age the soldiers claimed him emperor, after the murder of Caligula. At first he ruled well, but fell under the influence of his freedmen Pallas and Narcissus, who with his wife, Messalina, became the real rulers. Messalina was put to death in 48 A.D. Agrippina, his fourth wife, was suspected of poisoning him. He died A.D. 54.

CLAUDIUS II, Roman emperor surnamed Gothicus, was of Illyrian origin, and succeeded Gallienus 268 A.D. He died A.D. 270 at Sirmium in Pannonia.

CLAUDIUS, APPIUS, Roman general called Glaucus because he lost his sight in old age. He began the Appian Way during his censorship in 312 B.C. The ancients regarded him as founder of jurisprudence and grammar.—Another APPIUS CLAUDIUS was one of the decemvirs of ancient Rome.

CLAZOMENAE, one of the twelve Ionian cities in Asia Minor; birthplace of Anaxagoras.

CLEANTHES, Stoic philosopher, born c. 330 B.C. at Assus. He was pupil of Crates and Zeno, being a disciple of the latter for nineteen years. He earned his living by drawing water throughout the night, studying philosophy during the day. Having no

visible means of support he was called upon to give an account
of himself, which account so pleased his judges that they voted
him a sum of money which Zeno, however, would not allow him
to accept. In 263 B.C. he succeeded Zeno in his school. He died
of self-starvation in 230 B.C. at the age of 99.

CLEARCHUS, Spartan general who at the end of the Peloponnesian War persuaded his countrymen to send him to Thrace to
protect the Greeks against the Thracians. Having disobeyed their
orders the ephors recalled him and condemned him to death. He
however went and joined forces with Cyrus, gathering an army
of Greek mercenaries for him, in a bid to dethrone his brother
Artaxerxes. They marched into Upper Asia in 401 B.C. After the
battle of Cunaxa and the death of Cyrus, Clearchus was made
prisoner, with other Greek generals, by the treachery of Tissaphernes, and put to death.

CLEMENS, Bishop of Rome at the latter part of the first century, who wrote an epistle in Greek to the Corinthians.

CLEOBULUS, son of Evagoras, born c. 560 B.C.; was one of
the Seven Sages, celebrated for his skill in riddles.

CLEOMBROTUS, (a) son of Anaxandrides, King of Sparta,
who was regent after Thermopylae, 480 B.C. (b) King of Sparta,
son of Pausanias, reigned 380-371 B.C. He fell at the battle of
Leuctra in 371 B.C. (c) King of Sparta, son-in-law of Leonidas
II, reigned 242-c. 240 B.C. (d) an Academic philosopher of
Ambracia, referred to in Milton's *Paradise Lost*.

CLEOMENES, (a) King of Sparta, son of Anaxandrides. He
led the forces when Hippias was driven from Athens in 510 B.C.
Shortly after he aided Isagorus and the aristocratical party
against Clisthenes, q.v. He reigned 520-487 B.C. (b) King of
Sparta, son of Cleombrotus I, 370-309 B.C. (c) King of Sparta
son of Leonidas II, 235-222 B.C. He endeavoured to restore the
ancient Spartan constitution, which he accomplished, putting the
ephors to death. (d) Athenian sculptor: the Venus Medicean
was his work.

CLEON, an Athenian demagogue who was originally a tanner.
He opposed Pericles, afterwards becoming leader of the party

opposed to peace with Sparta. He was chiefly responsible for the decree to put to death the whole male population of Mitylene when the town revolted in 428 B.C. He was defeated by Brasidas, in a battle near Amphipolis, in which both commanders were killed in 422 B.C.

CLEONAE, ancient town of Argolis near Nemea, where Hercules slew the lion.

CLEOPATRA, Queen of Egypt, who on the death of her father, Ptolemy XIII Auletes, in 51 B.C. was appointed joint ruler with her younger brother. Three years later she was expelled by Pothinus and Achillas, her brother's guardians, but was reinstated by the intervention of Julius Caesar, who for a time yielded to her fascinations; she is believed to have borne a son, named Caesarion, by him. In 41 B.C. when Mark Antony and Octavian were dividing the Roman world between them, Cleopatra visited Antony, who fell under her spell. Octavian declared war on Cleopatra in 32 B.C. and Antony met his fleet commanded by Agrippa, at the battle of Actium. During the battle Cleopatra was seized with panic and fled, the lover leaving the fight to follow his mistress; and Agrippa's victory was complete. Antony on a report that she was dead, slew himself and Cleopatra died by her own hand, according to an improbable story, from the sting of an asp.

CLISTHENES, son of Megacles and Agariste; born at Athens. His mother was daughter of Clisthenes the tyrant of Sicyon. He was head of the Alcmaeonid clan after the banishment of Pisistratidae. Being unable to cope with his rival Isagoras, he increased the power of the commons. He abolished the four ancient tribes, establishing ten new ones in 510 B.C. This was in order to secure a representation of the whole people in the Council of Five Hundred. In addition each tribe had a local government. Clisthenes and his supporters eventually overcame Isagoras.

CLITOMACHUS, a Carthaginian, originally named Hasdrubal, who came to Athens about the middle of the second century B.C. He was a leader of the New Academy and well acquainted with Stoical and Peripatetic philosophy. He was pupil of Carneades. He died 110 B.C. by his own hand.

CLITUS, a Macedonian general who saved Alexander's life at the battle of Granicus in 334 B.C. Six years later, when both were inflamed with wine, Alexander slew him, for using insolent language, but later was filled with regret at the death of his friend.

CLOELIA, a virgin given to Porsena as a hostage; she escaped from the Etruscan camp and swam back across the river to Rome. The Romans returned her, but Porsena was so impressed by her bravery, that he set her free, together with other hostages, giving her a horse with fine trappings.

CLUSIUM, one of the greatest of the 12 Etruscan cities, first called Camers. It was the home of Porsena. At a later period Clusium was allied with Rome, and was considered a bulwark against the Gauls, but its siege by the Gauls in 391 B.C. led to the capture of Rome the following year.

CNIDOS, city of Asia Minor on the coast of Caria, where there was a Lacedaemonian colony; it was noted for wine. The great astronomer Eudoxus lived here. Cnidos also had a famous medical school.

CNOSSUS, town on the N. coast of Crete, famed as the residence of Minos. Variously mentioned by the poets as Gnossus, Cnosus, or Gnosus.

COCLES, HORATIUS, legendary hero of ancient Rome. When the Etruscan army under Porsena was about to attack the city, he stemmed the onrush, with two companions, while the Romans demolished the bridge, Horatius then swimming to the other shore in safety. As a reward he received as much land as he could plough in a day.

CODOMANNUS, *See* DARIUS (c).

CODRUS, hero of *Athenian Legend;* was last King of Athens, and belongs to the Eleventh Century B.C. It was prophesied that the Dorians would conquer Attica, if they spared the life of the Attic King. Codrus in disguise provoked a quarrel with some Dorian soldiers, he fell, and the Dorians retreated. No one was thought worthy to succeed this noble patriot; the title "King" was abolished, that of archon replacing it.

COELA, the west coast of Euboea, where part of the Persian fleet was wrecked in 480 B.C.

COELE-SYRIA, the valley between the two ranges of Mt. Lebanon. The name signifies "Hollow Syria." Later the name applied to all southern Syria.

COLCHIS, in *Ancient Geography*, triangular area of Asia Minor at the E. end of the Black Sea. The name was first applied to this district by the poets Aeschylus and Pindar. It was celebrated in *Greek Mythology* as the destination of the Argonauts, the home of Medea, and the special domain of sorcery. Colchis was subdued by the Romans under Trajan.

COLLATINUS, L. TARQUINIUS, son of Egerius, and nephew of Tarquinius Priscus. His surname was derived from the city of Collatia, where his father had been governor.

COLOPHON, one of 12 Ionian cities of Asia Minor, between Lebedos and Ephesus, lying near the coast; its harbour being called Notium. Supposed birthplace of Homer. Colophon was also the native city of Mimnermus, Hermesianax, and Nicander.

COLOSSAE, city of Phrygia, in Asia Minor. In the days of Herodotus it was a flourishing city, but declined with the rise of Laodicea. It was an early center of Christianity; S. Paul addressed one of his epistles to the church here.

COLOSSEUM, the larger of two amphitheatres in Rome. Vespasian began to build it in A.D. 72, and it was completed by Titus in 80. It was an oval building of large blocks of travertine. The exterior had four stories, the first three having arcades of the Doric, Ionic, and Corinthian orders: the fourth was a wall pierced with windows, and ornamented with Corinthian pilasters. Inside, the arena and surroundings formed an ellipse 600 ft. long and 500 ft. broad. It was built largely by Jewish prisoners, taken at the fall of Jerusalem. It was used for gladiatorial and wild beast fights. Many Christians were martyred there. Considerable ruins are extant.

COMITIA, the Roman legal assembly of the people, government being divided between the senate, magistrate and the people, (known as *populus*). The populus was not the same at all times. First it consisted of patricians alone, divided into 30 *curiae*. Later an amalgamation of patricians and plebs was instituted by King Servius Tullius. Servius in addition made a local division of all Roman territory into 30 tribes, whose assemblies were called *comitia tributa,* which eventually became national assemblies. In Republican times the functions of the comitia were:—*Comitia curiata,* who conferred the imperium, and the right of taking auspices upon magistrates after election. *Comitia centuriata,* had the right of electing higher magistrates, passing laws put before them by the Senate, and deciding upon war. *Comitia tributa,* had the right of electing inferior magistrates. In the 4th cent. B.C. the comitia centuriata and comitia tributa were merged. Under Julius Caesar their powers were greatly reduced.

COMITIUM, place in Rome used by the *Comitia* (assemblies), it later became part of the Forum.

COMMAGENE, district of Syria, between the Taurus and Euphrates, annexed to the Roman empire by Vespasian.

COMMODUS, LUCIUS AELIUS AURELIUS, Roman emperor, A.D. 180-192, born at Lanuvium in 161; was son of Marcus Aurelius by the younger Faustina. On his father's death in 180 Commodus hurried to Rome. His cruelty and misrule aroused public hatred which led to his murder.

COMUM, birthplace of the two Plinys; was in Gallia Cisalpina.

CONCORDIA, goddess of Rome having temples there. Camillus built the first, and in this the senate often met.

CONON, Athenian general, chosen as one of the ten who superseded Alcibiades in 406 B.C. In 405 B.C., the Athenian fleet was surprised by Lysander, at Aegospotami, and Conon fled to his friend, Evagoras, King of Cyprus. When war broke out between Sparta and the Persians, he obtained from Artaxerxes, joint command with Pharnabazus, of a Persian fleet, with which he defeated the Lacedaemonians near Cnidos in 394 B.C.

CONSTANS, youngest son of Alexander the Great, at whose death in A.D. 337, C. received Italy, Africa, Illyricum. At the death of his brother Constantine in 340 he became ruler of the West. The soldiers of Magnentius slew him in A.D. 350.

CONSTANTINOPOLIS (CONSTANTINOPLE), city built by Constantine the Great, on the site of ancient Byzantium, and founded as New Rome. It was commenced in A.D. 324, being completed in 330. Theodosius II later enlarged it, as did also Heraclius. For centuries it resisted invasion by Persians, Saracens, Ottomans, Goths, Huns, and Bulgars. It fell to the Turks in A.D. 1453. Until then it preserved its ancient civilization. Of its splendid buildings the most famous is the great church of Santa Sophia, built by Justinian in 532: this is now a museum.

CONSTANTINUS (CONSTANTINE), name of 11 Roman emperors who reigned in Constantinople, headed by Constantine The Great: he was son of Constantius Chlorus, and was born at Naissus in A.D. 272. When his father died at York in 306, the soldiers proclaimed him emperor. Another claimant, Maxentius, had seized power in Rome. In 312 Constantine defeated Maxentius, who was slain, Constantine having staked all on this battle, because in a dream he had seen a fiery cross in the sky with the words "by this conquer." Having been victorious, Constantine ordered his soldiers to wear a monogram of the Name of Christ on their shields, and decreed toleration of Christianity. He fought against Licinius, ruler of the East, gaining a total victory. He then founded a new capital at Byzantium, which was completed in 330, being renamed Constantinople. He died at Nicomedia in A.D. 337. CONSTANTINE II, son and successor of the foregoing, reigned A.D. 337-340, dividing the empire with his brother Constans, but the two quarrelled. CONSTANTINE III reigned only a few weeks in A.D. 641. (The last emperor of this name commenced to reign A.D. 1067.)

CONSTANTINUS, FLAVIUS CLAUDIUS, Roman soldier and usurper, declared emperor by the soldiers in Britain in A.D. 407, made himself master of Gaul, and was acknowledged by Honorius, as emperor of the West.

CONSTANTIUS, name of three Roman emperors. (a) CONSTANTIUS I, FLAVIUS VALERIUS, surnamed Chlorus (the

Pale), emperor A.D. 305-6; father of Constantine the Great. Under Diocletian's decentralization scheme he became ruler of Britain, Gaul, and Spain in A.D. 292, with title of Caesar. When Diocletian abdicated in 305, he received the title of Augustus. He died at York in A.D. 306. (b) CONSTANTIUS II, FLAVIUS JULIUS, emperor 337-361, was third son of Constantine The Great, on whose death he received the eastern part of the empire. He was much occupied with war in Persia. When his brother Constans was overthrown by Magnentius, Constantius was involved in a struggle ending with the defeat of Magnentius in 351, which left Constantius sole ruler of the Empire. War again broke out with the Persians in 359, and his Cousin Julian, commander in Gaul, was proclaimed emperor. Constantius decided to oppose him, but died in A.D. 361. (c) CONSTANTIUS III, commanded the troops in the reign of Honorius. On his marriage with Placidia, sister of Honorius, he was admitted to a share in the Empire, but died in A.D. 421, 7 months after his elevation.

CONVENAE, a race of mixed blood, settled by Pompey in Aquitania.

COPTOS, important commercial city under the Ptolemies, situated in Upper Egypt, E. of the Nile, below Thebes.

CORAX, of Sicily, first to write on the subject of rhetoric c. 467 B.C.

CORBULO, CN. DOMITIUS, Roman general who conducted successful campaigns against the Parthians in the days of Claudius and Nero: he committed suicide at Nero's instigation in A.D. 67.

CORCYRA, Latin form of Kerkyra, the Greek name of Corfu: this island was colonized by the Corinthians c. 733 B.C. Its alliance with Athens in 432 B.C. was a cause of the Peloponnesian War. Corcyra was taken by the Romans in 229 B.C.

CORDUBA, birthplace of the two Senecas and Lucan; founded by Claudius Marcellus in 152 B.C., being one of the greatest cities of Hispania Baetica.

CORFINIUM, town of Samnium, destined by the Italians, in the Social War, to replace Rome as capital, under the name of

Italica.

CORINNA, a lyric poetess of Tanagra, in Boeotia about 500 B.C. who instructed Pindar.

CORINTHIACUS ISTHMUS, was situated between the gulfs of Corinth and Saron, connecting the Peloponnesus with Hellas proper. The Isthmian games were held here. Demetrius Poliorcetes, Julius Caesar, Caligula, and Nero, all unsuccessfully attempted to construct a canal across the Isthmus.

CORINTHIACUS SINUS, gulf between the N. of Greece and Peloponnesus.

CORINTHUS (CORINTH), city of Peloponnesus, in ancient Greece, on the isthmus between the Corinthian and Saronic gulfs. Its two harbours, Lechaeum and Cenchreae, and its fortress, the Aerocorinth, made it of great importance. Cypselus made himself tyrant in 657 B.C.; under him and his son Periander, Corinth reached the height of its power. In 582 an oligarchy was restored. Jealous of Athens, Corinth brought about the Peloponnesian War in 431 B.C. The Macedonians occupied the Aerocorinth in 337 B.C., retaining it until 243 B.C. when Corinth became chief city of the Achaean League. The Romans destroyed Corinth in 146 B.C. Julius Caesar built a new city in 46, notable as one of the first places in Greece where a Christian Church was established.

CORIOLANUS, hero of *Roman Legend*, who received his name from the part he took in the capture of the Volscian town of Corioli. As an aristocrat he was banished for the part he took against the plebeians in a dispute with the patricians. He took refuge amongst the Volsci at Antium, and led them against Rome, advancing until he came to the Cluilian dike near Rome, where he camped in 489 B.C. The Romans in alarm sent several deputations to which he refused to listen. At last he yielded to the entreaties of a body of Roman matrons, headed by his mother, wife and two little children. He led his army back to Volscian territory where he remained until his death.

CORNELIA, (a) Daughter of P. Scipio Africanus the elder, and wife of T. Sempronius Gracchus, and mother of the tribunes

Tiberius and Gaius. (b) Daughter of Metellus Scipio, who married P. Crassus, son of the triumvir, and later, Pompey the Great, whom she accompanied to Egypt after Pharsalia, being a witness of his murder.

CORSICA, island of the Mediterranean called Cyrnus by the Greeks. The Iberians were its first inhabitants, while quite early Ligurians, Tyrrhenians, Carthaginians, and Greeks settled there. It was under Carthaginian rule until the beginning of the first Punic War, but soon after passed to the Romans.

CORTONA, one of the twelve cities of Etruria, situated on the N. W. of the Trasimene Lake, and one of the most ancient cities of Italy.

CORUNCANIUS, TITUS, was consul with P. Valerius Laevinus in 280 B.C. and first plebeian to be created pontifex maximus.

CORVUS, MARCUS VALERIUS, hero of ancient Rome, six times consul, and twice dictator. During single combat with a gigantic Gaul in 349 B.C., a raven attacked his enemy, so confusing him that Valerius gained the victory, hence the name Corvus (raven). He died aged 100.

COSA, ancient city in Etruria, near the sea, with a port (Herculis Portus). It became one of the 12 Etruscan cities after the collapse of Falerii.

COSSAEA, district of the Cossaei, who were never subdued by the Persians. Alexander overcame them in 325 B.C., but they regained independence after his death.

COSSUS, AULUS CORNELIUS, was consul in 428 B.C.; it was he who killed the king of Veii (Lars Tolumnius), in single combat.

COTISO, Dacian King, subjugated by Lentulus, in the reign of Augustus.

COTTA, AURELIUS, (a) was praetor in 40, when he passed the famous law entrusting the *judicia* to the senators, equites, and tribuni aerarii. (*Lex Aurelia Judiciaria*). (b) consul 75 B.C. He was a distinguished orator who is mentioned by Cicero.

COTTA, L. AURUNCULEIUS, a Gallican legate in the days of Caesar; killed in battle against Ambiorix in 54 B.C.

COTTIUS, king of a number of tribes of the Cottian Alps, who submitted to Augustus. He was granted the rule of twelve of his tribes. He built roads over the Alps, and a triumphal arch in honour of Augustus at Segusio in 8 B.C.

COTYS, several kings of Thrace were known by this name.

CRANTOR, academic philosopher who studied under Xenocrates and Polemon; author of several ethical books, which Cicero commends. He flourished about 300 B.C.

CRASSUS, M. LICINIUS, (a) Son of P. Licinius Crassus, probably born a little before 115 B.C. He was appointed to take command against Spartacus and the revolted gladiators of Capua, the battle of Rhegium ensued, with Crassus the victor, while Spartacus and 40,000 of his men fell. On his return he was awarded an ovation. In 70 B.C. he was consul with Pompey and again in 55 B.C. He received the province of Syria. He was later defeated by the Parthians near Carrhae in Mesopotamia: he was put to death by the Parthians in 53 B.C. (b) LUCIUS LICINIUS CRASSUS, considered the greatest orator of his time. Cicero pronounces him perfect. He was consul 95 B.C., censor in 92. He died 91 B.C.

CRATERUS, (a) One of Alexander's generals, upon whose death he received jointly with Antipater, the government of Macedonia and Greece. He died in a battle against Eumenes in 321 B.C. (b) A Greek physician, mentioned by Horace and Cicero.

CRATES, (a) Celebrated grammarian of Mallus in Cicilia, who founded a school of grammar at Pergamus, and wrote a commentary on Homer's poems in opposition to Aristarchus. (b) Athenian poet c. 450 B.C. (c) A pupil of the Cynic Diogenes c. 320 B.C. He was born at Thebes.

CRATINUS, son of Callimedes, a writer of old comedy, born at Athens in 519 B.C. He was adversary of Aristophanes, to whom on two occasions the judges gave him second place, and in 423 B.C. he gained first prize for his comedy *Wine-Flask;* the *Clouds* of Aristophanes being placed third. He died the following year. In his old age he was addicted to intemperance. The names of 40 of his comedies have been preserved.

CRATIPPUS, (a) Peripatetic philosopher born at Mitylene, friend of Cicero, who regarded him first philosopher of the age, and entrusted his son Marcus to his care at Athens. (b) Greek historian who continued Thucydides' history up to 394 B.C.

CREMONA, Roman colony near the confluence of the Addua and Po; founded with Placentia in 218 B.C., as a defence against Hannibal and the Gauls. Having espoused the cause of Vitellius, it was destroyed by Vespasian in A.D. 69.

CREON, (a) King of Corinth, whose daughter, Glauce, became wife of Jason. (b) Son of Menoecus; his sister was Jocaste, wife of Laius. Creon governed Thebes for a short time after the death of Laius, surrendering the kingdom to Oedipus.

CRESPHONTES, son of Aristomachus, and one of the conquerers of Peloponnesus, who was awarded Messenia. He and his two sons were killed in a Messenian insurrection, a third son, Aepytus, avenging their deaths.

CRESTONIA, a tract in Macedonia between the Axius and Strymon, occupied by a Thracian people, known as Crestonaei. The capital was Creston, founded by the Pelasgians.

CRETE, large island of the Mediterranean, sometimes known as *Candia,* lying across the S. end of the Aegaean Sea. It had a civilization of great antiquity and interest, as is shown by the ruins of Cnossus, Phaestus, and other cities. It was the first part of Europe to attain any high artistic achievement, this taking place between c. 2200-1600 B.C. (the Middle Minoan period). Invasions from Greece followed this period, resulting in another civilization, in which Asiatic influences were brought to bear, around 1000 B.C. The laws of this period show a social organization superior to that of the mainland. The rise of the maritime cities of Greece robbed Crete of its dominant position, and it became of little importance until the dawn of modern history. The island was conquered 68-66 B.C. by Q. Metellus, when it became a Roman province.

CRETHEUS, founder of Iolcus; was son of Aeolus and Enarete, and father of Aeson, Pheres, Amythaon, and Hippolyte.

CREUSA, daughter of Priam and Hecuba; wife of Aeneas, and mother of Ascanius; she perished at the capture of Troy.

CRISSA and CIRRHA, towns in Phocis, believed by some to be the same place. Others hold that Crissa was a town S. W. of Delphi, with Cirrha as its port in the Crissaean Gulf. The inhabitants taxed pilgrims who visited the Delphic oracle, and in consequence the Amphictyons made war on them in 595 B.C. eventually destroying them. The Crissaean plain was declared sacred to the Delphic god, cultivation being forbidden. The Amphissan's breach of this rule led to the Sacred War, in 338 B.C.

CRITIAS, one of the thirty tyrants sent to Athens by the Spartans in 404 B.C. He was a pupil of Socrates.

CRITOLAUS, (a) Head of the Peripatetic school of philosophy at Athens, in succession to Ariston. The Athenians sent him, in 156 B.C. as ambassador to Rome with Carneades, and Diogenes. (b) General of the Achaean League, who was defeated by Metellus.

CROESUS, last King of Lydia, son and successor of Alyattes. Powerful and wealthy he welcomed the Greeks to his court at Sardes, and gave handsome subscriptions to the temples of Apollo. It is said that the Athenian lawgiver Solon, told Croesus that no man could be called happy until his life had ended happily. Croesus was routed by Cyrus, and condemned to be burnt; at the stake he remembered the remark of Solon, and uttered his name three times, Cyrus hearing him, and learning the reason, spared him. He reigned 595-546 B.C.

CROTON or CROTONA, Greek city of Italy, founded by the Achaeans in 710 B.C., which became one of the richest and most powerful cities of Magna Graecia. Milo the athlete was born here. Pythagoras founded his society here about 540 B.C.

CTESIBIUS, an Alexandrian Greek, living about 150-120 B.C., the instructor of Hero (according to Pliny), and the inventor of hydraulic and other machines.

CTESIPHON, city of Assyria, on the E. side of the Tigris, 25 m. S. E. of Bagdad, which became capital of Parthia. It was conquered by the Romans in A.D. 116 and 199, and here Julian the Apostate defeated the Persians in 363.

CUMAE, ancient Greek settlement in Campania, founded about

750 B.C., 14 m. W. of Naples. It was one of the sources of Greek civilization in S. Italy, and acquired wealth and power. The rock of the Acropolis is honeycombed with caves, from one of which the Cumaean Sibyl brought the Sibylline Books to Rome.

CUNAXA, small town 50 m. N. of Babylon, where the battle between Cyrus the Younger and his brother Artaxerxes Mnemon was fought in 401 B.C., in which Cyrus was killed.

CURES, a town in the Sabines, birthplace of T. Tatius, and Numa Pompilius.

CURIA, *See* COMITIA.

CURIATII, *See* HORATIA GENS.

CURIO, C. SCRIBONIUS, (a) an enemy of Caesar; he supported P. Clodius when accused of violating the *sacra* of the Bona Dea. He was appointed pontifex maximus in 57 B.C. and died in 53 B.C. (b) Son of the foregoing; he married Fulvia who afterward became wife of Antony. He was made tribune of the plebs in 50 B.C. When civil war broke out he was sent by Caesar to Sicily as propraetor. He drove Cato from the island, then, crossing to Africa, he was killed by Juba and P. Attius Varus.

CURIUS, MANLIUS, Roman general who was three times consul; in 290 B.C. he defeated the Sabines and Samnites who had been at war with Rome for fifty years. By his victory at Beneventum in 275 B.C. he forced Pyrrhus, King of Epirus, to abandon his Italian campaign. His military talent and upright life made him one of the best representatives of the old Roman republic.

CURSOR, L. PAPIRIUS, was consul five times between 326 and 313 B.C., and dictator twice later. As a general he defeated the Samnites, and was ranked as a general, by Livy, with Alexander the Great.

CURSUS HONORUM, the order in which a Roman succeeded to the degrees of office.

CURTIUS RUFUS, Q., Roman historian, who wrote the life of Alexander the Great about A.D. 50, in 10 books, some of which are extant.

CYAXARES, king of Media, son of Phraortes, reigned 634-594

B.C., who introduced great military reforms. He made war with the Assyrians, Scythians, and with Alyattes, king of Syria.

CYCLADES, archipelago in the Aegaean Sea, about 20 in number, in ancient times supposed to form a circle round the sacred island of Delos. They were a center of Aegaean civilization in the second millennium.

CYDNUS, river on which Tarsus was built, noted for the coldness of its waters, in which while bathing Alexander nearly lost his life.

CYDONIA, place from whence quinces were first brought to Italy; situated on the N. W. coast of Crete.

CYLON, a noble Athenian who won an Olympic victory in 640 B.C., seizing the Acropolis with the intention of making himself tyrant of Athens. He and his followers were driven by famine to take refuge at the altar of Athena, whence they withdrew on a promise that they should be spared. Cylon escaped but the rest were slain.

CYNEGIRUS, distinguished himself at the battle of Marathon in 490 B.C., seizing one of the Persian ships to keep it back, (according to Herodotus). He was brother of the poet Aeschylus.

CYNOSARGES, gymnasium outside Athens, sacred to Heracles, where Antisthenes, founder of the Cynic school, taught.

CYPRIANUS, (CYPRIAN), Christian bishop and martyr, an early father of the Church was born in Africa. Being converted about 246 A.D. he became bishop of Carthage in 249 A.D. He suffered persecution under Decius and Valerian, being beheaded in 258 A.D. His writings have been preserved for us.

CYPRUS, island in the E. Mediterranean, 60 m. W. of Latakia, famous for its copper mines. It was colonized by the Phoenicians and then the Greeks, being subject at varying times to the Egyptians, Persians, and the Romans who made it a province in 58 B.C. Cyprus was a chief center of the worship of Aphrodite. Modern excavation has revealed a neolithic culture of the fourth millennium B.C.

CYRENE, ancient city of N. Africa, between Carthage and Alexandria. Originally a Greek colony, it became capital of Cyrenaica. It was birthplace of Aristippus, founder of the Cyrenaic philosophical school, also of Callimachus the poet. It was famed for its medical school. The city was founded by Battus about 630 B.C.

CYRESCHATA, (sometimes Cyropolis), town of Sogdiana, the furthest colony founded by Cyrus, and the furthest outpost of the Persian empire; it was destroyed by Alexander.

CYRRHESTICE, province of Syria in the days of the Seleucidae, bounded on the N. by Commagene, and on the S. by the plain of Antioch.

CYRUS, (a) THE ELDER, surnamed the Great, king of Persia, and founder of the Persian empire. According to his own statement in an inscription on a cylinder discovered in the ruins of Babylon, he was "son of Cambyses, the son of Cyrus, the son of Teispes, the son of Achaemenes." Cyrus overthrew Astyages in 549 B.C.; united Media and Persia, transferring the capital from Ecbatana to Susa. Afraid of his growing power, Croesus of Lydia, and Nabonidus of Babylon and Amasis of Egypt, combined against him. Cyrus overthrew Croesus in 546 B.C., making himself master of the coast of Asia Minor. Babylon fell to him in 539 B.C. without a blow. He was killed in 529 B.C. while fighting nomads. (b) THE YOUNGER, second son of Darius Nothus, king of Persia, who plotted against his brother, the reigning monarch, Artaxerxes Mnemon, who forgave him, restoring him as satrap of the coast of Asia Minor. But in the spring of 401 B.C. he raised an army against Artaxerxes and was killed at the battle of Cunaxa.

CYZICUS, ancient Greek city of Asia Minor, standing on an island in the Propontis, near the shore of Mysia, to which it was joined by two bridges, and later by a mole. It freed itself from the Persians after the peace of Antalcidas. Its resistance to Mithridates in 74 B.C., obtained for it the status of *libera civitas* (free state). The temple here was reckoned among the wonders of the world. Cyzicus was destroyed by earthquake in the reign of Justinian. Marble from the ruins was used in building S. Sophia at Constantinople.

D

DACIA, Roman province, bounded on the N. by the Carpathians, on the S. by the Danube, on the E. by Hierasus, and W. by Tysia. It was conquered and made a Roman province by Trajan. Under Aurelian it was given up to the Goths who were attacking hard on the N. E. frontier of the empire.

DADO, in *Classical Architecture*, the cubic block forming the body of a pedestal.

DAEDALA, Boeotian festival in honour of Hera, held at Plataea, consisting of a sacred marriage and a curious fire rite.

DAEDALUS, in *Greek Mythology*, an Athenian sculptor, architect, and inventor of tools and instruments. He was favoured by Minos, King of Crete, and built the subterranean labyrinth for housing the Minotaur. Daedalus and his son Icarus were confined in this labyrinth for having supplied Ariadne with the thread by which Theseus escaped from it. Daedalus then made wings of feathers fastened with wax, by means of which they flew across the sea. Icarus, rising too high, caught the heat of the sun, which, melting the wax, caused Icarus to fall and drown; Daedalus reached Italy in safety.

DAEMON, spirit holding a middle place between gods and men, as the daemon, or good spirit of Socrates.

DAHAE, Scythian nomadic people of the country E. of the Caspian and South of the Aral Sea: they were numerous and of some importance.

DALMATIA, district on the E. coast of the Adriatic, where lived a warlike people, who embarrassed the Romans. Metellus occupied their country in 119 B.C. and took the surname Dalmaticus, but the Dalmatians still managed to remain independent. Asinius Pollio defeated them in 39 B.C., and they were finally subdued in 23 B.C. by Statilius Taurus. Under the leadership of Bato they joined the Pannonian revolt, but after three years were again subdued by Tiberius in A.D. 9. Dalmatia was at first part of the province of Illyricum under the Romans, but towards the end of the 1st cent. A.D. it was made a province, and later Diocletian divided it into Dalmatia and Praevalitana.

DAMASCUS, this most ancient city existed in the time of Abraham, and was situated in what was afterwards called Coele-Syria. For centuries it was the center of the independent kingdom of Syria, which after being conquered by the Assyrians, came later under the domination of the Babylonians, and then successively, the Persians, the Greek kings of Syria, and the Romans. The Jewish historian Josephus traces the history of Damascus back to the Flood, thus making it one of the most ancient cities in the world. Its strategic position was unsurpassed, and most of the eastern caravan routes passed through it. It was a treasure city of Darius before he met Alexander at Issus. By 62 B.C. it was included in the Roman province of Syria. The city was one of Antony's gifts to Cleopatra. Later Augustus put it into the hands of Herod the Great. It became a stronghold of Judaism in the early days of Roman government. It early became a Christian stronghold, ranking first among the Churches under the Patriarch of Antioch. A great massacre of the Jews took place under Nero. The city suffered in the long struggle between Heraclius and the Persians, and was among the earliest conquests of Islam.

DAMOCLES, favourite of Dionysius The Elder, tyrant of Syracuse. He averred that Dionysius was the happiest man on earth, so Damocles was invited to take the tyrant's place at a banquet, where he saw above his head a sword suspended by a single hair; thereupon Damocles confessed himself mistaken.

DAMON AND PHINTIAS, (Note, not *Pythias*, as some suppose), two Pythagoreans, proverbial types of devoted friends. Phintias, having been condemned to die by Dionysius the tyrant, was allowed time to settle his affairs upon Damon offering himself to be put to death should Phintias fail to return. Phintias returned just in time, being pardoned by Dionysius, who was so impressed with the friendship that he asked to be included as a third in the brotherhood.

DAPHNE, a place 5 m. S. of Antioch noted for its great beauty, and famous for its temple and grove of Apollo. It also had pleasure grounds and theatres.

DARES, Trojan priest of Hephaestus in the days of the Trojan war, who is attributed with an ancient account of the war which was extant in the time of Aelian.

DARIUS, name of three Persian kings. Darius I, Hystaspes, was of the family of the Achaemenidae, and son of Hystaspes. He acquired the Persian throne after defeating the usurper Gaumata. Two Babylonian revolts were crushed, and by 519 B.C. Darius was complete master of his empire. Macedonia and Thrace were brought under Persian rule in 513 B.C., but in 501 B.C. Darius came into conflict with the Greeks. His first expedition against them was unsuccessful in 492 B.C. After further attempts he died in 485 B.C.—DARIUS II, OCHUS, rose against his illegitimate brother, Secydianus (who had murdered his brother, Xerxes II), and slew him. He reigned until his death in 404 B.C., being succeeded by his son Artaxerxes II. DARIUS III. CODOMANNUS was last of the Achaemenian dynasty, reigning 336-330 B.C.

DASSARETII, a people living on the borders of Macedonia, in Greek Illyria. Their capital was Lychnidus, on the N. of Lake Lychnitis.

DATAMES, a Carian who became a Persian General; was appointed a satrap of Cilicia by Artaxerxes II, against whom he revolted. After defeating armies sent against him he was assassinated in 362 B.C. He had a reputation for bravery.

DATIS, commanded the Persian army, (together with Artaphernes), which was defeated at the battle of Marathon, 490 B.C.

DATUM, town in Thrace, subject to Macedonia, having gold mines in its vicinity.

DECEBALUS, famous King of the Dacians, who was subsidized annually by Domitian. Trajan defeated him and he died by his own hand in A.D. 106.

DECEMVIRI, or Ten Men, the title of various magistrates or functionaries in ancient Rome. The name is particularly applied to a body of ten men who were appointed at Rome to make a code.

DECIUS, GAIUS MESSIUS QUINTUS, Roman emperor who succeeded Philip, was a violent persecutor of the Christians. He, with his sons, fell in an expedition against the Goths, c. A.D. 251.

DECIUS MUS, PUBLIUS, (a) Consul, with T. Manlius Torquatus, in 340 B.C. (b) Son of the above, and four times consul. (c) Son of (b) was consul in 279 B.C.

DEIOCES, first King of Media after the Assyrian yoke had been cast off: he built Ecbatana. He reigned 709-656 B.C. His son Phraortes succeeded him. q.v.

DEIOTARUS, King of Galatia, 52-40 B.C., who in the civil war supported Pompey, being present at Pharsalia in 48 B.C.

DELIAN, pertaining to *Delos,* q.v., in the Aegaean Sea, birthplace of Apollo and Artemis.

DELIUM, coastal town of Boeotia, in the district of Tanagra, where the Athenians were defeated in 424 B.C.

DELOS, smallest island of the Cyclades, in the Aegaean. In *Ancient Legend,* it was called from the deep Poseidon, and was a floating island until Zeus chained it to the ocean-bed, that Leto might rest there for the birth of Apollo and Artemis. Ionians settled there, and it became their centre of religious union, and their political seat in the 11th. cent. B.C. It became a naval base in Roman times. The sanctity of the island usually secured it from the raids, although not fortified.

DELPHI, town of ancient Greece, on the S. slope of Mt. Parnassus, famous for its oracle of Apollo. Its people were known as Dorians. It was the principal seat of Apollo worship, but was also associated with that of Dionysus. It was the scene of the Pythian games. The temple of Apollo was used as a treasure house by many of the Greek states. The oracular responses were given by a priestess, the Pythia, who sat on a tripod in the temple over a chasm, whence vapour arose from the river

Cassotis, this vapour being the source of inspiration. The oracle was noted for ambiguity.

DEMADES, Athenian orator contemporary with Demosthenes, who took the part of Philip in the Olynthian affair, being liberally rewarded. He was put to death by Antipater in 319 B.C.

DEMARATUS, (a) king of Sparta, 510-491 B.C., who was deposed by Cleomenes; going to Persia he was received by Darius. He joined Xerxes in the invasion of Greece. (b) a noble who was a merchant of Corinth; father of Aruns and Lucumo.

DEMETER, in *Greek Mythology*, goddess of Agriculture, whose Roman counterpart was Ceres. She was daughter of Cronus and Rhea, and became the mother of Proserpine, by Zeus. Pluto, the god of the underworld, carried away Proserpine, and her mother set out to seek her, refusing to allow the earth to produce its fruits until her daughter was restored. Proserpine eventually was allowed to spend six months of the year with her mother. This story is allegorical of the processes of nature, Proserpine being the seed which remains buried part of the year. When she returns she is the rising corn.

DEMETRIUS, POLIORCETES, son of Antigonus, king of Asia and Stratonice, who was continuously engaged in struggles with Cassander or Ptolemy. He besieged Rhodes in 305 B.C. using huge machines of war constructed at his orders; in 304 B.C. he made a treaty with the Rhodians. His father was slain at the battle of Ipsus in 301 B.C., after whose death the fortunes of Demetrius declined. In 294 B.C., however, the Macedonian army acknowledged him king, and he remained in possession of Macedonia for seven years. But in 288 B.C. his troops deserted him and proclaimed Pyrrhus King. Demetrius now went to Asia, and was later obliged to surrender himself to Seleucus, who confined him without harshness. In the third year of his imprisonment he died, in 283 B.C., aged 56.

DEMETRIUS SOTER, son of Seleucus IV Philopater, and grandson of Antiochus the Great. As a child he was sent as a hostage to Rome by his father, where he remained until he was twenty-three. He now escaped to Syria, being received as king by the Syrians. Balas the Impostor raised a rebellion against him, and slew him. He reigned 162-150 B.C.

DEMETRIUS NICATOR, son of Demetrius Soter, reigned for two periods, 145-141 B.C., and 129-126 B.C. He overthrew Balas with the aid of Ptolemy Philometor, but being detested by his subjects was driven from Syria, and Antiochus, infant son of Balas, was set up as pretender against him. Demetrius went to Babylon, and from there marched against the Parthians by whom he was captured in 138 B.C. He was ten years in captivity. Later he again secured the Syrian throne in 129 B.C. When he was absent on an expedition against Egypt, Ptolemy Physcon set up Alexander Zebina as pretender, who defeated Demetrius. Demetrius fled to Tyre where he was assassinated in 126 B.C.

DEMETRIUS PHALEREUS, was born of poor parents at Phalerum c. 345 B.C. He rose to high distinction at Athens as an orator, statesman, philosopher, and poet. Cassander entrusted him with the government of Athens in 317 B.C. He died in 283 B.C.

DEMOCEDES, famous physician of Crotona, who practised medicine at Aegina, Athens, and Samos. He was imprisoned with Polycrates, in 522 B.C., later being sent to the court of Darius by Susa; he made a name there by curing the king's foot and the breast of the queen, Atossa, who arranged that he should be sent with some nobles to explore the shores of Greece, to ascertain the most likely spot for attack. He escaped at Tarentum, settling at Crotona where he married the daughter of Milo, the wrestler.

DEMOCRITUS, Greek philosopher, born at Abdera, in Thrace, who taught the atomic theory of the universe, which has been reverted to by modern scientists. The atoms, taught Democritus, varied in size, shape and position. Falling together by force of gravity, impinging one upon another, and flying off in various directions as a result of impact, they produced a rotatory movement. Eventually they found their proper combinations, and thus the universe was formed. Democritus was known as the laughing philosopher on account of his optimism. He died, an old man, about 370 B.C.

DEMOPHON, son of Phaedra, by Theseus, who went with the

Greeks to Troy, and returning, gained the love of Phyllis, daughter of King Sithon of Thrace. Before the marriage had been celebrated he went to Attica, where he remained for so long that Phyllis thought she was forgotten, and ended her own life; afterwards she relived as a tree.

DEMOSTHENES, (a) Athenian general in the Peloponnesian War, was the son of Alcisthenes. He assisted Cleon in capturing the Spartans in the Isle of Sphacteria in 425 B.C. He was dispatched with a strong fleet to assist Nicias in 413 B.C. Both leaders were overcome and put to death by the Syracusans. (b) The most famous of the Athenian orators. He was early left an orphan, and in spite of natural disabilities studied law, and trained to become an orator. Having amassed sufficient money he was free to devote himself to politics by the year 355 B.C. He planned to regenerate Athens, so that she might lead the Hellenic world. From 351 B.C. he delivered telling speeches, vainly endeavouring to rouse his countrymen to the dangerous attitude of Philip of Macedon. They listened too late; Athens and Thebes were overcome at Chaeronea in 338 B.C., and this was the death blow of Greek independence. Ctesiphon proposed that a crown should be given to Demosthenes for services rendered. In 324 A.D., he was accused of receiving a bribe; he was found guilty and imprisoned. Making his escape, he lived abroad until the death of Alexander encouraged the Greeks to make a bid for independence. Demosthenes headed the revolt, but Greek hopes were shattered at the battle of Crannon in 322 B.C. To avoid falling into the hands of the Macedonians, Demosthenes took his life.

DERCETIS, DERCETO, Syrian goddess who offended Aphrodite, who in consequence inspired her with love of a youth, by whom she bore Semiramis. Shamed, she slew the youth, and exposed her child in the desert, and drowned herself. Doves fed the child, and she became a fish.

DEUCALION, in *Greek Mythology*, son of Prometheus, and king of Phthia in Thessaly. When Zeus sent an overwhelming flood, Deucalion and his wife escaped in a vessel, which after nine days' tossing rested on Mt. Parnassus. The oracle bid them to throw the bones of their mother over their shoulders. They thereupon threw stones behind them which became men and women. Deucalion, descending from Parnassus, built his first abode at Opus, and became by his wife, Pyrrha, father of Helen, Amphictyon, and Protogenia.

DEVA, the city of Chester, in England, which was a fortress of the Roman legion, near the mouth of the river Dee; it was built about A.D. 70.

DIADOCHI, the successors of Alexander the Great.

DIAGORUS of MELOS, also called the Atheist, was a Greek poet and philosopher, flourishing in the 5th. cent. B.C. He died at Corinth.

DIANA, in *Roman Mythology,* an Italian deity, identified with the Greek Artemis. Dianus and Diana are strictly two adjectives, derived from *dies,* 'day'. Dianus, by an easy change would become Janus, as Diana, we know, was corrupted by the rustics into Jana in their hymns to the new moon. Diana was patroness of the chase, and her aid was invoked in parturition.

DIANIUM, (now *Denia*), so named from the temple of Diana which stood here. The town was in Hispania Tarraconensis, being founded by the Massilians.

DIASIA, *See* GREEK FEASTS.

DIAULOS, the quarter of a mile double course for runners in Greek athletics.

DICAEARCHUS, disciple of Aristotle, and friend of Theophrastus, was born in Messana in Sicily. Besides philosophy, he studied geography and history.

DICAST, a juror under Attic law. There were six thousand of them, sworn annually, and divided into panels (dicasteries). They were paid for their services from the time of Pericles.

DICTATOR, the highest extraordinary magistrate in the Roman Republic; the office was instituted in 501 B.C. The dictator had the power of the two consuls, and the authority of all other magistrates, except that of the tribunes, ceased as soon as he was appointed. He possessed the whole administrative power of the state, and command of the army without restriction. The office was abolished in 44 B.C.

DICTE, MOUNT (CANDIA), was in eastern Crete, and it was here that Zeus was brought up, giving him name of Dictaeus.

DICTYNNA, an extra name, shared by Britomartis, Artemis, and Diana.

DICTYS CRETENSIS, the supposed author of *Ephemeris Belli Trojani*, in six books, which is still extant in a Latin translation.

DIDACHI, or the Teaching of the Twelve Apostles, a Christian writing of the early second century, the text of which was discovered by the patriarch of Constantinople in 1883.

DIDIUS JULIANUS, grandson of Salvius Julianus, was a famous jurist born about A.D. 133. He was educated by Domitia Lucilla, the mother of Marcus Aurelius. He rose to important offices, being successively, quaestor, praetor, and governor of Belgic Gaul; then, having defeated the Chauci, he became consul. After the murder of Pertinax, A.D. 193, the Praetorian soldiers, having put up the empire to auction, Didius was highest bidder, and was proclaimed emperor. He was murdered, after reigning two months, by the soldiers when Severus was marching against the city.

DIDO or ELISSA, legendary founder of Carthage, was daughter of Mutgo or Belus, king of Tyre, and wife of Sichaeus who was murdered for his wealth by Pygmalion, Belus' successor. Dido secured her dead husband's possessions and sailed for Africa where she purchased land on which she built a citadel, which formed the nucleus of Carthage. According to Virgil, Dido fell in love with Aeneas, q.v., committing suicide when he deserted her.

DIDYMUS, famous grammarian, son of a fish-seller of Alexandria. He was born in 63 B.C. in the consulship of Antonius and Cicero and lived in the time of Augustus. Macrobius calls him the greatest grammarian of all time.

DIFFARREATION, divorce from a Roman marriage by confarreation. (Confarreation was a patrician mode of marriage in which a spelt cake was offered up).

DIGENTIA, a small river in Latium, flowing into the Anio, through the Sabine farm of Horace.

DINARCHUS, one of the ten Attic orators, was born at Corinth about 361 B.C. He was a member of the Macedonian party. He was last of the ten orators and the least important. Only three of his speeches are extant.

DINDYMUS, mountain near the town of Pessinus, sacred to Cybele, mother of the gods.

DINOCRATES, Greek architect reputed to have restored the temple of Artemis at Ephesus. He worked in the 4th. cent. B.C.

DIO CASSIUS, Roman historian, born at Nicaea, in Bithynia in A.D. 155. His most important work was a history of Rome, in 80 books, from the landing of Aeneas to A.D. 229. 18 books of this work have come down to us.

DIOCLETIANUS VALERIUS (DIOCLETIAN), Roman emperor, 284-305 A.D., was born in Dioclea in Dalmatia of humble parents. He had a distinguished career in the army. He was proclaimed emperor by the soldiers on the death of Numerianus. Owing to the continued pressure of the barbarians on the frontiers, Diocletian thought it wise to appoint Maximian as a colleague, assigning the West to him in 286 B.C. This arrangement was followed by a further division in 292 A.D., when Constantius Chlorus and Galerius were appointed Caesars. This period of his reign was marked with several successes. Britain was regained in 296 A.D., affairs in Egypt were dealt with severely, and the barbarians were kept outside the frontiers. In the latter years of his reign Diocletian cruelly persecuted the Christians. He abdicated in 305 A.D. and died in 313. Under Diocletian the empire became in form what virtually it had been in fact—an absolute monarchy.

DIODORUS CRONUS, philosopher of the Megarian school, about 300 B.C. His most famous pupil was Zeus of Citium.

DIODORUS SICULUS, Greek historian, born at Agyrium in Sicily. He was in Egypt about 60 B.C. His history was written after the death of Julius Caesar and ended with the Gallic War, taking thirty years in the writing.

DIODOTUS, Stoic philosopher, teacher of Cicero: he died 59 B.C.

DIOGENES OF APOLLONIA, so called from his birthplace in Crete, was a pupil of Anaximenes, and contemporary with Anaxagoras. He lived in the 5th cent. B.C.

DIOGENES THE BABYLONIAN, Stoic philosopher, who succeeded Zeno as head of the Athenian school of the Stoics: he was pupil of Chrysippus. He was one of three ambassadors sent to Rome by the Athenians in 155 B.C.

DIOGENES THE CYNIC, was a native of Sinope. With his father Hicesius he was expelled from his native place on a charge of adulterating the coinage. According to another account, Hicesius was imprisoned and died there, while Diogenes escaped to Athens, where he came under the influence of Antisthenes. He was noted for his neglect of personal conveniences, and by his sarcastic expressions. He died at Corinth in the same year as Alexander the Great (323 B.C.).

DIOGENES LAERTIUS, born in Laertes in Cilicia, was biographer of the Greek philosophers. It is supposed that he lived in the reign of Severus of Caracalla, and that he was an Epicurean.

DIOMEDEAE INSULAE, five islands in the Adriatic Sea named after Diomedes. Julia, grand-daughter of Augustus, died on Trimerus, the largest of this group.

DIOMEDES or DIOMEDE, in *Greek Mythology,* King of Argos, one of the Greek heroes in the Trojan War, during which he was under the special protection of Athena, by whose aid he inflicted wounds even on the deities Ares and Aphrodite. He entered Troy in disguise, together with Odysseus, carrying off the city's sacred emblem. Diomedes is supposed to have died at Daunia in Apulia.—Another Diomedes was King of Thrace, who owned a herd of horses which he fed on human flesh.

DION, CHRYSOSTOMUS, (the golden-mouthed), was a sophist and Stoic, contemporary with Vespasian, Domitian, Nerva, and Trajan. Eighty orations attributed to him are extant.

DION of SYRACUSE, son of Hipparinus, one of the chief men of that city, lived in the reigns of both the Dionysii. He early be-

came a disciple of Plato, whom the elder Dionysius had invited
to Syracuse. The younger Dionysius proved to be a tyrant, and
Dion tried to influence him by prudent counsels and exhortations.
He persuaded him to invite Plato to revisit the Syracusan court.
The dissolute courtiers, fearing the good influence of Plato, recalled Philistus, who they thought would be a match for the
philosopher. Dion's enemies secured his banishment on suspicion of his loyalty. He went to Italy and Greece. Dionysius confiscated his lands, and forced his wife to marry another. When
Dion heard of this he determined to expel the tyrant. He assembled 800 troops privately on the isle of Zacynthus and sailed
to Sicily. He found that Dionysius was absent in Italy, but was
received by the people with joy. On his return Dionysius endeavoured to regain his power but was forced to quit the island.
Soon however, by the influence of Heraclides, Dion himself was
forced to leave. Later recalled he was murdered in 354 B.C. by his
supposed friend Calippus.

DIONYSIA, festivals held in honour of the god Dionysus, or
Bacchus, the most important being held at Athens and in Attica,
were the occasions on which all the dramatic exhibitions of the
Athenians took place.

DIONYSIUS THE ELDER, born at Syracuse c. 430 B.C., son of
Hermocrates, was Tyrant of Syracuse. He so distinguished himself in the war against Carthage that in 405 B.C. he was made
commander-in-chief of the Syracusan forces. He then made himself absolute ruler of Syracuse, and extended his rule to other
cities of Sicily. Having carried on a war with Carthage he forced
the Greek cities in Italy to acknowledge his authority. Though
oppressive and cruel, Dionysius was a great patron of the arts.
He died at Syracuse in 367 B.C.

DIONYSIUS THE YOUNGER, son of D. the Elder, who succeeded his father as tyrant of Sycacuse. He had neither the prudence nor experience of his father. At first he followed the advice
of Dion, q.v., and invited Plato to Syracuse. Dionysius not following Plato's advice the latter left Syracuse, and Dionysius gave
himself up to unrestrained debauchery. Dion, having been banished, returned with a small force, taking possession of the city.

Later Dion, by the influence of Heraclides, again was compelled to leave Syracuse, but was once more recalled, but treacherously murdered in 354 B.C. Then several tyrants succeeded each other until Dionysius himself came and retook Syracuse c. 346 B.C., but his cruelty drove many to Italy and Greece. Later he was compelled to surrender the citadel to Timoleon who came to Sicily to deliver the Greek cities from tyrants. He was allowed to go to Corinth in 343 B.C., where he spent the remainder of his life.

DIONYSIUS of COLOPHON, Greek painter in the time of Pericles. His works were known to Aristotle. Another painter of this name lived in Rome about the time of the first Roman emperors. He was known as the Anthropograph, because he painted nothing but men.

DIONYSIUS OF HALICARNASSUS, historian and critic, in the first century B.C. He came to Italy in 29 B.C. and for twenty-two years lived in Rome, learning the Latin language and collecting material for his history. His principal work was *Roman Antiquities.*

DIONYSIUS THE AREOPAGITE, was converted by S. Paul when he preached at Athens (*see* Acts xviii:34). He is said to have been martyred under Diocletian, after becoming the first bishop of Athens.

DIONYSUS, in *Greek Mythology,* alternative name for Bacchus.

DIOPHANTUS, of Alexandria, author of the only Greek work containing algebra. He flourished in the 3rd. cent. A.D.

DIOSCORIDES PEDACIUS, or PEDANIUS, a Greek writer on Materia Medica, was born at Anazarbus, in Cilicia, and flourished in the reign of Nero.

DIOSCURI, Castor and Pollux, sons of Zeus, known to the Greeks as Polydeuces.

DIOTIMA, woman sage of Mantinea, one of the instructors of Socrates.

DIPHYLUS, comic poet, contemporary with Menander.

DISCOBOLUS, name of the bronze statue by Myron, q.v., representing an athlete throwing a discus. There is a copy in the British Museum, and in the Vatican.

DISCUS, round or oval piece of stone or metal. Throwing the discus was one of the contests in the Greek Pentathlon.

DITHYRAMBUS, song and accompaniment at festivals of Dionysus.

DIVICO, led the Helvetians against Cassius in 107 B.C. Nearly fifty years later he headed the embassy sent to Julius Caesar, when he was anticipating an attack on the Helvetians.

DODONA, most ancient oracle of Greece, situated in the valley of Joannina in Epirus. The oracles were delivered from an oak. The temple at Dodona was destroyed by Dosimachus, the Aetolian praetor in 219 B.C.

DOLABELLA, name of a patrician family of the gens Cornelia. (a) CN. CORNELIUS D., consul 81 B.C., whom J. Caesar accused of extortion. (b) CN. CORNELIUS, praetor urbanus 81 B.C., condemned for plundering his province. (c) PUBLIUS CORNELIUS, son-in-law of Cicero; fought with Caesar at Pharsalia 48 B.C., was made consul 44 B.C. He died by his own hand in 43 B.C.

DOLIUM, Roman earthenware jar for wine, oil, grain, etc.

DOLON, the Trojan spy who was slain by Diomedes.

DOMITIANUS (DOMITIAN), whose full name was TITUS FLAVIUS DOMITIANUS AUGUSTUS, was younger son of Vespasian, and succeeded his brother Titus. He took a real interest in provincial government, misrule being almost unknown during his reign. He was a persecutor of the Christians. The military exploits of his reign were an expedition against the Chatti, campaigns in Britain under Agricola, and a war with the Dacians. He died by the hand of a freedman named Stephanus, at the instigation of his own wife Domitia, in A.D. 96.

DONATUS, AELIUS, grammarian of the fourth century, who wrote a Grammar which was long used in the schools. He also wrote notes on Terence and Virgil. He taught rhetoric and polite literature at Rome in 356, St. Jerome being one of his pupils.

DORIS, small mountainous country of Greece, with four towns, Boeum, Citinium, Erineus, and Pindus, forming the Dorian Tetrapolis. Doris was also the name of a district in Asia Minor.

DORISCUS, Thracian town; on the adjacent plain Xerxes reviewed his vast armies.

DRACHMA, ancient Greek weight, and a silver coin of different values.

DRACO, Archon of Athens, first to codify and commit to writing, the laws of state as formulated in judicial decisions, about 621 B.C. The severity of this code has made the word "draconian" synonymous with unmerciful. Its severity was mitigated by Solon.

DROMOS, Greek race-course.

DRUSILLA, LIVIA, wife of the Roman emperor Augustus, who had previously been wife of Tiberius Claudius Nero, whom Augustus compelled to divorce her. Her elder son by the first marriage became the Roman emperor Tiberius; her second son was Drusus. She should not be confounded with Drusilla, wife of Felix, procurator of Judaea, before whom S. Paul preached; nor with the daughter of Germanicus.

DRUSUS, NERO CLAUDIUS, Roman soldier, son of Livia Drusilla by her first husband, Tiberius Claudius Nero. He became a distinguished general of Augustus, Drusilla's second husband, and was father of Claudius, the emperor. He was called Senior, to distinguish him from his nephew, the son of Tiberius the Roman emperor.

DRYAS, father of Lycurgus, king of Thrace.

DUILIUS, gained a victory over the Carthaginian fleet by means of grappling irons. He was consul in 260 B.C.

DUMNORIX, Aedui chief who conspired against the Romans in 58 B.C. He was pardoned by Caesar who wished him to accompany him to Britain in 54 B.C., but Dumnorix fled and was killed.

DUROVERNUM, (Canterbury), a town of the Cantii in S. E. Britain.

DYRRHACHIUM, (EPIDAMNUS), town in Greek Illyria, established by the Corcyraeans. The Romans changed its name from Epidamnus.

E

EAGLE, (aquila), from a Roman standard-symbol, the eagle became the emblem of the rulers of the Eastern Empire.

EARTHWORK, ancient stronghold defended by earthen mounds. Many such are to be seen in England and Wales. Some were used successively by neolithic, Celtic, Roman, Saxon, and Norman occupants.

EBBSFLEET, hamlet of Kent, 3½ m. S.W. of Ramsgate; scene of the landing of Hengist and Horsa in 449-450 A.D.

EBORACUM, Roman name of the British town of York, used as a military station by Agricola, which became chief Roman settlement in the island, and the residence of the emperors, two of whom, Septimus Severus, and Constantius Chlorus, died here.

EBURONES, people of Germany, who later settled between the Rhine and the Mosa.

ECBATANA, capital of Media, the name of which in its Hebrew form Achmetha survives in the modern name, Hamadan. The town is 5,930 ft. above sea level; and was the summer residence of the ancient Persian and Parthian kings. There was a city of the same name in Syria, where Cambyses died.

ECCLESIA, a popular assembly of the Athenians, where the people exercised full sovereignty, and every male citizen above 20 years could vote. It was anciently held at the Agora, later at the Pnyx, and last in the theatre of Dionysus. Voting was by show of hands except when an individual's rights were affected. In such case the ballot was secret, a vote of at least 6,000 being required in favour of the motion.

ECHEDORUS, Macedonian river flowing through Mygdonia to the Thermaic Gulf.

ECHEMUS, Arcadian who killed Hyllus, q.v., in single combat.

ECHINADES, group of islands at the mouth of the Achelous, probably formed by alluvial deposits. The largest island was Dulichium, which belonged to the kingdom of Ulysses, who is sometimes known as Dulichius.

ECLECTICS, (Choosers), name applied to certain Greek philosophers in the 2nd and 1st cents. B.C., who were attached to no particular school.

EDESSA, ancient city of Mesopotamia founded by Seleucid I, and after the fall of the Seleucid empire was capital of an independent kingdom, which lasted from 137 B.C. to A.D. 216, when it became a Roman military colony, known as Colonia Marcia Edessenorum. When the Roman empire divided into East and West, Edessa became a center of Christianity.

EDICT, promulgation, by a Roman magistrate, upon entering office, particularly a praetor, on the principles upon which he intended to administer the law.

EGNATIA, coastal town of Apulia, famous for its miraculous stone, which of its own volition kindled wood and incense. The town was on the highroad from Rome to Brundisium, this highway being known as the Via Egnatia; this was part of the great military road between Italy and the East.

EGYPT, *See* AEGYPTUS.

EISPHORA, Athenian property tax.

ELAEA, ancient coastal city of Aeolis, which in later days was used as a port by Pergamos.

ELAGABALUS or HELIOGABALUS, Roman emperor A.D. 218-222, son of Sextus Varius Marcellus, and Julia, was made priest of Elagabalus, the Syrian sun-god, assuming his name. By pretending he was natural son of Caracalla, his grandmother, Julia Maesa, persuaded the legions in Syria to proclaim him emperor. He left the government to his mother and grandmother; devoting the first year of his reign to the introduction of sun-god worship. He was assassinated in A.D. 222. He was succeeded by his cousin Alexander Severus.

ELAPHEBOLIA, festival in honour of Artemis, held at Athens.

ELEPHANTINE, island in the Nile at Assuan, Upper Egypt, marking the S. limit of ancient Nile navigation. It contained the Old Kingdom frontier station towards Ethiopia, called Abu, or elephant town, on account of the Sudanese ivory trade. On the W. bank of the Nile, opposite the island, are rock-hewn tombs of Old and Middle Kingdom governors. Under Thothmes III, Rameses II, and other kings, its governor controlled the Assuan granite quarries. An interesting object is the nilometer, dating from the Ptolemaic period.

ELEUSIS, ancient city of Attica, said to have been founded by Triptolemus, standing 12 m. N. W. of Athens, with which it is still connected by the causeway called the Sacred Road. It was chief seat of Demeter worship in whose temple the Eleusinia were performed. These were rites symbolic of the death of nature in autumn and rebirth in spring. The city was destroyed by the Goths.

ELEUTHERIA, festival in honour of Eros, held at Samos.

ELIS or ELEA, district of the Peloponnesus included between Achaia, Arcadia, Messenia, and the sea; it was originally divided into three parts, N., called hollow Elis; S., Triphylia; and Middle, Pisatis. Eleans were first people in the Peloponnesus to experience Dorian invasion, their territory providing a landing place.

ELLOPIA, district, and town of northern Euboea. Also, the district about Dodona was anciently known by the same name.

ELYMAIS, district of Persia, between Susis and Media, its capital on the river Eulaeus being known by the same name. The inhabitants consisted of husbandmen who cultivated the plains, and a numerous army of archers who occupied the uplands.

ELYMUS, one of the Trojans who fled from Troy to Sicily. He was natural son of Anchises and brother of Eryx.

ELYSIUM, or THE ELYSIAN FIELDS, in *Classical Mythology,* the abode of good souls after death. Some legends make it part of the underworld, others make it an island in the Atlantic. Elysium is represented as a place of perpetual sunshine, with flowery meadows and cool streams.

EMATHIA, part of Macedonia, between Haliacmon and the Axius.

EMATHIDES, the nine daughters of Pierus, king of Emathia.

EMBALMING, art of preserving dead bodies. Among the ancient Egyptians, embalming originated in the idea of the resurrection of the body. Apparently there were three Egyptian methods each involving the use of aromatic and antiseptic preparations. The internal organs were usually embalmed separately and placed in jars. The Egyptians also embalmed cats, hawks, crocodiles, and other sacred animals and birds. The ancient Persians seem to have embalmed with wax and the Assyrians with honey.

EMESA, native city of Elagabalus, in Syria, on the E. bank of the Orontes.

EMPEDOCLES, Greek philosopher of Agrigentum in Sicily, who flourished about 460 B.C. He was first to teach that all natural substances are made up of the four so-called elements, fire, air, earth, and water. He is said to have thrown himself into the crater of Aetna so that the completeness of his disappearance might engender the belief that he had been translated alive to heaven, but the volcano threw up one of his sandals, thus revealing the manner of his death.

EMPORIAE, very ancient Greek colony in N. E. Spain.

ENNA, (sometimes HENNA), ancient town on the road from Catana to Agrigentum, in Sicily, occupied by the Siculi, was a chief seat of Demeter worship.

ENNIUS, QUINTUS, this old epic poet of Rome was born in Rudiae, in Calabria, in B.C. 239, two years after the first Punic War. He was Greek by birth and no doubt assumed his Latin name on becoming a Roman citizen (his Greek name is not known). In 204 B.C. he served as a Roman centurion in Sardinia, where he attracted the attention of Cato, whom he accompanied back to Rome. He soon had friends amongst the first men of Rome. Cato learned Greek from him. In 198 B.C. Ennius went with M. Fluvius Nobilior to the Aetolian campaign, and shared his triumph. He died in 169 B.C. aged 70, and was buried in the sepulchre of the Scipios. The Romans regarded him as the father of their poets. His most important work was entitled *Annales*, being a history of Rome written in dactylic hexameters.

EPAMINONDAS, Theban general and statesman, born about 418 B.C., won fame at the battle of Leuctra in 371 B.C., when he was chiefly responsible for the defeat which brought to an end the Spartan hegemony over Greece. He determined to break the power of Sparta in Peloponnesus, and united the cities of Arcadia in a league, founding the new city of Megalopolis as the capital. In 362 B.C. the Spartans attacked Arcadia, and were defeated at the battle of Mantinea, in which Epaminondas fell.

EPEUS, builder of the Trojan horse; he was son of Panopeus.

EPHEBI, general name by which youths over eighteen were called in Athens.

EPHESUS, a city of Asia Minor, and one of the twelve that belonged to the Ionian confederation, probably founded about 1000 B.C. It fell under the dominion of Croesus, king of Lydia in the 6th cent. B.C., and later under that of Cyrus the Great. During the Athenian hegemony it paid tribute to Athens. In the 4th cent. B.C. it again passed to the Persians. Later it acknowledged Macedonian supremacy, and after the Roman conquest of Greece became administrative capital of the Roman Province of Asia. Ephesus was noted for the worship of Artemis, whose temple, built in the 6th cent., was regarded as one of the seven wonders of the ancient world. The city was an early seat of Christianity, and was visited by S. Paul. 6 important councils of the Church were held here. S. John also visited Ephesus.

EPHETAE, name of certain Athenian magistrates, fifty in number, whose principal duty was to take cognizance of murders committed by accident. They had special privileges, and were superior to the Areopagites. Solon reduced their power, limiting their duties to trials for manslaughter, and conspiracy against the life of a citizen.

EPHORI, (overseers) board of five magistrates at Sparta, exercising great power. They were elected annually, the senior giving his name to the year. Every Spartan was eligible to the office.

EPHORUS, Greek historian, born at Cyme, in Aeolis in 405 B.C. He survived the passage of Alexander into Asia, in 333 B.C., which he mentions in his history.

EPHRAEM or EPHRAIM, ecclesiastical writer of the 4th cent. A.D., born either at Nisibis or Edessa. He died c. 378 A.D.

EPIC POETRY, the form of art which produces an imaginative description of external facts and events, as distinguished from lyric poetry, which registers, in an imaginative manner, all those internal facts and events which go by the name of feelings and emotions. Greek epic poetry falls naturally into two divisions, the heroic or romantic epos of Homer and the Cyclic poets, and the hieratic epos of Hesiod. The attention of that age centered on two grand ideas, the state and religion, and so we find a political and a hieratic epos. The Iliad and Odyssey are two specimens of the former kind, and stand in strong contrast to the Aeneid, which depends more on beauty of language and arrangement than on a story to excite interest of its readers, though it contains the adventures of an individual.

EPICHARMUS, chief comic poet of the Dorians, born in the island of Cos, went to Sicily about 485 B.C., is said to have been the pupil of Pythagoras. He spent his last years at Syracuse, at the court of Hieron. He died when he was ninety. Only fragments of his work are extant.

EPICTETUS, Stoic philosopher, living about 100 A.D. He was born at Hierapolis in Phrygia. He became an adherent and teacher of Stoicism. His pupil Arrianus, the historian, published his discourses and a Manual of his doctrines. According to Epictetus, we are only concerned with things that are under our control. The highest principles of life being patience, abstemiousness, and self-control. An Athenian potter of the 6th cent. B.C. also bore this name.

EPICURUS, Greek philosopher, 342-270 B.C. was born at Samos of Athenian parentage. Coming to Athens he founded his school in his garden. Epicurus divided philosophy into three parts:

Canonics (logic, the theory of knowledge), Physics, and Ethics. The basis of all knowledge is the evidence of sensual perception; all perceptions are true and irrefutable. In physics Epicurus agrees in the main with Democritus, founder of the atomic theory. In ethics he follows the Cyrenaics. Pleasure is the aim in life, and the only happiness. The virtuous man, he who rightly pursues pleasure, is alone happy.

EPIDAURUS, town of Argolis, in ancient Greece, on the Saronic Gulf, famous for its temple of Aesculapius, about eight miles away, which was visited by the sick from all parts of Greece.

EPIGONI, (descendants), name of the sons of the seven heroes who perished before Thebes.

EPIMENIDES, Greek legendary priest and miracle-worker; a native of Crete and associated with the worship of the Cretan Zeus and Apollo. He was summoned to Athens in 596 B.C. to purify the city from the curse of Cylon. He is thought to be the prophet of S. Paul's epistle to Titus (1:12), according to whom the Cretans were "always liars".

EPIPHANES, surname of Antiochus IV of Syria.

EPIPHANIUS, Greek ecclesiastical writer, born in a village near Eleutheropolis in Palestine, was made bishop of Constantia (formerly Salamis) in Cyprus. In A.D. 382 he was invited to Rome to give his vote in the case of Paulinus, bishop of Antioch. Epiphanius died on board ship in 402 A.D. Among his chief works was *Ancoratus,* that is, the anchor of faith against the heresies of the time, especially the Macedonian.

EPIRUS, (Greek, mainland), name given to the district in N. Greece which extended from the Ceraunian mountains on the N. to the Ambracian gulf on the south, and from the Ionian Sea to the chain of Pindus. The ancient geography of Epirus was attended with great difficulties even in the time of Strabo. The country had not then recovered from the destruction caused by Paulus Aemilius, in 167 B.C., when 70 towns were destroyed and 150,000 reduced to slavery, after which the remaining inhabitants had nothing but ruins and villages to dwell in. The people of Epirus were scarcely considered Hellenic, and in early times the population was Pelasgic. The oracle at Dodona was Pelasgic, and many place names were also borne by Pelasgic cities on the opposite coast of Italy. Theopompus divided the inhabitants into 14 tribes, the most renowned being Chaonians and Molossians. The Molossian princes, eventually obtained sovereignty over the whole country taking the title of kings of Epirus, the most famous being Pyrrhus, q.v.

EPITAPH, inscription on a tomb; some of the earliest extant are found on Egyptian sarcophagi, and were commonly used among the Jews. Various anthologies and the catacombs of Rome supply many Greek and Latin examples. A Greek epitaph composed before 216 A.D. by Abercius, bishop of Hierapolis, is of importance in connection with the sacramental system of the Christian Church.

EPOREDIA, Roman colony in Gallia Cisalpina, on the Duria.

ERASISTRATUS, born at Iulis, in Cos; he flourished as a physician and anatomist from 300-260 B.C. He founded the medical school at Alexandria.

ERATOSTHENES, distinguished contemporary of Archimedes, born at Cyrene in 276 B.C. He possessed a variety of talents, being proficient in mathematics, astronomy, and geography. The great Alexandrian library was entrusted to his superintendence by Ptolemaeus III (Euergetes). He died about 194 B.C., aged 80, having starved himself to death, being blind and tired of life.

ERECHTHEUM, Ionic temple on the Acropolis, at Athens, to the N. W. of the Parthenon. It was built partly in honour of the Greek hero, Erechtheus, the legendary king of Athens. It contained the shrine and image of Athena Pallas, guardian of the city, and the tomb of Cecrops. It is noted for its fine porch of the Caryatides.

ERETRIA, town of Euboea, on the Euripus, whose harbour, Porthmus, was established by the Athenians. It was important from early days on account of its commerce and navy, and it contended with Chalcis for supremacy in Euboea. The Persians destroyed it in 490 B.C., enslaving its inhabitants.

ERICHTHONIUS I, son of Hephaestus. Athena reared him, and entrusted him to Agraulus, Pandrosus, and Herse, concealed in a coffer, which they were forbidden to open. Disobeying they saw the child as an asp, and were seized with madness, throwing themselves from the rock of the Acropolis. Erichthonius became King of Athens, being succeeded by Pandion, his son. He introduced Athena worship and the festival of the Panathenaea, and built a temple on the Acropolis. He was worshipped as a god after death.

ERICHTHONIUS II, son of Pandion, whom he succeeded on the throne of Athens. He became father of Cecrops, Procris, Creusa, Chthonia, and Orithyia.

ERIDANUS, in *Classical Mythology*, a river, and river-god of Italy, identified with the Padus (Po), which rose in the alps and discharged into the Adriatic by several mouths.

ERINNA, Greek poetess: her birthplace is open to doubt, but was possibly Telos. Theocritus and Asclepiades, with whom she was contemporary, praised her work. Her fame rests on a poem called *The Distaff*, written in memory of Baucis. She died at the age of 19.

ERIPHYLE, wife of Amphiaraus, and daughter of Talaus. She was mother of Alcmaeon, q.v.

EROS, Cupido, god of love, son of Aphrodite, was represented as a beautiful, wanton boy. He is armed with arrows in a golden quiver, and is further represented with golden wings. Sometimes his eyes are covered so that he acts blindly.

ERYMANTHUS, mountain in Arcadia, haunt of the wild boar, slain by Heracles. A river of Arcadia bore the same name.

ERYTHRAE, one of the 12 Ionian cities of Asia Minor.

ERYTHRAEUM MARE, name anciently given to all the sea between Arabia and Africa, on the W., and India on the E., including the Red Sea and Persian Gulf. In later times the main body of water became known as Indicus Oceanus, while the Red Sea was named Arabicus Sinus, and the Persian Gulf, Persicus Sinus.

ESSENES, Jewish Sect founded in the 2nd. Cent. B.C., which sought to combine the ascetic practices of the Hebrew religion with eastern tenets and rites. They believed in one God and in eternal predestination. They accepted the doctrine of the immortality of the soul, but denied the resurrection of the body, and held a Greek view of the future rewards and punishments. They lived austerely, practised community of goods, dividing their time between prayer, study of the sacred writings, and agriculture. They were favoured by the Herods, but strongly opposed by orthodox Jews. The sect had died out before the 3rd Cent. A.D.

ESTHER, Book of the Old Testament, named from the chief character of the story. When Vashti, consort of the Persian King Ahashverôsh (Xerxes), was deposed, Esther, the adopted daughter of Mordecai, a Jewish exile, was chosen in her place. She was thus enabled to frustrate the plots of Haman, a powerful enemy of her people. The purpose of the books appears to be to explain the origin of the Jewish festival Purim.

ETESIAE, any periodical winds were known as the Etesian Winds, but especially the northerly winds of the Aegaean, which blow for 40 days from the rising of the Dog star.

ETRURIA or TUSCIA, country of central Italy, called Tyrrhenia by the Greeks. The Romans called the people Etrusci, or Tusci, and the Greeks Tyrrheni or Tyrseni; the people called themselves Rasena. The Etruscans' origin is in doubt: they may have come from Asia Minor before 800 B.C. They were governed by an aristocracy confined to the Lucumones, who were also priests. The Romans borrowed many of their religious and political institutions. The last three Kings of Rome were Etruscans. The later history of the Etruscans is a struggle against Rome to which they became subject in 283 B.C., being defeated by Cornelius Dolabella. They received Roman franchise in 91.

EUBOEA, EGRIPOS, or NEGROPONT, largest island of the Aegaean, 90 miles long, lying off the coast of Attica, Boeotia, and the S. of Thessaly. Homer calls the people Abantes. The Histiaei lived in the N., the Ellopii in central Euboea, and the Dryopes in the S. The Athenians planted the colony of Chalcis in central Euboea, also that of Eretria. After the Persian wars the island became subject to the Athenians.

EUCHARIST, (thanksgiving) is the Greek name for the Christian Sacrament of Holy Communion, particularly expressing the ideas of thankfully commemorating the mediatorial Sacrifice of Christ.

EUCLIDES, Greek mathematician familiarly known as Euclid. Little is known of his life except that he was of Greek descent, living and teaching in Alexandria. Besides the *Elements of Geometry,* Euclid wrote *De Divisionibus,* a collection of 36 problems on the division of areas, possibly the survivor of many such collections. He flourished 300 B.C. in the time of the first Ptolemy. Another of the same name was born at Negara, and became a pupil of Socrates.

EUDEMUS, Greek philosopher, pupil of Aristotle, who wrote histories of arithmetic, geometry, etc.

EUDOXUS, born at Cnidus, in Asia Minor, was son of Aeschines, and flourished about 370 B.C. He studied under Archytas, at Athens, and later in Egypt. Cicero says Eudoxus was the greatest astronomer who ever lived. He had an observatory at Cnidus. None of his works survived.—Another Eudoxus, born at Cyzicus, was sent by Ptolemaeus VII, on a voyage to India in 125 B.C.

EUERGETES, (benefactor), name bestowed by the Greek states, on those from whom they received benefits.

EUHEMERUS, born in Sicily, lived at the court of Cassander, in Macedonia about 316 B.C. He wrote a book called the *Sacred History,* in which he aimed to prove that all ancient myths were real events. Gods, he said, were originally men who had distinguished themselves, and after death received worship from a grateful people.

EULAEUS, river rising in Great Media, passing to the E. of Susa, and entering the Persian Gulf.

EUMENES, of Cardia, a town in the Thracian Chersonese, was an important actor in the troubled events following the death of Alexander the Great. He had served as private secretary to both Philip and Alexander, and after the death of the latter, obtained the government of Pontus, Paphlagonia, and Cappadocia. In 316 B.C. he was put to death by Antigonus.—Another of the same name was King of Pergamum from 197 to 159 B.C.

EUNUS, Sicilian slave leader in the Servile War in 134-132 B.C.

EUPATRIDAE, the Athenian nobility, a distinction abolished by Solon who founded an aristocracy of money.

EUPHORBUS, son of Panthous, who dedicated his shield in the temple of Hera. He was one of the bravest of the Trojans, and was slain by Menelaus.

EUPHORION, grammarian and poet, born at Chalcis. He was librarian to Antiochus the Great in 221 B.C.

EUPHRANOR, sculptor and painter, born at Corinth, but came to Athens where he flourished about 336 B.C.

EUPHRATES, one of the most notable rivers of antiquity, is in Asia. It rises in the highlands of Armenia, flowing through Asia Minor, at one point being only 60 m. from the Mediterranean. It then turns S.E. and at length enters Mesopotamia (Iraq). It is 1,800 m. long, and unites with the Tigris near Basra, and as the Shatt-al-Arab, the united streams fall into the Persian Gulf. The valley of the Euphrates and Tigris was one of the cradles of civilization, and, in ancient times, one of the most fertile areas of the world, due in part to an irrigation system mentioned by Xenophon.

EUPHRONIUS, Athenian potter, who employed the painters Panaetius, Onesimus, and Pistoxenus to decorate his work: he flourished 6th to 5th cent. B.C.

EUPOLIS, great Athenian poet of the old comedy, born at Athens c. 446 B.C., being contemporary with Aristophanes: these two were not on good terms, and Aristophanes speaks harshly of Eupolis in *The Cloud*, charging him with having pillaged from *The Knights* the material for his own *Maricas*, while Eupolis jeered at the baldness of the great comedian. He died about 411 B.C.

EURIPIDES, Athenian dramatist, born, according to tradition, on the island of Salamis on the day of the great naval victory over the Persians. He exhibited his first tragedy in 455 B.C., and in 441 gained the first prize. He was credited with over 90 plays, of which 18 survive. These are:—Alcestis, Medea, Hippolytus, Hecuba, Andromache, Ion, The Suppliants, Heracleidae, The Mad Heracles, Iphigenia Among the Tauri, The Trojan Women, Helen, The Phoenician Maidens, Electra, Orestes, Iphigenia at Aulis, Bacchae, Cyclops, the last being the only specimen of a satiric drama to come to us. He spent his last days at the court of King Archelaus in Macedonia, where he died in 406 B.C.

EURIPUS, the violent ebb and flow of the tide at any given place, especially the channel separating Euboea from Boeotia.

EUROTAS, river in Laconia, on which Sparta stood.

EURUS, Greek counterpart of the Latin Volturnus, the southeast wind.

EURYBATUS, the Ephesian, whom Croesus sent to Peloponnesus to collect mercenaries for his war with Cyrus. He deserted Eurybatus for Cyrus, his name becoming proverbial among the Greeks as synonymous with treachery.

EURYMEDON, son of Thucles, an Athenian general in the Peloponnesian War.—Eurymedon was also the name of a river in Pamphylia, famous for Cimon's victory over the Persians in 467 B.C.

EURYMUS, father of Telemus the seer.

EURYPON or EURYTION, grandson of Procles, and third King of that house at Sparta.

EURYPYLUS, one of the bravest Greek heroes at Troy, was son of Euaemon.—Another of the same name was son of Poseidon; was King of Cos, and killed by Heracles.

EURYSTHENES and PROCLES, twin sons of Aristodemus, who died just after the birth of his children. Both were made Kings at the instance of the oracle at Delphi. Two royal families in Sparta sprang from these brothers.

EUSEBIUS, ecclesiastical historian, often called Eusebius Pamphili, was probably a native of Palestine born about A.D. 264. His writings entitle him to be called the father of ecclesiastical history. He was made bishop of Caesarea about 315 A.D., and died about 340. His greatest work is his *Ecclesiastical History.*

EUTICHES, founder of the Eutichian heresy, was an abbot at Constantinople. The heresy denied that there are two natures in Christ. He died in 450 A.D.

EUTRESIS, ancient town of Boeotia, residence of Zethus and Amphion before they ruled Thebes. It had a temple and oracle of Apollo.

EUTROPIUS, Roman historian in the days of Constantine, Julian, and Valens. He wrote a Roman history in 10 books, dealing with the fortunes of Rome up till A.D. 364.

EVAGORAS, King of Salamis, 411-347 B.C. The Athenians gave him assistance against the Persians.

EVENUS, name of two rivers, one in Aetolia, rising in Mt. Oeta, and the other in Mysia, emptying into the Sinus Elaiticus near Pitane.

EXECIAS, potter and vase painter of Athens in the 6th cent. B.C.

F

FABIUS MAXIMUS, the Fabii were a powerful patrician gens of ancient Rome, which became subdivided, such as Fabii Maximi, Fabii Ambusti, Fabii Vibulani. They were of Sabine origin. Caeso Fabius, being quaestor with L. Valerius, impeached Spurius Cassius, in 486 B.C., and had him executed. For seven years after, one of the consulships was filled by three brothers Fabii in rotation. In 479 B.C., the whole house of the Fabii proposed to settle on the borders of Veii territory and undertake war against the Veientes. They left Rome with their followers and encamped on the banks of the Cremera, in sight of Veii, and began a harassing war against the Veientes and other people of Etruria, which lasted for nearly two years. At last they fell into an ambuscade and were all killed. Only one of the house escaped, he having remained at Rome. He became parent stock of all subsequent Fabii, was repeatedly consul, and later one of the decenviri with Appius Claudius. M. Fabius Ambustus was consul several times, and fought the Hernici and Tarquinians, left several sons, one of whom, Q. Fabius Maximus Rullianus defeated the Samnites. This Fabius was 5 times consul, and dictator twice. His son Q. Fabius Gurges was thrice consul, and was grandfather of Q. Fabius Maximus Verrucosus, who in his first consulship triumphed over the Ligurians. After the Thrasymenian defeat, he was entrusted with the salvation of the republic. The system he adopted to check the advance of Hannibal was by avoiding a general engagement, and harassing the enemy. This was new to the Romans, and earned for Fabius the name of Cunctator, or temporizer. Minucius, who shared the command with Fabius, having imprudently engaged Hannibal, was saved from destruction by Fabius. The following year, Fabius being recalled to Rome, the army was entrusted to the consul Terentius

Varro, who rushed unwisely into battle, being defeated at Cannae. Fabius was made consul in the next year, again keeping Hannibal in check. When he became consul for the 5th time Fabius re-took Tarentum. He died at a very advanced age.

FABIUS PICTOR, the historian, descended from Marcus Fabius Ambustus the consul.—Caius Fabius, one of the sons of Ambustus, was called Pictor, because about 304 B.C., he painted the temple of the goddess of health.

FABLE, *Fabula* in Latin, in its general sense means a fictitious narrative, but more particularly it means a didactic composition consisting of a short fictitious tale, which inculcates a moral truth or precept. The oldest collection of fables in any European language is in Greek prose, attributed to Aesop, but many fables associated with his name probably originated at a much earlier time in India. Babrius made a metrical version of Aesopian fables. Among the Latins, Phaedrus, who lived in the time of Tiberius, is the most famous fabulist.

FABRICUS, CAIUS, surnamed LICINIUS, was consul for the first time in 283 B.C., when he triumphed over the Boii and Etruscans. After the defeat of the Romans by Pyrrhus in 281 B.C., Fabricus was sent to the king, to treat for ransom of the prisoners. Pyrrhus is said to have tried to bribe him with large offers, which Fabricus, although poor, rejected with scorn, to the great admiration of the king. He again became consul in 279 B.C., and was sent against Pyrrhus, then encamped near Tarentum. The king's physician is said to have come secretly to the Roman camp, proposing to Fabricus, to poison his master for a bribe, at which the consul put him in fetters and sent him back to Pyrrhus. Fabricus, having defeated the Samnites, Lucanians, and Bruttii, who had joined Pyrrhus against Rome, had the honour of a triumph. Pyrrhus was finally defeated by M. Curius Dentatus in 276 B.C. Fabricus died poor, and the senate made provision for his daughters.

FAIR HAVENS, harbour on S. of Crete, where S. Paul's ship sheltered to escape the violent N. W. winds which had driven her from her course, and whence, contrary to the advice of the

Apostle, she sailed for Phenice, when she encountered the severe storm which ended in her wreck.

FALERII, town of Etruria, near Mt. Soracte, originally Pelasgic, but later one of the twelve Etruscan cities. The Falisci were of the same race as the Aequi, and were sometimes known as Aequi Falisci. They yielded to Rome through Camillus, in 394 B.C., after a long struggle, but revolted at the end of the first Punic War in 241 B.C., when the Romans destroyed their city. The white cows of Falerii were prized by the Romans, who used them in sacrifices. A new town was built near to the old site.

FALERNUS AGER, district of Italy famous for its wine, situated in N. Campania.

FANUM FORTUNAE, Umbrian town, famous for its temple of Fortuna, situated at the mouth of the Metaurus.

FARFARUS, river to which frequent reference is made by the Latin writers (sometimes under the name of Fabaris). It flowed across the district of Sabini, near Rome.

FASCES, symbol of authority borne by the lictors before a higher magistrate, consisting of a bundle of rods enclosing an axe.

FASTI, marble tables on which were inscribed the names of consuls, dictators, censors, and other principal magistrates of the republic. The word Fasti is often used as synonymous with the annals or chronicles of a nation. The Romans had another kind of Fasti, called Fasti Minores, a kind of almanac in which were registered the periodical festivals, games, official days of business, etc. Ovid wrote a poem explanatory of these Fasti, which he dedicated to Germanicus.

FATA MORGANA, form of mirage seen in the Straits of Messina, between Sicily and Calabria, so called because it was supposed from early times to be the work of a fata or fairy, named Morgana.

FATHERS, (secular, in ancient history) Father of Algebra, Diophantus; of Comedy, Aristophanes; of epic poetry, Homer; of Geometry, Euclid; of History, Herodotus; of Medicine, Hippocrates; of Tragedy, Aeschylus.

FAUNUS, in *Roman Mythology*, one of the most ancient gods, worshipped as the protector of agriculture, and shepherds, he also gave oracles. Later he became identified with Pan, and still later, Fauni are mentioned in the plural.

FAUSTA, CORNELIA, an infamous adultress, wife of Milo, and daughter of the dictator Sulla.

FAUSTINA, the elder, the licentious wife of Antoninus Pius.

FAUSTINA, the younger, daughter of the above, wife of M. Aurelius, and also a profligate.

FAVONIUS, the Latin equivalent of Zephyrus, the west wind.

FAVONIUS, M., known as Cato's ape, on account of his imitation of Cato Uticensis.

FEBRUUS, ancient Roman divinity from whom the name of the month February is derived, which month was sacred to him.

FECIALES, messengers, or heralds of war and peace in ancient Rome. They belonged to the order of the priesthood. They were also employed in demanding satisfaction for wrongs done to the state. The rules which regulated their duties were known as the Jus Feciale.

FELICITAS, the personification of good luck, symbolized by a matron, bearing the staff of Mercury and a cornucopia, often used by the Romans as a mascot.

FELIX, ANTONINUS, brother of the freedman Pallas, minister of the Roman emperor Claudius. He was procurator of Judaea. He persuaded Drusilla to leave her husband, and she was still living with him, when S. Paul preached before them in A.D. 60.

FENNI, a barbarian people, of German origin (according to Tacitus) who dwelt in the extremity of Prussia, and corresponded with the modern Finns.

FERIAE, holy days (holidays) dedicated to the worship of a divinity.

FERONIA, goddess of ancient Rome whose chief seat of worship was at Terracina. A fair was held at her festival, during which an offering of first-fruits was made to her.

FESCENNIUM, town of Etruria from which the Romans derived the lewd songs which were sung at harvest festivals and weddings.

FESTUS, PORCIUS, procurator of Judaea in succession to Felix about A.D. 58. He heard in the presence of Herod Agrippa II and Berenice, the case of S. Paul, whom he sent to Rome for trial. He died in A.D. 62.

FESTUS, SEXTUS POMPEIUS, Roman grammarian in the second century A.D. He compiled an epitome of the voluminous work *De Verborum Significatione*, of Marcus Verrius Flaccus, a grammarian of the Augustan age mentioned by Suetonius.

FETIALES, group of twenty men whose duty was to maintain the laws of international relationship: they were elected for life in Italy.

FIBULA, term used among the Romans for the brooch, or buckle, with which their vests were usually fastened.

FIDEICOMMISSUM, in the Roman law, something given by will or codecil, not directly to the person beneficially interested in it, but to another, with a request that he would transfer it to the party for whom it was intended. The person so entrusted was called Haeres Fiduciarius, and the person for whom it was intended Haeres Fideicommissarius.

FIDENAE, ancient town of the Sabines, a few miles N. E. of Rome, built on high ground, between the Anio and the Tiber, said to have been colonized by Romulus. It revolted on several occasions and was frequently reduced by the Romans. It revolted last in 438 B.C. Destroyed by the Romans, it was later rebuilt.

FIDIUS, in the expression *Medius Fidius*, is equivalent to "So help me the god of truth." This god of faith was a Sabine deity, Semo Sancus.

FIGULUS, P. NIGIDIUS, Pythagorean philosopher, who became a Senator, flourishing about 60 B.C.

FILIBI, or PHILIPPOPILI, town of Roumelia, founded by Philip of Macedon. Under the Romans it was one of the most important towns of the country.

FIMBRIA, C. FLAVIUS, consul in 104 B.C. He was an orator and jurist. His son, of the same name, was a partisan of Marius and Cinna during the civil war. In 86 B.C. he was sent to Asia as legate of Valerius Flaccus, whom he incited the soldiers to put to death. He fought against Mithridates, but was himself attacked by Sulla in 85 B.C. when he took his own life.

FIRE ENGINE, under the Roman emperors there were bands of trained firemen kept. Ctesibius is believed to have invented an engine for the extinction of fires in the time of the Ptolemies.

FISC, FISCUS, means a basket of wicker-work such as would hold a sum of coined money. Under the Roman empire it was used to signify the treasury of the emperor, as distinguished from that of the state.

FLACCUS, name of a notable Roman family. (a) Quintus Fulvius F., Roman general in the second Punic War. (b) Marcus Fulvius, one of the commissioners appointed to carry out the agrarian measures of Tiberius Gracchus. (c) Marcus Verrius, a grammarian in the time of Augustus. The poets Horace and Valerius belonged to this family.

FLAMEN, FLAMINES, an order of priesthood in ancient Rome, like the Salii, the Feciales, and others; instituted, according to tradition, by Numa Pompilius. The several Flamines were destined to the service of some particular diety. There were the Flamen Dialis, who were consecrated to the worship of Jupiter, and held first rank; the Flamen Martialis, who attended the worship of Mars; and others.

FLAMININUS, TITUS QUINTUS, was made consul in 198 B.C., having the province of Macedonia, with charge of continuing the war against Philip, whom he defeated in 197 B.C. at the battle of Cynoscephalae, in Thessaly.

FLAMINIUS, C., Roman statesman, during whose censorship in 220 B.C. the great Circus Flaminius was built. He also extended the Via Flaminia to Ariminum, making it the first Roman road to cross Italy.

FLAVIA GENS, famous family to which Vespasian belonged. The name Flavius descended from one emperor to another after the time of Constantius, who was first to bear this name.

FLORENTIA (FLORENCE), town in Etruria, on the Arnus, which became a Roman colony.

FLORIANUS, M. ANNIUS, brother of the emperor Tacitus, whom he succeeded in 276 A.D. He was assassinated by his soldiers at Tarsus, two months after his succession, while marching against Probus.

FLORUS, L. ANNAEUS, Roman historian in the time of Trajan and Hadrian, who wrote a summary of Roman history.

FONTEIUS, M., propraetor in Narbonese Gaul; he was charged in 69 B.C. with extortion in his province, being defended by Cicero.

FORMIAE, ancient town on the Appia Via, near which were clustered the villas of the nobles, the best known of these being the Formianum of Cicero. It was a noted vintage area.

FORNACALIA, movable feasts among the Romans, the celebration of which was proclaimed by the Curio, on the 12th of the Kalends of May. They were first instituted by Numa, in honour of the goddess Fornax, from whom they received their name.

FORTUNATAE, (the Islands of the Blessed), alternative name for the Elysian Fields of early Greek mythology. They were vaguely spoken of as beyond the Pillars of Hercules, i.e. the Straits of Gibraltar. It has been generally accepted that the Canary Islands are the Fortunate Islands of the ancients.

FORUM, among the ancient Romans any open space used for public business. More particularly the term was used for the open space in Rome between the Palatine and Capitoline hills, known as Forum Romanum. The people met here, while magistrates and others addressed them from the tribunal or rostra. Other fora were introduced as the city grew, the Forum Julium by Julius Caesar, the Forum Augustum, and the Forum Pacis, where Vespasian built a temple of peace. The Forum Trajanum, erected by the emperor Trajan, surpassed the others in size and magnificence, and remains the greatest monument of Roman architecture.

FOSSAE (canal) CLUILIA, (a) a trench 5 m. from Rome, probably dug to protect the camp of the Alban King Cluilius, when he marched against Rome in the time of Tullus Hostilius. (b) DRUSIANA, a canal uniting the Rhine and the Yssel, dug by Drusus in 11 B.C. (c) MARIANA, connected the Rhone and the Mediterranean, dug by Marius during his war with the Cimbri. (d) XERXES.

FRENTANI, Samnite people of the Adriatic coast, from the Sagrus to the Frento, who came under Roman rule in 304 B.C.

FRETUM GADITANUM, the Straits of Gibraltar.

FRETUM GALLICUM, the English Channel.

FRISII, German people of the coast from the E. mouth of the Rhine to the Amisia.

FRONTINUS, SEXTUS JULIUS, was praetor in A.D. 70, and five years later was sent by Vespasian to Britain, where he conquered the Silures. About A.D. 78 he was succeeded by Agricola in the command of the troops in Britain.

FRONTO, MARCUS CORNELIUS, born at Cirta in Africa, of an Italian family, came to Rome in the reign of Hadrian, acquiring a great reputation as a rhetorician and grammarian. Antoninus Pius appointed him to educate his two adopted sons, Marcus Aurelius, and Lucius Verus. He died in the reign of Marcus Aurelius at an advanced age.

FUCINUS LACUS, central lake of Italy, in the country of the Marsi, 30 m. in circumference into which the Apennine mountain streams flowed. To avoid flooding the emperor Claudius constructed a channel for carrying the waters from the lake to the river Liris.

FULLING, the art of fulling was not unknown to the ancients. According to Pliny it was invented by Nicias, a governor of Greece, during the Roman domination. Among the Romans the fullers scoured, washed, and fitted up clothes; their art was considered of importance, laws being promulgated for its regulation.

FULVIA, mistress of Q. Curius, a Catilinian conspirator, who divulged the plot to Cicero. Another of this name was daughter of M. Fulvius Bambalio; she became wife of P. Clodius, and later successively married C. Scribonius Curio, and M. Antony. She died in 40 B.C.

FUNERAL ORATIONS, the second book of Thucydides contains the harangue delivered by Pericles at the funeral of the Athenians who fell at the beginning of the Peloponnesian War. It was also the Roman custom to deliver such harangues. Nero pronounced a funeral oration over his wife Poppaea. Funeral orations were also common over Christian martyrs.

FUNERAL SHOW, or GAMES, frequently followed public funerals among the Greeks and Romans. An early example occurs in the funeral games celebrated by Achilles in honour of Patroclus. The *Adelphi* of Terence was produced for the first time at the funeral of Lucius Aemilius Paulus.

G

GABII, town of a colony from Alba Longa, where traditionally, Romulus was brought up. It was subdued by Tarquinius Superbus, and was in ruins by the time of Augustus. Remaining inscriptions indicate a flourishing town in the reign of Hadrian. The fashion of wearing the toga at Rome, *cinctus Gabinus,* was derived from this town. From the neighbouring stone quarries part of Rome was built.

GABINIUS, tribune of the plebs in 67 B.C. when a law was passed assigning to Pompey the command of the war against pirates. He was consul in 58 B.C., playing his part in the banishment of Cicero. He fought for Caesar in the civil war. He died in 48 B.C. in Illyricum.

GAD, seventh son of Jacob, by Zilpah, the handmaid of his wife Leah. It is also the name of a prophet who counselled David, and wrote a history of his reign.

GADES, ancient town of the Phoenicians in Hispania Baetica, which received its franchise from Julius Caesar. (Now CADIZ).

GAEA or GE, in *Greek Mythology,* the earth goddess, daughter of Chaos, and mother of Uranus, Pontus, and the Titans. Her Roman counterpart was Tellus.

GAETULIA, or the land of the Gaetuli, an ancient district of somewhat uncertain limits in N. Africa. The Gaetulians were one of the two great aboriginal races of N. Africa.

GAIUS, Roman jurist, living during the period from Hadrian to Marcus Aurelius. Fragments of his *Institutiones* are preserved in Justinian's *Digest* and other works.

GALATIA, territory in Asia Minor, comprising part of Phrygia and Cappadocia. Its people were an offshoot from the host of Gauls who overran Asia Minor until halted by Attalus I, King of

Pergamum (241-197 B.C.), who compelled them to settle in the country later known as Galatia, which became a Roman province under Augustus.

GALATIANS, EPISTLE TO THE, one of the four principal letters written by S. Paul; like that to the Romans, it sets forth the main points of the Apostle's teaching, with some autobiographical matter, supplementing the biographical statements in Acts. It has been supposed that the epistle is addressed to the Church in South Galatia, so was probably written from the Syrian Antioch about A.D. 53.

GALBA, SERVIUS SULPICIUS, born of a patrician family in the time of Augustus. After serving with distinction in Germany, he was proconsul, first in Africa, and afterwards in the Tarraconensis province of Spain, where he was when Julius Vindex, proconsul of Celtic Gaul, rose against Nero in A.D. 68, and urged Galba to do the same. Upon Galba declaring against Nero, the soldiers proclaimed him emperor, but he declared that he was only acting as lieutenant of the senate and people of Rome, to put an end to Nero's tyranny, but the praetorian guards and senate acknowledged him as emperor. He returned to Rome and called to account Nero's favourites, and exercised an administration of great parsimony, and tried to restore discipline among the soldiers. Otho caused a conspiracy among the guards, and Galba was put to death by the soldiers, after a reign of seven months, in A.D. 69. He was succeeded by Otho.

GALENUS, CLAUDIUS, (GALEN), Greek physician, born at Pergamum, in Asia Minor, about A.D. 130, was friend of Marcus Aurelius, and author of some 500 treatises on medical and philosophical subjects, of which 83 are extant. He ranks second only to Hippocrates as a physician. He was a great practical anatomist, but as a physiologist erred on the side of theory. He co-ordinated all the medical knowledge of his time. He died about A.D. 200 at the age of 70.

GALERIUS, VALERIUS MAXIMIANUS, Roman emperor A.D. 305-311, also known as Maximianus II. At the quadripartite division of the empire by Diocletian in 239, Galerius became one of the Caesars, and on the abdication of Diocletian became senior emperor.

GALESUS, river of Italy, emptying into the Gulf of Tarentum, and flowing through sheep pasturage; the wool of these animals was much prized in antiquity.

GALGACUS, Caledonian chief who commanded the native tribes when Caledonia was invaded by Agricola. After determined resistance he was defeated about A.D. 85 at the battle of Mons Graupius.

GALILEE, province of N. Palestine, which after the Captivity was ceded by the Assyrians to the Israelites. Tiberias was its chief city, and it contained Nazareth. The Sea of Galilee, also called the Lake of Tiberias, and the Lake of Gennesareth, is formed by an expansion of the Jordan: it is subject to sudden and violent storms. Tiberias and Capernaum stood on its shores.

GALINTHIAS, (sometimes GALANTHIS), friend of Alcmene, and daughter of Proetus of Thebes. When Alcmene was about to give birth to Heracles, and the Moerae and Ilithyiae, were trying to stay the birth, Galinthias rushed in with the false news that Alcmene had delivered a son. The hostile goddesses dropped their arms in surprise, and so was the charm broken. The goddesses avenged themselves by changing Galinthias into a weasel, but Hecate took pity on her making her an attendant upon herself.

GALLAECIA (GALICIA), district in the N. W. of Spain, occupied by the Gallaeci, the most civilized people of Spain. Under D. Brutus, consul in 138 B.C., they were defeated with great slaughter, after which victory Brutus was given the name Gallaecus.

GALLI, priests of the goddess Cybele, so called from the river Gallus, in Phrygia, of which they were in the habit of drinking before they began their festivals, it being supposed that the water infused the divine madness which accompanied their sacrifices. They were also called Corybantes, who, in their orgies, beat their cymbals, and acted as if delirious.

GALLIA, broadly speaking, all country occupied by the Galli, or Celtae, but in its restricted sense, the name was used to indicate two countries, GALLIA TRANSALPINA, and GALLIA CISALPINA. The former, in the time of Augustus, was bounded S. by the Pyrenees and Mediterranean, E. by the Varus and the Alps and the Rhine, N. by the German Ocean and English Channel, and W. by the Atlantic. In 600 B.C. the Greeks founded the important town of Massilia, q.v. The Romans started the conquest of Gaul in 125 B.C. and soon after the S. E. part became a Roman province. Caesar subdued the remainder of the country between 58-51 B.C. Now Gaul became divided into Aquitania, Celtica, and Belgica. Gaul was divided into four under Augustus, Gallia Narbonensis, G. Aquitania, G. Lugdunensis, G. Belgica. Latin became the language of the inhabitants, and Roman customs prevailed. The rhetoricians and poets of Gaul rank high in later Roman literature. On the crumbling of the Roman empire the barbarians overran Gaul and most of the country became subject to Clovis, King of the Franks.—GALLICA CISALPINA or CITERIOR was a Roman province in northern Italy, divided by the Po into Gallia Transpadana, and Gallia Cispadana. Originally it was peopled by Ligurians, Umbrians, Etruscans, and others, but its fertility attracted the Galli, who crossed the Alps and settled, after expelling the inhabitants. The Romans conquered the whole country after the first Punic War and made it a Roman province.

GALLIENUS, PUBLIUS LICINIUS, son of the emperor Valerianus, was made Caesar and colleague to his father in A.D. 253. He defeated the Alemanni near Milan, and other northern tribes which had entered N. Italy. He was an orator and poet. When Valerianus was made prisoner by the Persians in 260, Gallienus was acknowledged as Augustus. He became profligate and neglected the empire. Usurpers arose in Egypt, and in almost every province, from which circumstance this period has been styled the reign of The Thirty Tyrants. Gallienus was murdered by his own soldiers in A.D. 268, while besieging Milan.

GALLIO, proconsul of Achaia, in the Ist cent. A.D., brother of the Stoic philosopher Seneca. S. Paul was brought before him at

Corinth. He typified Roman impartiality towards the controversies around him as implied by the phrase "he careth for none of these things" (Acts xviii. 17).

GALLUS, C. CORNELIUS, Roman poet, orator, and politician, born of humble parents at Forum Julii, in Gaul, about 66 B.C. Early in life he came to Rome where he was taught by the same master as Virgil and Varius. In politics he espoused the cause of Octavianus, and was rewarded by being made prefect of Egypt. His conduct in this position later brought him into disgrace with Augustus, and dreading exposure, threw himself on his sword in 26 B.C.

GALLUS SALONINUS, C. ASINIUS, son of C. Asinius Pollio, was made consul in 8 B.C. He married Vipsania, former wife of Tiberius, who hated him in consequence, keeping him in prison for three years, where he died of starvation in A.D. 33.

GALLUS, TREBONIANUS, Roman emperor A.D. 251-253. He was governor of Lower Moesia during the campaign of his predecessor, Decius, against the Goths, with whom, when he had been proclaimed, he concluded peace. He was defeated in 253, being slain at Interamma by the usurper Aemilianus.

GAMALIEL, Jewish rabbi, grandson of Hillel, and a member of the Sanhedrin. S. Paul attended his school at Jerusalem when a youth. Gamaliel died about A.D. 52.

GANYMEDES (GANYMEDE), in *Greek Mythology*, a Phrygian youth, carried to heaven to be the cup-bearer of Zeus. Later he was identified with the spirit of the sources of the Nile.

GARAMANTES, people of Phazania, living in the south part of N. Africa. Herodotus refers to them as a weak unwarlike race.

GARGETTUS, a 'parish' (demus), in Attica, where Neocles, father of Epicurus was born.

GARUMNA, river of Gaul, the S. W. boundary of Aquitania. It flowed through Lugdunum, Tolosa, and Burdigala; it is the modern *Garonne*.

GAURUS MONS, volcanic range in Campania, between Cumae and Neapolis. Here the Samnites were defeated by M. Valerius

Corvus, in 343 B.C.

GAZA, town of Palestine, in Biblical times one of the five chief cities of the Philistines. It was captured by Alexander the Great in 332 B.C., and later figured in the chronicles of the Maccabees.

GE, *See* GAEA.

GEDROSIA, the limit of the Persian empire to the S. E.

GEHENNA, name in Biblical, and other Literature of a place of fiery torment. The name is derived from Ge. Hinnom, a valley to the W. of Jerusalem, where criminals were burned, also the refuse of the city and the bodies of animals.

GELA, wealthy and powerful coastal town of S. Sicily, which later declined and by the time of August was not inhabited. Aeschylus died here.

GELLIUS AULUS, Latin grammarian, sometimes called Agellius, who wrote the *Noctes Atticae*, during the winter evenings in Attica, to amuse his children. It is divided into 20 books which are still extant, except the 8th and beginning of the 7th. He lived about A.D. 123-165.

GELON, tyrant of Gela, rose from a private citizen to be ruler of Gela and Syracuse. He had previously commanded the cavalry and distinguished himself in the wars of Hippocrates against the Grecian cities of Sicily. On the death of Hippocrates Gelon seized supreme power in 491 B.C., and in 485 B.C. was supreme in Syracuse. In 480 B.C. he defeated the Carthaginians at Himera. He reigned 7 years at Syracuse, and died 478 B.C.

GEMONIAE, stairway, cut from the Aventine, down which executed prisoners were dragged, before being thrown into the Tiber.

GENABUM, (sometimes CENABUM), town on the Ligeris, in Gallia Lugdunensis, being chief town of the Carnutes, later renamed Civitas Aurelianorum, now known as *Orleans*.

GENESIS, first book of the Pentateuch, or rather Hexateuch. The name is taken from the Septuagint title, the *Generation of the World*. The Hebrew title is *In the Beginning*. The book falls into two main divisions. (1) Creation stories and primeval history. (2) History and stories of the patriarchs. It is composed of a number of narratives, more or less independent in origin, based on tradition.

GENEVA or GENAVA, town of the Allobroges on the border of the Helvetti, on the S. bank of the Rhone.

GENIUS, in *Roman and Greek Mythology,* every man was supposed to be accompanied from the cradle to the grave by his genius, his higher and better self, by whom he was protected and influenced.

GENSERIC, King of the Vandals, was illegitimate brother of Gonderic, whom he succeeded in A.D. 429. He left Spain the same year for Africa, at the request of the Roman governor there, who had been induced to rebel against Valentinian III, emperor of the West. The governor soon repented having sent for Genseric as he was joined by the Moors and the sect of the Donatists, so that the governor (Bonifacius) was obliged to retire into Hippo Regius, which he later abandoned to the barbarians and sailed for Italy. In 435 a peace was concluded by which Africa to the W. of Carthage went to the Vandals, notwithstanding the Vandals took Carthage in 439. Invited by Eudoxia he sailed up the Tiber in 455, allowing his soldiers to pillage Rome for 14 days. He was an Arian who persecuted his Catholic subjects. He died in A.D. 477.

GENTILES, scriptural term used variously in the O.T. and N.T. Sometimes rendered *nations* and sometimes *heathen.* It was originally employed by the Jews in a general sense to mean any nation but themselves. With the advance of the Hebrew idea of "the chosen people," this division was emphasized.

GENTIUS, King of Illyria, who in 168 B.C. conquered Rome.

GENUA, (GENOA), Ligurian town on the Gulf of Genoa, which became a Roman municipium.

GERENIA, Nestor's birthplace, was situated in Messenia.

GERMANIA, country bounded by the Rhine on the S. W., the Carpathians on the E., the German Ocean and Baltic on the N., and the Danube on the S. Tacitus states that Germani was the name of the Tungri, who were the first German people to cross the Rhine, and the first with whom the Romans came into contact. They were a branch of the Indo-Germanic race, who, with the Celts came to Europe from the Caucasus long before historical records were kept. They were fair with blue eyes, tall and strong. They were nomadic and the men were warlike; women were held in honour. There seem to have been four classes, nobles, freemen, vassals, and slaves. The chief was elected from the nobles, but he had only limited authority. They first appear in history in the expeditions of the Cimbri and Teutones in 113 B.C. Campaigns against the Germans were undertaken by Julius Caesar, Drusus, Verus, and by Germanicus, who was recalled by Tiberius when gaining continued victories. The Romans made no further attempts to reduce Germany, rather they had to defend their empire from invasion by German tribes, especially the Alemanni and Franks, who gained a number of Roman provinces.

GERMANICUS, CAESAR, distinguished Roman general, and provincial governer in the reign of Tiberius, who was born 15 B.C. and died 19 A.D. His father was Claudius Drusus Nero, and his mother the younger Antonia: he married Agrippina, granddaughter of Augustus. He was adopted by Tiberius, and raised to honour. He assisted Tiberius against the Pannonians and Dalmatians in A.D. 7-10, and the Germans in 11 and 12 A.D. He was commanding the legions in Germany when mutiny broke out upon the death of Augustus in A.D. 14. Having restored order he set out to conquer Germany, with such success that he needed only a year to reduce the country from Rhine to Elbe. It was at this juncture he was recalled to Rome by Tiberius, who gave him charge of the eastern provinces, but secretly instructed Cn. Piso to check and thwart Germanicus. It is thought, and so he thought himself, that he was poisoned by Piso, in Syria A.D. 19. In any case Tiberius had to sacrifice Piso to the public indignation.

GEROUSIA, the supreme legislative body of Sparta.

GERRA or GERRHA, ancient city of Arabia Felix, on the west of the Persian Gulf, described by Strabo as inhabited by Chaldaean exiles from Babylon, who built their houses of salt, repairing them by application of salt water. Gerra was a great center of trade between Arabia and India.

GERRHA, among the Greeks, a kind of hurdle or shield, covered with wicker-work, which the soldiers in sieges held over their heads, to protect them from beams and falling stones. They resembled the vineae of the Romans. The soldiers who carried these shields were termed Gerrhophoroi.

GETA, ANTONINUS, younger son of the emperor Septimus Severus, born about A.D. 190; was made Caesar with his father and brother in 208. He was distinguished for his mildness of character.

GETAE, name of a northern tribe mentioned in Roman history, living on both banks of the Danube, and W. shores of the Euxine. Those on the south of the river were brought into some sort of subjection in the days of Augustus. The Getae are described by Herodotus as living in his time S. of the Ister (Danube).

GIDEON, Hebrew judge and warrior, son of Joash, who overthrew the altars and groves of Baal, routed the Midianites, and judged Israel for 40 years.

GILGAMESH, Hero of a Babylonian epic, a man of mighty strength, a great hunter, and ruler of Erech. The epic narrates the Babylon story of the flood.

GIRASOL, called by the ancients *Asteria,* a precious stone of value and beauty, found in various colours, emerald-green and yellow, etc., but usually bluish white.

GLABRIO, ACILIUS, M., defeated Antiochus at Thermopylae, when he was consul in 191 B.C.—Another of the name was praetor urbanus in 70, who presided at the impeachment of Verres. He was made consul in 67, and succeeded L. Lucullus in command of the war against Mithridates, but was superseded by Cn. Pompey.

GLADIATORS, were men who fought with swords, and other weapons in the amphitheatres and other public places for the entertainment of the Romans. They were either slaves, prisoners, or convicts, and as such obliged to fight, or volunteers, who exhibited for money. The practise was defended as serving to promote a martial spirit, and a contempt of death among the people. Constantine prohibited gladiators' fights in A.D. 325, but the practise was not extinct till the time of Theodoric. In 76 B.C. 74 gladiators at Capua rose against their master, overpowered the guards, and fled to the mountains, where they were joined by thousands of runaway slaves. Being led by Spartacus, they defeated several Roman armies. They were finally mastered by M. Crassus, Spartacus being killed.

GLASS, the place where glass was first made is not known, but its origin in Egypt is dated about 1550 B.C.

GLAUCUS, in *Greek Mythology,* name of three personages: the builder of the Argo, the ship of the Argonauts; the father of Bellerophon; and a Lycian hero, slain by Ajax.

GLYCERA, favourite name of courtesans.

GLYCERIUS, emperor of the West A.D. 473, dethroned by Julius Nepos, and compelled to take Holy Orders. He became bishop of Salona, in Dalmatia.

GNATIA, *see* Egnatia.

GOLDEN AGE, in *Classical Mythology,* the period when Saturn or Cronus, after being dethroned by Zeus, reigned in Latium as king. Saturn taught agriculture and the arts of civilization to his subjects, and his reign came to be known as the Golden Age.

GOMPHI, fortress town in Thessaly on the Epirus, commanding a pass between Thessaly and Epirus.

GORDIANUS, MARCUS ANTONINUS, name of three Roman emperors, father, son, and grandson. The father governed Africa for many years, being proclaimed emperor at 80. His son was killed in battle. His grandson was proclaimed emperor by the soldiers, in A.D. 238, after the murder of Balbinus and Pupienus, when he was 12 years old, he reigned six years, and was murdered by the troops at Zaitha, Philip the Arab then seized the throne.

GORDIUM, chief city of ancient Phrygia, on the Sangarius, where the kings of the dynasty of Gordius lived. It was the scene of Alexander's "cutting the Gordian knot." The knot of bark, fastening the yoke to his wagon pole was cut by Alexander, an oracle having declared that whoever should loose the knot should be ruler of Asia.

GORDIUS, a king of ancient Phrygia, father of Midas, and of humble origin.

GORGIAS, of Leontini, in Sicily, a statesman, sophist and orator. He came to Athens in 427 B.C., to seek assistance for his native city whose independence was menaced by Syracuse. He was born about 480 B.C., and died in 376 B.C.

GORGONES (Gorgons), in *Greek Mythology*, three monsters named Sthenmo, Euryale, and Medusa, who dwelt in Libya. Instead of hair their heads were covered with crawling serpents, which had the property of turning into stone anyone who looked upon them. Medusa, who alone was mortal, was killed by Perseus, who struck off her head, while looking at her reflection in a mirror as he did so. Perseus presented the head to Athena, who set it in the middle of her shield.

GORTYNA or GORTYN, an important ancient city on the S. side of Crete, standing on the river Lethaeus (Mitropolipotamo), a short distance from the sea with which it communicated by means of its two harbours, Mettalam, and Labena. It had temples of Apollo-Pythius, Artemis, and Zeus. The "Code of Gortyn" dating from about 450 B.C. was an inscription discovered in 1884.

GOTHI, GOTHONES, GUTTONES (Goths), Teutonic people of the Scandinavian branch. In the first century A.D. they seem to have been inhabiting the neighbourhood of the Baltic and the river Vistula. In the 3rd century they had moved S. and were spreading along the N. of the Black Sea and lower Danube. Later in that century they cut up the army of the emperor Decius, but later were defeated by Claudius. Aurelian finally allowed them to settle in Dacia. There they became known as the Visigoths, while the tribes remaining in the E. were called Ostrogoths. Under Alaric, the Visigoths rebelled, invading Western Europe in 400 A.D., by way of N. Italy. Rome was captured in 410 A.D., and sacked. In all, under Alaric's successor, Ataulf, they withdrew into S. Gaul, setting up the Gothic Kingdom of Toulouse (Tolosa). From here they invaded Spain, founding another kingdom, which lasted two centuries, until overthrown by the Arabs. The Ostrogoths also extended their territory nearly as far as Constantinople, and adopted Christianity.

GRACCHUS, TIBERIUS, born 163 B.C., son of Tiberius Sempronius G., who was twice consul, and of Cornelia, daughter of Scipio Africanus. He served his first campaign in Africa, under Scipio, and later served as quaestor under Mancinus in the Numantine War. He was elected tribune of the Plebs in 133 B.C. Tiberius Gracchus attempted the revival of the Licinian Rogations (Agrarian Law), which enacted that no citizen should hold more than 500 jugera of land. Gracchus added a clause, whereby a father and two sons might hold together up to a 1000. This was opposed by the aristocracy, but was passed. The following year he was assassinated by P. Scipio Nasica, when he was about 35 years old.

GRACCHUS, GAIUS, brother of the preceding and 9 years younger, was tribune of the Plebs in 123 B.C. He carried out extensive reforms, and renewed the promulgation of the Agrarian Law. He was elected tribune a second time in 122 B.C. The Senate, determined to destroy his influence with the people, persuaded M. Livius Drusus, to propose more popular measures still. So the popularity of Gaius waned, and he failed to be elected tribune the next year. Several of his enactments were repealed, and he came to the Forum to oppose these measures upon which disorder broke out; while his friends fought in his defence Gaius fled to the grove of the Furies, across the Tiber, and commanded his servant to destroy him in 121 B.C.

GRAECIA or HELLAS (GREECE), country of Europe inhabited by the Graeci or Hellenes. The term Hellas was applied to any place, regardless of geographical situation, where Hellenes might have settled; e.g. Greek colonies in Smyrna, Tarentum, and Cyrene were said to be in Hellas. In earliest times

Hellas was a small district of Phthiotis, in Thessaly. During the prosperous times of Greek independence, Peloponnesus was regarded as distinct from Hellas proper, but was later, together with the Greek islands, included under the name Hellas, in contradistinction to the land of barbarians. The country was called Hellenes Graecia by the Romans. The length of Greece is 250 m. from Mt. Olympus to Cape Taenarus, and the width from the W. coast of Acarnania to Marathon is 180 m., an area somewhat less than Portugal; the Cambunian and Ceraunian mountains separated it from Macedonia on the N., on the other three sides it was bounded by the sea. It is a very mountainous country, with but few plains and continuous valleys. This division contributed to the establishment of separate political communities. Latterly the N. of Greece was divided into 10 districts:—Epirus, Thessalia, Acarnania, Aetolia, Doris, Lorcis, Phocis, Boeotia, Attica, and Megaris. The Peloponnesus, or S. Greece was divided into eight districts, Corinthia, Sicyonia, Achaia, Elis, Messenia, Laconia, Argolis, and Arcadia. The Greek population seem to have been descendants of the Pelasgians, the best known of the earliest inhabitants. The Hellenes, had a mythical ancestor Hellen, from whose sons and grandsons they were divided into four tribes, Dorians, Ionians, Aeolians and Achaeans.

GRAECIA MAGNA, the districts in S. Italy, populated by the Greeks, chiefly applied to the cities of the Tarentine Gulf, Tarentum, Sybaris, Croton, Caulonia, Siris, Metapontum, Locri, and Rhegium, and the Greek cities on the W. coast.

GRATIANUS, AUGUSTUS, eldest son of Valentinian I, succeeding his father, in 375, in a share of the Western empire, having for his lot Gaul, Spain, and Britain; his brother Valentinian II, then an infant, had Italy, Illyricum, and Africa, under the guardianship of Gratianus, who was in reality ruler of the west. His uncle, Valens, had the empire of the E. He was murdered by the usurper Maximus.

GRATTIUS, FALISCUS, Greek poet, contemporary with Ovid, who wrote a poem on the chase, entitled *Cynegetica,* which has been preserved.

GRAVISCAE, ancient Roman colony of Etruria, noted for its unhealthy climate.

GREEK ARCHITECTURE, not till the 5th cent. did Greek architecture assume the combined stability and grace which are its characteristics. Its chief expression was the hexastyle temple, an oblong structure enclosed by rows of columns, of a single storey with low-pitched roofs ending in a pediment. The exterior was decorated with bright primary colours, sometimes gilded. The sculpture was painted, and fine marble covered with coloured stucco. Greek architecture was dominated at successive periods by three orders, Doric, Ionic, and Corinthian. The Doric was the simplest form of column and capital, as illustrated by the finely preserved temple of Theseus at Athens. Ionic is known by its volute capitals, and Corinthian by its foliated capitals, the latter being a late Hellenistic development. Theatres were built on a grand scale, that at Dionysus being 443 ft. in diameter.

GREEK ART, the very ancient civilization and art in the Aegaean, which discoveries have revealed, came to an end about 1000 B.C., leaving but doubtful traces in the Greek art that followed. This early period produced masterpieces of decoration, and some remarkable naturalistic works, such as the gold cups unearthed at Vaphio; but the symmetry and sobriety of the Greek art are lacking. The early 6th cent. brought the beginnings of Greek sculpture. Rude images like the Apollo statue at Amyclae, rapidly gave way to intimate studies of the human form. A mythical sculptor, Daedalus, is said to have founded a school. Better authenticated early practitioners were Achermus of Chios, Dipoenus and Scyllis of Crete; and Rhoecus and Theodorus, the inventors of bronze casting. The sculptures of the Parthenon, and the paintings of Polygnotus belong to the 5th cent. Vase painting was developed at Athens by Euphronius, Duris, and Hieron. In the 4th cent. came Praxiteles, Scopas, and Lysippus of Sicyon in sculpture, and Apelles, Protogenes, Zeuxis, and Parrhasius in painting. The best known sculptures of the Hellenistic age (after the death of Alexander), were the Colossus of Rhodes by Chares, the Victory of Samothrace, Apollo Belvedere, and Laocoon. It was also the age of the Tanagra Statuettes in terra cotta.

GREEK DRAMA, arose from the festivals of Dionysus, the god of wine, which were held from the beginning of winter to the beginning of Spring. A group of rustics would gather round the altar of the god, and sing a hymn in his honour. "Tragedy" meant "the goat song," a goat being sacrificed to Dionysus before the hymn was sung. Thespis is thought to have transformed the Dionysiac song to a simple drama, introducing an interlocutor, embodying in himself a number of characters. Aeschylus and Sophocles introduced a second and third character respectively. Three tragedies were usually presented together, followed by a satire. "Comedy" was the same Dionysiac song regarded as an occasion for rustic jest, its form developing on the lines of tragic drama. Attic comedy began about 470 B.C., and was brought to perfection by Aristophanes who wrote from 427-388 B.C.

GREEK FEASTS, the unity of the Greeks was cultural rather than political and found expression in four great festivals, that of Zeus at Olympia; Zeus at Nemea; Pythian Apollo at Delphi; and Poseidon on the Isthmus. Every Greek had a right to take part. The Olympian festival was held every fourth year at midsummer, the Pythian in Aug. and Sept. in the 3rd year of each Olympiad; the Isthmian, in the spring of each second year; and the Nemean, two months later than the Isthmian. The feasts were famous for the athletic contests, valuable prizes being offered, but the highest honours were the crown of wild olive at Olympia, and the chaplet of bay at Delphi. At Athens there were six chief festivals, (a) The greater *Panathenaea,* in Aug. each fourth year. (b) The greater *Dionysia.* (c) The great *Mysteries.* (d) *The Anthesteria,* in spring. (e) The *Diasia.* (f) And the *Thesmophoria* (celebrated by women only).

GREEK PHILOSOPHY, the first seat of Greek philosophy was the colonies of Magna Graecia in Italy and Asia Minor. By 600 B.C. men were becoming interested in origins, and the whys and wherefores of the universe, and half a century later speculative enquiry began in Greece proper. The first name of importance was Thales of Miletus, who moved from myth to science, and propounded that water is the substance of all things. Anaximander took as his principle "The infinite," out of which were produced the four elements. Anaximenes chose air for his principle, to which he gave the name of God. The greatest of the Ionians, however, was Heraclitus, who regarded fire as the first principle, and held that "all things are in a state of flux." Two eastern Greeks, Pythagoras, and Xenophanes, followed, Pythagoras being the founder of a mystic concept of the world, the key to which could be found in numerals. He taught immortality and the preexistence of the soul. Xenophanes founded the Eleatic school, opposed polytheism, and anthropomorphism, and stressed the distinction between *Opinion* and *Knowledge*. But Parmenides was a greater figure, of scientific mind, inspired by religious enthusiasm and moral courage. He believed the world to be spherical, identified thought and being, and that the "One" is imperishable, immutable, indivisible. His pupil Zeno was famous for puzzles relating to space and motion. Then came Empedocles who rejected the theory of the "One," and discovered four elements, separated and combined by "hatred" and "love." The doctrine of Anaxagoras was that of a divine "nous" (intelligence), bringer of order out of chaos. Democritus proposed the "atomic" theory of matter. Humanism of the Sophists now supplanted philosophy for a time, represented by Protagoras and Gorgias. The sophists did not care for philosophy, but rather professed a liberal education. The greatest name in Greek philosophy was Socrates 470-399 B.C. He brought philosophy from heaven to earth, teaching men how to reason inductively by patient cross-examination. His teaching was ethical: of metaphysics he was sceptical in a reasoned manner. Antisthenes was the founder of the Cynic school, who taught most men are fools; only the wise can lead them; the wise man alone being happy and self-sufficient. There is no good but virtue; and no evil but vice. Aristippus founded the Cyrenaic school holding that objective knowledge being unattainable, the one thing that mattered was whether our feelings were agreeable or not. Therefore the only sound practice was to enjoy the present. Plato and Aristotle have influenced the thought of all later ages. To Plato we owe the word *idea;* his philosophy is idealism. Everything we see is the copy of a perfect original in the supra-sensual world. The perfect archetype alone *exists.* From God, the first cause, proceed all "ideas". Aristotle, 384-322 B.C., is a scientific enquirer, an analytic systemizer, profound thinker, taking all human knowledge as his province. Happiness consists in the harmonious exercise of man's best powers according to their own law of excellence. Virtue is a state of the *will,* not of the *reason.* A new epoch now opened with Stoicism and Epicureanism. Zeno founded the Stoic school, and was succeeded by Cleanthes, he in turn by Chrysippus. Epicurus founded Epicureanism, his greatest pupil being Lucretius. "Duty was the keyword of the Stoics"; pleasure of the Epicureans.—The tendency in later thought was to combine and recombine systems, and it was not until after the establishment of the Roman empire that the last school of philosophy arose, that of Neoplatonism, Plotinus being the outstanding figure of this period. The Stoic system, as a force, died with Marcus Aurelius; from now on Oriental influence is felt. Christianity had become a power. The diffusion of Neoplatonism is seen in the works of Porphyry, and Iamblichus. The master thought is that all things proceed from the "One" and hunger for reabsorption into that "One." Beauty, Truth, and Goodness all mount up to God.

GREGORIUS (Gregory), was born near Nazianzus in Cappadocia, about the year A.D. 329. He is usually known as Gregory Nazianzen. When he was a student at Athens he became the friend of Basil. Returning home in A.D. 356 he was ordained, being appointed to assist his father, who was bishop there. He went to Constantinople in A.D. 379 to contest with the Arian heretics, being made bishop of Constantinople in A.D. 380. He died in his native town in 389.—Another Gregory, surnamed Nyssenus, was bishop of Nyssa in Cappadocia, and was born at Caesarea about A.D. 331. He worked in defence of orthodoxy. His death took place some time subsequent to A.D. 394.

GRYLLUS, son of Xenophon, slain in battle at Mantinea in 362

B.C., after inflicting a mortal wond on Epaminondas.

GRYNIUM, ancient city of southern Mysia, with temple and oracle of Apollo.

GRYPS or GRYPHUS (GRIFFIN), mythical monster, part lion, part eagle, supposed to typify strength and vigilance. It figures in Persian sculpture as a guardian of treasure, also on Greek coins, and in classical architecture. It is represented in heraldry with a body, tail, and hind legs of a lion, and head, neck, breast, fore legs, and wings of an eagle, and with forward ears.

GYARUS, small island, of the Cyclades group, S.W. of Andros. It was a place of exile under the Roman emperors.

GYGES, first ruler to be named "tyrant"; was King of Lydia who founded the Mermnadae dynasty. He reigned 685-657 B.C., sending costly presents to Delphi. The first use of coinage was established in his reign.

GYLIPPUS, Spartan commander who went to Syracuse to oppose the Athenians in 415 B.C. He defeated the Athenians, taking Demosthenes and Nicias prisoners. He was entrusted by Lysander, after the defeat of Athens, to take home the treasure. Part of this he stole, and being discovered, was exiled.

GYNDES, Assyrian river, from which Cyrus the Great is supposed to have drawn off the waters by 360 channels.

H

HABAKKUK, one of the twelve minor Hebrew prophets, who prophesied in the reign of Jehoiakim, 609 B.C. He lived at the time when Judah was invaded by the Chaldaeans, and taught that they were the instruments of God's punishment. He was contemporary with Jeremiah.

HADES, in *Greek Mythology*, strictly the name of the god who ruled the underworld, also called Pluto. He was son of Cronus and Rhea, and brother of Zeus and Poseidon; his wife was Proserpine, daughter of Demeter.—In later mythology the name Hades came to be used for the realms of the god, the river Styx being the boundary, over which the dead were ferried by Charon. On the opposite bank was a three-headed dog, Cerberus, vicious guardian of Pluto's realm. Three judged the dead, Minos, Rhadamanthus, and Aeacus.

HADRIANOPOLIS, town founded by the emperor Hadrian, on the right bank of the river Hebrus, in Thrace.

HADRIANUS, P. AELIUS, (HADRIAN), Roman emperor A.D. 117-138. He was born at Italica in Spain in A.D. 76. He was adopted and brought up by Trajan and designated his successor. He made peace with the Parthians, Trajan's war against whom had ended so disastrously, and is said to have contemplated retirement from Dacia. The greater part of Hadrian's reign was spent in travel. He carried out civic and legal reforms, was a man of wide culture, and a leader in a movement which sought its literary models in the past. The Jews revolted during the last years of his reign which resulted in their virtual extermination in Judaea. He died July 10th, 138.

HADROSAURUS, the great Cretaceous Dinosaur.

HAEMON, son of Creon, who was in love with Antigone, and died by his own hand on hearing she was condemned to be entombed alive, by her father.

HAEMUS, mountain range in Thrace, noted for its cold climate. The most used passes of antiquity were called Succi, and Porta Trajani.

HAGGAI, one of the minor prophets of the Hebrews, who returned from the Babylonian captivity with Zerubbabel, and began prophesying in his old age. His design was to encourage the people to rebuild the Temple.

HALESUS, chief of the Auruncans and Oscans, and an ally of Turnus, who was killed by Evander. Halesus' father was a soothsayer.

HALIACMON, river forming the boundary between Eordaea and Pieria, in Macedonia, falling into the Thermaic Gulf, and rising in the Tymphaean mountains.

HALIARTUS, ancient Boeotian town to the S. of lake Copias, was destroyed by Xerxes in 480 B.C., and later rebuilt. Lysander was killed under its walls in 395 B.C.

HALICARNASSUS, Greek city of Asia Minor which was built by the Dorians from Troezen, about 1000 B.C., in the S. W. part of Caria, opposite Cos. In the 4th cent. B.C. it was the seat of a dynasty; on the death of Mausolus, one of that dynasty, his widow Artemisia raised a magnificent monument to his memory known as the Mausoleum: it was considered one of the seven ancient wonders of the world. The historians Herodotus and Dionysius were born here. Modern *Budrum* occupies the site.

HALL-MOTE, a term among the Anglo-Saxons which signified a convention of citizens in the general hall where they were in the habit of assembling. It was sometimes called *folk-mote.* At other times the name was applied to the manorial court of the lord, where disputes between tenants were settled.

HALLSTATT, of the transition from the Bronze to the Iron Age, from the finds at *Hallstatt* in Upper Austria.

HALONESUS, Aegaean island off Thessaly. Philip and the Athenians were often in dispute over its possession.

HAMADAN, *See* ECBATANA.

HAMAN, chief minister and favourite of Ahasuerus, King of Persia. Because a Jew named Mordecai paid him no reverence, he resolved to destroy him and all other Jews in the kingdom. The plot was discovered by Esther, with the result that Haman himself was hanged.

HAMILCAR BARCA, leader of the popular party at Carthage, was appointed in the 18th year of the first Punic War, 247 B.C., to command the Carthaginian forces. He ravaged the coasts of the Bruttii and Epizephyrian Locrians with his fleet, and seized upon a fortress in Sicily, between Eryx and Panormus, where he maintained himself some years. He frequently ravaged the S. coasts of Italy as far as Cumae, and defeated the Roman army in Sicily. Then the Romans fitted out a fleet to cut off all communication between Hamilcar and Carthage; the Carthaginian fleet sent to his assistance was defeated by the Roman consul, Lutatius Catulus in 241 B.C., and the Carthaginians sued for peace, which was granted by the Romans; Hamilcar led his troops to Lilybaeum, whence they were conveyed to Africa. The Carthaginian treasury being exhausted, it was proposed to the troops that they should give up part of the pay due to them; this proposal they rejected and enforced their demands. They were joined by native tribes and defeated Hanno the Carthaginian general sent against them, bringing Carthage to the verge of ruin. Hamilcar succeeded in subduing them after three years. Hamilcar was sent to Spain in 238 B.C., where he remained nine years extending the dominion of Carthage over the southern and eastern parts of that country. He was killed in battle in 229 B.C., being succeeded by his son-in-law Hasdrubal (not the brother of Hannibal). Several other Carthaginian generals were named Hamilcar.

HAMMURABI, KHAMMURABI, or HAMMURAPI, King of Babylon about 2,100 B.C., the Amraphel, King of Shinar, mentioned in Genesis. He left a remarkable code of laws which throw light upon the economic and political conditions of his times. It was inscribed on a black diorite stele for the temple of the sun-god Shamash at Sippara, and carried thence to Susa, about 1,200 B.C. It was discovered in three fragments in 1901-2.

HANGING GARDENS, a term commonly applied to the celebrated gardens of Babylon, which are frequently mentioned in ancient history, and fully described by Herodotus, Diodorus, and other Greek writers. So magnificent and extensive was their structure, that they have been classed among the wonders of the world. They were constructed by Nebuchadnezzar for the gratification of his favourite wife, Amytis. The whole structure was sustained by stupendous arches, and the soil laid on them was deep enough to support the largest of trees.

HANNAH, wife of Elkanah, and mother of the Hebrew prophet Samuel.

HANNIBAL, son of Hamilcar Barca, was born in 247 B.C. When nine he went with his father to Spain, his father first making him swear never to be a friend to the Romans. At an early age he was associated with Hasdrubal, who succeeded his father in command of the Carthaginian army in the country. On Hasdrubal's death in 221 B.C., he took command of the armies, quickly conquering many Spanish tribes. The people of Saguntum, alarmed at his success, appealed to Rome. An embassy was sent to Hannibal, who was passing the winter at New Carthage, to announce that the independence of Saguntum was guaranteed by a treaty between Carthage and Rome, concluded in 226 B.C. Hannibal paid no regard to the treaty, taking Saguntum in 219 B.C. He then prepared to invade Italy. He set out from New Carthage, in 218 B.C. with 80,000 foot, and 12,000 horse. Before crossing the Pyrenees he left Hanno to secure his recent conquests leaving him 11,000 men. The same number of Spanish troops he sent to their own cities. Now with an army of 50,000 foot, and 9,000 horse, he advanced to the Rhone. Two Roman armies had been levied, one, commanded by Scipio, was to oppose Hannibal in Spain, and a second, under Sempronius, was designed for an African invasion. Scipio was delayed by a revolt of the Boian and Insubrian Gauls, against whom he had to send his army. Raising a new army he sailed to the Rhone, but Hannibal had already crossed. He sailed back to Italy to meet Hannibal when he descended from the Alps. Scipio sent his brother (Cmaeus), into Spain, with the greater part of the troops to oppose Hasdrubal. Hannibal, crossing the Alps, probably by the Little S. Bernard, entered the Dora Baltea valley and went on to the territory of the Insubrian Gauls. His march from Carthage had taken 5 months, and he had lost many men. With 12,000 Africans, 8,000 Spaniards, and 6,000 horse, his first battle with Scipio was on the right bank of the Tieinus. Defeated, Scipio retreated, crossed the Po, and camped at Placentia. The army under Sempronius was recalled, and after the union of the two armies Sempronius, against the advice of Scipio, decided to risk another battle and more armies, and was defeated, retreating to the fortified cities. Hannibal now had all Cisalpine Gaul (N. Italy). In 217 B.C., the Romans raised two more armies, posting one at Arretium, and the other at Ariminum. Hannibal's army had suffered much in the swamps, and he had lost the sight of an eye. He marched past Arretium to engage the other army, which was defeated at Lake Trasimenus. Q. Fabius Maximum was now appointed dictator, and in 216 B.C., raised an army of 86,000, the Carthaginians now having 50,000 men. A battle ensued and the Romans were utterly defeated with fearful slaughter, Hannibal losing only 4,700 men. So lower Italy was in Hannibal's power. Capua was retaken by the Romans in 211 B.C. Cnaeus Scipio was joined in Spain by P. Cornelius Scipio and war went on there until the Roman army was completely defeated by Hasdrubal in 212 B.C. Both Scipios fell in battle. In 207 B.C., Hasdrubal crossed the Alps to join his brother, arriving at Placentia before the Romans knew he had entered Italy. Before he could join Hannibal he was attacked by Claudius Nero and M. Livius, in Umbria, and his army destroyed, he himself falling. Hannibal was now on the defensive and from this time until his departure from Italy in 203 B.C., he was confined to the country of the Bruttii. Scipio now passed to Africa, and with the aid of Massinissa, a Numidian prince, gained two victories over the Carthaginians, who recalled Hannibal to defend his native state. Returning he was completely defeated by Scipio in 202 B.C. The

Carthaginians sued for peace, and so ended the Second Punic War in 201 B.C. Hannibal took refuge at the court of Antiochus III, who was on the eve of war with Rome. On the defeat of Antiochus, the surrender of Hannibal was a condition of peace. Hannibal aware of his danger fled, eventually taking poison to avoid falling into Roman hands, about 183 B.C.

HANNO, a common Carthaginian name. HANNO the GREAT was the leader of the aristocrats, and chief adversary of Hamilcar Barca and his family; whom he ceaselessly sought to thwart. —Another of the name was a Carthaginian navigator, who wrote *Periplus,* being an account of a voyage taken beyond Gibraltar, in order to found Libyphoenician towns.

HARMODIUS AND ARISTOGITON, two devoted Athenian friends. When the sister of Harmodius had been insulted by Hipparchus, brother of the tyrant Hippias, they resolved to murder Hipparchus at the festival of Panathenaea, in 514 B.C. Hipparchus was slain, but Harmodius was killed and Aristogiton died under torture. They were honoured as martyrs by the Greeks.

HARPAGINES, naval implements of war, used by the ancients for hooking on to the enemy's ships, and raising them up in the air, by which means they were frequently sunk or destroyed.

HARPALUS, Macedonian treasurer to Alexander the Great, and satrap of Babylon. He went to Greece in 325 B.C. having embezzled large sums, and bribed leading men at Athens to support him against his master. He later fled to Crete, where he was murdered in 323 B.C.

HARPOCRATES, *See* HORUS.

HARPOCRATION, Greek lexicographer of the second century, who wrote, *Lexicon of the Ten Orators.*

HASDRUBAL, or ASDRUBAL, a Carthaginian name, the most famous holder being the Carthaginian soldier left in Spain by his brother Hannibal (q.v.), when going on his expedition against Rome in 218 B.C. Hasdrubal carried on the war against the two Scipios, whose object it was to prevent him from rejoining Hannibal. In 208 B.C. he crossed the Pyrenees, and in 207 the Alps, reaching Italy with his army. He was defeated however, at Metaurus, Hasdrubal being killed. Another Hasdrubal was son-in-law of Hamilcar. It was he who founded New Carthage.

HEADBOROW, term applied by the Saxons to the head of the frank-pledge in boroughs. He was chief of the ten pledges, as the other nine, being inferior pledges, were designated *handborows*. (Note: A frank-pledge was a mutual suretyship by which the members of a tithing were made responsible to one another.)

HAZOR or HAZUR, name of several places in Palestine, the most important being a city in Naphtali, just S. of Kedesh, which was taken and destroyed by Joshua, and rebuilt and fortified by Solomon. It was later taken by Tiglath Pileser, King of Assyria: *see* 2 Kings xv. 29.

HEBREWS, EPISTLE TO THE, one of the canonical books of the N.T. In the English version it bears the title "The Epistle of Paul the Apostle to the Hebrews," but can hardly have been written by S. Paul, since it differs in style, language, and thought from the other Pauline writings. The use made of the O.T. by the writer suggests that his purpose was to save his readers from a relapse into Judaism. It seems to have been written towards the end of the first century.—The Gospel according to the Hebrews is one of the more important of the N.T. Apocryphal books, which has survived only in fragments found in the writings of the fathers of the Church. It seems to have been written originally in Aramaic, and intended for the Jewish Christian congregations of Palestine.

HEBRON, the ancient Kirjath-Arba, town in Palestine, in the valley of Mamre, 16 m. S.S.W. of Jerusalem. One of the oldest cities of Palestine, it was the abode of Abraham, Isaac, and Jacob, besides other patriarchs; its old walled mosque of Machpelah, is supposed to cover the tomb of Abraham.

HEBRUS, most important river in Thrace, on the banks of which Orpheus was torn to pieces by the Thracian women. It was closely associated with the worship of Dionysus.

HECATAEUS, of Miletus, was one of the earliest Greek prose writers. He was present at the deliberation of the Ionians in

501 B.C., and tried to dissuade them from revolting against the Persian King. He is mentioned by Herodotus as being alive at the time of the flight of Aristagoras in 497 B.C.

HECATE, ancient Greek divinity, daughter of the Titan Perses and Asteria, according to Hesiod. Her attributes correspond in most respects with those of Artemis.

HECATESIA, festival celebrated by the Greeks, especially the Athenians, in honour of Hecate.

HECATOMB, Greek word signifying the sacrifice of a large number of victims, usually a hundred. Strictly speaking the sacrifice should consist of a hundred bulls, but inferior animals were often substituted. In the time of Homer it was usual only to burn the legs, fat, and intestines, the remainder being eaten at the feast following the hecatomb. Hence at Athens it was the most popular form of sacrifice as it pleased not only the gods, but fed both priests and people.

HECTOR, greatest of the Trojan heroes, was son of Priam and Hecuba; he married Andromache. In the Iliad he is not only a bold warrior, but a hero ennobled by the more tender and human virtues. He finally fell by the hand of Achilles, who gave up his body to Priam. His remains were buried at Troy, where funeral sacrifices were offered to him as a hero.

HECUBA, wife of Priam, King of Troy, by whom she was mother of Hector, Paris, Cassandra, and many other children. At the taking of Troy she was carried away captive by the Greeks to Thracian Chersonese. Eventually she was changed into a dog, and threw herself into the sea, at Cynossema, (the tomb of the Dog).

HEGESIAS, Greek rhetorician and historian, born at Magnesia, who lived about the time of the historian Timaeus, 250 B.C. He wrote a history of Alexander the Great. His style was jerky and was parodied by Cicero.

HEGESIAS, the Cyrenaic Philosopher, lived in the reign of Ptolemaeus Philadelphus. His doctrines were similar to those of Aristippus, founder of the Cyrenaic school, who maintained that pleasure was the great object of life. But Hegesias denied that kindness, friendship, and benevolence had any independent existence, but arise and disappear with our feeling of the want of them.

HEGESIPPUS, Athenian orator, contemporary with Demosthenes.

HELENA and HELENE (Helen), in *Greek Legend,* a woman of surpassing beauty whose seizure by Paris was the cause of the Trojan War. According to earlier stories she was daughter of Tyndareus and Leda, Castor and Pollux being her brothers. In a later version, Leda was visited by Zeus in the form of a swan, and gave birth to an egg, from which Helen, Castor, and Pollux came forth. Helen became wife of Menelaus, King of Sparta, and when Paris, son of Priam, King of Troy, came there on a visit, Aphrodite, in fulfilment of a promise to give Paris the most beautiful women in the world, caused her to fall in love with the visitor. After the capture of Troy, Helen returned to Sparta with her husband.

HELENA, FLAVIA JULIA, wife of the emperor Constantius Chlorus, and mother of Constantine the Great, was born of humble origin in Nicomedia, becoming famous for her devotion to Christianity. She made a pilgrimage to Jerusalem in her old age, and, according to a legend, she discovered the Holy Sepulchre, and the wood of the Cross.

HELENUS, son of Priam and Hecuba, famous for prophecy. On the death of Paris Helenus and Deiphobus contended for Helena. Helenus, being overcome, fled to Mt. Ida, where he was made prisoner by the Greeks. He foretold the sufferings which awaited the Greeks who returned by sea.

HELEPOLIS, a ponderous movable machine, used by the ancients for besieging towns, forts, etc., consisting of numerous stories, whose dimensions lessened as they ascended. Bodies of soldiers occupied each compartment from which they discharged their missiles from small openings. The machine was pushed forward on castors by the strongest men of the army.

HELIAEA, Athenian court of justice, next in importance to the

Areopagus. It was generally composed of 500 members. The judges, in awarding their verdict, made use of black and white beans which were cast into urns, the votes being counted by the presiding magistrate: a majority of white beans gave an acquittal.

HELICON, Mt. in S.W. Boeotia; its beautiful scenery caused it to be known as the home of the Muses, to whom there was a temple, and in whose honour games were celebrated. The well of Aganippe at its base, and the fountain of Hippocrene were also sacred to them.

HELIODORUS, was born at Emesa in Syria, in the 3rd Cent. A.D. He became Bishop of Tricca, in Thessaly. In his youth he wrote a romance in Greek which he called *Aethiopica*, which is an account of the adventures of Chariclea, daughter of Hydaspes, King of Ethiopia, and Theagenes, a noble Thessalian, who were lovers. This work served as a model for later Greek writers of romance.

HELIOGABALUS, *see* ELAGABALUS.

HELIOPOLIS, (City of the Sun), town of ancient Egypt, chief seat of religious learning, formerly containing a university for the training of priests. It is the On of the Bible (Gen. XLI. 45), to the Egyptians it was known as Annu. Ruins of the great temple of the sun remain.

HELLANICUS, early Greek prose writer, born at Mitylene in the island of Lesbos, in 496 B.C. He wrote several historical books which are quoted by ancient writers.

HELLAS, HELLENES, *see* GRAECIA.

HELLE, daughter of Athamas and Nephele, and sister of Phrixus, after whom the Hellespont was named.

HELLESPONTUS, (Hellespont, Straits of the Dardanelles), in *Ancient Geography*, strait separating the Thracian Chersonese from Asia. It is supposed to have derived its Greek name of Hellespontus (sea of Helle) from Helle, daughter of Athamas, who in her flight from her step-mother, Ino, on the ram with the golden fleece, fell into the sea and was drowned.

HELOT, lowest section of the community in Sparta, analogous to the medieval villeins in England, and of the Russian serf before his emancipation. They belonged to the state, not to individuals, and could not be removed from the land. The ruling class of Spartans employed them to cultivate their farms, and they had to hand over a fixed amount of the produce of the farm each year; any surplus they retained. In time of war they served as light-armed infantry, or oarsmen.

HELVETII, a Celtic people which formerly occupied a part of Europe corresponding to modern Switzerland. We learn from Caesar that they had twelve towns, and 400 villages, all of which they burned, in 58 B.C., previous to their attempted invasion of Southern Gaul, to prevent which Caesar had to destroy the bridge at Geneva, and build a long wall along the Rhone. Failing to pass the barrier the Helvetii took another route, but were met and repulsed, two-thirds being killed, and the remainder obliged to return to their country, and subject themselves to the Romans. After the death of Nero they gradually became extinct as a race.

HELVIA, mother of Seneca, the philosopher.

HELVIDIUS PRISCUS, *see* PRISCUS.

HEPHAESTION, friend of Alexander the Great, who was a Macedonian; he died at Ecbatana in 324 B.C. Another of the name was a writer of the 2nd Cent. A.D.

HEPHAESTUS, in *Greek Mythology,* god of fire, and the working of metals. He was son of Zeus and Hera, but was so disliked by his mother that she threw him out of Olympus. He is represented as having been lame from birth. In art he is depicted as a strongly-built man with a beard, holding a smith's hammer and tongs. Hephaestus was identified by the Romans with Vulcan.

HERA, in *Greek Mythology,* sister and wife of Zeus, and daughter of Cronus and Rhea, was one of the major deities of ancient Greece. She became mother of Ares, Hephaestus, and Hebe, by Zeus. She is represented as of a jealous disposition. She had frequent quarrels with her husband and on one occasion plotted with Athena and Poseidon to put him in chains. For this she was beaten by Zeus, and herself put in chains. Her annoyance

with Paris for his judgment against her led her to side with the
Greeks in the Trojan War. She is represented as a woman of
stately beauty. The Romans identified her with Juno.

HERACLEA, or HERACLEIA, (the city of Heracles), was the
name of several cities of Greek colonization. (a) A city in Magna
Graecia, between the rivers Aciris and Siris, near the shore of
the Gulf of Tarentum. Pyrrhus was victorious in the vicinity, in
280 B.C. (b) City of Sicily, at the mouth of the Halycus, not far
from Capa Bianco; it was distinguished by the surname Minoa,
it being founded by Minos of Crete. (c) H. Pontica, city on the
Phrygian coast, founded by a Megarian colony. (d) H. Sintica,
town in Thracian Macedonia, S. of the Strymon. (e) a town on
the borders of Caria and Ionia, near Mt. Latmus. Endymion was
buried near here.

HERACLES, called by the Romans Hercules, hero in *Greek
Mythology,* son of Zeus by Alcmene, wife of Amphitryon, King
of Thebes. The famous Twelve Labours of Hercules are:— 1. The
slaying of the Nemean lion. 2. The destruction of the Hydra of
Lernae. 3. The capture of the Arcadian stag. 4. The capture of
the Erymanthian boar. 5. The cleansing of the stables of Augeas.
6. The destruction of the Stymphalian birds. 7. The capture of
the mad bull of Minos. 8. The capture of the man-eating horses
of Diomedes. 9. The taking of the girdle of Hippolyte. 10. The
seizure of the oxen of Geryon. 11. The taking of the three golden
apples from the garden of Hesperides. 12. The bringing of Cerberus from the lower world.—Besides these labours Hercules
performed many other deeds.

HERACLIDAE, the descendants of Heracles, or Hercules. According to tradition, after Hercules' death, his children took refuge in Attica, to escape persecution from Eurystheus, where
they were well received. In conjunction with the Dorians, they
conquered Peloponnesus 80 years after the fall of Troy. (According to mythical chronology 1104 B.C.)

HERACLIDES PONTICUS, Greek miscellaneous writer, flourished in the 4th Cent. B.C., was born at Heraclea in Pontus.
Going to Athens he became disciple first of Speusippus, then of

Plato, also of Aristotle. Plato, on departing for Sicily, left his scholars in charge of Heraclides. He is said to have been vain and fat, and maintained such state that wits changed his name to Pompicus (the Showy).

HERACLITUS of EPHESUS, surnamed the Naturalist, belonged to the dynamical school of Ionian philosophy. He was born about 500 B.C., dying when 60 years of age. He assumed the title of 'self-taught', but this title refutes the claims of various masters whom he is said to have had. His work, *On Nature*, was so complex, that it earned him the title of 'the Obscure'. According to Heraclitus, the end of wisdom is to discover the ground and principle of things. The physical doctrines of Heraclitus formed no inconsiderable portion of the eclectical system of the Stoics.

HERCULANEUM, ancient Italian coastal town, between Naples and Pompeii, at the foot of Mt. Vesuvius. It was badly damaged by an earthquake in the days of Nero, and in the autumn of 79 was totally destroyed together with Pompeii, by an eruption from Vesuvius. It was buried by lava from 70-100 ft. beneath the present level. The city was discovered accidentally in 1720 when a well was being sunk. One of the interesting finds was the library of an Epicurean.

HERCULES, *see* HERACLES.

HERMAE, small pillars, surmounted by a head, usually that of Hermes. In Greece they were set up in large numbers in public places. It was the alleged mutilation by Alcibiades of the Hermae of Athens on the eve of the expedition to Sicily in 415 B.C. that led to his disgrace.

HERMAPHRODITUS, in *Greek Mythology*, son of Hermes and Aphrodite. The nymph of a fountain by Halicarnassus fell in love with the youth, and the two combined to form a being with the characteristics of both sexes.

HERMARCHUS, rhetorician, born at Mitylene, about 270 B.C. He became a disciple of Epicurus, who appointed him as his successor.

HERMAS, early Christian writer, supposed brother of Pope

Pius I. He appears to have flourished in the first half of the 2nd cent., when he wrote his allegory *The Shepherd*, giving a valuable picture of the state of Christianity of Rome during that period.

HERMES, in *Greek Mythology*, son of Zeus, became an adept in robbery, stealing the trident of Poseidon, the girdle of Aphrodite, and the sword of Ares. He found favour with Zeus who made him his messenger. He became god of eloquence and good fortune; the patron of merchants, travellers, and thieves. He is represented as a handsome youth in art. He wears the petasus, or broad-brimmed hat, bears the caduceus, and has winged sandals.

HERMES TRESMEGISTUS, the Egyptian Thoth, Tauut, or Tat, who was identified by the Greeks more or less completely with their own Hermes.

HERMESIANAX, elegiac poet of the Alexandrian school, was born at Colophon, flourishing in the time of Philip and Alexander, or a little later. He was friend and admirer of the poet Philetas, whom he outlived. Part of his *Leontion* is extant.

HERMETICA, writings ascribed to Hermes Trismegistus, q.v.; they are really Neoplatonist documents of the 3rd cent. A.D.

HERMIONE, daughter of Menelaus and Helena, had been promised to Orestes before the Trojan war, but married Neoptolemus, q.v., after whose murder Hermione married Orestes, by whom she bore Tisamenus.

HERMOGENES, of Tarsus, Greek rhetorician, flourished in the reign of Marcus Aurelius. His ability secured him an appointment as public teacher of his art, while yet a boy. At the age of 25 his faculties failed. In the few years of his activity he composed a whole series of treatises on rhetorical matters, which became popular text books.

HERMOGENES, heretic of the early Church against whom Tertullian has written a treatise; was probably a native of Africa.

HERMOLAUS, Macedonian youth, page to Alexander the Great. He conspired against the king's life, in 327 B.C. but was discovered and stoned to death.

HERMOPOLIS MAGNA, one of the most ancient of the Egyptian cities, standing on the W. bank of the Nile; was chief seat of Anubis worship. Excavation has discovered here Graeco-Egyptian murals, and interesting papyri.

HERNICI, people of Sabine origin, living in Latium, a warlike tribe who offered resistance to the Romans, who subdued them in 306 B.C.

HERO, See LEANDER.

HERO, or HERON, there were two of this name, both writers on mechanical subjects. Hero the Elder, was pupil of Ctesibius, and lived at Alexandria, in about 100 B.C. The country of the younger is uncertain. The Elder is mentioned by Gregory Nazianzen with Euclid and Ptolemaeus. The Younger wrote on Practical Geometry, and Military science.

HERODES (HEROD), the name of seven Jewish princes. (a) HEROD the GREAT was second son of Antipater, by whom he was appointed governor of Galilee at the age of 25. When the Parthians invaded Judaea in 40 B.C., Herod escaped to Rome, where by the influence of M. Antonius, he was appointed King of the Jews. The Roman generals in Syria gave him but poor support, and it was not until the year 38 B.C. that Jerusalem was taken by Sossius. In that year Herod married Mariamne, granddaughter of Hyrcanus, hoping for the support of this family which was popular in Judaea. He made his wife's brother, Aristobulus high priest, but soon he was secretly put to death at Herod's instigation. Cleopatra, being informed of the murder Herod was accused before M. Antonius, whom he bribed. In the war between Octavianus and M. Antonius, Herod favoured the latter. After the battle of Actium, he went to meet Octavianus at Rhodes: he was well received, and confirmed in his kingdom. Herod and his wife now became estranged, and Mariamne, being accused of adultery was executed. His disregard of the Jewish law caused hatred amongst his subjects. To secure himself against rebellion he fortified Samaria, and built Caesarea. In 17 B.C. he began to rebuild the temple, which was completed in 8 years, apart from decoration. He died in March of 4 B.C. in the

34th year of his reign at the age of 70. The birth of Jesus Christ took place in the last year of his reign. (b) HEROD ANTIPAS, son of Herod the Great, was appointed, by his father's will, Tetrarch of Galilee and Peraea. About A.D. 26 he divorced the daughter of Aretas, King of Arabia, marrying his sister-in-law, Herodias. John Baptist protested against the union, was imprisoned, and later put to death. Aretas marched against Antipas, and defeated him. In A.D. 39 Antipas was accused by Agrippa, King of Judaea, of a secret understanding with the Parthians, and was banished by Caligula to Lyon. (c) HEROD AGRIPPA, son of Aristobulus, and grandson of Herod the Great. When Antipas was banished he was appointed to his tetrarchy. He was popular with the Jews, to please whom he persecuted the Christians. He died of a loathsome disease at Caesarea in the 3rd year of his reign, in A.D. 44. (d) HEROD AGRIPPA, son of the above, was 17 years old at the time of his father's death, and 4 years later Claudius bestowed the kingdom upon him. His dominions were enlarged by Nero. The trial of S. Paul took place before him in A.D. 60. Agrippa exerted himself to keep down the spirit of revolt among the Jews. When war broke out Agrippa joined the Romans. After the taking of Jerusalem he retired with his sister Berenice to Rome, when he died when about 70.

HERODES, ATTICUS TIBERIUS CLAUDIUS, Greek rhetorician, born at Marathon, about A.D. 101; he taught rhetoric at Athens and Rome. M. Aurelius, and L. Verus were his pupils. He became consul in A.D. 143. He added greatly to the embellishment of Athens. He died A.D. 177, aged 70.

HERODIANS, probably a political party in Judaea, who were anxious to preserve the government in the hands of Herod's family. Many believe the Herodians to have been a religious sect, connected with the Sadducees, since that which is called by S. Mark, 'the leaven of Herod,' is styled by S. Matthew 'the leaven of the Sadducees.'

HERODIANUS, Greek author, who wrote a history, in eight books, of the Roman emporors who reigned in his lifetime, beginning with the death of M. Aurelius in 180, and ending with the accession of the younger Gordianus, in 238.

HERODOTUS, a native of Halicarnassus, born about B.C. 484. He was son of Lyxes and Dryo, of illustrious family. Not liking the rule of Lygdamis, tyrant of Halicarnassus, he retired for a time to Samos, where he cultivated the Ionic dialect of Greek. Before he was 30 he joined the successful attempt to expel Lygdamis. He now joined the colony which the Athenians sent to Thurii, in S. Italy, where he died, and was buried in the Agora, or Public Place. Herodotus was a traveller and observer as well as an historian. The extent of his travels may be ascertained from his History. He frequently does not say that he was at a place, but uses words which are as conclusive as any statement. The nine books of Herodotus contain a great variety of matter, the unity of which is not perceived till the whole work has been carefully examined. His object was to combine a general history of the Greeks and the Barbarians with the history of the wars of the Greeks and Persians. So, in the execution of his main subject, he traces the course of events from the time when the Lydian kingdom of Croesus fell, 546 B.C. until the capture of Sestos, in 478 B.C., an event which crowned the triumph of the Greeks over the Persians. He has earned the well-merited appellation of the Father of History. His style is simple, pleasing, and generally perspicuous, and often highly poetical in expression and sentiment. It bears the marks, however, of belonging to a period when prose composition had not yet become a subject of art. His sentences are often ill-constructed and hang loosely together, but his clear comprehension of his own meaning, and the value of his matter, have saved him from the reproach of diffuseness and incoherence.

HEROIC VERSE, in its ancient sense, means that which was the vehicle of Greek, and subsequently of Latin, epic poetry, of which the actions of the heroes were the appropriate subject.

HEROOPOLIS, city of Lower Egypt, E. of the Delta, near the canal which connected the Nile with the W. head of the Red Sea, (Sinus Heroopoliticus).

HEROSTRATUS, it was he who set fire to the temple of Artemis at Ephesus on the night that Alexander the Great was born, in 356 B.C., in order to immortalize himself.

HESIODUS (HESIOD), Greek diadactic poet, who flourished about 700 B.C. He lived at Ascra, at the foot of Mt. Helicon, in Boeotia. He was a farmer by profession. One of his poems, *Works and Days,* is a didactic poem, part of which is largely a manual of agriculture, to which Virgil was much indebted. His other surviving poem, *Theogony,* is an account of the Creation, and a history of the gods, and demi-gods. As Homer represents the Ionic school of poetry in Asia Minor, so Hesiod represents the Boeotian.

HESPERIDES (Daughters of Evening), in *Greek Mythology,* nymphs who guarded the golden apples of Hera. Different legends placed their gardens variously in the Far West. The quest of three of these apples was one of the 12 labours of Hercules, q.v. Some writers mention three Hesperides:—Aegle, Arethusa, and Hesperia; others four, Aegle, Crytheia, Hestia, and Arethusa; while some mention seven.

HESSENES, or ESSENES, one of the three great sects into which the Jews were divided in the time of Christ. They generally lived away from large towns, in communities which bore resemblance to monkish societies of later times. They had all things in common, ate at a common table, were abstemious, never taking food before sunset. They sent gifts to the Temple but never offered sacrifice there. They held the Scriptures in great reverence, explaining them allegorically.

HESTIA, *See* VESTA.

HESYCHIUS, flourished 5th cent. A.D., author of a valuable Greek lexicon, which contains chiefly short explanations of unusual Greek words, or forms of words, and technical terms. It was unknown until the 16th cent.

HETAIRA, concubine, or woman-companion, as opposed to the legal wife, but the word had several connotations. They were often accomplished, sometimes enjoying more privileges than the legal wife.

HETEROSCII, ancient term in astronomy for persons living in such parts of the earth that their shadows at noon were always turned contrary ways.

HEXAMETER, most common form of dactylic verse, consisting of six feet, either dactyls or spondees, with no limit in their arrangements, except that the fifth is usually a dactyl, and the sixth invariably a spondee.

HEZEKIAH, King of Judah; he succeeded his father, Ahaz, at the age of 25, was a notable reformer, who abolished centers of idolatrous worship, restoring the worship of Jehovah. He was a man of literary and poetic gifts, regarded by the Jews as one of their most famous kings.

HIBERNIA, IVERNIA, or IERNE, name given to Ireland by Latin writers. It is mentioned by Eratosthenes and Caesar.

HIEMPSAL, (a) son of Micipsa, King of Numidia, who was murdered by Jugurtha in 118 B.C. (b) King of Numidia, descendant of Masinissa, and father of Juba. He was expelled by Cn. Domitius Ahenobarbus, but restored by Pompey in 81 B.C.

HIERAPOLIS, city of Phrygia, near the Meander; it was an early seat of Christianity.

HIEROGLYPHICS, name for the picture characters which the ancient Egyptians used in writing. In ancient texts they are called 'the words of the god' (Hieroglyphic—'sacred writing'). There are three forms 1. Hieroglyphic; 2. Hieratic; 3. Demotic. In the first the characters are recognizable pictures; in the second only the most salient features of the pictures are preserved; in the third the characters are so modified that in many instances they are mere conventional representations of the hieroglyphics. Early in the Roman period the knowledge of hieroglyphics was lost, all attempts at deciphering proving unsuccessful until the beginning of the 19th cent. when Thomas Young deduced correct values of several characters. Thanks to Zoega (1755-1809), it became known that a king's name was always written within an oblong cartouche with rounded ends, but it was uncertain at which end the name began. Two monuments cleared up the difficulty, the Rosetta stone, and a stone obelisk from Philae. Each contains a Greek as well as an Egyptian inscription, as it was customary for kings to publish their edicts in two languages. On the Rosetta stone the Greek text shows that the inscription is an edict of the priests of Egypt, met in the temple of Ptah, in Memphis, in March, 196 B.C. who decreed that special honours should be paid to Ptolemy V. Epiphanes.

HIEROGRAMMATISTS, among the ancient Egyptians, certain priests who presided over religion and learning. Their special duties were to expound religious mysteries, and preserve the history and hieroglyphics of the land.

HIERON or HIERO, name of a tyrant and King of Syracuse. Hieron I was Tyrant of Syracuse 478-467 B.C. He gained a decisive naval victory over the Etruscans near Cumae, in 474 B.C. He was a generous patron of art and literature, Aeschylus, Pindar, Bacchylides, and Simonides, all residing at his court under his patronage. Hieron II, King of Syracuse 270-216 B.C., distinguished himself in wars against Pyrrhus.

HIERONYMUS, (a) grandson of Hieron II, King of Syracuse, who succeeded him at the age of 15, in 216 B.C. Under him the court became profligate. After the battle of Cannae, Hieronymus, made war against the Romans, but his soldiers conspired, and he was murdered, after reigning 13 months. (b) Of Cardia, who went to Asia with Alexander, and after his death served under Eumenes. He later fought under Antigonus, Demetrius, and Antigonus Gonatas. He died aged 104. (c) Better known as S. Jerome, one of the Latin Fathers, who translated the Bible into that language. He died A.D. 420.

HIEROSOLYMA, See JERUSALEM.

HIEROPHANTES, high priests of the Eleusinian mysteries, who for many generations were chosen from the family of the Eumolpidae. The name was also applied priests or priestesses who had care of the sacrifices and sacred things.

HILARION, SAINT, the founder of monastic institutions in Palestine, was born at Tabatha, about A.D. 291.

HILARIUS, born in Sardinia, was made deacon at Rome about A.D. 354. He is frequently mentioned by Jerome.

HIMERA, city of Sicily, founded by Zanclaeans of Mylae in

648 B.C. After existing for 240 years it was destroyed by the Carthaginians, its treasure being carried away. The surviving inhabitants established themselves at Thermae. Upon the capture of Carthage, Scipio restored to the people the monuments of art plundered by the Carthaginians.

HIPPALUS, navigator who discovered the S. W. monsoons and instituted the Arabia-India sea route, about 150 B.C.

HIPPARCHUS, Greek astronomer, flourished about 160-125 B.C., was born at Nicaea in Bithynia; he chiefly carried out his observations in Rhodes and Alexandria. His *Commentary on the Phaenomena of Eudoxus and Aratus,* is extant. His chief title to fame was his catalogue of 1,080 stars. He was inventor of trigonometry, and originated the method of fixing terrestrial positions by means of circles of latitude and longitude.

HIPPIAS, Greek sophist, native of Elis and contemporary with Socrates, famous for his extensive knowledge and remarkable memory. He regarded law as opposed to nature and driving man to act contrary to his natural instincts.

HIPPO or HIPPO REGIUS, ancient city of N. Africa, founded by the Phoenicians, was the favourite residence of the Kings of Numidia. Under Rome Hippo flourished as a trading center, and became the see of S. Augustine, who died there in A.D. 340. Hippo was sacked by the Vandals. Finally it was destroyed by the Moslems in the 7th cent.

HIPPOCRATES, Greek physician, Father of Medicine. One of the first scientific medical men, he was born in Cos, about 460 B.C., and was a member of the celebrated family of priest-physicians, the Asclepiadae. He was an acute observer and practised both as physician and surgeon. More than 70 of his essays have come to us. He died at Larissa in Thessaly about 357 B.C., in his 104th year.

HIPPOCRENE (Fountain of the Horse), was in Mt. Helicon in Boeotia, and was sacred to the Muses.

HIPPODAMIA, daughter of Oenomaus, King of Pisa. The wife of Pirithous, q.v., also bore this name.

HIPPODROME, large enclosed space in ancient Greece, set

apart for their horse and chariot races. There was little difference between the Roman circus, q.v., and the Greek hippodrome, except that the circus was narrower.

HIPPOLYTE, in *Greek Legend,* queen of the Amazons, who wore a famous girdle, gift of her father Ares, to obtain which was one of the twelve labours of Hercules, q.v.; refusing to give it up she was slain by him. Another legend says, Hippolyte invaded Attica at the head of her Amazons, but was defeated by Theseus, and became his wife.—The wife of Acastus also bore this name.

HIPPOLYTUS, in *Greek Legend,* son of Theseus who rejected the advances of his step-mother, Phaedra, who in consequence took her own life, leaving a letter accusing Hippolytus as the offender. Theseus called upon Poseidon to kill his son, but Aesculapius restored him to life. Afterwards he ruled in the grove of Egeria under the name of Virbus.

HIPPOMENES, son of Megareus, who conquered the Boeotian Atalanta in a running-race. Another of the name was a descendant of Codrus, last of the decennial archons.

HIPPONAX, of Ephesus, iambic poet, about 546-520 B.C.

HIPPOPOTAMUS, Roman name for the River Horse.

HIRPINI, inhabitants of the S. of Samnium of Samnite origin, with their chief town at Aeculanum.

HIRTIUS, A., consul with Pansa, in 43 B.C., and friend of Caesar. With his colleague he was killed at the battle of Mutina, when fighting against Antony.

HISPALIS, town of Hispania Baetica, founded by the Phoenicians, became important under the Romans.

HISPANIA (SPAIN), country of Europe, occupying the greater part of the peninsula which is divided from France by the Pyrenees. There is evidence that Spain was well-known to the Phoenicians at least by 1000 B.C. Its original inhabitants seem to have been Celts and Iberians, who were later called the Celtiberians. The history of Spain really starts from the founding of the Carthaginian colony of Barceno, about 300 B.C. After the second Punic War the Romans resolved to carry their arms to a country endowed with natural wealth, as Spain was. The subjugation of Carthage had made them masters of the Mediterranean, and their fleets easily transported their legions to the Spanish coasts. They managed to establish themselves on the E. and S. coasts, but inland met sturdy resistance. While Rome was engaged in the third Punic War, several tribes, formerly allied to Carthage, united under Viriathus, attacking the Romans at Lusitania. Here they defeated Vetitius, the praetor, with a loss of 4000 men. A second Roman army was sent but was defeated, and Viriathus made himself master of the country. Carthage fell, and Rome immediately set out to recover supremacy in Spain, but her legions were often repulsed. At last Scipio Aemilianus, the destroyer of Carthage, was sent to close the war. He besieged the principal stronghold, which eventually submitted. All Spain now acknowledged Roman rule and was divided into Baetica, or Hispania Ulterior, and Tarraconensis, or Hispania Citerior. But the spirit of revolt was only dormant. When Sulla had crushed Marius at Rome in 81 B.C., the Marian chief Sertorius, fled to Spain, collected a great army and successfully defended himself from the forces of the republic under Gaius Annius and Metellus, and gradually wrested the whole peninsula from Rome. The rule of Sertorius was mild and conciliatory. He maintained his position against Cnaeus Pompeius (Pompey the Great), but the struggle was great and Sertorius fell victim to the duplicity of his lieutenant, and was assassinated in 72 B.C. The traitor assumed his victim's place but the Iberians deserted him, and he was no fit antagonist for Pompeius. He was defeated and captured in the first battle and put to death. Isolated revolts occurred for many years until Agrippa exterminated the rebellious tribes. Augustus developed the country founding colonies at Caesar Augusta, and Augustus Emerita. Spain prospered and gave birth to many great men, such as, Pomponius Mela, Seneca, Lucan, Trajan, and Theodosius the Great. This period came to an end and the Gothic tribes of Vandals, Alans, and Suevi, poured into the peninsula. The kingdom of the Visigoths was founded about 420. The Vandals from whom Andalusia received its name, retired before Wallia, the Visigoth conqueror. The Romans were compelled to fly by his successor, Eurie in 484. Finally the unity of the Spanish nation under a Visigoth king was established by Leovigild in 583.

HISTIAEUS, tyrant of Miletus; when Darius invaded Syria, in 513 B.C., Histiaeus was left, with other Ionians, to guard the bridge of boats over the Danube. He opposed the proposal to destroy the bridge, which was made by Miltiades, being rewarded with a district in Thrace; there he founded Myrcinus, with a view to establishing an independent kingdom. This made Darius suspicious, and he persuaded Aristagoras to induce the Ionians to revolt. Darius allowed Histiaeus to depart on his engaging to subdue Ionia. He was killed by Artaphernes, satrap of Ionia.

HISTRIONES, pantomimic actors among the ancient Romans, considered inferior to the regular actors of drama. Hence was derived the term *histrionic,* as applied to the modern stage.

HOLOCAUST, among the classical ancients, a religious sacrifice, in which the whole instead of a portion of the victim was burnt. The custom was similar to the burnt-offering of the ancient Jews.

HOMERUS (HOMER), the great epic poet of Greece, reputed author of the Iliad and the Odyssey. Some scholars regard him as a mythical figure, but there seems no reason to doubt that a poet named Homer existed, and tradition describes him as blind. Seven cities, Smyrna, Chios, Colophon, Salamis, Rhodus, Argos, and Athens, claimed to have been his birthplace. His period is variously placed between 1200 and 850 B.C., or later. The original home of the poems was the west coast of Asia Minor. The Iliad, of about 15,500 lines, relates the events of 51 days of the last year of the siege of Troy by the Greeks. The Odyssey, of 12,000 lines, describes the wandering of Odysseus, (Ulysses), on his way back from the Trojan War, and the vengeance he took with the suitors of his wife Penelope. Many scholars think that the Iliad and Odyssey are not by the same author and that they belong to different periods.

HONOR or HONOS, personification of honour at Rome, to whom Marcellus and Marius reared Temples.

HONORIUS, FLAVIUS, emperor of the west from 397-425

A.D. His reign was one of the most eventful in Roman annals; the weakness and timidity of the emperor co-operated with the attacks of the Goths and Vandals in promoting the rapid distintegration of the empire. His influence on current events was purely negative.

HOPLITES, Greek heavy armed infantry. It was also a term for such candidates at the public games as ran races in armour.

HORACE, *See* HORATIUS FLACCUS, Q.

HORATIA GENS, ancient Roman patrician gens, three brothers of which fought the three Curiatii, from Alba, to decide whether Rome or Alba was to be supreme. The battle was protracted, two of the Horatii falling, and all the Curiatti receiving severe wounds. The surviving Horatius pretended to flee, and overcame his wounded opponents by meeting them one at a time. Returning in triumph, as he approached the Capene gate, he was met by Horatia, his sister, when she recognized, on his shoulders, the mantle of one of the Curiatii who was her betrothed. Her extreme grief, made Horatius so angry that he stabbed her, exclaiming, 'So perish every Roman woman who bewails a foe.' He was summoned before the duumviri, and condemned to be hanged; but the public acquitted him but forced him to be led, by his father, under a gibbet.

HORATIUS COCLES, *See* COCLES.

HORATIUS FLACCUS, Q., (HORACE),   Roman poet, born Dec. 8th, 65 B.C., at Venusia, in S. Italy, and died in Rome, Nov. 27th, A.D. 8. After six years' schooling in Rome he was sent to Athens to complete his studies. During the civil war he served as an officer in the Republican army, being present at its defeat at Philippi in 42 B.C. About 38 B.C. he was introduced by Virgil to Maecenas, the generous patron of letters. The crowning work of Horace is found in his immortal odes. The maturity of his genius is also reflected in his epistles, including the *Ars Poetica,* which, like the satires, are in hexameter verse. As a literary artist he is unsurpassed, and hundreds of the phrases, in which he has crystallized his thoughts, have passed into the currency of the educated of all times.

HORTENSIUS, QUINTUS, born in 114 B.C., of an equestrian Roman family, had gained a great reputation as an orator when Cicero made his appearance in the Forum. From that time Cicero and Hortensius were considered as professional rivals, but they lived on friendly terms. At the beginning of his book *De Claris Oratoribus,* Cicero pays an eloquent tribute of praise to the memory of Hortensius, who had lately died. Hortensius was successively quaestor, aedile, praetor, and consul with Q. Caecilius Metullus Creticus, in 69 B.C. He acquired great wealth, which he spent liberally, leaving ample for his children. He died in 50 B.C. His son was put to death by M. Antony after the battle of Philippi.

HORUS, called Harpocrates by the Greeks; son of Osiris and Isis, Egyptian deity, hawk-headed, perhaps the totem of a hawk clan, whose victory originated the Horus-name borne by the dynastic kings, afterwards being deemed a sun-god.

HUNNI, Asiatics inhabiting the plains of Tartary, who harassed the Chinese empire. Part of them came to Europe in the days of Valens and were allowed to settle in Thrace in 376 A.D. Under Attila, their king, they ravaged the fairest parts of the empire. After Attila's death their empire faded away.

HYBLA, name of several cities in Sicily, named after Hyblaea the Sicilian goddess. The most important city was founded by the Megarians, about 726 B.C. It flourished for a time, and a century after its own establishment, founded in its turn the colony of Selinus. It was completely destroyed by Gelon, tyrant of Syracuse, about 481 B.C. Most of the people were sold as slaves, and the richer transported to Syracuse as citizens. Among these was Epicharmus of Cos, who had been brought up in Megara. During the Athenian expedition to Sicily, Lamarchus urged that they should occupy the deserted site. An older city of the name belonged to the Siculi, and lay on the S. slope of Mt. Aetna; it is mentioned in the history of the Second Punic War. Hyblaean honey is often praised by the Latin poets.

HYCCARA, Sicanian town on the coast of Sicily, near Panormus, the Athenians conquered it, selling the inhabitants as slaves in 415 B.C.; Timandra, wife of Alcibiades, and mother of Lais, was among the captives.

HYGINUS, GAIUS JULIUS, a freedman of Augustus Caesar, and a grammarian, who was, some say, a native of Spain, others saying Alexandria. He was placed by Augustus in charge of the library on the Palatine Hill, and also gave instruction to numerous pupils.

HYKSOS, loose confederation of W. Asian people which dominated Egypt between the 12th and 16th dynasties. Inaccurately called the shepherd kings, they established a defensive line from Avaris. Their camp at Tell-el-Yehudiya has been excavated. About 1580 B.C. Aahmes I, finally expelled them, and inaugurated the new empire.

HYLE, town of Boeotia, on lake Hylice.

HYLLUS, son of Hercules by Deianira, who with the other sons of Hercules was expelled from Peloponnesus by Eurystheus. He was slain by Echemus, King of Arcadia, on attempting to re-enter Peloponnesus.

HYMEN or HYMENAEUS, was originally the song sung at marriages among the Greeks. As usual the name gradually produced the idea of an actual person whose adventures gave rise to the custom of the song. He occurs often in association with Linus and Ialemus, who represent similar personifications, and is generally called a son of Apollo and a Muse. In Attic legend he was a beautiful youth.

HYMETTUS, mountain of Attica, near Athens, famous for honey and marble.

HYPATIA, daughter of Theon, the mathematician, born at Alexandria, about 370 A.D. She was instructed by her father, and succeeded him in the chair of Philosophy at Alexandria. Being beautiful she attracted a numerous auditory. Magistrates frequently consulted her on important cases. S. Cyril, the bishop often came into conflict with the authority of Orestes, the prefect, whose hostility to the bishop and clergy was, by them, falsely attributed to the influence of Hypatia. In A.D. 415 the monks seized her in the street, dragged her in front of the chief church of the city, stripped her and stoned her to death, and after scraped her flesh from the bone with oyster shells, and carried her limbs to Cinaron, to be burnt. Cyril has not been held guiltless of her blood, but to what extent he was implicated is uncertain.

HYPERBOREI MONTES, at first the name of a range of imaginary mountains in the north, and later applied to the Caucasus.

HYPERIDES, one of ten Attic orators, son of Glaucippus. He was probably younger than Lycurgus (born about 385 B.C.). Having studied under Isocrates, he began as a writer of speeches for the courts, and in 360 B.C., prosecuted Autocles, a general charged with treason in Thrace. Hyperides supported Demosthenes in the struggle against Macedon; but in the affair of Harpalus, he was one of the ten public prosecutors of Demosthenes. He was chief promoter of the Lamian War against Antipater and Craterus. After the defeat of Crannon, in 322 B.C. Hyperides and the other orators were condemned to death by the subdued Athenians, but fled to sanctuary, whence he was dragged and put to death.

HYPERMNESTRA, daughter of Danaus, and wife of Lynceus, q.v.

HYPSIPYLE, daughter of Throas, King of Lemnos, who saved her father, when the women killed all the men on the island. She bore twin sons to Jason, when the Argonauts landed there. When the women discovered Throas alive, they compelled Hypsipyle to leave the island. She was taken by pirates who sold her to the Nemean King, Lycurgus, who entrusted her to the care of his son Opheltes.

HYRCANUS, Greek surname of unknown origin, borne by several Jews of the Maccabaean period. (a) JOANNES, prince and high priest of the Jews, son of Simon Maccabaeus, restorer of Judaean independence. (b) High priest, and King of the Jews: put to death by Augustus. He was succeeded by Herod.

HYRCANIA, ancient Persian province, on the southern shores of the Caspian.

HYRTACUS, Trojan to whom Priam gave his first wife, Arisba, when he married Hecuba.

I

IACCHUS, in *Greek Mythology*, a mystic deity who played an important part in the Eleusinia. Later he was confused with the younger Dionysus, son of Zeus and Demeter.

IAMBLICHUS, Neo-platonist of the 4th cent. A.D., was born at Chalcis, in Coele-Syria. His reputation among contemporaries eclipsed the fame of his teacher Porphyry, whom he was really far from equalling in powers of mind. His literary career extends from Constantine the Great to Julian the Apostate, whose favour he obtained for his *Life of Pythagoras,* in which he ascribed to the Greek philosopher signs and wonders upon which the Christians not only founded the divine authority of their creed, but to which they still laid claim. Iamblichus made the perfection of man's moral nature to consist in a state of contemplative innocence, and asserted the existence of several classes of spiritual essences, and tried to determine the ways of their manifestation.

IAMBUS, a foot of two syllables, a short followed by a long, or an unstressed by a stressed.

IAMUS, son of Apollo and Evadne: he was a prophet, and supposed to be ancestor of the Iamidae at Olympia.

IAPETUS, in *Greek Mythology*, one of the Titans. When Zeus defeated this race of giants, Iapetus was imprisoned in Tartarus. —Iapetus is also the name of the eighth moon of Saturn, counting outwards from the planet.

IAPYDIA, district of N. Illyricum conquered by Augustus, situated between the Arsia and Tedanius, and peopled by the Iapydes, a mixed race, of warlike disposition.

IAPYGIA, a Greek appellation for S. of Apulia.

IAPYX, a wind blowing off the coast of Apulia (Iapygia), favourable to those crossing to Greece.

188

IARDANES, father of Omphale, who is therefore called Iardanis.

IAZYGES, a Sarmatian people who once lived on the coast of Pontus Euxinus, and Palus Maeotis, and in the time of Claudius settled near the Quadi, in Dacia. They were a powerful race.

IBERIA, name given by the Greeks to the S. W. peninsula of Europe, called Hispania by the Romans, and is still referred to as the Iberian peninsula. The name Iberia was also borne by the region between the Caucasus and Armenia, corresponding to modern Georgia. Iberian Mountains is the name sometimes given to the mountains of central and east Spain, particularly the ranges which include the Sierra de Guadamarra and those south of the Ebro.

IBERUS, principal river of N. E. Spain, now the Ebro.

IBYCUS, Greek lyric poet, who flourished about 540 B.C., was a native of Rhegium in Italy, but spent most of his life at the court of Polycrates, tyrant of Samos. It is said that, while travelling near Corinth, the poet was waylaid and mortally wounded by robbers. As he lay dying he saw a flock of cranes overhead, and called upon them to avenge his death. The murderers went to Corinth, and while sitting in the theatre, saw the cranes above. One ejaculated, 'Behold the avengers of Ibycus,' thus giving the clue to the detection of the crime. The phrase 'The cranes of Ibycus' passed into a proverb among the Greeks. Of the seven books of lyrics by Ibycus, only a few fragments remain.

ICARIUS, a man of Athens who received Dionysus kindly, and was taught by him how to cultivate the vine. The peasants, intoxicated by his wine, slew Icarius as they thought they had been poisoned by him. Erigone, his daughter, was conducted to his grave by his faithful dog, Maera, and from grief hanged herself over his grave.—Another Icarius was a Lacedaemonian, the son of Oebalus of Sparta.

ICARUS, in *Greek Mythology,* son of Daedalus. While accompanying his father on his flight from Crete, he was drowned near Samos, in the sea called after him, Icarian.—There was an island of this name in the Aegean, also connected with the myth.

ICENI, a powerful race in Britain living to the N. of the Trinobantes, in a district corresponding to Suffolk and Norfolk. Their capital was Venta Icenorum, sited near where Yarmouth now stands.

ICHTHYOPHAGI, primitive coastal peoples, reputed by ancient geographers to live on sea-food. Nearchus, Alexander the Great's admiral, described those of the Gedrosian coast—the Baluchistan Makran—as giving fish to animals also, and as living in whalebone and conch-shell huts.

ICHTHYOSAURUS, genus of extinct fishlike reptiles found in the Rhaetic, Jurassic, and Cretaceous strata in Europe, Africa, and other countries. The reptile was from 4-40 ft. long, having a round and tapering body, and a large head with long jaws, armed with sharp conical teeth. The neck was short, the limbs like flappers, and the tail a vertical fin.

ICILIUS, patronym of a plebeian family. L. Icilius, was tribune of the plebs in 456 and 455 B.C., and a leader of the outbreak against the decemvirs in 449 B.C.

ICKNIELD WAY, early English name for a prehistoric track from near Wantage to Dunstable.

ICONIUM, chief city of Lycaonia, a flourishing city, visited by S. Paul.

ICTINUS, Greek architect, contemporary with Phidias and Pericles, during the 5th cent B.C., who designed the Parthenon at Athens, and temple of Apollo at Bussae, also the second Telesterion at Eleusis.

IDA, mountain range of Asia Minor. This name was given in classical times to a range stretching from Phrygia through Mysia into the Troad. It was also, the name of a mountain in Crete, connected with the worship of Zeus.

IDALIUM, town in Cyprus, sacred to Venus Idalia.

IDES, in the Roman calendar, the name of the 13th day of the month, except in March, May, July, and October, when the Ides fell on the 15th.

IDOMENEUS, in *Greek Legend,* King of Crete, grandson of

Minos, was caught in a storm while returning from the Trojan war, and vowed to sacrifice to Poseidon the first thing that met him if he arrived home safely. This proved to be his son, whom he was compelled to sacrifice. As a result a plague descended on the country, and Idomeneus was exiled.

IDUMAEA, (Edom of the Old Testament), the district of Mt. Seir. The decline of Judaea enabled the Edomites to extend over Judaea as far as Hebron. What had been their first home was occupied by the Nabathaean Arabs. The Idumaea of Roman history is the S. of Judaea and part of N. Arabia Petraea.

IDYIA, mother of Medea, and wife of Aeëtes, King of Colchis.

IGNATIUS, patriarch of Antioch, and Apostolic Father. Eusebius, the ecclesiastical historian, says he was second bishop of Antioch after S. Peter. He was seized during the Trajan persecution in A.D. 116, taken to Rome, and thrown to the lions. He wrote the Ignatian Epistles, addressed to various churches, while on the journey.

IGUANODON, prehistoric, extinct land reptile, belonging to the Dinosaurs. Its fossil is found in the Jurassic and lower Cretaceous rocks of Europe. It was 15 to 25 ft. long, with small head, heavy jaws, and strong flexible lips. It supported itself on its two hindlegs and tail, its forelimbs being small; it was an herbivorous feeder.

IGUVIUM, Umbrian town on the southern slope of the Apennines. Nearby was a temple of Jupiter, in the ruins of which nine brass tables were discovered, lettered with Umbrian inscriptions. Referred to as the Eugubian Tables, they were inscribed between 400 and 90 B.C.

ILERDA, town in Hispania Tarraconensis, N. of the Sicoris, inhabited by the Ilergetes. Pompey's legates Africanus and Petreius, were defeated here by Caesar in 49 B.C.

ILIAD, *See* HOMERUS.

ILISSUS, stream in Attica, rising in Mt. Hymettus, and flowing to the E. of Athens.

ILLIBERIS, river in Gallia Narbonensis, falling into the Mare Gallicum, and called by the Romans, Techum. Also, the name of a town, at the foot of the Pyrenees, whose name Constantine changed to Helena.

ILLYRICUM, (ILLYRIA), term used in ancient times for the country on the Adriatic coast N. of Epirus, extending as far as the river Dravus, and bounded E. by Macedonia and Upper Moesia. It included, more or less, the more modern, Montenegro, Bosnia, Herzegovina, Dalmatia, and S. W. Hungary. It was annexed by the Romans in 168 B.C., being made a province in A.D. 9.

ILUS, son of Tros and Callirrhoe, and great-grandson of Dardanus. He was father of Laomedon, and grandfather of Priam, and believed to be founder of Ilium, which was named Troy after his father.

IMAGINES, portrait masks of ancestors, executed in wax.

IMAUS, in *Ancient Geography* a mountain range in Asia, the situation of which is not very definite, but probably used to denote the W. Himalayas.

IMPERATOR, strictly, commander-in-chief. From the 2nd cent. B.C. this distinction was given to a general by his army, following a victory. Under Augustus all honours of war belonged to the emperor, and from the days of Vespasian, Imperator became title of the emperor.

INACHIS, a name of Io, daughter of Inachus: the goddess Isis is also known by this name.

INACHUS, son of Oceanus and Tethys, was first King of Argos.

INAROS, leader of an Egyptian revolt in 461 B.C., which was first successful, but was subdued by the Persians in 455 B.C. Inaros was son of Psammetichus, a Libyan.

INDIA, the external history of India starts with the Greek invasion in 327 B.C., but direct trade between India and the Levant existed from very ancient times. The first Greek historian to speak clearly of India was Hecataeus of Miletus (549-486 B.C.); the knowledge of Herodotus (450 B.C.) ended at the Indus; Ctesias, the physician (401 B.C.) brought from Persia a few facts about Indian dyes, fabrics, monkeys, and parrots. India E. of the Indus was first known in Europe through those who accompanied Alexander in 327 B.C., their narratives being quoted by

Strabo, Pliny, and Arrian. Soon after Megasthenes, as Greek ambassador at a court in central Bengal (306-298 B.C.), had opportunity of close observation. The real knowledge of the Greeks and Romans concerning India practically dates from his researches, about 300 B.C.

INDUS, river of Asia, rising in the Tibetan Himalayas and flowing N.W. through Ladakh, bending S. 20 miles S.E. of Gilgit, and proceeding in a S. W. direction to its delta in the Erythraeum Mare (Indian Ocean). Its length is about 1,800 miles.—Another river of this name rises in Phrygia, flowing through Caria, into the Mediterranean.

INDUTIOMARUS, chief of the Treviri in Gaul, who was defeated and slain by Labienus in 54 B.C.

INFAMIA, Roman law term indicating the effects of condemnation for certain offences. The consequences of infamia included loss of right to vote, or to put up for office, and of personal status. Disabilities in marriage and making of wills were included, also disqualification from acting for another at law.

INSUBRES, a Gallic race, dwelling in N. Italy, subdued by the Romans just prior to the second Punic War. Their chief town was Mediolanum, q.v.

INTERAMNA, town in Umbria, on the Nar, birthplace of Tacitus.—Also the name of a town in Latium at the junction of the Casinus with the Liris.

INTERNUM MARE, (MEDITERRANEAN), sea that washes the shores of Europe, Asia, and Africa, extending from the Straits of Hercules (GIBRALTAR), to the coasts of Syria and Asia Minor. From its washing the coasts of Greece and Italy, the Greeks and Romans called it "Our Sea." The Nile is the only great river which feeds the sea directly. The Mediterranean is almost tideless.

IO, daughter of Inachus, King of Argos, whose beauty excited the admiration of Zeus, and the jealousy of Hera. The queen of heaven, therefore, transformed her into a heifer, intrusting her to the care of Argos Panoptes, who was slain by Hermes. Hera then sent a gadfly who stung the heifer into madness, and drove her wandering over the earth. The legend is related to a much earlier Egyptian myth.

IOBATES, King of Lycia.

IOLAUS, in *Greek Mythology,* the faithful companion and charioteer of Hercules. He assisted at the slaying of the Lernaean hydra and helped his children in their fight for the Peloponnese, killing Eurystheus in battle.

IOLCUS, ancient town in Magnesia, famous as the residence of Pelias and Jason, and as the place from whence the Argonauts set sail.

IOLE, daughter of Eurytus, who was loved by Heracles, after whose death she married his son Hyllus.

ION, legendary founder of the Ionian race, was son of Apollo by Creusa, wife of Xuthus. On reaching manhood he narrowly escaped being poisoned accidentally by his mother.

IONIA, ancient district of Greece, so-called from having been colonized by Greeks of the Ionian branch of the Hellenic race. The Ionians spoke a dialect different from Aeolic and Doric, and the name Ionian was applied to the people of Attica and Euboea, to the Ionian colonies in Asia Minor, and to offshoots from these.

IONIAN SCHOOL, includes several of the earliest philosophers of Greece, whose speculations were chiefly of a physical character, and who, with a few exceptions, were natives of the Ionian colonies in Asia Minor.

IONIC ORDER, second of the three orders of Greek architecture. It is more slender and graceful than the Doric order; the fluting of the column is finer, and its square capital can easily be distinguished from both Doric and Corinthian, by its volutes, or spirals. The mouldings, also, are more delicate.

IOPHON, son of Sophocles, who became a tragic poet. (*See* Sophocles).

IPHICRATES, Athenian general, who introduced an innovation upon ancient Greek tactics in the war that ended in 387 B.C. Laying aside the weighty panoply of the regular infantry he substituted a light target and quilted jacket, and doubled the length of the sword. The men carried missile javelins and ventured within throw of the enemy, the weight of whose charge they could not have resisted, trusting their agility. When the enemy column was broken its individual soldiers were overmatched by the longer weapons. Many successes were so gained.

IPHIGENIA, in *Greek Legend,* daughter of Agamemnon, and Clytaemnestra. The Greek fleet, destined for Troy being becalmed at Aulis, because Artemis had been offended because Agamemnon had killed a stag sacred to her, Calchas, the soothsayer, declared that Agamemnon must sacrifice his daughter to appease the goddess. Iphigenia was fetched under the pretext that she was to be married to Achilles; at the moment of sacrifice Artemis bore her to the Tauri, where she became a priestess.

IPHIMEDE, wife of Aloeus.

IPSUS, where the battle took place in 301 B.C., which ended the wars between Antigonus and his rivals.

IRA, mountain stronghold of Messenia, where Aristomenes defended himself against the Spartans for eleven years, until its capture in 668 B.C. ended the second Messenian War.

IRENAEUS, lived from about A.D. 120-202, was bishop of Lyons. Supposed to have been born at Smyrna he went to France, and became a priest, succeeding Pothinus to the bishopric in A.D. 177. He assisted in the dispute between the Bishop of Rome and the Asiatic Churches about the date of Easter. He is said to have been martyred under Severus: he was later canonized.

IRENE, in *Greek Mythology,* goddess of peace, daughter of Zeus and Themis. The Romans worshipped her under the name of Pax.

IRIS, in *Greek Mythology,* daughter of Thaumas and Electra, and messenger of the gods, particularly of Hera; she was also the personification of the rainbow.

IRIS, stream in Asia Minor, flowing through Pontus into the Sinus Amisenus in the Euxine.

ISAAC, one of the Hebrew patriarchs, inheritor of the promises made by God to his father Abraham. A prosperous farmer and shepherd in S. Palestine, he is said to have been forty years old when he married Rebekah, his sons Jacob and Esau being born twenty years later. He owned many cattle, and is the first patriarch mentioned as sowing seed: he was a famous well-digger. He is said to have died at the age of 180, and was buried with his father in the cave of Machpelah.

ISAEUS, one of the ten Attic orators, who founded a school of rhetoric at Athens: Demosthenes may have been his pupil. He lived 420-348 B.C. A number of his orations have come down to us.

ISAGORAS, was opposed to Clisthenes, as leader of the oligarchical party at Athens.

ISAIAH, Hebrew prophet, author of a Biblical Book, son of Amoz, he lived in the 8th cent. B.C. He seems to have spent his life at Jerusalem, receiving his call about 740 B.C. Seemingly a man of rank and influence, his activity was at its height in the great crisis that agitated the nations from the Syro-Ephraimitish war in 735-734 B.C., to the invasion of Sennacherib in 701 B.C. Isaiah's great task was to warn the people that, in consequence of their neglect of Jehovah, severe punishment at the hand of Assyria was about to overtake them. He warned them that salvation lay in a return to Jehovah, and in renewed confidence in him.

ISARA, river in Gallia Narbonensis, rising in the Graian Alps, and flowing into the Rhone.

ISAURIA, district of Asia Minor, N. of the Taurus, whose people, the Isauri, were notorious robbers. The Roman consul L. Servilius defeated them in 75 B.C.

ISCA SILURUM, a military post of the Second Legion from about A.D. 75 till late 3rd cent.

ISIA, festivals held among the Romans in honour of the Egyptian goddess Isis, q.v.; the priests were called Isiaci.

ISIS, one of the chief Egyptian deities, wife of Osiris, was represented as the goddess of fecundity, the cow being sacred to her. Her annual festival lasted seven days, during which a general purification took place. The priests of Isis were celibate, their heads shaved, and they went barefooted. She was often represented as a woman with the horns of a cow. She also appears with the lotus on her head, and in some instances is covered with a hood. By the Greeks she was identified with Ceres.

ISMARUS, town in Thrace, near Maronea, noted anciently for wine.

ISOCRATES, one of the ten Attic orators, was born at Athens in 436 B.C. He had been a pupil of Socrates, but gave up philosophy and started as a writer of speeches for clients to deliver in law cases, later composing speeches dealing with public affairs, and intended for reading, not speaking. He might be said to be the first political pamphleteer. Of 20 speeches extant the finest is the *Panegyricus*, in which he extols Athens as natural leader of Greece. Isocrates died at Athens in 338 B.C., aged 98.

ISSA, island of the Adriatic off the coast of Dalmatia, with a town of the same name.

ISSUS, town in the S. E. end of Cilicia, where Alexander defeated Darius Codomannus in 333 B.C.

ISTHMIAN GAMES, were one of the four great national festivals of Greece, the others being Olympian, Pythian, and Nemean. They were celebrated under the presidency of the Corinthians, near Corinth, on the isthmus which connects Peloponnesus with the continent, and were celebrated at intervals of three or four years. The victor's crowns were of pine leaves.

ISTRIA, the peninsula at the N. of the Adriatic, separated from Venetia by the Timavus, and from Illyricum by the Arsia. Its people were called Istri, and were a warlike race, subdued by C. Claudius Pulcher, the consul, in 177 B.C. The chief towns were Tergeste and Pola.

ISRAEL, (Heb. for Perseverer with God), name given by God to Jacob, which became a synonym for Jew or Hebrew.

ITALIA (ITALY), from the time of Augustus, all the country S. of the Alps; originally the name was used of a much more restricted area. It probably took its name from the ancient King Italus, and was the land of the Itali or Vitali, an ancient race, better known as Siculi. According to the Greeks Italia was originally only the most southerly part of what was later called Bruttii. They later gave the name to the whole country S. of Posidonia on the W., and Tarentum on the E. After the Romans had conquered Tarentum and the south, about 272 B.C., Italia was the name used of all the country subject to Rome, from the Straits of Sicily to the Arnus and Rubico. N. of the rivers the country was still called Gallia Cisalpina and Liguria, until the end of the republic. Augustus first extended the name Italia to include, the territory from the Maratime Alps to Pola, in Istria. The country was called by various other names, particularly by the poets. Italy gave residence to a large number of different races who had entered the country at very early periods, even the remains of palaeolithic man have been found there. When Roman history began the following races inhabited Italy. The Etruscans lived from the mouth of the Tiber, between its right bank and the sea, and extended N. to the Alps; the Umbrians lived between the left bank of the Tiber and the Adriatic. The Sacrani, Casci, or Prisci, lived on the S. of the Etruscans; the Opici lived still farther S., and were also known as Ausones or Aurunci; the Oenotrians lived in the S. of the peninsula, but were later driven to the interior by the numerous Greek colonies founded on the coasts. The various Sabellian tribes, the Sabines proper, the Peligni, Marsi, Marrucini, Vestini, and Hernici lived S. of the Umbrians, extending to Mt. Garganus; the Daunians or Apulians, Peucettii, Messapii, and Sallentini lived between Mt. Garganus and the S.E. end of the peninsula. All were eventually subdued by the Romans. In the days of Augustus the following were the main divisions of Italy. I. UPPER ITALY, from the Alps to the Macra on the W. and the Rubico on the E. Upper Italy included Liguria, Gallia Cisalpina, Venetia, Carnia, and Istria. II. CENTRAL ITALY, from the Macra on the W. and the Rubico on the E. to the Silarus on the W. and the Frento on the E. Central Italy included Picenum, Etruria, Umbria, Samnium, Latium, and Campania. III. LOWER ITALY, the remainder of the peninsula S. of the Silarus and the Frento. Lower Italy included Apulia,

Lucania and Bruttium. Later Augustus divided Italy into 11 Regiones, Latium and Campania; the land of the Hirpini, Apulia, and Calabria; Lucania and Bruttium; the land of the Frentani, Marrucini, Peligni, Marsi, Vestini, and Sabina, together with Samnium; Picenum; Umbria, and a district of Ariminum; Etruria; Gallia Cisalpina; Liguria; the E. of Gallia Transpadana, Venetia, Carnia, and Istria; the W. of Gallia Transpadana. *See* under various headings.

ITALICA, town of Hispania Baetica, on the Baetis, N. W. of Hispalis, established by Scipio Africanus during the second Punic War; birthplace of Hadrian and Trajan.

ITHACA, small island of Epirus in the Ionian Sea, birthplace of Ulysses. It consists of two parts joined by a narrow isthmus. There is a mountain ridge in each part. The northern one is Neritum, and the southern, Neium. The city was built on a conical hill, occupying the breadth of the isthmus.

ITHOME, stronghold in Messenia, on a mountain of the same name.

ITIUS PORTUS, a port of the Morini, on the N. coast of Gaul, whence Caesar sailed for Britain.

ITURAEA, N. E. district of Palestine, which Augustus gave to the family of Herod.

ITYS, *See* TEREUS.

IXION, in *Greek Mythology,* King of Lapithae in Thessaly. Having murdered his father-in-law, he was taken to heaven by Zeus for purification. For attempting the virtue of Hera, wife of Zeus, he was condemned to be bound to a continuously rolling wheel in the under world.

IXIONIDES, a name for Pirithous, son of Ixion. The centaurs were called Ixionidae.

J

JABBOK, river in Gilead, a tributary of the Jordan, separating the territory of the Amorites from that of Bashan. It was on the banks of this stream that Jacob wrestled with the angel.

JABESH-GILEAD, a chief city in Gilead, where the inhabitants were slain for refusing to aid Israel against the Benjaminites. Saul and his sons were buried near here.

JACOB, younger son of Isaac and Rebekah, who obtained his elder brother's birthright, and his father's blessing by deception, thereby becoming heir, and one of the three great patriarchs of Israel. For fourteen years he served his uncle Laban, obtaining Leah and Rachel as his wives. His youngest and dearest son, Joseph was sold to Egypt, causing bitter grief, only relieved when famine caused him to send his other sons to Egypt to buy corn, when the high position of Joseph was discovered. He later went with his family to Egypt, was honourably received by Pharaoh, and henceforth prospered.

JAEL, wife of Heber the Kenite. When Jabin's army was defeated by Israel, under Barak and Deborah, Jabin's general, Sisera, fled to the tent of Jael for refuge. Choosing between the laws of hospitality and betrayal of Israel, Jael killed Sisera.

JANICULUM, hill of Rome on the W. bank of the Tiber, with an altitude of 275 ft., was connected with the E. bank by a wooden bridge, the Pons Sublicius. Many villas were built on the river front, mostly housing Jews and foreigners. It was named from Janus, mythical King of Latium, who was supposed to have built a citadel on the ridge.

JANUARIUS, saint and martyr, said to have been a native of Naples, and bishop of Beneventum, in the days of Diocletian. Having visited Christians imprisoned for their faith at Pozzuoli, he was taken and thrown to the lions who refused to molest him: he was afterwards beheaded.

JANUS, in *Mythological History,* earliest of the Italian kings, reigned in Latium, being contemporary with Saturn. He was, by some accounts, son of the sun, and his attributes connect him with sun worship. He was porter of heaven, and opened the year, the first month of which was named after him; he also presided over the seasons, whence he is sometimes represented with four heads, as Janus Quadrifrons, his temples in that capacity being built with four equal sides, but only one entrance. He was keeper of earth, sea, and sky; guardian deity of gates, on which account he is represented with two heads, because every door looks two ways. He is usually represented with a key in his left hand, and a staff in his right. In time of war the gates of the principal temple at Rome, that of Janus Quirinus, were always open; in peace they were closed, to retain the wars within. They were shut once only between the reigns of Numa and Augustus.

JAPHETH, one of the sons of Noah, whose son Javan, was reputed ancestor of the Ionians. The name Japhetic, now replaced by Aryan or Indo-European, was formerly used to designate the Caucasian people of Europe and parts of Asia, as contrasted with the Hamitic and Semitic.

JASON, in *Greek Mythology,* the leader of the Argonauts, was son of Aeson, King of Iolcus in Thessaly, who had been usurped by his brother Pelias, who had persuaded him to organize an expedition to fetch the famous Golden Fleece from Colchis on the Black Sea. Jason on his return found that Pelias had murdered his father, to avenge which Medea, Jason's wife, persuaded the daughters of Pelias to cut their father in pieces and boil him in a cauldron. Expelled for this deed Jason and Medea went to Corinth where Jason deserted his wife for Creusa. Medea avenged herself by sending Creusa a poisoned robe which burned her to death, and by killing her children by Jason.

JAVELIN, short, light spear, for throwing, used for military purposes in classical times. Its estimated range was from 30-40 yards.

JAXARTES, river of central Asia, flowing into the Sea of Aral. In ancient days it was supposed to fall into the N. side of the Caspian Sea. It was the boundary between Sogdiana and Scythia.

JEHOIACHIN, King of Judah, succeeded his father Jehoiakim, who reigned only for three months, in 597 B.C., and was carried captive to Babylon by Nebuchadnezzar, being released after 37 years.

JEHOIADA, high priest at Jerusalem in the reigns of Ahaziah, Athaliah, and Joash. He put down the worship of Baal, and raised funds to restore the temple, and was buried among the kings.

JEHOIAKIM, King of Judah, son of King Josiah, was made king by Pharaoh Necho, the country at that time being under Egyptian domination. He reigned from 608 to 597 B.C. During three of these years he was vassal of Nebuchadnezzar.

JEHOSHAPHAT, King of Judah, 876-851 B.C., who succeeded his father Asa. He did much to exterminate idolatry, and built a number of strongholds. As an ally of Ahab, King of Israel, he took part in the battle of Ramoth Gilead, and was later at war with Moab and Ammon. With Ahaziah he sent a maritime expedition to Tarshish to get gold from Ophir, but the fleet was destroyed at Ezion-Geber.

JEHOVAH, proper name of the God of Israel, by which he revealed Himself to Moses at Horeb. Jehovah is an artificial pronunciation of the Hebrew consonants JĤVH, or YHWH, arrived at by giving the consonants the vowels of another divine name, Adonai, which means My Lord: According to tradition the name was pronounced Ya—be. This seems to indicate Jahveh or Jahweh, Yahweh or Yahveh, a pronunciation adopted by modern teachers. This treatment gives a suitable meaning either 'he who causes to be'; or 'he who is.'

JEHU, son of Jehoshaphat, and King of Israel from 843-815 B.C. He was a general under Jehoram, during whose illness he was acclaimed king by the armed forces. He formed an alliance with Shalmaneser II of Assyria to protect himself against the Syrians. Reference in the Bible to his furious driving has made his name a synonym for a driver of horses.

JEPTHA, judge of Israel, illegitimate son of Gilead, who was asked by the elders to command an army against the Ammonites, defeating the enemy at Rabbath-Ammon. He had solemnly vowed, if successful, to sacrifice the first thing he met on his return, which proved to be his own daughter. (c.f. Idomeneus)

JEREMIAH, prophet of Judah, writer of the book in the Hebrew canon which bears his name. He was of priestly family, son of Hilkiah the priest, who lived at Anathoth, a city of Judah, 3 m. N. of Jerusalem. He received his call in the 13th year of King Josiah, and continued in office till the 11th year of King Zedekiah. His book is a collection of prophecies and exhortations, mingled with historical events consisting of 1. Prophecies written by Jeremiah; 2. biographical chapters, written by another person, probably after the prophet's death, 3. a few chapters and verses by a third person. Jeremiah did his best to dissuade his countrymen from following the counsels of false prophets, and gave inspired advice.

JERICHO, was first city W. of Jordan occupied by the Israelites. It was destroyed and was not rebuilt as a fortified place till the reign of Ahab, when it became seat of a prophetical society, and appears in the history of Elisha. Elisha's narrative of the healing of the waters is mentioned by Josephus in connection with the copious fountain which lies on the W. margin of the Jordan valley. Jericho shared the calamities of the Babylonian exile, was reoccupied on the restoration, and fortified by Bacchides in the Maccabeans' wars. In the time of Strabo there were two forts, Threx and Taurus, protecting the pass above Jericho. Antony gave the groves of Jericho as a rich gift to Cleopatra, from whom they passed to Herod the Great who made the city his winter residence. It was here that the tyrant died.

JEROBOAM, name of two Kings of Israel. One, the son of Nebat, became king after Solomon. It was he who set up the worship of the golden calf at Dan and Bethel. Jeroboam II was King of Israel from 761-740 b.c.; he was famous as a warrior, under whose leadership Israel defeated the Syrians.

JEROME, SAINT, accounted the most learned of the Latin

fathers of the Church, was born about 340 A.D. and died in 420. He was a native of Pannonia, and came early to Rome where he studied under the grammarian Donatus. He visited Gaul, Thrace, Pontus, Bithynia, Galatia, and Cappadocia, also Jerusalem. He returned to Rome in 382, having visited Constantinople on the way. At Rome he became secretary to Pope Damasus. Eventually he returned to the neighbourhood of Jerusalem, taking up his abode in a monastery at Bethlehem, where he is believed to have died. Many of his writings are extant, amongst the most valuable being *Lives and Writings of the Elder Christian Fathers,* and *Commentaries on the Prophetical Books of the Old Testament,* etc. His greatest work is a translation of the Bible into Latin, known as the *Vulgate.*

JERUSALEM or **HIEROSOLYMA,** chief city of Palestine, 33 m. from the Mediterranean, and 15 from the Dead Sea, occupying a plateau with two southward-pointing spurs, and bounded by the Hinnom and Kidron valleys. Pottery found on the E. hill proves a pre-Semitic settlement before 2500 B.C. Later the E. hill became a fortified town, and is mentioned in the Amarna correspondence, about 1,400 B.C. Jerusalem remained a Canaanite city until about 1,000 B.C., when its Jebusite population was subdued by David. After the division of the kingdom of Israel under Rehoboam, Jerusalem was capital of Judah, until destroyed by Nebuchadnezzar in 588 B.C. On the return of the exiles in 538 B.C., Cyrus permitted them to rebuild the city and Temple, a task which occupied about 24 years. After the death of Alexander, Jerusalem was first subject to the Greek kings of Egypt, and, after, to those of Syria. In consequence of attempts by Antiochus IV Epiphanes, to eradicate the national religion, the Jews rebelled under the Maccabees and after a struggle established their independence. Jerusalem then became capital of a separate kingdom under the Maccabees. The Jews rebelling against the Romans, in A.D. 70, caused Titus to destroy the city which was rebuilt by Hadrian in 135 A.D.: he renamed it AELIA CAPITOLINA, and built a temple of Jupiter on the old Temple site. The advent of Christianity restored to the city its sacred character.

JESUS CHRIST, all that we know of His life is contained in the four Gospels. Mary, His mother, described His birth thus. An angel came and said "The Holy Ghost shall come upon thee, and the power of the Most High shall overshadow Thee, wherefore also that which is to be born shall be called holy, the Son of God." When at the age of twelve He achieved the status of manhood, He explained to His mother, and to Joseph, that He was bound to be "about His Father's business." For 18 years, however, He lived in obscurity at Nazareth, working as a carpenter. The emergence of His cousin John as a prophet called Him from retirement. Gathering a few disciples, He began a ministry of teaching and healing at Capernaum. His teaching was summed up in the Sermon on the Mount. The power and independence of His message brought Him in collision with the religious authorities. Jesus made it a practice to go up to Jerusalem for festivals; and going up for the Passover in the third year of His ministry He was conscious that He went to die. By the treachery of a disciple He was arrested: an illegal trial was hurried through in the night, and on the morning of the Paschal Feast the authorities of Judaism demanded of Pilate that He should be crucified. The Roman procurator was unwilling, but public pressure compelled him to assent. Jesus was crucified but the third day He rose alive from the tomb.

JEWS, in its widest acceptation, a term used as synonymous with Hebrews or Israelites, but in a restricted sense, in the time of Jesus, applied to the people of Judaea. Their ancestor Abraham, called "the Hebrew," by birth a Chaldaean, emigrated with his wife Sarah, and nephew Lot, his servants and flocks, to Canaan, where he settled about 1921 B.C. His son Jacob, surnamed Israel, had 12 sons, and from these descended the 12 tribes. One tribe, Levi, was set apart for religious service. The history of the Jews, before the days of Christ, is set forth in the Old Testament, and in Josephus.

JEZEBEL, daughter of Ethbaal, King of the Sidonians, married Ahab before his accession, being the first Canaanitish woman to share the throne of Israel. Ahab was but a puppet in her hands; she established Phoenician worship, had Naboth stoned, and persecuted the prophets. Thrown from her window at the command of Jehu, she was trampled under his chariot horses. Her name has even been a title of reproach.

JEZREEL, Canaanitish city, about 11 m. from Nazareth, where Ahab had his capital.

JOAB, David's nephew who was made a general in the army of Judah, and the king's intimate adviser. After the death of David he supported the claim of Adonijah to the throne, and was executed by order of Solomon.

JOB, hero of the Biblical Book of that name, which is mainly a poem, with a prologue and epilogue in prose, which give an account of Job's fortunes and misfortunes. He is a blameless, upright character, fortunate and prosperous, which things have been noted by Satan, who attended a session held by Jehovah in heaven. When Job's piety is praised, Satan suggests that his motive is ulterior and that if God turned from him he would curse Him to His face. Misfortunes and afflictions were sent to try Job's faith. He lost stock, servants, children, and was himself smitten with disease, but Job refused to curse God. Three friends bemoan and comfort him, whose words only serve to add to his trials. Job remains faithful to the end, so that "The patience of Job" is proverbial.

JOCASTA, in *Greek Legend,* wife of Laius, King of Thebes, mother of Oedipus. She unwittingly became wife of her own son, and overwhelmed with horror, hanged herself.

JOEL, minor Hebrew prophet, whose book in the O. T., was written about 500 B.C. or later and is inserted between Hosea and Amos. He was son of Pethuel, and resided at Jerusalem. He deals with divine judgment, and calls for repentance.

JOHN, Saint and Apostle, son of Zebedee and Salome, a sister of Mary, the mother of Jesus; was a master fisherman on the Sea of Galilee, and came under the influence of John Baptist, and was with James his brother, among the earliest followers of Jesus. John was prominent at the Last Supper and was present at the trial of Jesus. It was to him that Jesus committed the care of His mother as He hung on the Cross.

JOHN BAPTIST, Christian saint and last of the prophets under the old dispensation, was son of Zacharias and Elisabeth,
being born in Judaea. He was a Nazarite from birth, and lived
apart in the wilderness. Soon he began to preach that the Kingdom of God was at hand, proclaiming the advent of the Christ,
calling the people to repentance, and introducing baptism as a
symbol of repentance. Herod was moved by his preaching, but
when the Baptist reproved him for unlawful marriage he was
imprisoned and later beheaded.

JONAH, author of a Book of the Old Testament belonging to
the group known as the twelve minor prophets. The book is in
narrative form, representing the prophet Jonah as having preached
in Nineveh.

JOPPA or JOPPE, ancient coastal city of Palestine, S. on the
boundary between Judaea and Samaria.

JORDANES, (sometimes, less correctly, JORNANDES), historian of the Goths. He belonged to the Alani, a tribe akin to the
Goths. He wrote, in Latin, two works, one a compendium of history from the Creation to his own times, and the other a history
of the Goths based on a lost work by Cassiodorus. He presents
the Goths as the most enlightened of the barbarians. He lived
during the reign of Justinian.

JORDANES, (JORDAN), river of Palestine, rising in the Mt.
Hermon range, flowing S. into the Sea of Galilee, and thence to
the Dead Sea.

JOSEPH, son of Jacob, the eldest by his wife Rachel, and
brother of Benjamin, and favourite son until Benjamin's birth.
His jealous brethren sold him to Ishmaelite merchants, who in
turn sold him to Potiphar, an official at Pharaoh's court. A false
charge by his master's wife led him to prison, where his art of
interpreting dreams brought him to Pharaoh's notice. The king
gave him charge of the arrangements to meet an anticipated
famine, and so he became chief officer of the realm. When his
brothers came to buy corn, he discovered himself to them, and
received his father and family into Egypt, where they settled in

Goshen.

JOSEPH, Spouse of the Blessed Virgin Mary, native of Bethlehem, and a carpenter at Nazareth. We hear nothing of him after he accompanied Mary to Jerusalem when Jesus was twelve years old.

JOSEPH OF ARIMATHEA, wealthy Jew, a member of the Sanhedrin, and secret disciple of Jesus. He used his influence to procure the body of Jesus, which he buried in his own tomb.

JOSEPHUS, FLAVIUS, Jewish historian and revolutionary leader, born at Jerusalem in 37 A.D. After a gallant defence at Iotapata he was made prisoner, but later released. After the fall of Jerusalem in A.D. 70, he went to Rome and was under the patronage of Vespasian, Titus, and Domitian. He wrote *The Jewish War,* in seven books, a *Jewish Antiquities,* in 20 books. He died about A.D. 100.

JOSHUA, author of an Old Testament Book giving an account of his exploits, when he succeeded Moses as leader of Israel into the Promised Land. The book has three divisions:—(a) History of the conquest of Canaan. (b) Division of the conquered territory. (c) Joshua's addresses to the tribes; with an account of his death and burial.

JOSIAH, King of Judah, who succeeded his father Amon when eight years old. During repairs to the Temple the lost book of the law was found. Greatly impressed by its contents, he set out to cleanse the land of idolatry. Peace and prosperity ensued until Pharaoh Necho came to fight the Assyrians; Josiah attacked him, and fell at the battle of Megiddo.

JOVIANUS, FLAVIUS CLAUDIUS, (JOVIAN), elected emperor by the army in June A.D. 363: he was compelled to conclude a humiliating peace with Persia. He was found dead at Dadastana, in Bithynia, less than eight months after his accession. Jovian was a Christian.

JUBA, King of Numidia, who was of Pompey's party, gaining a victory over Curio, Caesar's legate, in 49 B.C. After Thrapsus, in 46 B.C., he took his own life.—Also, Juba, son of the above, was taken to Rome by Caesar and became a great scholar writing many books on a variety of topics: only fragments survive. Augustus reinstated him in his father's kingdom of Numidia in 30 B.C. and gave him Selene, daughter of Antony and Cleopatra, for his wife. In 25 B.C. Augustus gave him Mauretania in exchange for Numidia. He died in Mauretania about A.D. 23.

JUBAL, son of Lamech and Adah; traditionally the inventor of musical instruments.

JUBILEE, (Hebrew, YOBEL—a ram's horn trumpet), Jewish festival celebrated every 50th year in pre-Captivity days: it commemorated the release from Egyptian bondage and was proclaimed by the sounding of trumpets, and commenced on the day of Atonement. Land was always allowed to lie fallow during the year. Slaves were released, property reverted to its original owner, and each returned to his family.—*The Book of Jubilees* is a non-canonical O. T. Pseudepigrapha.

JUDAEA, district comprising the S. of Palestine after the exile. When the Jews returned they settled here. They were mostly of the tribe of Judah so named the district Judaea. Sometimes the term is used of the W. part of Palestine generally.

JUDAS ISCARIOT, Apostle of Jesus who betrayed Him to the priests, was the only Judaean Apostle, the rest being Galileans: after the betrayal Judas hanged himself.

JUDAS MACCABAEUS, succeeded his father Mattathias in 166 B.C. as leader of the Jews in their attempts to throw off the yoke of the Syrian kings. He was successful against Antiochus, and his successor Antiochus Eupator. Anxious to render Judaea independent, and feeling the difficulty of continuing the contest against the whole power of the Syrian empire, Judas sent envoys to Rome to seek alliance with the Roman people, which was readily granted. Before assistance could be received from his new allies, Judas ventured to attack the Syrian army under Bacchides, with a force of only 800, and after an obstinate struggle was defeated in 160 B.C.

JUDE, THE EPISTLE OF, N. T., Catholic epistle, i.e. addressed to Christians in general as opposed to being addressed to one particular Church: its probable date is between 60 and 70 A.D.

Jude's epistle is so like Peter's second epistle that one must have borrowed from the other, or else both must have used a common source.

JUDGES, THE BOOK OF, in the Bible so called because it relates the history of the Israelite tribal chiefs who led the people in peace and war from the settlement in Canaan under Joshua until the birth of the prophet Samuel. The book is in four sections: 1. Introduction describing the state of Canaan at the beginning of the period of the judges. 2. A moralising prelude to the history. 3. History of the judges. 4. Appendix describing some special episodes. Some of it was probably compiled, with the help of other sources, as early as the 7th cent. B.C.

JUDITH, THE BOOK OF, apocryphal book of the O.T., originally written in Hebrew, about the end of the 2nd cent. B.C. Its form is a religious romance recounting the adventures of a good and patriotic Jewess, at the period of the return from captivity.

JUGUM, among the Romans, a humiliating kind of punishment inflicted on their vanquished enemies. It consisted of two upright spears, with a third laid across, in the shape of a gallows; those who had surrendered were compelled, by way of ignominy, to pass under the erection without arms or military accoutrements.

JUGURTHA, illegitimate son of Mastanabal, and grandson of Masinissa, and King of Numidia. His uncle Micipsa having left his kingdom to be divided equally between his two sons, Hiempsal and Adherbal, Jugurtha put both to death and became sole ruler. He defied the power of Rome until defeated by Metellus and finally subdued by Marius: he was taken to Rome and starved to death. His life and campaigns were the subject of a work by Sallust, the Roman historian. Jugurtha died in 104 B.C.

JULIA, (a) Caesar's aunt, wife of Marius the elder. (b) Mother of the triumvir Antonius. (c) Sister of Caesar, wife of Balbus, and grandmother of Augustus. (d) Daughter of Caesar by Cornelia. (e) Daughter of Augustus, and his only child. (f) Daughter of the preceding. (g) Youngest child of Germanicus and Agrippina. (h) Daughter of Drusus and Livia.

JULIAN CALENDAR, reformed calendar of Julius Caesar, revised in 1582 by Pope Gregory XIII, has been superseded by the Gregorian calendar.

JULIANUS, FLAVIUS CLAUDIUS (JULIAN), Roman emperor A.D. 361-363, called the Apostate. He was born at Constantinople in 331, being nephew of Constantine the Great. In 335 Constantine gave Julian the title of Caesar, placing him in command of Gaul and the W., where he was victorious over German tribes. He became emperor in A.D. 361. He asserted a policy of religious toleration, but discouraged Christianity by making it clear that pagans would be preferred in office. He sent an expedition against the Persians in A.D. 363, but pushing too far into a waterless country, he had to retreat, and in rearguard actions received a mortal wound. A number of his letters, speeches, and satirical writings have come down to us.

JULIUS AFRICANUS, Christian writer, whose *Chronographiae* formed the basis of Eusebius' *Chronicle*. He died A.D. 240.

JUNO, in *Roman Mythology*, a major deity, identified with the Greek Hera, was sister and wife of Jupiter, and queen of heaven, and as such her power was greater than Hera's. Juno, Jupiter, and Minerva were a trinity which protected the Roman state. Matronali was a festival celebrated in her honour by married women on March 1st.

JUPITER, in *Roman Mythology*, an Italian divinity identified with the Greek Zeus. His name signifies "light-father," and he was especially associated with the heavens, rain, thunder, lightning, and growth of the fruits of the field. He came to be regarded as the god of hospitality, truth and justice in local and international relations. He was also a war god and giver of victory. In early times he had a temple on the Alban mount. After the worship of Janus declined, Jupiter became chief god of the Romans. His temple on the Capitoline Hill, was regarded as the heart of the Roman state.

JURASSUS MONS or JURA, mountain range N. of Lake Lemanus, and the boundary between the Sequani and Helvetti.

JUSTIN, name of two Byzantine emperors. Justin I, who was probably a Goth, commanded the imperial guards and was proclaimed emperor by the soldiers after the death of Anastasius. He reigned 518-527. Justin II, nephew of the above, became emperor in 574, he became subject to fits of insanity, and took Tiberius to him as joint ruler. He died in 578.

JUSTINIAN I, Roman emperor, born at Illyricum, May 11th, A.D. 483, was probably of Thracian descent. His generals Belisarius and Narses, pushing back the Persians, recovered the mastery of the African provinces by destroying the Vandal Kingdom, and for a time established imperial dominion in Italy by overthrowing the Ostrogoths. Justinian's fame rests upon his codification of Roman law which became the basis of all European systems, except in England. He died Nov. 14th, A.D. 565.

JUSTIN MARTYR, Christian apologist, born about A.D. 100, in Samaria, of Greek parents. As a youth he studied Stoicism and Platonism. He became a Christian through study of the O.T., but continued to lecture on philosophy in Rome, Ephesus, etc. He was martyred about A.D. 165. In his famous *Apologies,* he defended Christianity against the charges of pagan writers.

JUVENALIS, DECIMUS JUNIUS (JUVENAL), Roman satirist, living from the reign of Nero to that of Antoninus Pius. The best known of his satires is on *Women.* A fine piece of work is his satire on *Rome.* He lived from about A.D. 60-140.

L

LABARUM, the famous standard of Constantine the Great, which he designed in remembrance of the vision of a cross in the heavens that occurred to him on his march against Byzantium. The Greek historians describe it as a long pike surmounted by a crown of gold, the crown inclosing a monogram of the first two letters of Christ's Name. From its shape it also served as an emblem of the Cross. A silken banner hanging from it was embroidered with figures of the emperor and his family. It was carefully preserved for generations and carried before the armies in emergencies to ensure the safety of the empire.

LABEO, ANTISTIUS, one of Caesar's assassins, who was a Roman jurist. He ended his own life after the battle of Philippi, in 42 B.C.—His son, of the same name, was also a jurist, whose republican views were disliked by Augustus. He founded a legal school.

LABERIUS, DECIMUS, born about 115 B.C. was a Roman eques and writer of mimes, and was compelled by Caesar to appear on the stage to contend with Syrus, a professional mimus; he took his revenge by pointing his wit at Caesar. He died at Puteoli, in Campania, in 43 B.C.

LABIENUS, tribune of the plebs in 63 B.C., legatus of Caesar in his wars against the Gauls, and his friend. However, he joined Pompey in 49 B.C., at the outbreak of civil war. He was killed in battle at Munda in 45 B.C.—His son invaded Syria leading a Parthian army in 40 B.C. The Parthians were defeated by Antony's legate, Ventidius, and Labienus fled to Cilicia, where he was put to death.

LABYNETUS, name of several Babylonian kings. The one mentioned by Herodotus, is the same as Nebuchadnezzar. Another mentioned by the historian is the same as Belshazzar, so that

'Labynetus' would appear to be a kind of title.

LABYRINTH, in Greco-Roman times a confusing net-work of paths or passages, often underground, designed to make it difficult for anyone who entered to get out again. The Egyptian labyrinths were the most famous in ancient times. They were sited near Lake Moeris, being built about 2300 B.C.

LACEDAEMON, in ancient Greece, alternative name for Laconia, a district of the Eurotas valley in S. Peloponnesus. *See* SPARTA.

LACHESIS, one of the Parcae, or Fates, who presided over futurity, represented as spinning the thread of life.

LACHISH, ancient fortified town of Palestine E. of Gaza. It has been called the Mound of Many Cities by excavators. A tablet found dating 1400 B.C. belongs to the Tell el-Amarna correspondence. Various levels have been dated as contemporary with Joshua, Rehoboam, Sennacherib (who besieged it in 701 B.C.), and Nebuchadnezzar.

LACINIUM, headland on the coast of Bruttii, south of Croton: here was a temple of Juno.

LACONICA, called by Roman writers, LACONIA, a country of ancient Greece, bounded W. by Messenia, N. by Arcadia and Argolis, being washed by the sea E. and S. The district from N. to S., between two mountain masses, drained by the Eurotas which falls into the Laconian Sea. Sparta q.v., was the only town of importance in the country.

LACONICUS SINUS, gulf of S. Peloponnesus.

LACTANTIUS, LUCIUS CAELIUS FIRMIANUS, Latin father living at the end of the third and beginning of the fourth centuries, generally thought to be an African. On the invitation of Diocletian, he went to Nicomedia where he taught rhetoric. Later Crispus, son of Constantine, was his pupil. His chief works are the *Divine Institutions,* in seven books, written in reply to two pagans who wrote against Christianity at the beginning of Diocletian's persecution; a treatise on the *Workmanship of God;* on the *Wrath of God;* also a work entitled *Symposion,* which he wrote when very young.

LACYDES, born at Cyrene, was president of the Academy at Athens, succeeding Arcesilaus. He died about 206.

LADAS, name of two famous ancient athletes. One of unknown date, belonged to Laconia, and won the long race at the Olympic games. The sculptor Myron carved a statue of him. The other Ladas won the short race at the games in 280 B.C.

LADE, island off the W. coast of Caria.

LAELIUS, friend of Scipio the elder, with whom he fought in his campaigns. He was consul in 190 B.C.—His son LAELIUS SAPIENS, was friend of Scipio the younger. He was born about 186 B.C., was tribune in 151, praetor in 145, and consul in 140. He is made principal interlocutor in Cicero's dialogue, *De Amicitia,* and a speaker in *De Senectute* and *De Republica.*

LAENAS, name of a Roman family, notorious for cruelty, sternness, and haughtiness.

LAERTES, in *Greek Legend,* King of Ithaca, husband of Anticlea, and aged father of Ulysses. When Ulysses returned after 20 years' absence from Ithaca, his father still lived, their meeting being described by Homer.

LAESTRYGONES, the cannibalistic race encountered by Ulysses during his wanderings.

LAEVINUS, VALERIUS, consul in 280 B.C., who was defeated by Pyrrhus on the banks of the Siris.—Another of the name was praetor in 215 B.C., and consul in 210 B.C., he captured the town of Agrigentum.

LAGASH, Sumerian town at Tello, S. Babylonia. The earliest name associated with it is the patesi Lugalshagengur, who ruled under Mesilim, King of Kish. Later Lagash was made capital of S. Babylonia by Eannatum. This dynasty closed with the reformer Urukagina. From this time the city was ruled until 2400 B.C. by patesis under Akkad, Erech, and Ur.

LAIS, there were two Greek courtesans of this name, one living during the Peloponnesian War, was accounted the most beautiful woman of the age.—The other was born at Hyccara, and was daughter of Timandra.

LAIUS, son of Labdacus, husband of Jocasta, and King of Thebes, was father of Oedipus.

LALAGE, common Greek term of endearment for courtesans.

LAMACHUS, colleague of Alcibiades and Nicias, in the Sicilian expedition of 415 B.C.: he was an Athenian.

LAMENTATIONS, Biblical book belonging to the Megilloth (rolls) group. It consists of five poems, four of which are alphabetic, written in a metre consisting of three beats followed by two. They lament over the destruction of Jerusalem by Nebuchadnezzar. Ancient tradition ascribes them to Jeremiah.

LAMIA, Roman family name: this family claimed descent from the legendary hero Lamus. L. Aelius Lamia was consul in A.D. 3, and son of the Lamia who supported Cicero in suppression of the Catilinarian conspiracy.

LAMIA, (a) Town in Thessaly, on the Achelous. (b) In *Greek Mythology,* a fabulous monster supposed to devour children. (c) An old Libyan queen who avenged the death of her children, slain by Hera, by slaying all other children she could lay hands on. In later legend she became a beautiful woman, gaining the affection of handsome young men, whose blood she sucked, before eating their flesh.

LAMPSACUS, city of Asia Minor, famous for wine: here was the center of the worship of Priapus.

LAMUS, Cicilian town and river.

LANUVIUM, birthplace of the emperor Antoninus Pius.

LAOCOON, in *Greek Mythology,* a Trojan priest who warned his countrymen of the wooden horse. After his warning two serpents, sent by Poseidon, came from the sea while the priest was offering a sacrifice, and crushed him and his two sons to death. The incident is recorded in the celebrated piece of statuary discovered in Rome, now in the Vatican museum.

LAODAMIA, in *Greek Mythology,* wife of Protesilaus. After her husband had fallen at Troy, she requested the gods that he might return from Hades to converse with her for three hours.

When Protesilaus returned to Hades, Laodamia died and accompanied him.

LAODICEA, name of at least eight cities, founded or renovated in the later Hellenic period; most of them were founded by the Seleucid Kings of Syria.

LAOMEDON, in *Greek Mythology*, King of Troy. Poseidon and Apollo, having offended Zeus, were ordered to render their services to Laomedon. When the period of service ended the two gods claimed from Laomedon their promised reward. This being refused, Poseidon, in revenge sent a sea monster to ravage the neighbourhood of Troy, to which a virgin had to be sacrificed from time to time. The king's daughter, Hesione, was saved by Hercules, who slew the monster. But the king was faithless a second time, refusing Hercules a promised reward. Hercules in his wrath attacked Troy and slew Laomedon and all his sons except Priam, who became king.

LAPITHAE, a mythical race whose conflict with the Centaurs is one of the most famous events in Greek Mythology. The site of the legend is the district round Mt. Pelion.

LAR, LARS, an Etruscan prefix-name signifying hero or king. It was adopted by the Romans, e.g. Lar Herminius, consul in 448 B.C.

LARES, in *Roman Mythology*, originally divinities who watched over agricultural pursuits; they were worshipped at cross roads where a yearly festival was held in their honour. Also every household had a private Lar, or household god, (latterly increased to two), whose image was kept on the hearth or in the lararium, a kind of chapel set apart for this purpose. They were also tutelary deities of travellers, of streets, and of districts, towns and cities.

LARISSA, the name of a number of Pelasgian towns.

LARIUS LACUS (Como), lake in Gallia Transpadana: Pliny the Younger had a villa on its shores.

LARSUS, the mentor of Pindar, was a poet born in Hermione in Argolis.

LATIFUNDIA, large estates, built up from the distribution of public land. They were farmed by slaves, labouring under the worst conditions. When slave labour became too expensive, tenants occupied the lands, but these in turn fell into the condition of serfs.

LATINI, name of one of the most ancient nations of Italy, said to have descended, before the building of Rome, from the central Apennines into the lower country between the Anio, the Tiber, the Alban mountains, and the sea, which was afterwards called Latium.

LATINUS, King of Latium, father of Lavinia, who married Aeneas.

LATIUM, country of the ancient Latins, (*See* Latini), had at first for its boundaries on the W. the Tiber; on the N. the Anio; on the S. the Tyrrhenian Sea; to the E. the boundary is not so clear. Later the name of Latium was extended to the whole country inhabited by the Volsci, Hernici, and Aurunci, in addition to the country of the old Latins, and this was called Latium Novum. Under Augustus, Latium and Campania constituted the first of the eleven regions into which Italy was divided by the emperor.

LATMICUS SINUS, an Ionian gulf in Asia Minor, into which the Maeander flowed.

LATMUS, mountain of Caria.

LAURENTUM, town of Latium, where lived the mythical Latinus. It was built on a height between Ostia and Ardea, being surrounded by a grove of laurels.

LAURIUM, mountain of Attica, famous for its silver mines, which were a great source of wealth to the Athenians.

LAUS POMPEII, town in Gallia Cisalpina.

LAUSUS, son of Mezentius, king of the Etruscans, who was killed by Aeneas.—Another of the name was son of Numitor; he was slain by Amulius.

LAVINIUM, town in Latium, on the Via Appia, founded by Aeneas.

LEANDER, in *Greek Legend*, the lover of Hero: in order to visit her he used to swim the Hellespont each evening. One night he was drowned, and Hero threw herself into the sea.

LEBADEA, place in Boeotia, famous for the oracle of Trophonius.

LECTISTERNIUM, a feast at which a god or gods were present, who were represented by statues or sheaves of herbs.

LECYTHUS, a tall urn with a handle, constructed for putting in tombs: they were often decorated.

LEDA, in Greek Mythology, wife of Tyndareus, King of Sparta, with whom Zeus fell in love, and visited in the form of a swan, as a result Leda brought forth two eggs, from one of which sprang Castor and Pollux and from the other Helen.

LEGIO, (legion), chief unit of the Roman army. The original number of 3000 infantry was increased in the time of Servius Tullius to 3000 heavy, and 1200 light armed troops, and from the days of Marius consisted of 6000. A legion was divided into 30 maniples, or companies, each under the command of two centurions. The legionary soldier was equipped with a helmet, shield, cuirass, sword, dagger and a missile weapon. Under the empire the standing army consisted of 25 to 30 legions.

LEGIO, town in Hispania Tarraconensis, at one time H. Q. of a legion.

LEITOURGIA, duties imposed by the state at Athens. Among others, were the office of choregus (choirmaster); of gymnasiarch, and public entertainer; of periodic (the sacred mission to Delos); of extraordinary, such as missions to the oracle at Delphi, etc.

LELEGES, with the Pelasgians, the most ancient inhabitants of Greece. They were warlike and roving, first settling on island coasts, and later moving inland.

LEMANNUS, lake formed by the Rhodanus.

LEMNOS, large island in the Aegaean, Thracian Sinties being its first inhabitants. The island was conquered by one of Darius' generals, but it was recovered by Miltiades, and made subject to Athens. In ancient mythology, it is known as the spot on which

Vulcan fell after being hurled from heaven.

LEMURES, shades of the dead. Apparently the term covered all the spirits of the dead who were divided into two classes, (a) the Lares, being souls of good men, and (b) Larvae, souls of the wicked. The Romans held a yearly festival of the Lemuralia on three days in May, in order to propitiate them.

LENTULUS, PUBLIUS CORNELIUS, surnamed Sura, was a member of one of the proudest patrician families in ancient Rome. He was consul in 71 B.C. but was expelled from the senate for his extravagant immorality. He joined Catiline in his conspiracy in 63 B.C., but carried on negotiations with the envoys of the Allobroges, who afterwards sold their information to Cicero. He was arrested, with his accomplices and put to death.

LEO THE GREAT, Pope from 440-461 A.D. was by tradition a native of Tuscany, and succeeded Sixtus III. His chief care was promotion of the unity of the Church, by putting down heresy, and by maintenance of Papal Supremacy over the whole Church. His widespread influence turned back Attila, King of the Huns, in his march on Rome, and saved Rome from being sacked after the capture of the city by the Vandals. The Latinity of his sermons equalled that of the best Latin classics. He died Nov. 10 A.D. 461.

LEO, Roman emperor of the East 457-474, was called the Great, but had but little claim to that title. In later times there were 5 other Eastern emperors of that name.

LEOCHARES, Greek sculptor of the 4th cent. B.C. He produced a group in bronze of Ganymede rapt by the eagle. He also worked on the Mausoleum.

LEONIDAS, King of Sparta, commanded the Grecian troops sent to maintain the pass of Thermopylae against Xerxes in 480 B.C. He had 4200 men, besides the Opuntian Locri, and 1000 Phocians. During two days' fight he defended the pass, but the enemy discovering by treachery a circuitous pass, crossed Mt. Oeta. On hearing this Leonidas dismissed all his troops except 300 Spartans, the Thebans, and the Thespians, 700 in number. Being attacked front and rear, the Spartans and Thespians fell to a man after inflicting great slaughter. The Thebans asked and obtained quarter. The corpse of Leonidas was mutilated and exposed on a cross by Xerxes. A stone lion was afterwards erected on the spot where he fell, and the slain honoured with monumental pillars. Two inscriptions ran thus: "Here 4000 men from Peloponnesus once fought 3 millions." "Stranger, tell the Lacedaemonians that we lie here, obeying their laws."

LEONNATUS, a Macedonian of Pella, general to Alexander, who crossed to Europe in 322 B.C. to aid Antipater against the Greeks but was defeated, and killed by the Athenians.

LEONTINI, town in Sicily N. W. of Syracuse, established by Chalcidians in 729 B.C. To the N. of the city were fertile plains known as Leontini Campi. Gorgias was born here.

LEOTYCHIDES, King of Sparta, commanded the Greek fleet in 479 B.C., defeating the Persians at the battle of Mycale.—Another of the name was reputed son of Agis II, who was excluded from the throne on grounds of doubtful parentage. His uncle, Agesilaus II, became king.

LEPIDUS, MARCUS AEMILIUS, renowned Roman triumvir, was elected aedile in 52 B.C., and praetor in 49 B.C. in which year Caesar quarrelled with the senatorian party. On the first expedition of Caesar into Spain, Lepidus was left in charge of Rome, and proposed a law by which Caesar was created Dictator. After Caesar's death, Lepidus was courted by both parties. He promised support to the Senate, but carried on secret negotiations with Antonius. When ordered by the Senate to join Decimus Brutus, he refused and united his forces with those of Caesar's successor. In 43 B.C. the famous triumvirate of Antonius, Lepidus, and Octavianus was established, Lepidus receiving Spain and Gallia Narbonensis. The war against Brutus and Cassius was assigned to Antonius and Augustus, while the city was intrusted to Lepidus, who was again elected consul in 43 B.C. After the defeat of Brutus and Cassius, in a new division of the empire Spain and Gallia Narbonensis were taken from Lepidus, he receiving Africa instead. Lepidus had now lost all authority but was again included in the triumvirate when renewed in 37 B.C. The year after he was summoned from Africa to aid Augustus in Sicily against Sextus Pompeius. He arrived with a large army by means of which he sought to reestablish his power, but was deserted by his troops and obliged to implore mercy of Augustus, who spared him, allowing him to retain his property and the dignity of pontifex maximus, though he banished him to Circeii. Lepidus died in 12 B.C.

LEPTINES, an Athenian who proposed a law taking away all special exemptions from the burden of public charges, against which the speech of Demosthenes was directed.

LERNA, district of Argolis, where Hercules slew the Lernean Hydra.

LESBOS, island in the Aegaean, of importance in early Greek history, as the home of the Aeolian school of lyric verse. Sappho, Alcaeus, and Terpander the poets were born here, also Pittacus the sage, Hellanicus the historian, and Theophrastus the philosopher.

LETHE, in *Greek Mythology,* the underworld river of oblivion, those who drank thereof forgetting the whole of their former existence.

LETO, in *Greek Mythology,* mother of Apollo and Artemis by Zeus. His love for her aroused the jealousy of Hera who sent the serpent Pytho to pursue Leto. She fled far and wide, finding no rest. At last Poseidon in pity fixed the floating island of Delos, and there Leto gave birth to Apollo and Artemis. She was Latona to the Romans.

LEUCAS, island of the Ionian Sea.

LEUCIPPUS, founder of Atomism in Greek philosophy about the middle of the 5th cent. B.C. Two others of the name were, (a) the lover of Daphne, and (b) son of Perieres, prince of the Messenians, and father of Phoebe and Hilaira.

LEUCOPHRYS, city of Caria, with a warm-water lake, and having a temple of Artemis.

LEVI, third son of Jacob and Leah, who with Simeon massacred the Schechemites in revenge for an injury to his sister

Dinah. His descendants were the Levites.

LEVIATHAN, in ancient Jewish belief, a water monster. The Septuagint renders the word dragon, and there may be a connection with the serpent of Babylonian mythology. In Job 41 the crocodile is described under this name.

LEVITES, one of the 12 tribes of Israel, forming a sacred caste. Traditionally descended from Levi, they acted as assistants to the priests in Tabernacle and Temple. They had no specific territory, but 48 cities were allotted them, they receiving titles and alms.

LEVITICUS, third book of the Pentateuch or Hexateuch, the name signifying 'that which concerns the Levites.' The book deals with the priests, and legal and ceremonial institutions. The Book falls into five divisions 1. Sacrifices, and duties and privileges of priests. 2. Consecration of the priests. 3. Clean and Unclean, and the Day of Atonement. 4. Holiness. 5. Vows and tithes.

LEX DUODECIM TABULARUM (Twelve Tables of the Law), oldest code of Roman law, promulgated about 450 B.C., by the Decemviri. The tables were written in archaic Latin, on copper tablets, which were set up in the Forum at Rome. The code was a summary of the old criminal and civil law, but contained no constitutional enactments. The twelve tables were later venerated by the Romans.

LIBANIUS, born at Antioch, between A.D. 314 and 316, was a Sophist, and the most distinguished writer of the 4th cent. He studied at Athens and spent his early manhood in Constantinople and Nicomedia. His private classes were more popular at Constantinople than those of the public professors, who in consequence found means to expel him, in 346, on a charge of studying magic. He was recalled after 5 years, but ill health compelled him to retire to Antioch. Though a pagan he enjoyed favour with the Christian emperors. S. John Chrysostom and S. Basil were among his pupils. He died about 395 A.D.

LIBANUS, mountain range, dividing Phoenice from Coele-Syria.

LIBETHRUM, ancient town in Pieria, in Macedonia of Thracian origin.

LIBERTINUS, in Rome polity, persons were divided, with respect to status or condition, into freemen (liberi) or slaves (servi). Freemen were again divided into persons born in a state of freedom (ingenui), and libertini, or those who had been manumitted. A manumitted slave was called *libertus,* i.e. *liberatus,* "freed," with reference to the act of manumission, and to his master, who, by manumitting him, became his patron, (patronus): he was called 'libertinus' with reference to the class, to which, by the act of manumission, he belonged. A manumitted slave might either become a full Roman citizen or a Latinus or might obtain no higher privileges than the class Dediticii.

LIBRA, Roman unit of weight nearly equal to 12 oz. avoirdupois.

LIBURNIANS, a people who at different times were prominent on the Adriatic coasts, most likely one of the homogeneous Illyrian tribes. They were famous for swift boats with a large sail, the Romans adopted them, and it was to these boats that Augustus was indebted for his victory at Actium.

LIBYA, Greek name for the African continent.

LIBYPHOENICES, people of the cities founded by Phoenicia on the Carthaginian coasts, a mixed race of colonists from Phoenicia and Libyan natives.

LICINIUS, PUBLIUS FLAVIUS GALERIUS VALERIUS LICINIANUS, Roman emperor of Dacian peasant origin was born about A.D. 250, and was elevated after the death of Severus to rank of Augustus by Galerius, receiving charge of Illyricum. On the death of Galerius in A.D. 311, he shared the empire with Maximinus. In 313 he entered into alliance with Constantine at Milan, and inflicted a decisive defeat on Maximinus at Heraclea, thus making himself master of the East, while Constantine was supreme in the West. He in his turn was defeated by Constantine in 315. A second war between Licinius and Constantine broke out in 323, in which Licinius lost his throne. Constantine put him to death the following year.

LICTORES (LICTORS), officers who walked in front of certain of the higher magistrates of ancient Rome. On their left shoulder they bore the fasces, a bundle of rods with an axe bound in the middle, symbolising the magistrates' power of corporal and capital punishment.

LIGURIA, division of ancient N. W. Italy including the districts which border on the Tyrrhenian Sea, from Gaul to Etruria. Of the origin of the Ligurians nothing is known. The principal Ligurian tribes were 1. the Apuani, inhabiting the valley of the Magra; 2. the Friniates on the N. slope of the Apennines; 3. the Briniates, in the valley of the Vara; 4. the Genuates, around Genoa; 5. the Veturii, west of the preceding; 6. the Ingauni, whose capital was Albium Ingaunum; 7. The Intemelii; 8. the Vediantii.

LILYBAEUM, Sicilian port, founded by Carthage in 396 B.C.

LIMITES ROMANI, continuous fortifications erected by the Romans along the Rhine and Danube as a protection against the Germans.

LINDUM, (LINCOLN), Roman colony in Britain, peopled by the Coritani.

LINGONES, a people in Transalpine Gaul, whose chief town was Andematurinum. A branch of this race migrated to Cisalpine Gaul.

LINUS, saint of the Gregorian canon, and according to *Breviarium Romanum,* successor of S. Peter in the see of Rome. He was born at Volterra, and developed such a high degree of sanctity and faith that he could cast out devils and raise the dead. He was beheaded by order of the ungrateful consul Saturninus, whose daughter he had freed from demoniac possession, after a pontificate of eleven years, two months, and twenty-three days.

LIRIS, river of central Italy, rising in the Apennines, and falling into the Sinus Caietanus, and forming the boundary between Latium and Campania. More anciently it had been called the Clanis.

LISSUS, town of S. Dalmatia, at the mouth of the Drilon, founded by Dionysius of Syracuse in 385 B.C., with an acropolis named Acrolissus.

LITANA SILVA, a forest of the Apennines in Cisalpine Gaul.

LITERNUM, coastal town of Campania, at the mouth of the Liris, where Scipio Africanus the elder retired when about to be brought to trial by the tribunes.

LIVIA, (a) was married first to Porcius Cato, and after to Q. Servilius Caepio, by whom she bore Servilia, the mother of M. Brutus, Caesar's assassin. (b) LIVIA DRUSILLA, married first T. Claudius Nero, and afterwards Augustus, who had compelled her husband to divorce her. (c) LIVIA, wife of Drusus junior; she was seduced by Sejanus, who persuaded her to poison her husband. (d) Julia LIVILLA, daughter of Germanicus and Agrippina.

LIVIUS, TITUS, (LIVY), Roman historian, born at Patavium in 59 B.C. He spent most of his time in Rome, and was on intimate terms with Augustus, who used to call him a Pompeian, on account of the praises which he bestowed upon Pompey and his followers. He also encouraged the studies of Claudius, who became emperor. He died in A.D. 17, in his seventy-sixth year. Livy's great work was originally published in 142 books, and was a history of Rome, from the earliest period till the death of Drusus in 9 B.C. Of these books 35 are extant, viz., the first 10, containing the history of the city to 293 B.C.; and from the 21st to 45th, inclusive, which commence with the Second Punic War, in 218 B.C., and continue to the conquest of Macedon, in 167 B.C. Brief epitomes of the lost books exist. Tacitus and Seneca speak in the highest terms of the beauty of Livy's style, and the fidelity of his history, praises constantly repeated by modern writers.

LIVIUS ANDRONICUS, the earliest Roman poet, was a Greek, the freedman of M. Livius Salinator. He wrote Latin tragedies and comedies, his first drama being presented in 240 B.C.; also he translated the Odyssey into Saturnian verse.

LOCRI, people of Greece found in two different districts, on the Aegaean coast, opposite Euboea, and on the Corinthian Gulf, between Phocis and Aetolia. The former are divided into the northern Locri Epicnemidii, and the southern Locri Opuntii, whose chief town was Opus; but the name Opuntii is applied to the whole district by Thucydides, Herodotus, and others. They were considered by Aristotle to be a Lelegian tribe; but they became Hellenized at an early time, ranking in Homer with the other Greek tribes before Troy. The Locri Ozolae on the Corinthian Gulf were a barbarous race who make no appearance in Greek history until the Peloponnesian war. A colony called Locri Epizephyrii settled in the S. W. extremity of Italy at the end of the 8th cent. B.C.

LOCUSTA, a poisoner employed by Agrippina to poison Claudius, and by Nero, to kill Britannicus. She was put to death in the reign of Galba.

LOGIA, name given to several fragmentary 'Sayings of Jesus,' on 3rd cent. papyri, found in Egypt.

LONDINIUM, (LONDON), town of the Cantii, in Britain which became capital of the province. Its first site was probably on an eminence near the Walbrook. The town is first mentioned in Nero's days as prosperous, being visited by Roman merchants. In the revolt of Boudicca, the town was taken and the people killed in A.D. 61. London Wall was built in A.D. 140, running from a fort, near the site of the Tower, along the Minories to Cripplegate, Newgate, and Ludgate. The town covered about 330 acres, a bridge connecting it with the S. bank. All the Roman roads converged on London. Part of a Roman milestone may still be seen in the wall of S. Swithun's church in Cannon St.

LONGINUS, (1) traditional name for unknown author of the Greek treatise, *On the Sublime,* due to its mistaken association with (2) Also another later author Cassius Longinus said to have been born in Syria or at Athens. His education was superintended by his uncle, Fronto, a famous teacher of rhetoric; he received instruction from Ammonius and Origen. He later settled at Athens, where he taught philosophy, rhetoric, and criticism. Porphyry was one of his pupils. He finally went to Palmyra at the invitation of Queen Zenobia, to educate her sons, and took an active part in public affairs. After the capture of

Palmyra by Aurelian in 273, Longinus was put to death by order of the emperor.

LONGUS, author of a Greek pastoral, *The Loves of Daphnis and Chloe,* noted for elegance and simplicity. He lived in the 4th or 5th cent.

LORIUM, village in Etruria where Antoninus Pius died.

LOTOPHAGI, (LOTUS EATERS) in *Greek Mythology,* a people with whom Ulysses came into contact during his wanderings. Eating the lotus caused those who did so to lose all desire to return to their native country.

LUCANIA, district of Lower Italy, separated from Campania by the Silarus, and from Bruttium by the Laus.

LUCANUS, M. ANNAEUS, (LUCAN), Roman poet born at Corduba, in Spain, a nephew of Seneca, under whose influence Lucan started his career under the best auspices, first attracting attention by a panegyric of the emperor. Later he incurred the jealousy of Nero, and with others formed a conspiracy to assassinate the emperor. This was discovered, Lucan being compelled to commit suicide at the age of 26 in A.D. 65. His *Pharsalia,* an epic dealing with the fall of the Roman republic, abounds with passages of brilliant rhetoric.

LUCCEIUS, L., friend of Cicero, who wrote a history of Rome, beginning with the Social war.

LUCIANUS (LUCIAN), Greek satirist, born at Samosata, on the Euphrates, in Syria. He became a travelling rhetorician, lecturing and teaching in various cities in Asia Minor, Greece, Italy, and Gaul. Towards the end of his life he received an official appointment in Egypt, where he died in A.D. 180.

LUCIFER, name given to the planet Venus as the morning star, in mythology, the son of Aurora.

LUCILIUS, C., Roman satirist, born at Suessa, in 180 B.C. He died in 102 B.C. at Naples.

LUCRETIA, in *Roman Legend,* wife of Lucius Tarquinius Collatinus. Sextus Tarquinius, son of Tarquinius Superbus, inflamed by her beauty, forced her to yield to his desires. On the following day Lucretia stabbed herself, whereupon Junius Brutus, cousin of Tarquinius, seized the dagger and raised it as a standard of revolt.

LUCRETIUS, CARUS, T., Roman poet and philosopher, born 94 B.C. He was contemporary with Cicero and Caesar, little is known of his life, although his great poem, in six books, *De Rerum Natura*, ranks as a world masterpiece. It attempts to express the author's system of Epicurean philosophy. He is said to have perished by his own hand in 55 B.C.

LUCULLUS, LUCIUS LICINIUS, Roman soldier and epicure. In the third Mithridatic War, he was in chief command for eight years, and was successful in driving Mithridates from his kingdom of Pontus. In 69 B.C., he overcame Tigranes, King of Armenia, and overran Mesopotamian Armenia, but soon retired to enjoy his wealth. He was a great patron of the arts. His gardens were far famed, and his banquets proverbial.

LUGDUNUM, town at the junction of the Arar and the Rhodanus, colonized by the Romans in 43 B.C. Under Augustus it became capital of the province and seat of the Roman governor (the modern Paris).

LUKE, one of the four evangelists. He tells us in his Gospel, that he obtained his information from eye-witnesses of the facts, and from written accounts.

LUNA, an Etruscan town, with harbour (called Lunae Portus). It became a Roman colony in 177 B.C.

LUPERCALIA, ancient Roman festival in honour of Lupercus, on Feb. 15th. Originally it was pastoral.

LUSTRUM, name applied to a period of five solar years among the Romans, the termination of which was marked by religious Solemnities.

LUTETIA, capital of the Parisii, where Julian was proclaimed emperor in A.D. 360 (the modern Lyons).

LYCAONIA, district of Asia Minor, first mentioned by Xenophon, as extending E. from Iconium in Phrygia to the borders of Cappadocia. In the days of Strabo, the name was applied to the S. E. part of Phrygia.

LYCEUM, gymnasium, sacred to Apollo Lycius, situated just outside Athens to the S. E., famous as the place where Aristotle and his successors taught. The name was applied to the school of philosophy in which Aristotelian teaching was expounded.

LYCON of TROAS, Peripatetic philosopher, pupil of Straton, whom he succeeded as head of the school in 272 B.C.

LYCOPHRON, born at Chalcis in about 300 B.C., was grammarian and poet, residing at Alexandria, under Ptolemy Philadelphus.

LYCOREA, ancient town, beneath Mt. Lycorea.

LYCURGUS, flourished about 800 B.C., reputed founder of the constitution of Sparta. Tradition has it that after acting as regent for his young nephew King Charilaus, he left Sparta to travel. On his return he was called upon to rescue the state from confusion into which it had fallen. This he did with success, and left, never to return.—Another Lycurgus was an Athenian statesman and orator (c. 396-323 B.C.), with Demosthenes and Hypereides he belonged to the national party. He administered Athenian public finance with great success for 12 years.

LYDIA, ancient district of Asia Minor, bounded N. by Mysia; E. by Phrygia; S. by Caria; and W. by the Aegaean. In Homeric times it was known as Maeonia, this name disappeared about 700 B.C. when Gyges seized the throne. His dynasty lasted 150 years, during which Lydia became prosperous, reaching its zenith with Croesus, under whom the Lydian empire extended from the Aegaean to the river Halys, and the Greek cities of Asia Minor were tributary. In 546 B.C. dominion passed to Cyrus. After Persia's overthrow by Alexander, Lydia became independent again, but was later subject to Syria, then to Pergamum. It became part of the Roman empire in 133 B.C.

LYNCEUS, one of the 50 sons of Aegyptus, saved by his wife, Hypermnestra, when his brothers were killed by the daughters of Danaus.

LYSANDER, Spartan general and statesman, who rose to fame during the latter period of the Peloponnesian War. As commander of the Spartan fleet he ingratiated himself with Cyrus the Younger, receiving considerable subsidies for the Spartans, which helped them in their triumph. In 405 B.C., his fleet defeated the

Athenians at Aegospotami. The year following he took Athens, destroyed the Long Walls, and established the rule of the Thirty Tyrants.

LYSIAS, (458-380 B.C.). Greek orator, author of over 200 forensic speeches. Noted for his simplicity and lucidity of style.

LYSIMACHUS, one of Alexander's generals, son of Agathocles, a Thessalian in the service of Philip of Macedon, was born about 361 B.C. Thrace was allotted to him after the death of Alexander, in 323 B.C., he assuming the title of king in 306. He joined the other generals in opposing Antigonus, and he and Seleucus gained the decisive victory at Ipsus over Antigonus in 301 B.C. In 288 Lysimachus and Pyrrhus expelled Demetrius from Macedonia. Towards the end of his reign Lysimachus put his son Agathocles to death, which deed alienated his subjects, and Seleucus invaded his dominions. The two kings met on the plain of Corus, when Lysimachus fell in battle in 281 B.C.

LYSIPPUS of SICYON, Greek sculptor, contemporary with Alexander the Great.

LYSIS, Pythagorean philosopher who taught Epaminondas.

LYSTRA, city of Lycaonia, famous as a chief scene of the preaching of SS. Paul and Barnabas.

M

MAAT, Egyptian goddess, associated with Ra and Thoth, personifying physical and moral law. As goddess of truth she was identified by the Greeks with Themis. She had neither temples nor offerings, but presided in the judgment hall of Osiris when the souls were weighed. Judicial officials were allegorically called priests of Maat.

MACCABAEI (MACCABEES), later name of the Hasmonaeans, or Asmonaeans, an aristocratic family of Jews. In the 2nd cent. B.C. they overcame the Syro-Hellenic yoke, and established a line of priest-kings. Their history starts with Mattathias, an aged priest, who when ordered to sacrifice to the gods, killed the Syrian commissioner and a Jew about to obey the order, and, with his five sons, escaped to the mountains. The last of the race was Mariamne, by whose marriage with Herod the dynasty passed to the Herodians.

MACCABEES, BOOK OF, four books of the Biblical Apocrypha. The first and second are valuable historical writings, one covering the period of Jewish history from Antiochus Epiphanes to the death of Simon, i.e., from 175-135 B.C. The other covers part of the same period but is of less historical value. The third book is by way of being an historical romance, while the fourth is philosophical rather than historical.

MACEDONIA, a country of Europe which was bounded S. by Thessaly and the Aegaean; E. by Thrace; and W. by Illyria. Its principal towns were Edessa, Pella, Pydna, Philippi, Potidaea, and Thessalonica, the first two being capital in turn. The country was renowned for salt, gold, and silver mines, and for its vineyards. Macedonia did not become important until the reign of Philip II, 359-336 B.C. It reached its zenith under his successor, Alexander the Great, at whose death in 323 B.C. the Macedonian empire included Macedonia, Greece, Thrace, Asia Minor, Syria, Egypt, Babylonia, Assyria, part of Persia, Afghanistan, Baluchistan, and central Asia. Under the Diadochi (the successors of Alexander), these colonies were contested among a number of claimants. In 278 B.C. Antigonus Gonatus established himself on the throne, but in 146 Macedonia became a Roman province.

MACER, AEMILIUS, Roman jurist, who lived under Alexander Severus, or a little later. He was either a contemporary of, or wrote after Ulpianus, for he cites him several times.

MACHAON, surgeon to the Greeks in the Trojan war, was son of Aesculapius. He led, with his brother Podalirius, the Thessalian troops. He was killed by Eurypylus, son of Telephus.

MACRINUS, MARCUS OPELLIUS SEVERUS, Roman emperor from A.D. 217-218, who instigated the murder of Caracalla, and ascended the throne. After a disastrous Parthian campaign the soldiers proclaimed Elagabalus emperor. Macrinus was defeated and killed.

MACROBIUS, AMBROSIUS THEODOSIUS, Roman grammarian and philosopher, who wrote towards the beginning of the 5th cent. A.D.

MAEANDER, in *Ancient Geography*, a river of Asia Minor, rising near Celaenae, in Phrygia, flowing W. by a devious course, and after being joined by the Lycus, crossing Caria, fèll into the Icarian Sea. The word 'meander' is used literally and figuratively to denote a winding course.

MAECENUS, GAIUS CILNIUS, Roman patron of letters, born between 73-63 B.C., of an old Etruscan family, was a man of great wealth and culture, who became friend and adviser of Augustus. He died in 8 B.C. Was friend and patron of Horace and Virgil, q.q.v.

MAECIANUS, LUCIUS VOLUSIUS, Roman jurist of the 2nd cent. A.D., holding office under Antoninus Pius and Marcus Aurelius, who had been his pupil.

MAEDICA, district in the W. of Thrace.

MAELIUS, S., rich plebeian who purchased corn in Etruria during the great famine in Rome in 440 B.C. This was sold to the poor at a low price, or sometimes given to them. The patricians accused him of an ulterior motive. C. Servilius Ahala, commanded Maelius to appear before the dictator Cincinnatus. He refused to do this, so Ahala slew him; his estate was confiscated and his house pulled down.

MAENALUS, a mountain in Arcadia, famous as the haunt of Pan.

MAENIUS, C., with L. Furius Camillus, was consul in 338 B.C. It was he who captured the Antiate fleet.

MAEOTIS PALUS, inland sea, N. of the Black Sea: it was also known as Cimmerium or Bosporicum Mare, and now known as the Sea of Azov.

MAGI, caste of learned priests in ancient Persia. They were an aboriginal Median tribe who became predominant by their development of central Asian shamanism, practising exposure of the dead, and next-of-kin marriage. After their Aryan subjugation they assumed control of Zoroastrianism. Their supremacy was maintained throughout the Sassanian empire. They ultimately declined into jugglers, hence the English word magic.

MAGNENTIUS, emperor of the West from A.D. 350 to 353, who murdered Constans to obtain the throne. Being defeated by Constantius he committed suicide.

MAGO, one of the most common Carthaginian names, and borne by the reputed founder of the military power of Carthage, also the Punic admiral in the war with the elder Dionysius. The most famous of the name was the youngest of three sons of Hamilcar Barca who accompanied his brother Hannibal on his Italian expedition, and held important commands in the great victories of the first three years. After the battle of Cannae he marched through S. Italy and sailed to Carthage to report success. He was about to return to Italy with strong reinforcements, when he was ordered to go to aid his brother Hasdrubal, who was hard pressed in Spain. After various other engagements he was defeated in Cisalpine Gaul by the Romans in 203 B.C. Returning to Carthage he died on the way of wounds received in battle.

MAJORIANUS, JULIUS VALERIUS, emperor of the West from A.D. 457-61.

MALACA, coastal town of Hispania Baetica, founded by the Phoenicians.

MALACHI, minor Hebrew prophet, generally accepted author of the last O.T. Book, and possibly contemporary with Ezra and Nehemiah. The writer deplores the degeneracy of the priesthood and the falling off of religious observance, and urges repentance. He deals with the prosperity of the ungodly, and foretells the coming of another Elijah (John the Baptist) to prepare the way for the Messiah.

MALEA, headland of S. E. Laconia.

MALIS, part of S. Thessaly on the Maliacus Sinus, whose inhabitants were Dorians, and were members of the Amphictyonic League.

MAMURRA, Roman eques, born at Formiae was prefect in Caesar's army in Gaul and Spain.

MANASSEH, elder son of Joseph, over whom his younger brother Ephraim took precedence. The tribe of his descendants, which settled on both sides of the Jordan, were famous as warriors.—Another of the name was King of Judah, and son and successor of Hezekiah. He reigned from about 697-642 B.C., restored idolatry, persecuted the prophets, and was carried captive to Babylon.

MANCINUS, C. HOSTILIUS, was consul in 137 B.C. He was defeated by the Numantines and purchased safety by making peace, which the Senate refused to recognize, handing him over to the enemy, who would not accept him.

MANES, name given by the Latins to souls separated from the body. They were generally identified with the Lares, and so received the name Dii Manes. Public rites in their honour took place in February. Stones in Roman burial-places, and their funeral urns, were generally inscribed with the letter D. M. S., that is, *Dis Manibus Sacrum* ('sacred to the Manes Gods').

MANETHO, Egyptian writer, born at Diospolis, said to have lived in the days of Ptolemaeus Philadelphus at Mende or Heliopolis, and to have been a man of great learning. He was a priest, and interpreter or recorder of religious usages, and of religious and historical writings. There was probably more than one of this name. The only work of Manetho which has come down to us complete is a poem, in six books, in hexameter verse, on the influence of the stars. We have fragments of a history of the ancient kings of Egypt.

MANILIUS, (a) Consul 149 B.C., besieged Carthage. (b) Tribune 67 B.C., carried law conferring the command of the Mithridatic War to Pompey. (c) Author of didactic poem "Astronomica".

MANLIUS, name of a Roman gens, chiefly patrician. (a) MARCUS MANLIUS CAPITOLINUS, a distinguished soldier, one of the garrison of the Capitol while besieged by the Gauls. (b) TITUS MANLIUS IMPERIOSUS TORQUATUS, he went to the tribune Pomponius, who had arraigned his father for overstepping the limits of office, and threatened to kill him unless he desisted from the accusation in 365 B.C. (c) TITUS MANLIUS TORQUATUS, in 235 B.C., in his first consulship subjugated Sardinia. (d) CNAEUS MANLIUS VULSO, consul in 189 B.C., received Asia as his province.

MANTINEA, ancient town in Arcadia, on an elevated plain bounded N. by the plain of Orchomenus, and S. by that of Tegea. The Mantineans had a democratic form of government, and were closely connected with Argos. In 385 B.C. the Spartans took Mantineia and destroyed the city. After the battle of Leuctra, the inhabitants rebuilt the city, and in the vicinity of their town, the Spartans and Thebans fought their battle in 362 B.C., in which Epaminondas fell. The Mantineans joined the Achaean League. Pausanias visited the city in the 2nd cent. and found it large and flourishing.

MANTO, daughter of Tiresias, and mother of Mopsus, was a prophetess.

MANTUA, town in Gallia Transpadana, regarded by Virgil as his birthplace.

MARATHON, BATTLE OF, was fought in 490 B.C. between Greeks and Persians, on the plain of Marathon, on the N. E.

coast of Attica, about 22 m. from Athens. The Greek army was made up of 9,000 Athenians and 1,000 Plataeans, under Callimachus and Miltiades; the Persian army was five or six times stronger, being led by Datis and Artaphernes, generals of Darius. Most of the Persians succeeded in re-embarking in their ships, but some 6,000 lay dead, while the Greek losses were only 192 killed. The actual direction of the battle seems to have been in the hands of Miltiades.

MARCELLUS, MARCUS CLAUDIUS, nephew, and adopted son of Caesar, destined to be the successor of Augustus, whose daughter, Julia, he married; his early death in 23 B.C. was deeply mourned.

MARCIUS, Roman seer, whose prophetic verses were discovered in 213 B.C.; being placed among the Sibylline books in the Capitol.

MARCOMANNI, a German people, living originally between the Rhine and Danube, under Maroboduus, their chief: later they migrated to Bohemia and part of Bavaria with other tribes they carried on war with Marcus Aurelius, until peace was made by Commodus in A.D. 180.

MARDONIUS, son of Gobryas and nephew of Darius Hystaspis, was a Persian general. He was sent by Darius, in 492 B.C. to punish Eretria and Athens for the help given by them to the Ionians. His fleet was destroyed in a storm off Mt. Athos, while his land force was partly destroyed while passing through Macedonia. Under Xerxes he instigated an expedition against Greece. After Salamis, in 480 B.C., he was left to conquer Greece, being defeated in 479 B.C., near Plataea, by Pausanias, and slain.

MARIUS, GAIUS, Roman general and statesman, born at Cereatae, near Arpinum, of humble parents, he served under the younger Scipio Africanus in Spain; in Africa against Jugurtha; crushed the Cimbri and Teutones; and was hailed as saviour of the state being elected consul for the 6th time in 100 B.C. In the Social War, Marius rendered more service to the state. When war broke out with Mithridates, he was passed over in favour of Sulla, whom he tried to deprive of command. For a time a refugee, he came back, and with the aid of revenge on the

MAROBODUUS, king of the Marcomanni.

MARPESSA, mountain in Paros from whence came the Parian marble.

MARRUCINI, a warlike people of Italy, living along the right bank of the Aternus, their capital being Teate; they submitted to Rome in 304 B.C.

MARS, in *Classical Mythology*, Roman god of war and agriculture, was extensively worshipped by the Romans who claimed him as father of their founder Romulus. An altar to the god stood on the Campus Martius, which was the place of exercise for youths. He was identified by the Romans with the Greek Ares.

MARTIALIS, M. VALERIUS,   poet, born at Bibilis, about A.D. 40, who came to Rome in A.D. 64, and after remaining 35 years, returned to Bibilis in A.D. 100. He was famous, and had for patrons Titus and Domitian. He died in A.D. 104.

MASINISSA, Numidian prince whose history is intertwined with that of the wars between Rome and Carthage. In the second Punic War he fought on the side of the Carthaginians in Spain in 212 B.C., but later joined the Romans. On his return to Africa he was attacked by the Carthaginians, but held his ground until Scipio arrived in Africa in 204 B.C. With Scipio he reduced Cirta, capital of Syphax. In the battle of Zama in 202 B.C. Masinissa commanded the cavalry of the right wing. After the war he received most of the territories which had belonged to Syphax. Apart from disputes with Carthage, for the next half century Masinissa reigned in peace, dying in the first year of the third Punic War, in 149 B.C.

MASSAGETAE,   people of central Asia living on the peninsula between the Sea of Aral and the Caspian. Cyrus the Great was defeated and slain by them.

MASSICUS, mountain of Campania, famous for the celebrated Falernian wine, coming from the eastern slope.

MASSILIA (MARSEILLES),   Greek city in Gallia Narbonensis, founded by the Phocaeans, about 600 B.C., and one of the most important cities of commerce in the ancient world. In the war between Caesar and Pompey, in 49 B.C., it supported the latter, but was obliged to submit to Caesar. It became a seat of learning under the early emperors.

MATINUS, Apulian mountain jutting into the sea, is mentioned by Horace.

MATRONALIA, name given in ancient Rome to a festival celebrated by married women in honour of Juno on March 1st.

MATTHEW, GOSPEL OF SAINT, is compiled from two main sources, Mark and the Logia, with additional matter, especially at the beginning and end. It was written for Jewish readers. Its earliest date is A.D. 60-70, some place it 10 years later.

MAURETANIA, Roman province of N. W. Africa, roughly corresponding to Morocco and W. Algeria, was bounded E. by the province of Numidia. The Romans came into contact with the country during the war with Jugurtha, in 106 B.C.; Claudius formed it into a province.

MAUSOLUS, king of Caria. *See* MAUSOLEUM.

MAUSOLEUM, name given to a tomb or cenotaph of unusual size and importance. It was first used of the tomb of King Mausolus of Caria, Asia Minor, erected by his wife at Halicarnassus, in 353 B.C. This was accounted one of the seven wonders of the ancient world, and was 111 ft. in circumference, and 140 ft. high, crowned with colossal statues of Mausolus and his wife, Artemisia.

MAXENTIUS, MARCUS AURELIUS VALERIUS, Roman emperor from A.D. 306 to 312, was son of Maximian, who was colleague of Diocletian. He had seized power with the assistance of the praetorian guard and his reign came to an end when he was defeated by Constantine and drowned in course of his flight, in Oct. 312.

MAXIMIANUS I, MARCUS AURELIUS VALERIUS, Roman emperor from A.D. 286-305, was a Pannonian of humble parentage who was chosen by Diocletian to be his colleague, with the west as his portion. When the empire was divided into four, in 293, Maximianus had charge of Italy and Africa. When Diocletian abdicated in 305 he compelled Maximianus to follow his example. In 306 his son, Maxentius became Augustus, which induced Maximianus to resume the crown. He died by his own hand in A.D. 310—MAXIMIANUS II, Roman emperor from A.D. 305-311, is better known as Galerius.

MAXIMINUS, GAIUS JULIUS VERUS, Roman emperor from A.D. 235-38, was by birth a Thracian peasant, who rose to high command in the army. He was proclaimed emperor by the legions on the Rhine, and the assassination of Alexander Severus, within a month, cleared his way to the throne. He was successful against the Germans, but alienated his subjects by his tyranny, which caused an African revolt. He was murdered by the army.

MAXIMUS, MAGNUS CLEMENS, Roman emperor from A.D. 383-88, was born in Spain, and proclaimed emperor by the soldiers in Britain. He crossed to Gaul and defeated Gratian, his rule beyond the Alps being recognized by both Theodosius and Valentinian II. In 387 he invaded Italy, but was captured and put to death at Aquileia, by order of Theodosius.

MAXIMUS, PETRONIUS, Roman emperor who murdered Valentinian III, and married his widow in A.D. 455. He committed suicide the same year.

MAXIMUS TYRIUS, born at Tyre, was a Greek rhetorician and platonic philosopher, living during the time of the Antonines.

MEDAURA, city of N. Africa, the birthplace of Appuleius.

MEDIA, ancient country of W. Asia, S. and S. W. of the Caspian, whose capital was Ecbatana (Hamadan). Soon after 700 B. C., the Medes threw off the Assyrian yoke and became a great nation. In 549 B.C. Cyrus, who was subject to Astyages, rebelled, and by 500 B.C. was ruler of the empire of the Medes and Persians. With the Persian defeat by Alexander, Media became part of Alexander's empire. After his death in 323 B.C. it formed part of the kingdom of the Seleucidae, until the Parthians conquered it in 147 B.C.

MEDIAE MURUS, wall which ran from the Euphrates to the Tigris, dividing Mesopotamia and Babylonia.

MEDIOLANUM (MILAN), a town of the Insubres captured by the Romans in 222 B.C., and became a colony. From the days of Diocletian until it was taken by Attila, it was residence of the Western emperors. It became the see of S. Ambrose.

MEDON, son of Codrus, first Athenian archon.

MEDUSA, See GORGONES.

MEGALOPOLIS, city of S. Arcadia, on a plain, 20 m. S. W. of Tegea, on the Helisson, owing its origin to Epaminondas who founded it in 370 B.C., the year following Leuctra, as a defence against Sparta, and as the seat of the Arcadian federal diet, which consisted of 10,000 men.

MEGARA, city of ancient Greece, opposite the island of Salamis, 30 m. from Corinth. It was chief city of Megaris, early becoming important, and founding the colonies of Chalcedon, Byzantium and the Sicilian Megara. It became a member of the Athenian alliance. During the Peloponnesian War Megara supported Sparta.

MELA, ANNAEUS, father of Lucan, brother of L. Seneca, the philosopher, and youngest son of M. Annaeus Seneca, the rhetorician.

MELA POMPONIUS, born in Spain, in the time of Claudius, wrote a work on geography, *De Chorographia.*

MELAMPUS, introduced the worship of Dionysus into Greece; he was son of Amythaon, physician and prophet.

MELANIPPIDES, OF MELOS, a dithyrambic poet, flourishing about 480 B.C.

MELANTHIUS, painter of the 4th cent. B.C., was of the Sicyonian school.

MELAS, name of at least six rivers, whose waters were dark.

MELCHIZEDEK, priest-king of Salem, described as Priest of the Most High God: Abraham received his blessing and paid him tithes. As priest-king he is regarded as a prototype of the Messiah.

MELEAGER, in *Greek Legend,* famous hero and hunter. The goddess Artemis, offended by his father Oeneus, sent a boar to Aetolia, and all the heroes were asked to assist in killing it, among them came Atalanta. The boar was finally killed by

Meleager, who presented Atalanta with the skin and head, as she had given the animal its first wound.

MELIBOEA, coastal town of Thessaly, in Magnesia, of which Philoctetes was king; was situated between Mts. Pelion and Ossa.

MELISSA, village of Phrygia Magna, burial place of Alcibiades, to whom Hadrian ordered a statue to be erected there.

MELISSUS, a Greek philosopher of Samos; was of Ithagenes. —There was another of this name who was a Latin grammarian and comic poet, who arranged the library in the portico of Octavia, by order of Augustus.

MELITA, Mediterranean island, belonging to Carthage, and colonized by Phoenicians. The Romans took possession of it in the second Punic War. This island now called Malta, was scene of S. Paul's ship wreck.

MELOS, island of the Aegaean, being the most westerly of the Sporades. Its first occupants were probably Phoenicians, but it was Hellenized at an early date by Mynians and Dorians from Laconia. These sent a contingent to the Greek fleet at Salamis, but did not join the Attic League, and sought to remain neutral during the Peloponnesian War. In 416 B.C. the Athenians attacked the island, killing all capable of bearing arms, enslaved the women and children, and introduced 500 Greek colonists. Lysander restored the island to its old Dorian possessors.

MELPOMENE, *See* MUSAE.

MEMMIUS, (a) C. MEMMIUS, tribune of the plebs, in 111 B.C., opposed the oligarchic party at Rome, during the war against Jugurtha. He was killed by a mob. (b) C. GEMELLUS M., tribune of the plebs in 66, was accused of bribery, and left Rome. His wife, Fausta, was daughter of Sulla.

MEMNON, in *Greek mythology*, son of Tithonus and Eos, who came to assist the Trojans against the Greeks towards the end of the war. He was slain by Achilles.

MEMPHIS, ancient capital of Lower Egypt, on the left bank of the Nile, 14 m. S. of Cairo. It was founded by the first historic King of Egypt, Menes. Before Menes' days there had been a city here called White Wall. Under various dynasties it was embellished with pyramids and palaces, and, in spite of invasions, remained an important place until the rise of Alexandria, although not constantly the country's capital. The existing monuments include the colossal statues of Rameses II. The ruins were mostly employed for building Cairo.

MENANDER, an Athenian comic poet, chief representative of the New Comedy, said to have written 105 comedies. He was especially strong in moral maxims. Terence, called by Caesar the "half Menander," adapted four of his comedies from Menander.

MENAPIA, city of Bactriana, on the Zariaspis.

MENAPII, powerful people of N. Gallia Belgica, who originally dwelt on both sides of the Rhine, near its mouth, but were later driven from the right bank by the Usipetes and Tenchteri.

MENAS, also known as MENDORUS, a freedman of Pompey the Great, and one of the principal commanders of the fleet of Sextus Pompey in his war against Octavianus and Antony in 40 B.C.

MENDE or MENDAE, town of the W. coast of the Macedonian peninsula of Pellene, was a colony of Eretrians, who were celebrated for their wine.

MENDES, city of the Egyptian Delta, on the bank of a tributary of the Nile. Mendes, a he-goat, identified by the Greeks with Pan, was worshipped here.

MENECRATES, (a) Syracusan physician, in the court of Philip of Macedon, 359-336 B.C. (b) a physician mentioned by Galen, who wrote over 150 medical works.

MENEDEMUS, Greek philosopher who established the Eretrian school, and later went to Antigonus in Asia, where he committed suicide by fasting, about 265 B.C.

MENELAI PORTUS, ancient city of N. Africa, founded by Menelaus, where Agesilaus died.

MENELAIUM, mountain of Laconia, near Therapne, S. E. of Sparta, on which the heroum of Menelaus was situated.

MENELAUS, in *Greek Legend,* King of Sparta, brother of Agamemnon, and husband of Helen. At the Spartan court Paris was hospitably received but during the absence of Menelaus in Crete he carried off Helen, from which resulted the Trojan War. At the fall of Troy, Menelaus took Helen back.

MENENIUS LATANUS, (a) AGRIPPA, consul in 503 B.C., conquered the Sabines. (b) T., consul in 477 B.C., was defeated by the Etruscans.

MENES, according to Egyptian tradition, first king of Egypt. Herodotus says that he built Memphis, on ground reclaimed by turning the river from its course, and there built a magnificent Temple to Hephaestus (Pthah). Diodorus adds that he introduced the worship of the gods and their sacrifices, and a more luxurious form of living. Eusebius quotes an extract from Manetho describing him as a conquerer. Some have tried to identify him with Mizraim of the Bible. He is said to have been killed by a crocodile.

MENESTHEI PORTUS, harbour of Hispania Baetica, with an oracle of Menestheus.

MENESTHES, Greek warrior, slain by Hector, at the siege of Troy.

MENESTHEUS, (a) son of Peteus, King of Athens, who led against Troy. (b) Charioteer of Diomedes.

MENESTHUS, (a) son of Areithous, King of Arne in Boeotia, slain by Paris. (b) Son of Sperchius, nephew of Achilles, and a leader of the Myrmidons at Troy.

MENESTRATUS, a sculptor. His statues of Hercules and Hecate are famous; the latter stood in the opisthodomus of the temple of Diana at Ephesus.

MENIPPUS, Cynic philosopher, and a native of Gadara in Coele-Syria: his date is uncertain.

MENODOTUS, physician of Nicomedia, was pupil of Antiochus of Laodicea, and tutor of Herodotus of Tarsus, probably living at the beginning of the 2nd cent. A.D.

MENOECEUS, (a) A Theban, grandson of Pentheus, and father of Hipponome, Jocasta, and Creon. (b) Son of Creon, above, who ended his life because Tiresias had declared that his death would bring victory to his country, when the Argive heroes marched against Troy.

MENOETES, (a) Pilot of the ship of Gyas, who threw him overboard, for delaying his vessel at the games in honour of Anchises. (b) An Arcadian who fought for Aeneas in Italy, being slain by Turnus.

MENOETIUS, (a) son of Iapetus and Clymene, brother of Atlas, who was killed by Zeus, by lightning, in the battle of the Titans. (b) Son of Actor and Aegina, and father of Patroclus.

MENON, (a) Trojan soldier, slain by Leonteus. (b) Menon of Pharsalus, in Thessaly, who assisted the Athenians at Eion with twelve talents and 200 horsemen, being rewarded with the freedom of the city. (c) A Thessalian general of the Greek mercenaries in the army of Cyrus the Younger, when he marched into upper Asia, against his brother, Artaxerxes, in 401 B.C. He is the same as the Menon introduced into the Dialogue of Plato, which bears his name.

MENTOR, in *Greek Mythology*, the faithful and prudent friend of Ulysses to whom, when he left home for the Trojan War, he entrusted the care of his affairs and the education of Telemachus. The name Mentor has become synonymous with a wise counsellor.

MENTORES, people on the coast of Liburnia who also possessed the islands in the Adriatic, called Insulae Mentorides.

MERCURIUS, Roman divinity of commerce and gain. He had a temple near the Circus Maximus, as early as 495 B.C. He was identified by the Romans with the Greek Hermes. His festival was celebrated on May 25th, chiefly by members of the merchant guilds.

MERIONES, Cretan hero, son of Molus, who with his friend Idomeneus, led the Cretans in 80 ships against Troy.

MERMERUS, (a) son of Jason and Medea, was murdered with his brother Pheres, by his mother at Corinth. (b) Son of Pheres, above. (c) A Trojan slain by Antilocus. (d) A centaur present at the nuptials of Pirithous.

MERODACH-BALADAN, name of three kings of Babylon.

The second was a Chaldaean chief who, while Sargon II was occupied with the affairs of Samaria, captured Babylon, reigning from 721-710 B.C. He was then overthrown and retired to the Sealand; he reappeared in 703 B.C. and was defeated by Sennacherib. The other two kings were of no particular importance.

MEROE, ancient Nubian city, near the right bank of the Nile, 28 m. N. E. of Shendi, was founded on an earlier site after, 650 B.C., by Aspelut from Napata. During this early period a sun-temple, and a temple of Ammon were built, and Egyptian culture was dominant. A "middle period," starting about 300 B.C., showed Hellenistic influence, such as royal baths, frescoed chambers, cremation, and non-Egyptian native art. After a short Roman occupation, there followed in 10 B.C., the commencement of a "late" period of artistic decline lasting until A.D. 700.

MEROM, WATERS OF, ancient name for Lake Huleh, an expansion of the Jordan, N. of the Sea of Galilee. Joshua fought the Canaanites near here.

MEROPE, (a) one of the sisters of Phaeton (the Heliades). (b) Daughter of Atlas, and one of the Pleiades. (c) Daughter of Cypselus, and mother of Aepytus.

MEROPS, (a) King of Cos, whom Hera turned into an eagle, and placed among the stars. (b) King of the Æthiopians. (c) King of Rhyndacus, on the Hellespont, who was a celebrated soothsayer. (d) A Trojan, companion of Aeneas; was slain by Turnus in Italy.

MESAMBRIA, peninsula, near the Padargus, on the coast of Persis.

MESCHELA, big city on the coast of N. Africa, founded by Greeks returning from the Trojan war. It was captured by Eumachus, lieutenant of Agathocles.

MESEMBRIA, (a) famous town of Thrace on the Pontus Euxinus, at the foot of Mt. Haemus, founded by the people of Chalcedon and Byzantium, in the days of Darius Hystaspis. (b) Less important town of Thrace on the Aegaean, in the territory of the Cicones.

MESOMEDES, epigrammatic and lyric poet, under Hadrian

and the Antonines, was born in Crete, and was a freedman of Hadrian.

MESOPOTAMIA, district of Asia, between the Tigris and Euphrates, first so-called by the Greeks in the days of the Seleucidae. In Persian days it belonged to the satrapy of Babylonia.

MESPILA, city of Assyria on the E. side of the Tigris, mentioned by Xenophon as having been formerly an important city of the Medes, but in his days fell into decay.

MESSSALA, name of a distinguished Roman family. (a) M. Valerius Maximus Corvinus Messala, was consul in 263 B.C. and fought against the Carthaginians in Sicily. (b) M. Valerius Corvinus, fought on the republican side at Philippi in 42 B.C. was pardoned by the triumvirs, and became friend of Augustus, and one of his generals. There were several others of this name.

MESSALINA, VALERIA, wife of the Emperor Claudius, whom she dominated, and with his freedmen Pellas and Narcissus, virtually ruled the empire. Matters came to a head when, having become enamoured of Gaius Silius, she openly married him. Claudius ordered Messalina to be put to death.

MESSANA, coastal town of Sicily, was originally an abode of the Siceli, being called by them Zancle (sickle) on account of the shape of the harbour. It was colonized by the Chalcidians, being later captured by the Samians, who came to Sicily after the capture of Miletus by the Persians in 494 B.C. They in turn were driven out by Anaxilas, who changed the name, and brought a body of Messenians there from Rhegium. It was destroyed by the Carthaginians in 396 B.C. being rebuilt by Dionysius. Later it was captured by Agathocles. Among his mercenaries were some Mamertini, who had been sent from home under the protection of Mars, to seek their fortune. These were quartered in Messana. After the death of Agathocles, in 289 B.C. these mercenaries killed the male inhabitants, and took their wives, children, and property. The town was now named Mamertina, and the people Mamertini, but the term Messana was in more general use. The new occupants became involved in a war with Hieron of Syracuse; the Carthaginians came to assist the Mamertini, who had also applied to Rome for aid. This the Romans welcomed, as it gave them opportunity to get a footing in Sicily. So Messana became the cause of the first Punic War, in 264 B.C. The Mamertini turned out the Carthaginians and accepted the Romans, who retained their hold until the latest times.

MESSAPIA, Greek name of Calabria.

MESSAPIUM, mountain of Boeotia, near Anthedon, from which Messapus is said to have sailed to Italy.

MESSE, town and harbour of Laconia.

MESSEIS, (a) Famous fountain in Pherae in Thessaly. (b) A fountain in Laconia, near Therapne.

MESSENIA, country of ancient Greece, bounded E. by Laconia, N. by Elis and Arcadia, and surrounded by the sea on the W. and S. It was separated from Laconica by the mountain chain Taygetus, and from Elis and Arcadia by the Neda, and the high land which runs between the Neda and the source of the Pamisus. Messenia is said, by Pausanias, to have been the most fertile province of Peloponnesus. On the division of the Peloponnesus, after the Dorian conquest under the Heraclidae, Messenia fell to the share of Cresphontes, who had his capital in Stenyclerus, and divided the country into five districts. The history of Messenia belongs to the general history of Greece, and is particularly connected with Sparta. The chief towns were Pylos and Mothone, the bay of Pylos being the best harbour in the Peloponnesus. The only important inland town was Messene, at the foot of Mt. Ithome, on the summit of which was the citadel, which Strabo refers to as one of the two strongest places in Peloponnesus.

MESSENIACUS SINUS, a broad gulf washing the S. shore of Messenia.

MESSIUS, C., tribune of the plebs in 56 B.C., when he introduced a bill for Cicero's recall from exile, also the Messian law assigning extraordinary powers to Cm. Pompey.

MESSIUS CICIRRHUS, an ugly disfigured Oscan, whose wordy war with Sarmentus is humorously described by Horace, in his Brundisian journey.

MESTLETA, Iberian city, in Asia, on the Cyrus.

MESYLA, town of Pontus, between Tavium and Comana.

METABUS, father of Camilla, and chief of the Volsci.

METAGENES, (a) Athenian comic poet, contemporary with Aristophanes. (b) Architect, son of Chersiphron. (c) An Athenian architect in the time of Pericles, who was engaged among others, in erecting the great temple at Eleusis.

METALLINUM, Roman colony in Lusitania, on the Anas, near Augustus Emerita.

METANIRA, wife of Celeus, and mother of Triptolemus.

METAPONTIUM, famous Greek city in S. Italy, on the Tarentine Gulf, later destroyed by the Samnites, and peopled by a colony of Achaeans. It fell into the hands of the Romans in the war against Pyrrhus, but revolted to Hannibal after Cannae. No mention is made of the city after the second Punic War.

METAURUS, river of Umbria, scene of Hasdrubal's defeat in 207 B.C.

METELLUS, plebeian family of Rome. (a) L. Caecilius Metellus, consul in 251 B.C., when he defeated the Carthaginians in Sicily, and again in 247 B.C., he was afterwards pontifex maximus. He rescued the Palladium from the fire in the temple of Venus, losing his sight. (b) Q. Caecilius M. Macedonicus, grandson of the above, was praetor in 148 B.C., when he defeated Andriscus in Macedonia. He built two temples in Rome. (c) Q. Caecilius M. Numidicus, nephew of the above, consul in 109 B.C. fought against Jugurtha in Numidia successfully. He was censor in 102 B.C., being banished two years later through intrigues, but was recalled. (d) Q. Caecilius M. Pius, son of the above, was praetor in 89 B.C., and commander in the Social War. (e) Q. Caecilius M. Pius Scipio, adopted son of the above, who fought for Pompey in the civil war, and after Pharsalia, crossed to Africa, and commanded the Pompeian troops. He was defeated at Thrapsus by Caesar in 46 B.C., and took his own life. (f)

Q. Caecilius M. Creticus, grandson of (b) was consul in 69 B.C., and fought against Crete, which was subdued in three years. (g) L. Caecilius Metellus, brother of the above, was praetor in 71 B.C. (h) M. Caecilius Metellus, cousin of the above, was praetor in 69 B.C., and presided at the trial of Verres.

METHODIUS, surnamed Patarensis, was bishop of Olympus, then at Patara, in Lycia, and later of Tyre in Phoenicia. He lived in the 3rd cent. A.D., and died in the beginning of the 4th.

METHONE, (a) Town of S.W. Messenia, with a good harbour, which after the conquest of Messenia became one of the Lacedaemonian harbours. (b) Greek town in Macedonia, on the Thermaic Gulf: Philip lost an eye at the siege of this place. (c) Town of Sicily, mentioned by Homer. (d) Ancient town of Argolis, on the peninsula of the same name.

METHUSELAH, son of Enoch and grandfather of Noah, is stated in the O.T. to have lived 969 years, the greatest age among the patriarchs; the Samaritan text gives his age as 720 years.

METHYDRIUM, small town of Arcadia, on the road from Olympia to Orchomenus.

METHYMNA, second city of Lesbos, at its N. extremity, having a good harbour. The poet Arion, and historian Hellanicus, were born there. In the Peloponnesian War it remained faithful to Athens. It was sacked by the Spartans in 406 B.C., and did not recover its former prosperity.

METIOCHUS, (a) Son of Miltiades, taken prisoner by the Phoenicians, and carried to the Persian court. Darius received him kindly and gave him a Persian lady for his wife. (b) Athenian author, friend of Pericles.

METIC, a resident alien. In Athens and other places such had no rights of citizenship but had to pay the metic taxes. He was required by law to have a guardian, or patron. Occasionally special privileges were granted to individuals.

METIS, in Greek Mythology, daughter of Oceanus, the first wife of Zeus, who was so wise and prudent that Zeus, fearing he might have a child destined to become wiser than himself, devoured her when she became pregnant, with the result that Athena was born from the head of Zeus.

METON, Athenian astronomer, introducer in about 432 B.C., of the sytem of a cycle of nineteen years by which he adjusted the course of the sun and moon.

METOPUS, a Pythagorean of Metapontum, who wrote a work on virtue, fragments of which have been preserved by Stobaeus.

METROBIUS, favourite actor of the dictator Sulla; he performed in women's parts.

METRODORUS, born in Lampsacus, in 330 B.C., was one of four principal exponents of Epicureanism.

METROPHANES, general of Mithridates, who sent him with troops to aid Archelaus in 87 B.C. He was at last defeated by the Roman general Brutius Sura.

METROPOLIS, (a) Most ancient city of Phrygia. (b) City in the plain of the Cayster, in Lydia, between Ephesus and Smyrna. (c) A town of Thessaly, in Histiaeotis, near the Peneus. (d) Town of Acarnania, between the Ambracian Gulf and the Achelous.

METTIUS, dictator of Alba, torn asunder by chariots, by order of Tullus Hostilius, third king of Rome, for treachery.

METULUM, chief town of the Iapydes in Illyricum, where Augustus nearly lost his life in subduing the place.

MEVANIA, ancient city of Umbria, on the Tinea, between Rome and Ancona, famous for white oxen. It had brick fortifications.

MEZENTIUS, King of the Etruscans, at Agylla, expelled by his subjects for cruelty, taking refuge with Turnus, King of the Rutulians, whom he aided in war against Aeneas and the Trojans.

MICAH, minor Hebrew prophet, born at Moresheth, near Gath, and a younger contemporary with Isaiah, who prophesied in the reigns of Jotham, Ahaz, and Hezekiah. The early chapters of his book denounce oppression and drunkenness and predict the ruin of the nations. Messianic predictions of restoration and future glory follow, while the closing chapters deal with the controversy between God and His people.

MICCION, a painter, disciple of Zeuxis, who is mentioned by Lucian.

MICIPSA, King of Numidia, and eldest son of Masinissa, after whose death in 148 B.C., the sovereignty was divided between Micipsa and his brother Gulussa and Mastanabal. His two brothers dying, he was left with undivided power, which he held to his death in 118 B.C., leaving the kingdom to his sons Adherbal and Hiempsal, and their adopted brother Jugurtha.

MICYTHUS, son of Choerus, a slave of Anaxilas, tyrant of Rhegium, who rose in his master's confidence, and at whose death, in 476 B.C., he left him guardian of his infant sons, and regent until their majority. This task he rendered faithfully, then settled at Tegea for the remainder of his life.

MIDAEUM, city of Phrygia Epictetus, where Sextus Pompeius was captured by Antony's troops, in 35 B.C.

MIDAS, legendary King of Phrygia, who, having done a favour to Silenus, asked that all he touched should be turned into gold. Finding that even his food turned to gold before it reached his lips, he asked Bacchus to revoke the gift. By command of the god he bathed in the springs of the river Pactolus, and the baleful power left him.

MIDEA, town in Argolis, perhaps originally Persepolis, is said to have been named after the wife of Electryon, who resided here. It was destroyed by Argos, soon after the Persian wars.

MIDIAS, wealthy Athenian, and violent enemy of Demosthenes. In 354 B.C., Midias assaulted Demosthenes, during the festival of Dionysia. Demosthenes accused him, but the speech he wrote for the occasion was not delivered, since Demosthenes dropped the case, in consequence of receiving the sum of thirty minae. The speech is extant.

MIEZA, Macedonian town in Emathia, S.W. of Pella, near the frontiers of Sicily.

MILETOPOLIS, city of Mysia, in Asia Minor, at the junction of the Rhyndacus and Macestus.

MILETUS, son of Apollo and Aria, being beloved of Minos and Sarpedon, he accepted the latter, and fled from Minos to Asia, where he built the city of Miletus.

MILETUS, great and ancient city of Asia Minor on the Gulf of Latmos, near the mouth of the Meander, was capital of the Ionian colonies of Greece. It was famous for woollen goods, and traded with the whole Mediterranean coast, establishing many colonies on the Propontis and Euxine, as well as Naucratis, in Egypt. It was captured by Croesus, and in 557 B.C., by the Persians, it headed the great Ionian revolt against Persia, but was destroyed on its suppression in 49 B.C. Alexander captured it, and it passed to the kingdom of Pergamum, and finally to Rome. It was birthplace of Thales, and other Greek writers.

MILICHUS, Phoenician god, represented as son of a satyr and the nymph Myrice, and with horns.

MILICHUS, freedman of Flavius Scaevinus, who gave Nero first information of Piso's conspiracy, in A.D. 66, and was liberally rewarded, assuming the surname of Soter.

MILLEARIUM AUREUM,   a sheathed gilt bronze column in the Roman forum, giving the distances to chief towns on the roads radiating through the 37 gates. It was reared by Augustus in 29 B.C.

MILO, famous athlete of ancient times, belonging to Crotona, S. Italy, who gained many victories at the Olympic and other games. In 511 B.C., he was general of the army which defeated the Sybarites.

MILTAS, a Thessalian, called by Plutarch a seer, was contemporary with Plato and a follower of his philosophy. He served in the army of Dion against Dionysius the younger, encouraging the troops when alarmed by an eclipse.

MILTIADES, Athenian soldier, son of Cimon q.v., who succeeded his brother Stesagoras as tyrant of the Thracian Chersonese. He incurred the hostility of Darius, who then made war on Greece. Miltiades sought refuge in Athens. He was one of the ten generals chosen, and under him the Greeks won the battle of Marathon, in 490 B.C. He was later entrusted with 70 ships to carry on the war against the Persians, and he attacked the island of Paros. He failed, and was condemned to pay a fine. Not being able to do so he was thrown into prison, where he died of a wound. Cimon, his son, later paid the fine.

MILTO, name of the favourite mistress of Cyrus, also known as Aspasia.

MILTOCYTHES, Thracian officer, of Cyrus the younger, who, after the death of Cyrus, deserted the Greeks, and went over to the side of the King with 30 cavalry and 300 infantry.

MILYAS, originally the name of all Lycia, but later applied to the tableland in the N., between Cadmus and the Taurus, and extending into Pisidia.

MIMAS MONS, (a) Mountain chain of Ionia. (b) Mountain chain of Thrace.

MIMNERMUS, a native of Smyrna, who became a Greek elegiac poet, flourishing from about 634-600 B.C., being contemporary with Solon. Only a few fragments of his works remain.

MINCIUS, river of Gallia Transpadana, flowing through Lake Benacus, and emptying into the Po, below Mantua.

MINDARUS, a Lacedaemonian who succeeded Astyochus as commander of the fleet in 411 B.C., and was defeated and killed by the Athenians near Cyzicus.

MINERVA, in *Classical Mythology,* the Italian goddess, whom the Romans identified with the Greek Athena; she was one of the chief Roman deities, worshipped in the Capitoline temple, and regarded as goddess of wisdom, and patroness of arts and crafts. After her identification with Athena she became goddess of war. Her festival was held from 19th to the 23rd day of March.

MINERVAE ARX, a hill on the coast of Calabria, where Aeneas is supposed to have landed.

MINERVAE PROMONTORIUM, rocky headland of Campania, S.E. of Surrentum, on the top of which was a temple of Minerva, said to have been built by Ulysses. The Greeks regarded this promontory as the N.W. boundary of Oenotria.

MINOS, in *Greek legend,* king and law-giver of Crete, son of Zeus by Europa, and husband of Pasiphae, daughter of Helios, who brought forth the Minotaur. He is represented by some as a monster of cruelty, and by others as an able monarch, who made Crete a great sea-power, cleared the sea of pirates, and by wise government promoted the welfare of his people. After death he was made one of the judges of the dead.

MINOTAUR, in *Greek Legend,* a monster with the head of a bull, and the body of a man. He was offspring of Pasiphae, wife of Minos, and a bull sent to Minos from Poseidon. It was kept in a labyrinth, and given a yearly tribute of seven youths, and seven maidens from Athens. Finally Theseus slew it.

MINTHE, mountain of Elis, in Triphylia, near Pylos.

MINTURNAE, town of Latium, near a grove sacred to Marica, the nymph. It was close to the marshes, formed by the overflow of the Liris, where Marius was captured.

MINUCIA, a vestal priestess in 337 B.C., whose passion for gay dress made her conduct suspect. An inquiry proving this to be so, she was buried alive.

MINUCIANUS, (a) Greek rhetorician, contemporary with Hermogenes of Tarsus, with whom he quarrelled. (b) Son of Nicagoran, an Athenian, was a rhetorician in the reign of Gallienus, 260-68 A.D.

MINUCIUS, FELIX M., first Latin Christian apologist, of the third century, who wrote the *Octavius,* in defence of Christianity.

MINYAE, ancient Greek people of Thessaly, whose ancestral hero, Minyas, migrated to N. Boeotia, establishing the empire of the Minyae, with its chief town Orchomenus, q.v. As the Argonauts were nearly all descended from the Minyae, they were called by that name. The Minyae founded a colony in Lemnos, whence they went to Elis Triphylia, and to the island of Thera.

MIOCENE, in *Geology* name given to an era between the Oligocene and Pliocene periods. The rocks of the era are chiefly unconsolidated clays and sands, limestones, and conglomerates, being found in France, Belgium, Switzerland, Austria and the Mediterranean (also America); the animals of this period included the mastodon, dinotherium, rhinoceros, the three-toed proto-hippus, and the hippotherium.

MIROBRIGA, (a) Coastal town of the Celtici, in Lusitania. (b) A Roman municipium in the territory of the Turduli, in Hispania Baetica, on the road from Emerita to Caesaraugusta.

MIRRORS, of polished bronze were used by the Egyptians, Greeks, and Romans.

MISENUM, headland in Campania, S. of Cumae, taking its name from Misenus, companion and trumpeter of Aeneas, who was drowned and buried here. Under Augustus Misenum became chief Roman naval base in Italy.

MISENUS, (a) Companion of Ulysses. (b) Pilot of Aeneas' fleet.

MISHNA, Jewish code embodying the oral law, was compiled and edited by Rabbi Jehudah el Nasi, about 200 A.D. It is in six parts. The Mishna, long handed down orally, is written in late Hebrew. Further commentaries were embodied in the Gemara, and the two works form the Talmud.

MITHRADATIS REGIO, district of Sarmatia Asiatica, W. of the Rha, so called because Mithridates took refuge there in the days of Claudius.

MITHRAS, god of light and wisdom among the Persians. Under the emperors his worship was introduced to Rome.

MITHRIDATES or MITHRADATES, (a) Kings of Pontus, the best known being Mithridates VI, the Great, famous for his wars with the Romans. His reign was from 120-63 B.C. He is said to have known 25 languages. After extending his empire, he ventured against Rome. The first Mithridatic war was from 88-84 B.C. He drove Ariobarzanes from Cappadocia, and Nicomedes from Bithynia, and at last made himself master of the Roman province of Asia. During the winter he ordered all Roman and Italian citizens in Asia to be slaughtered; 80,000 are said to have been killed in one day. Now Sulla had received command of the war against Mithridates, and went into Greece in 87 B.C. Archelaus, Mithridates' general, was defeated twice by Sulla in Boeotia in 86 B.C., the King himself being defeated by Fimbria, in Asia, about the same time. Mithridates sued for peace which was granted in 84 B.C. The second Mithridatic War (83-82 B.C.) was caused by unprovoked attacks on Murena, who had been left in command in Asia by Sulla. Murena invaded Mithridates' dominions, but was defeated, and was ordered by Sulla to discontinue. The third Mithridatic War lasted from 74 B.C., to the death of Mithridates in 63. It came about owing to the King seizing Bithynia, which had been left by Nicomedes III to the Roman people. The consul Lucullus conducted the war with success, and in 73 B.C., relieved Cyzicus, which was besieged, and in two years drove the King from Pontus, compelling him to take refuge with his son-in-law, Tigranes, King of Armenia, who espoused the cause of his father-in-law, whereupon Lucullus marched into Armenia, defeated Tigranes and Mithridates in 69 and 68 B.C., but his soldiers having mutinied Lucullus could not follow up his successes, and Mithridates recovered Pontus. In 66 B.C., Lucullus was succeeded by Pompey in his command. Pompey defeated Mithridates, whose son-in-law now refused him sanctuary, so he marched into Colchis, and made his way to Panticapaeum, capital of the Cimmerian Bosporus. He intended to march around the N. and W. coasts of the Euxine, and invade Italy, having collected the Sarmatians and Getae (two wild tribes) on the way. But his followers were becoming disaffected, and his son Pharnaces rebelled against him, and was joined by all the army and the citizens of Panticapaeum, who proclaimed him King. Mithridates took his own life, in 63 B.C., after reigning 57 years. (b) Kings of Parthia.

MITHROBARZANES, (a) Father-in-law of Datames, whom he joined in revolt from the King of Persia, but afterward, having deserted with his troops, was slain by Datames. (b) General of the Cappadocian forces in the Persian army at the battle of the Gronicus, where he was slain. (c) A general of Tigranes, who was sent to oppose the Romans under Lucullus, but was slain by them.

MITRA, (a) Article of male attire consisting of a brazen belt, stuffed with wool, lined with leather, and worn between the breastplate and kilt of a soldier. (b) In female attire, a covering for the head.

MITYS, river of Macedonia, N. of the Haliacmon, falling into the Thermaicus Sinus.

MITYLENE, see MYTILENE.

MNASALCAS, epigrammatic poet of Sicyonia, of uncertain date.

MNASEAS, born at Patara, in Lycia, was pupil of Eratosthenes, and a famous grammarian, who wrote two works, one entitled *Periplus,* the other being a collection of oracles given at Delphi.

MNASIPPUS, Spartan admiral who led the fleet of 60 ships against Corcyra, in 373 B.C. At first successful, he became careless, being defeated and slain by the Corcyreans.

MNESARCHUS, (a) Son of Euthyphron, and father of Pythagoras. (b) Grandson of the above, and son of Pythagoras and Theano. (c) Stoic philosopher, disciple of Panaetius, taught at Athens about 110 B.C. Antiochus of Ascalon was among his pupils.

MNESICLES, Greek architect of the Propylaea of the Acropolis which took five years to build (437-433 B.C.).

MNESILOCHUS, (a) Tyrant of Athens. (b) Son of Euripedes by Choerile.

MNESIMACHUS, comic poet of middle comedy, some fragments of whose plays are extant.

MNESITHIDES, tyrant of Athens.

MNESITHEUS, a native of Athens, who practised as a physician in the 4th cent. B.C. He is mentioned by Galen.

MNESTER, famous pantomime actor in the days of Caligula and Claudius, and one of the lovers of the Empress Messalina, who was executed upon the ruin of the latter.

MNESTHEUS, Trojan who went to Italy with Aeneas.

MOABITES, ancient Semitic people related to the Hebrews, and, according to Gen. 19, were descended from Moab. They were often at war with Israel and Judah, and were defeated by David. Solomon married Moabite wives, and introduced the worship of their god Chemosh into Jerusalem. The Moabites again became independent, and Mesha, who set up the Moabite stone, won victories over Israel. The history of Moab ends with the Babylonian conquest.

MOABITE STONE, a stone of black basalt from Dibon, Moab, discovered in 1868, by Klien, and shattered by its Beduin custodians. It was recovered and reconstructed. There are 34 lines of primitive Hebrew script, in the Moabite dialect of about 850 B.C., describing Israel's conflict with Mesha.

MOAGETES, tyrant of the Cibyrates in Upper Phrygia, who was at enmity with Rome during the war with Antiochus the Great, for which he was condemned by the consul, to pay a large fine.

MOCA, city of Arabia Petraea, which was regarded as a holy city under the Roman supremacy, having its own laws. Coins from this city of the era of the Antonines and Septimus Severus are still extant.

MODICA, town of Gallia Transpadana, on the Lamdrus, N. of Mediolanum, where Theodoric built a palace, and Theodolinda, queen of the Langobards a magnificent church.

MOERAE, called Parcae by the Romans; the Fates, who were three in number—Clotho, the spinning Fate; Lachesis, who assigned to man his fate; Atropos, who broke the thread of life.

MOERIS, very ancient King of Egypt, mentioned by Herodotus as reigning 900 years before his own visit to Egypt in about 450 B.C. Moeris is said to have fashioned a lake, and to have connected it by a canal to the Nile. He built two pyramids in the Lake, with stone statues, seated on thrones, surmounting them, intended to represent himself and his wife.

MOERO, poetess of Byzantium, wife of Andromachus, and mother of the poet Homer. (Not the epic one.)

MOEROCLES, Athenian orator, born at Salamis, and contemporary with Demosthenes.

MOESIA, country of Europe, bounded S. by Thrace and Macedonia, W. by Illyricum and Pannonia, N. by the Danube, and E. by the Pontus Euxinus. It was conquered in the reign of Augustus, being made a Roman province in 44 A.D.

MOGONTIACUM, (MAINZ), town on the left bank of the Rhine, in the territory of the Vangiones, and subsequently capital of the province of Germania Prima. It was a Roman municipium, fortified by Drusus, and until the downfall of the empire, one of the chief Roman fortresses on the Rhine.

MOLOCH, Canaanite god of fire, a Semitic word meaning king.

MOLORCHUS, mythical founder of Molorchia, near Nemea, who entertained Hercules when he went against the Nemean lion.

MOLOSSI, people occupying a strip of country in Epirus, along the W. bank of the Arachthus. They were the most powerful inhabitants of Epirus. Their first king was Alexander, who was killed in Italy in 330 B.C. Their chief town was Ambracia. Famous hounds were bred here.

MOLYCRIUM, town in the extreme S. of Aetolia, founded by the Corinthians, but after acquired by the Aetolians.

MONA, (Anglesey), island of the coast of the Ordovices in Britain, a chief seat of the Druids. It was invaded by Suetonius Paulinus and conquered by Agricola in 78 A.D.

MONAESES, (a) Parthian general, thought to be the same as Surenas, the general of Orodes, who defeated Crassus. (b) Parthian noble who went over to Antony. (c) General of Vologeses I, a Parthian king, in the reign of Nero.

MONIMA, wife of Mithridates, a Greek woman, who was put to death by the king's orders when he fled to Armenia in 72 B.C.

MONOECI PORTUS or HERCULIS MONOECI PORTUS, port on the Ligurian coast, founded by the Massilians. The town had a temple of Hercules.

MONTANUS, CURTIUS, was exiled in 67 A.D., by Nero, but recalled at his father's petition. In the early days of Vespasian he attacked the notorious delator Aquilius Regulus in the Senate.

MONTANUS, VOLTIENUS, rhetorician in the reign of Tiberius, who died in exile in the Balearic Islands in A.D. 25.

MOPSIA or MOPSOPIA, ancient name of Attica.

MOPSUESTIA, city of Cicilia of which Theodore, the great exegete, was Bishop.

MOPSUS, in *Greek Legend,* (a) Son of Manto, the daughter of Tiresias and Apollo. Having built the city of Mallos in Cicilia, together with Amphilochus, a quarrel arose about its possession, in which both were slain. (b) One of the Lapithae. Son of Apollo and a nymph, he took part in the voyage of the Argonauts, for whom he acted as seer.

MORGETES, ancient people of S. Italy, dwelling near Rhegium.

MORIMENE, N.W. district of Cappadocia, assigned by the Romans to Galatia, was famous for its grazing pastures.

MORINI, people of N. Gaul, living on the coast of Gallia Belgica.

MORITASGUS, brother of Cavarinus, King of the Senones at the arrival of Caesar in Gaul.

MORMO, hobgoblin with which the Greeks used to threaten their children.

MORPHEUS, son of Sleep, and god of dreams.

MORS, god of death: Thanatos to the Greeks.

MORSIMUS, son of Philocles, and brother of Melanthius, a tragic poet; the brothers were made the object of bitter attack by Aristophanes, on account of the quality of Morsimus' poetry, and his depravity.

MORYCHUS, tragic poet, contemporary with Aristophanes, notorious for gluttony.

MOSCHA, sea-port on the N.E. coast of Arabia Felix, a chief center of trade between Arabia and India.

MOSCHUS, of Syracuse, a Bucolic poet, some of whose verses have come down to us.

MOSELLA, river in Gallia Belgica, rising in Mt. Vogesus, flowing N.E. and joining the Rhine at Confluentes.

MOSES, Hebrew law-giver, and leader of the Israelites from Egypt, was son of Amram, a Levite, and Jochebed, and was younger brother of Miriam and Aaron. He was adopted by Pharaoh's daughter. After slaying an Egyptian task-master, who had ill-treated an Israelite, he fled to Midian. He received a Divine call at Horeb to return to Egypt, from which he later led the Israelites to Canaan, receiving the Decalogue from Jehovah, on Mt. Sinai. After glimpsing the Promised Land from Pisgah, he died at the age of 120, leaving two sons, Gershom and Eliezer.

MOSTENI, city of Lydia, S.E. of Thyatira, destroyed by an earthquake in 17 A.D.

MOSYNOECI, people dwelling in Pontus, E. of Cerasus, described by Xenophon as being warlike. Their houses were of wood, and conical. They chose their own king, who was guarded in a house higher than the rest, and was maintained by public money. If he displeased the commons, they cut off supplies and starved him until he died.

MOTYA, ancient town of N.W. Sicily, on an island, close to the coast, with which it was connected. It was of Phoenician foundation, possessing a good harbour. It passed to the Carthaginians and was later taken by Dionysius of Syracuse; it was finally captured by Himilco, a Carthaginian general, who carried the inhabitants to Lilybaeum, which he had founded in the vicinity in 497 B.C. From now on nothing is heard of Motya.

MUCIA, wife of Cn. Pompey, from whom she was divorced in 62 B.C. She later married Aemilius Scaurus, stepson of Sulla. Mucia went to Sicily in 39 B.C., to mediate between Sextus (her son by Pompey), and Augustus, who treated her with great respect.

MUCIANUS, (a) P. LICINIUS CRASSUS DIVES, son of P. Mucius Scaevola, and adopted by P. Licinius Crassus Dives, was consul in 131 B.C., when he was defeated by Aristonicus in Asia. He succeeded Scipio Nasica as pontifex maximus. (b) LICINIUS MUCIANUS, consul in 52, 70, and 75 A.D. He had command of Syria after the death of Nero.

MULCIBER, a surname of Vulcan, frequently used by Latin poets.

MUMMIUS, (a) L., tribune of the plebs in 187 B.C., and praetor in 177 B.C. (b) L. Achaicus, son of the above was praetor in

146 B.C., established the province of Achaia, defeated the army of the Achaean League, and destroyed Corinth.

MUNDA, Roman colony and town in Hispania Baetica, scene of the victory of Cn. Scipio over the Carthaginians in 216 B.C., and of Julius Caesar over Pompey's sons in 45 B.C.

MUNYCHIA, one of the three harbours of Piraeus, fortified by Themistocles.

MURENA LICINIUS, (a) P., Killed in the wars of Marius and Sulla, in 82 B.C. (b) L., brother of the above, served under Sulla in Greece. (c) Son of the above, served under his father in the second Mithridatic war, and under Lucullus in the third. (d) A. Terentius Varro, probably son of the preceding, was adopted by A. Terentius Varro, whose name he took. He subdued the Salassi in the Alps, in 25 B.C., and founded the town of Augusta: was consul suffectus in 23 B.C.

MUSA, ANTONIUS, famous physician at Rome, was brother to Euphorbus, and physician to Augustus.

MUSAE, in *Greek Mythology,* divinities who presided over liberal art. They were supposed to be daughters of Zeus, and companions of Apollo. The muses were at first three in number, and nine in later legend. They were: Clio, muse of history, represented with an open scroll; Euterpe, of lyric poetry, with a flute; Thalia, of comedy and pastoral poetry; Melpomene, of tragedy; Terpsichore, of dancing; Erato, of love songs; Polyhymnia, of sacred song; Urania, of astronomy; and Calliope, of epic poetry, represented with stylus and tablet.

MUSONIUS RUFUS, C., famous Stoic philosopher, son of a Roman eques, was banished by Nero to the island of Gyaros in A.D. 66, under pretext of having knowledge of the conspiracy of Piso, but returned under Galba.

MUSTI, Carthaginian town, near the Bagradas, where Regulus killed an enormous serpent.

MYCENAE, ancient Greek city in Argolis in Peloponnesus, the center of the so-called Mycenaean civilization, and residence and burial place of Agamemnon. It was destroyed in 468 B.C., by the Argives.

MYCERINUS, son of Cheops, King of Egypt, who succeeded his uncle to the throne. He began to build a pyramid, but died before it was finished.

MYCHUS, harbour in the E. of Phocis, on the Crissaean Gulf.

MYCI, a people of Asia, of the fourteenth satrapy of Persian empire.

MYGDONIA, name of three districts, one in E. Macedonia, the second in N. Asia Minor, and the other in N.E. Mesopotamia.

MYLAE, (a) Coastal town of Sicily, on a headland jutting far into the sea, with a harbour, was founded by Messana. It was here that Agrippa defeated the fleet of Sextus Pompeius, in 36 B.C. (b) Town in Thessaly.

MYOS HORMOS, important trading center on the Red Sea, built by Ptolemy II.

MYRON, Greek sculptor, born about 480 B.C., at Eleutherae, in Boeotia. With Polycletus he was a disciple of Ageladas. He was younger contemporary of Phidias. His most famous works were the *Discobolus,* and the statue of Marsyas.

MYRTOUM MARE, part of the Aegaean probably taking its name from the small island of Myrtus.

MYS, one of the most distinguished engravers of ancient times, who executed the battle of the Lapithae and the Centaurs, and other figures, on the shield of Phidias' bronze statue of Minerva, in the Acropolis at Athens.

MYSIA, name of an ancient division of Asia Minor, forming the N.W. extremity of that peninsula, bounded N. by the Propontis, W. by the Hellespont and Aegaean, S. by Lydia, and E. by the river Rhyndacus. Mysia became subject to the Lydian monarchy, after the fall of which it became part of one of the satrapies of the Persian empire, which also included Lydia. It was later, in turn, under the Macedonians, the kings of Pergamum, and the Romans, under whom it was part of the province of Asia. The principal towns were Pergamum, Cyzicus, Abydos, Lampsacus, and Adramyttium.

MYTILENE or MITYLENE, capital of Lesbos, on the E. of

the island. It was early colonized by the Aeolians, and gained importance as a naval power, founding colonies in Mysia and Thrace. About the beginning of the 7th cent. B.C., the Mytilenaeans and the Athenians disputed possession of one of these colonies, Sigeum, at the mouth of the Hellespont. After the Persian war Mytilene became allied with Athens, but headed a revolt in 428 B.C., the suppression of which robbed Mytilene of its power.

N

NAARDA, a Babylonian town, where there was a Jewish academy.

NAARMALCHA, sometimes NAHRMALCHA, the largest canal joining the Tigris and Euphrates, running just S. of the Median wall. Its digging was ascribed to Gobares, a governor. The canal was repaired when Seleucia was built by Nicator, at its junction with the Tigris. Further repairs were executed under Trajan, Severus, and Julian.

NABATAEI, Arabian people, descendants of Ishmael's eldest son, first living in the N.W. of the peninsula, with the Moabites and Edomites on the E. and S.E. Under Trajan their country was included in the Roman province of Arabia.

NABIS, tyrant of Lacedaemon, on the death of Machanidas, in 207 B.C., was notorious for his cruelty and rapacity. With a large body of villainous mercenaries, he extended his influence over a good deal of Peloponnesus, his further progress being stayed by Flamininus in 193 B.C. He retained sovereignty of Sparta. At the departure of Flamininus he renewed hostilities, being opposed by Philopoemen, general of the Achaean League. Soon after Nabis was slain by some Aetolians in 192 B.C.

NABONASSAR, King of Babylon, 747-734 B.C., seems to have been vassal of Tiglath-Pileser IV, who permitted his defeated foe to remain in nominal independence.

NABONIDUS, last ruler of the Chaldaean empire, and father of Belshazzar; succeeded to the throne 556 B.C., but gave more time to building temples than to preparing for resistance to the Persians, who took him prisoner in 538 B.C.

NABOPOLASSAR, King of Babylon, 625-605 B.C., founder of the Chaldaean empire; aided by Medes he captured Nineveh in 606 B.C.; he was father of Nebuchadnezzar.

NABOTH, owner of a vineyard coveted by Ahab, and obtained by Jezebel by murderous fraud, *see* I. Kings XXI.

NACOLIA, town of Phrygia Epictelus, on the Thymbrius, where Valens defeated Procopius in A.D. 366.

NAEBIS, river of Hispania Tarraconensis, running between the Durius and the Minius.

NAENIA, funeral dirge, personified by the Romans, and worshipped as a deity. Her place of worship was outside the walls, near the Porta Viminalis.

NAEVIUS, GNAEUS, first Roman epic poet. He was of the plebeian party, and attacked Scipio and the Metelli in his writings, being arraigned by Q. Metellus, and imprisoned, only being released on his recanting. He died in exile about 201 B.C.

NAHARVALI, tribe of the Lygii, in Germany, in whose territory was a grove dedicated to the worship of the two Alces, comparable, according to Tacitus, with Castor and Pollux.

NAHUM, Hebrew minor prophet, born at Elkoah, probably in Galilee; he flourished about the 7th cent. B.C. His book predicts the fall of Nineveh which took place in 606 B.C. The reference to the capture of No-Amon, (Thebes) by Ashurbanipal, King of Assyria, further shows that it must have been written after 666 B.C.

NAIN, Galilean city, to the S. of Mt. Tabor. It was the home of a youth whom Jesus raised from the dead.

NAISUS, or NAESUS, town of Upper Moesia, on an eastern tributary of the Margus, where Constantine the Great was born. The city was destroyed by Attila, being rebuilt and fortified by Justinian.

NALITAE, CAUPONES, STABULARII,   the well-known edict of the Roman praetor, by which shipmasters, tavern-keepers, and stablers were held responsible for the goods and effects of travellers and passengers received into their vessel, inn, or stable.

NAMNETAE, people of W. Gallia Lugdunensis, whose chief town was Condivincum, later changed to Namnetes.

NAMUSA, AUFIDIUS, Roman jurist, and pupil of Servius Sulpicius.

NAPAEADS, in *Greek Mythology,* nymphs of the valleys.

NAPOCA or NAPUCA, Dacian Roman Colony, between Patavissa and Optatiana.

NAR, Italian river, rising in Mt. Fiscellus, being the boundary between Umbria and the Sabini, and flowing into the Tiber.

NARAGGARA, inland city of Numidia, between Thagura and Sicca Veneria, scene of Scipio's interview with Hannibal after Zama.

NARBO MARTIUS, town of S. Gaul, made a Roman colony by the consul Q. Martius in 118 B.C. Veterans of the 10th legion were settled here by J. Caesar.

NARCISSUS, In *Greek Mythology,* a beautiful youth, beloved of the nymph Echo, whose passion he was unable to return. Echo died of grief, and as a punishment the gods caused Narcissus to fall in love with his own reflection in a spring. This fruitless love made him pine away, until he was changed into the flower.

NARCISSUS, freedman and secretary to Claudius, who had turned a blind eye to the irregularities of Messalina. Later, when he feared she was planning his death, he told Claudius of her marriage with C. Silius. Messalina was slain in 48 A.D. After the murder of Claudius, Agrippina put Narcissus to death in 54 A.D.

NARISCI, tribe in S. Germany of Suevic race, living W. of the Marcommanni and E. of the Hermunduri.

NARONA, Roman colony in Dalmatia, on the Naro, and on the road to Dyrrhachium.

NARSES, General and administrator under Justinian. He was a Persarmenian eunuch who rose to high position, and for some time shared the command in Italy with Belisarius. His own military triumphs included a series of victories over the Goths, Alamanni, and Franks, as a result of which Italy was recovered as a province of the empire, governed by Narses himself from Ravenna.

NASAMONES, a Libyan people, originally of the shores of the Great Syrtis, but later driven inland by Greek settlers of Cyrenaica, and again by Romans.

NASIDIUS, Q., was sent by Pompey, with a fleet of 16 ships, in 49 B.C., to the relief of Massilia, then besieged by Brutus. Being defeated he went to Africa, where he commanded the Pompeian fleet. After serving Sextus Pompey, he joined Antony, commanding part of his fleet in the war with Octavianus in 31 B.C.

NASTES, son of Nomion, leader of the Carians at Troy.

NASUA, a leader of the Suevi in their irruption into Gaul, about the date of Caesar's arrival in that country.

NAUBOLUS, King of Tanagra, one of the Argonauts.

NAUCLIDES, (a) Leader of the party who invited and opened the gates for the Thebans, who seized Plataea in 431 B.C. (b) A Spartan ephor sent with Pausanias into Attica, in 403 B.C., when the Athenians were hard-pressed by Lysander.

NAUCRATES, of Erythrae, Greek rhetorician, disciple of Isocrates, who competed for the prize of Artemisia for the best funeral oration over Mausolus in 352 B.C.

NAUCRATIS, city of the Egyptian Delta on the E. bank of the Canopic branch of the Nile. It was colonized by Milesians, remaining a pure Greek city. It was the only town in Egypt where Greeks might settle and trade. It was birthplace of Julius Pollux, Polycharmus, Phylarchus, and Lyceas, also of Athenaeus. It was a seat of the worship of Aphrodite.

NAUCYDES, Greek sculptor, son of Mothon, and brother of Polycletus II. He flourished around 420 B.C.

NAUPACTUS, ancient fortified town of the Locri Ozolae, with the best harbour on the N. coast of the Corinthian Gulf. After the Persian wars it was held by the Athenians, who peopled it with Messenians. During the Peloponnesian War it was Athenian H.Q. At the close of the war the Messenians had to leave and the town went to the Achaeans. After passing to Aetolia it was again given back to Locris by the Romans.

NAUPLIA, port of Argos, on the Saronic Gulf.

NAUPLIUS, King of Euboea, father of Palamedes, Oeax, and Nausimedon. To avenge the death of Palamades, q.v., he waited for the Greeks to return from Troy, and, as they neared Euboea, lighted torches on a dangerous rock, the sailors being wrecked thereby.

NAUSTATHMUS, (a) Port on the E. coast of Sicily. (b) Port on the Pontus Euxinus. (c) Port in Cyrenaica.

NAXOS, (a) Aegaean island, largest of the Cyclades, halfway between Greece and Asia Minor, was famous for wine. The island was conquered by Pisistratus, who sent Lygdamis as tyrant in about 540 B.C. The Persians attempted to subdue Naxos in 501 B.C., failing to do so, they did conquer it in 490, enslaving the people. They recovered independence after Salamis in 480 B.C., but the Athenians subjected them in 471 B.C., after which little is heard of them. (b) Greek city on the E. coast of Sicily founded by the Chalcidians of Euboea in 735 B.C.

NAZARETH, town of Galilee, on the slope of a hill, halfway between the Lake of Galilee and the sea. It is famous as the early home of Jesus Christ.

NAZARITES, word meaning separated, and applied to certain Jews. These devoted themselves to the service of God, abstained from wine, allowed their hair to grow long, and avoided contact with dead bodies. As a rule the vow was only temporary, usually taken for a month, at the end of which certain sacrifices were offered, and the head ceremonially shaved.

NAZARIUS, Latin rhetorician, author of a panegyric on Constantine, delivered before Crispus and Constantine.

NAZIANZUS, Cappadocian city, famous as the seat of Gregory Nazianzen, Father of the Church.

NEAETHUS, river of Bruttium, in S. Italy, emptying into the Tarentine Gulf. Captive Trojan women are said to have burnt the Greek ships here.

NEALCES, a painter, living in the days of Aratus, 245 B.C.

NEANTHES, of Cyzicus, a writer, principally of history, who lived about 241 B.C., and was a disciple of the Milesian Philiscus.

NEAPOLIS, city of Campania, founded by the Chalcidians of Cumae. When first mentioned it consisted of two sections, divided by a wall, Palaeopolis, the old city, and Neapolis, the new. The city was taken by the Samnites in 327 B.C., Rome acquiring it in 290 B.C., but it remained a Greek city to the latest times. There were nine other towns of this name.

NEARCHUS, son of Androtimus, and a Cretan by birth, but an inhabitant of Amphipolis. He accompanied Alexander in his invasion of Asia, being appointed to conduct to the Persian Gulf, the fleet which had been built on the Hydaspes. The narrative of this voyage was written by Nearchus.

NEBO, god of the ancient Babylonians, son and interpreter of Merodach, he was regarded as writer of the first book, and instructor of mankind in letters and science. He had a temple at Borsippa.

NEBO, mountain in Moab, near the N. end of the Dead Sea, from which Moses viewed the promised land before his death. It is sometimes called Pisgah.

NEBRODES MONTES, the mountain chain of Sicily, a continuation of the Apennines.

NEBUCHADNEZZAR, more properly NEBUCHADREZZAR, name of three kings of Babylon. The most famous, Nebuchadrezzar II, son of Nabopolassar, reigned 604-561 B.C., invaded Judah three times, taking Jerusalem and carrying many Jews into captivity, in 586 B.C. He captured Tyre after a siege of twelve years and invaded Egypt. He restored many temples and rebuilt Babylon.

NECO or NECHU, succeeded his father, Psammetichus, to the throne of Egypt in 617 B.C. He started a canal to connect the Nile with the Arabian Gulf, but, Herodotus tells us, ceased on the advice of an oracle, on the grounds that it would be used by an invader. Phoenicians in his service, sailing from the Arabian Gulf, circumnavigated Africa, in just over two years, entered the Mediterranean, returning by the Straits of Gibraltar. Neco marched against the Babylonians and Medes, who had recently destroyed Nineveh, and was met at Megiddo (Magdolus) by

Josiah, King of Judah, a vassal of Babylon. Josiah was defeated and mortally wounded, Neco advanced to the Euphrates, conquered the Babylonians, and captured Carchemish, where he left a garrison. After Megiddo he took the town of Cadytis (Jerusalem?). Nebuchadnezzar defeated Neco in 606 B.C. Neco died in 601 B.C., after reigning 16 years, being succeeded by his son Psammis.

NECTANABIS, (a) King of Egypt, first of the Sebennite Dynasty, succeeded Nepherites c. 374 B.C. Kept out the Persian invaders Pharnabazus and Iphicrates. He was succeeded by Tachos. (b) Nephew of Tachos. He defeated the attempts of Artaxerxes III Ochus to recover Egypt for a time but was at length defeated, and fled to Aethiopia, in 350 B.C. (c) Nectanabis, past king of the Sebennite dynasty, and last native king of Egypt.

NEDA, river of Peloponnesus, emptying into the Ionian Sea, and the boundary between Arcadia and Messenia.

NEGRANA or NEGRA, town of Arabia Felix, destroyed by Aelius Gallus.

NEHEMIAH, reputed author of an O.T. book, closely related to Ezra and Chronicles, recording the work in Jerusalem of a Jewish cupbearer to Artaxerxes, who in 444 B.C., was appointed Persian governor of Judah. Nehemiah made two journeys to Jerusalem, where he inspected the rebuilding of the walls, and introduced reforms.

NELEUS, son of Poseidon, and twin brother of Pelias, both of whom were exposed by their mother, but they were discovered, and finally seized the throne of Iolcos. Pelias later expelled Neleus, who went with Melampus and Bias to Pylos, of which he obtained the throne. Neleus' twelve sons were all slain by Hercules, with the exception of Nestor.—Another of the same name was son of Codrus, last king of Athens.

NEMAUSUS, important town of Gallia Narbonensis, and capital of the Arecomici, was a Roman colony. It was sited on the high road from Italy to Spain.

NEMESIANUS, M. AURELIUS OLYMPIUS, Roman poet, at

the court of the Emperor Carus (283 A.D.), was esteemed second to Prince Numerianus alone. His verse dealt with fishing, hunting, and aquatics.

NEMESIS, in *Greek Mythology,* daughter of Night, and one of the deities of the underworld. She was goddess of vengeance, punishing the guilty, but at the same time rewarding virtue, and thus became the personification of respect for law and justice.

NEMETES, people in Gallia Belgica, on the Rhine, with Noviomagus as their chief town.

NEOCAESAREA, (a) Under the Roman empire, capital of Pontus Polemoniacus, in Asia Minor. A Church Council was held here in 314 A.D. (b) Fortress on the Euphrates, built by Justinian.

NEON, ancient town of Phocis, destroyed by the Persians under Xerxes, but rebuilt, and named Tithorea. This city was destroyed in the Sacred War, but was again rebuilt.

NEONTICHOS (New Wall), (a) one of the twelve cities of Aeolis. (b) A stronghold near the Chersonesus.

NEOPTOLEMUS (PYRRHUS), son of Achilles and Deidamia, carried by his father to Scyros, where he was reared in the palace of Lycomedes, and was taken by Ulysses to aid the Greeks in the Trojan War, because Helenus had prophesied that Neoptolemus and Philoctetes were necessary for the capture of Troy. Neoptolemus was one of the heroes in the wooden horse. At the fall of Troy he killed Priam, and sacrificed Polyxena to the spirit of his father. He was given Hector's widow, Andromache. Returning home he gave up his native kingdom and went to Epirus, there becoming ancestor of the Molossian kings. He married Hermione, being slain in consequence by Orestes, to whom she had been promised.

NEPHERIS, fortified town, built on a rock, near Carthage.

NEPOS, CORNELIUS, Roman historian, friend of Catullus, Cicero, and Pomponius Atticus, said to have written a universal history under the title *Chronica,* letters to Cicero, and other works, including a series of biographies styled *De Viris Illustribus.*

NEPOS, JULIUS, last but one of the Roman emperors of the West, from 474-5 A.D., was nephew of Marcellinus who had established a semi-independent principality in Dalmatia. He was deposed by Orestes, and fled to Dalmatia where he was killed in 480 A.D.

NEPOTIANUS, FLAVIUS POPILIUS,   son of Eutropia, Constantine the Great's half-sister. He was proclaimed emperor in 350 A.D., but was killed by Marcellinus, after reigning for only twenty-eight days.

NEPTUNUS (NEPTUNE), called Poseidon by the Greeks, was chief marine deity of the Romans. At his festival the people formed tents of branches, in which they feasted and drank. When a naval commander set sail he first sacrificed to Neptune, the sacrifice being cast into the sea.

NERATIUS PRISCUS, Roman jurist in the days of Trajan and Hadrian. He was highly esteemed by Hadrian, and was one of his consiliarii.

NEREIDES, a name by which the fifty daughters of Nereus and Doris were known.

NEREIS, daughter of Pyrrhus I, king of Epirus, and wife of Gelon of Syracuse, and last descendant of the royal house of the Aeacidae.

NERIUM, headland in the N.W. corner of Spain, in the territory of the Nerii, a tribe of the Celtic Artabri.

NERO, name of a family of the Claudia gens. (Nero - brave in the Sabine tongue). (a) C. Claudius, consul in 207 B.C., who defeated Hasdrubal, whom he slew. (b) Tib. Claudius N., husband of Livia, father of Tiberius and Drusus. (c) Roman emperor. Originally named Lucius Domitius Ahenobarbus, he was stepson of the Emperor Claudius, by whom he was adopted in 50 A.D., thenceforth bearing the name of Nero. On the death of Claudius in 54 A.D., Nero was made emperor. For the five years of his minority the empire was well administered. Then Nero threw aside his tutors and ministers, and for nine years indulged in that orgy of tyranny which has made his name a byword. The horror grew till Galba, one of the provincial generals, led his troops upon Rome. The emperor fled, and when he heard the tramp of the approaching troops, died by his own hand in 68 A.D.

NERUSII, a people among the Alpes Maritimae in Gallia Narbonensis, with their chief town at Vintium.

NERVA, MARCUS COCCEIUS, Roman emperor, on the assassination of Domitian in 96 A.D., after whose tyranny his mild rule was a welcome relief. He took an oath that he would put no senator to death, and suppressed the worst of the informers who had disgraced the latter part of Domitian's reign. He adopted Trajan, and died Jan. 27th, 98 A.D.

NERVII, warlike people of Gallia Belgica, with territory extending from the Sabis to the sea, part of which was covered by the forest of Arduenna. They were sub-divided into the Centrones, Grudii, Levaci, Pleumoxii, and Geiduni. Caesar defeated them in 58 B.C., leaving alive only 500 of the 60,000 men capable of bearing arms.

NESACTIUM, town on the Arsia, captured by the Romans in 177 B.C.

NESIS, a favourite residence of the Roman nobility, was an island of Campania, opposite Mt. Pausilypus.

NESSONIS, lake in Thessaly, near Lake Boebeis. These lakes were regarded by the ancients as remnants of a vast lake which was supposed to have covered all Thessaly until an outlet was made through the rocks of Tempe.

NESTOR, in *Greek Legend,* King of Pylos, who in spite of his years took part in the Trojan War, being one of the few Greek leaders to reach home safely after the fall of Troy. As a young man he had taken part in several adventures, including the expedition of the Argonauts, and the hunt for the Calydonian boar.

NESTOR, academic philosopher, son of Octavia, and mentor of Marcellus.

NESTORIUS, famous Haeresiarch, made patriarch of Constantinople in 428 A.D., but in consequence of his heresy, deposed by the Council of Ephesus in 431. His opponent was S. Cyril.

He was banished to Egypt, dying in exile, probably before 450. He distinguished between the divine and human nature attributed to Jesus and refused to apply the title Mother of God to the Blessed Virgin Mary; his doctrine is still held by Nestorian Christians.

NEURI, people of Samatia Europaea, described by Herodotus, as not of Scythian race, though they emulated their customs. They had been driven from earlier quarters by a plague of serpents, before they settled N.W. of the sources of the Tyras. They had a reputation as enchanters.

NEW TESTAMENT, the collection of books in the Bible which contain accounts of the life and teaching of Jesus, the beginnings of Christianity, and the faith of the early Church. These books were written to meet the needs of the Christians of the 1st cent., and it was a considerable time before they were added to the Canon of Scripture. By the year 200 the majority of the documents of the N.T. had secured universal recognition in the whole of Christendom. The Western Church, however, rejected S. James and Hebrews, and the Eastern Church 2 and 3 John and Jude, while 2 Peter had not yet won recognition at all. Some doubt, too, was expressed about the Apocalypse.

NICAEA, famous city of Asia, on the E. side of Lake Ascania, in Bithynia, on a site occupied in very ancient times by a town called Attaea, and later by a settlement of Bottiaeans, called Hellicore, which the Mysians destroyed. Soon after the death of Alexander, Antigonus built a city here, naming it Antigonea, but Lysimachus changed the name to Nicaea, in honour of his wife. It was a royal residence of the kings of Bithynia, and disputed with Nicomedia the prestige of being capital. Roman emperors bestowed honours and benefits upon it. Several chief roads through Asia Minor to Constantinople merged here, making it the center of much traffic. It is most famous in ecclesiastical history as the scene of the great oecumenical council convoked by Constantine in 325 A.D., chiefly for a decision on the Arian controversy, and which drew up part of the Nicene Creed. The Council also settled the date of Easter. A second Council, in

787 A.D., decided in favour of images. In 326 A.D., Nicaea was destroyed by earthquake, but restored by Valens in 368. Under the emperors of the East, Nicaea served as the bulwark of Constantinople, against Arabs and Turks.—There was another town of the same name in Illyria, and it was the ancient name of Mariana in Corsica. Another Nicaea was a city on the coast of Liguria, which first became of importance as a stronghold of Christianity, which was preached there by Nazarius.

NICANDER, Greek poet, physician, and grammarian, succeeded his father Damnaeus or Xenophanes as hereditary priest of Apollo at Clarus. He wrote many books in prose and verse, two of which are preserved; the longest, *Theriaca,* is a poem of about 1000 hexameters on the nature of venomous animals and the wounds they inflict. The other, *Alexipharmaca,* has 600 hexameters treating of poisons and their antidotes. He seems to have flourished about 185-135 B.C.

NICANOR, (a) Son of Parmenion, and an officer of Alexander, who died in the advance into Bactria, in 330 B.C. (b) Macedonian officer, who gained the government of Cappadocia in 321, on the death of Perdiccas. (c) Macedonian officer under Cassander, sent at the death of Antipater, in 319, to command the Macedonian garrison at Munychia.

NICE, (to the Romans, Victoria), goddess of victory.

NICEPHORIUM, fortified town on the Euphrates, S. of Edessa, built by command of Alexander.

NICEPHORIUS, Armenian river tributary of the Upper Tigris on which Tigranes built his residence Tigranocerta.

NICERATUS, (a) Son of Nicias, the Athenian general. (b) Son of Nicias, slain by the thirty tyrants. (c) A follower of Asclepiades of Bithynia, who wrote about plants.

NICIAS, leader of the aristocratic party at Athens and one of the foremost figures in Athenian history during the Peloponnesian War. Although opposed to the democratic tendencies which gave the tone to Attic politics at this period, his high character, wealth, and influence, gained the confidence of the people, and he was raised to the highest offices in their gift. His abilities were not equal to the duties he was called to perform, and in the severe trial of the Sicilian expedition his conduct showed such timidity in critical situations, that the disastrous end of the Siege of Syracuse must be mainly laid to his charge.—Another Nicias was physician to Pyrrhus, King of Epirus, who offered to poison the King for a Roman reward. Still another of the name was a Coan grammarian living at Rome in the days of Cicero.

NICIPPUS, a native of Cos, who made himself tyrant of the island.—Another of the name was ephor of the Messenians in 220 B.C.

NICOCHARES, Athenian poet of Old Comedy, contemporary with Aristophanes, was son of Philonides.

NICOCRATES, (a) native of Cyprus, who owned an extensive library at a very early date. (b) Archon of Athens, 333 B.C.

NICOCREON, King of Salamis at the time of Alexander's expedition to Asia.

NICOLAUS DAMASCENUS, historian of the age of Augustus, and friend of Herod the Great, tetrarch of Judaea, is mentioned by Josephus, Athenaeus, Eusebius, and others. He wrote various works in Greek, among them one on universal history.

NICOMACHUS, (a) Father of Aristotle. (b) Son of Aristotle by a slave. (c) called Gerasenus, writer of a life of Pythagoras, now lost. (d) of Thebes, a famous painter, brother and teacher of Aristides.

NICOMEDES I, son of Zipoetes, succeeded his father as King of Bithynia in 278 B.C. He enlarged the kingdom which had been founded by his father in 288 B.C. He was founder of Nicomedia.

NICOMEDES II, fourth in descent from the above, was son of Prusias II. He was so popular that his father sent him to Rome, where he was so much favoured that his father sought to have him assassinated. The plot being discovered Nicomedes successfully rebelled against his father, ordering him to be slain before the altar of Zeus in Nicomedia. Nicomedes reigned from 149-91 B.C.

NICOMEDES III, son and successor of the above. Socrates, his brother, contended the kingdom with him, but Nicomedes was established by Roman aid in 90 B.C., but expelled by Mithridates in 88 B.C., after defeat of Paphlagonia. He died 94 B.C., bequeathing his kingdom to the Romans.

NICOMEDIA, city of Bithynia, at the head of the gulf of Astacus in the Prepontis, was founded by Nicomedes I, in 264 B.C. Under the emperors it became a chief city of the empire. Hannibal died here, and it was birthplace of the historian Arrain.

NICON, (a) A Tarentine who betrayed his city to Hannibal during the second Punic War in 212 B.C., but fell in the defence of the city. (b) Leader of the Sicilian pirates, was captured by P. Servilius Isaurieus. (c) Comic poet. (d) Architect of Pergamus in Mysia, father of Galen.

NICOPHON, Athenian comic poet, contemporary with Aristophanes.

NICOPOLIS or ACTIA NICOPOLIS, ancient city of Epirus, founded in 31 B.C., by Octavian in memory of his victory at Actium. The colony composed of mixed settlers proved successful, and the city was considered capital of S. Epirus and Acarnania.

NICOSTRATUS, (a) Athenian general, son of Diitrephes, was colleague of Nicias at Cythera. (b) An Argive, possessed of great strength, and distinguished for prudence, who was sent with 3000 men to aid Darius Ochus against Egypt.

NIGER, C. PESCENNIUS, governor of Syria towards the end of Commodus' reign, at whose death he was proclaimed emperor by legions of the East in 193 A.D. He was defeated the year following and put to death by Severus.

NIGRITIAE, Aethiopian peoples of the most northerly part of Central Africa.

NILUPOLIS, city of the Heptanomis, (Middle Egypt), built on an island in the Nile, with a temple where the river was worshipped as a god.

NILUS (NILE), *see* Aegyptus.

NINEVEH, (Ninus), Assyrian city on the left bank of the

Tigris opposite Mosul. Its walls, enclosing 1,800 acres, with fifteen gates and many towers, were protected on three sides by a moat filled from the Choser tributary. A Mitannian domination, about 1400 B.C., preceded the outburst of Assyrian conquest under Shalmeneser I, about 1,300 B.C., who restored the temple, but made Calah his capital. It became a royal residence about 1100 B.C. Nineveh owed its chief renown to Sennacherib, who built a magnificent palace at Kuyunjik and an arsenal at Nebi Yunus, the traditional tomb of the prophet Jonah, and laid out a park wherein he acclimatized exotic animals and plants. Esarhaddon widened the streets and built a palace at Nebi Yunus. The fall of the city, foretold by Nahum and Zephaniah, was achieved by the Medes and Babylonians in 612 B.C., and a Sassanian village grew upon the mounds.

NINUS, reputed founder of Nineveh.

NIOBE, in *Greek Mythology*, wife of Amphion, King of Thebes, by whom she bore twelve children. She was so proud of this that she mocked the goddess Leto, who had only given birth to two children, whereupon the offended goddess incited her son Apollo, and her daughter Artemis, to slay all the children of Niobe with their arrows. Niobe was changed into a stone. Her story has often been treated in art.

NIPHATES, mountain range of Armenia. Niphates was also the name of one of the Persian generals at the battle of the Granicus.

NIPPUR, city of Babylonia; a Sumerian center, was on the Shatt-en-Nil, 20 m. E.N.E. of Diwaniya, central Babylonia. Among tablets discovered is one representing part of a Babylonian version of the Deluge.

NISIBIS, city of Mesopotamia, capital of Mygdonia, on the Mygdonius, S.W. of Tigranocerta, was a trading center and military post. In wars between the Romans and Tigranes, the Parthians, and Persians, it was successively taken and retaken, until it fell into Persian hands in the days of Jovian.—There was another city of the same name, at the foot of Mt. Paropamisus.

NISYRUS, island in the Carpathian Sea, off Caria, famous for its hot springs, wine, and millstones.

NITETIS, daughter of Apries, King of Egypt, who was deposed by Amasis.

NITIOBRIGES, Celtic people in Gallia Aquitanica, whose chief town was Aginnum.

NITOCRIS, Queen of Babylon, probably the wife of Nebuchadnezzar.—Nitocris was also the name of a queen of Egypt, and last monarch of the VIth dynasty.

NITRIAE, the famous natron lakes of Lower Egypt. The district in which they were situated was a chief seat of Serapis worship.

NIXI DII, the Roman divinities who assisted at child-birth.

NOAH, Biblical patriarch, son of Lamech, and father of Shem, Ham, and Japheth, who by divine command built an ark in which he and his family, and a certain number of every kind of animal were preserved in the Deluge.

NOBILIOR, FULVIUS, family of plebeians, originally called Paetinus, the name Nobilior being taken by Ser. Fulvius Nobilior to indicate that he was more noble than others of this name. The most outstanding of this family was M. Fluvius Nobilior, who was consul in 189 B.C., who defeated the Aetolians.

NOEGA, coastal city of the Astures, in Hispania Tarraconensis, on the borders of the Cantabri.

NOES, tributary of the Ister, in Thrace.

NOLA, ancient town of Campania, was founded by the Ausonians, but passed to the Tyrrheni. Nola sent 2000 troops to the assistance of Neapolis in 327 B.C. The town was captured by the Romans in 313 B.C. It was here that Augustus died.

NOMENTUM, Latin town founded by Alba, in a district near Rome famous for its wine.

NOMION, father of Amphimachus and Nastes, who led the Carians to the Trojan war.

NONNOSUS, Byzantine historian and ambassador, sent by Justinian I on an embassy to the Aethiopians, Saracens, etc., who on his return wrote an account of his mission.

NORA, an early city of Sardinia, founded by Iberian settlers on the coast of the Sinus Caralitanus.—Nora was also the name of a fortress in Cappadocia.

NORBA, fortified town of Latium, belonging originally to the Latin League, whence it passed to the Volscian League. There was a Roman colony at Norba as early as 492 B.C.

NOREIA, ancient capital of the Norici, in Noricum, situated S. of the river Murius, on the road from Virunum to Ovilaba, famous as the place where Carbo was defeated by the Cimbri in 113 B.C.

NORICUM, Roman province S. of the Danube, between Raetia and Vindelicia, and Pannonia, incorporated with the empire about 16 B.C.

NOSSIS, Greek poetess, author of twelve epigrams, who lived about 310 B.C.

NOVATIANUS, heretic; he insisted on perpetual excommunication for all who fell from the faith under persecution.

NUDIUM, settlement of the Minyae in Elis, destroyed by the Eleans.

NUITHONES, people of Germany, on the right bank of the Albis.

NUMA POMPILIUS, second of the seven legendary kings of Rome, reputed to have reigned from 715-673 B.C. He first established the priestly offices of the Roman state. He also divided the land among the people, and the craftsmen into guilds, according to occupation.

NUMANA, town of Picenum, founded by the Siculi, which became a municipium.

NUMANTIA, capital of the Arevaci in Hispania Tarraconensis, destroyed by Scipio Africanus the Younger in 133 B.C.

NUMBERS, fourth book of the Pentateuch, or, rather, Hexateuch. It takes its title from the Septuagint, the book being so called because it contains accounts of two numberings of the children of Israel. The Hebrew title is *In the Wilderness.* Three divisions may be distinguished: 1. The first census, and other events preparatory to the departure from Sinai. 2. The journey from Sinai to Moab. 3. The second census, the appointment of Joshua as Moses' successor, and other events.

NUMENIUS, of Apamea in Syria, was a Pythagoreo-Platonic philosopher, well thought of by Plotinus and Origen. He probably belongs to the time of the Antonines.

NUMERIANUS, M. AURELIUS, younger son of the Emperor Carus, who went with his father on the Persian expedition in 283 B.C. After his father's death he became joint emperor with his brother Carinus. He was murdered a few months later. Arrius Aper the deceased's father-in-law was accused, and without being allowed to defend himself, was stabbed to death by Diocletian, who the troops had proclaimed emperor.

NUMICIUS, TIB., tribune of the plebs in 320 B.C., was given over with his colleague Q. Maelius, to the Samnites when the Romans resolved not to adhere to the peace made at Caudium.

NUMIDA PLOTIUS, friend of Horace, who addressed an ode to him, to commemorate his safe arrival in Italy, after a campaign in Spain.

NUMIDIA, Roman province in N. Africa. The name means land of nomads, and the country corresponded roughly with the eastern part of Algeria. Masinissa united it with Roman aid in 201 B.C. On the overthrow of Jugurtha the Romans conquered Numidia, but left it under its own kings. Juba I, having sided with Pompey, Julius Caesar made Numidia a Roman province, in 46 B.C., but in 25 B.C., Augustus gave the W. part to Juba II. The Numidians provided light cavalry for the Carthaginians, and later for the Roman army.

NUMISIANUS, physician of Corinth, whose lectures Galen attended about 150 A.D. Galen esteemed him the most celebrated of all the pupils of Quintus.

NYMPHAE, in *Classical Mythology,* localized female nature spirits, regarded as minor divinities. There were sea and water nymphs, such as the Oceanids, the Nereids, and the Naiads; Oreads, or mountain nymphs; Dryads and Hamadryads, or tree nymphs. They had no temples, but offerings were made to them of milk and honey in grottos, at fountains, trees, etc.

NYMPHIDIUS SABINUS, commander of the praetorian troops, who on the death of Nero, tried to seize the throne, but was murdered by friends of Galba.

NYMPHODORUS, citizen of Abdera, whose sister married Sitacles, King of Thrace. The Athenians made him proxenus in 431 B.C.

NYX, (called NOX by the Romans), *in Greek Mythology,* the personification of night. She was daughter of Chaos, and is represented as a winged goddess in a chariot.

O

OANUS, stream of southern Sicily.

OARACTA, fertile island off Carmania, in the Persian Gulf. Here Erythras, for whom the Erthraean Sea was named, was buried.

OARUS, river, rising, according to Herodotus, in the country of the Thyssagetae, emptying into the Palus Maeotis, E. of Tanais.

OASIS, (Island in the sea of sand), fertile spots found in various parts of the great sandy deserts of Africa. The ancient Romans often used such places as sites for banishment. The most noted oases are in the Libyan desert, viz., Angila, Siwah, the great oasis W. of Thebes, called El-Khargeh, the little oasis, or Wah-el-Bahryeh, and several smaller ones a few days' journey W. of the Nile. Fezzan may also be considered as a great oasis of the Sahara. These oases seem to be depressions in the table-land of Libya. The desert is an elevated plain, and the oases are valleys sunk into this plain, and are similar in fertility to the plain of Egypt, but surrounded by steep hills of limestone. It would seem that where the limestone superstratum is removed, the water rises and fertilizes the land.

OAXUS, town of Crete, on the Oaxes, near Eleutherna.

OBADIAH, Minor Hebrew prophet. His book in the O.T. predicts the utter ruin of Edom, and the coming of the Day of the Lord.

OBELISK, tapering pillar-stone, especially in ancient Egypt. Usually a four-sided monolith of pink syenite, with a base width one-tenth its height, and a copper-sheathed pyramidal apex, it bore incised hieroglyphs upon each face. Obelisks stood in pairs before the temple portals, indicative of sun worship. One remains at Heliopolis, also that of Hatshepsut at Karnak. The tallest extant, 105½ ft., is in Rome.

OBOLUS, ancient Greek silver coin, alloyed with copper. It was equivalent to about 1½d. in English money: six obols made a drachma.

OBULCO PONTIFICENSE, Roman municipium in Hispania Baetica.

OCALEA, ancient town of Boeotia, between Haliartus and Alalcomenae.

OCALEA, daughter of Mantineus, wife of Abas, and mother of Acrisius and Proetus.

OCCIA, vestal virgin who exercised her priesthood for 57 years. She died 19 A.D., in the reign of Tiberius.

OCEANUS, in *Greek Mythology*, the god of the ocean, and father of all things. The name was also given to the river supposed to encircle the whole earth, which was regarded as being flat.

OCELIS, famous harbour and trading center on the S.W. point of Arabia Felix, at the entrance to the Red Sea.

OCELLUS LUCANUS, Pythagorean philosopher, born in Lucania.

OCHA, highest mountain of Euboea, in the S. of the island.

OCHESIUS, an Aetolian prince, father of Periphas, who was killed in the Trojan War.

OCHUS, river of Central Asia, possibly the same as the Oxus.

OCNUS, son of Tiberis and Manto, is reputed to have founded Mantua.

OCRICULUM, municipium in Umbria, on the Tiber, with an aqueduct, amphitheatre and temples.

OCTAVIA, sister of Octavian, who was afterwards the Roman emperor Augustus, and wife, first of C. Marcellus, by whom she was the mother of Marcus Marcellus, and secondly of Antony, the triumvir. The desertion of Octavia by Antony for Cleopatra was an important factor in causing the war between Octavian and Antony.—Another Octavia was daughter of Claudius and Messalina, and wife of Nero, who divorced her that he might marry his mistress Poppaea, and was later put to death by Nero's orders in 62 A.D.

OCTAVIUS, name of the gens to which the Emperor Augustus belonged.

OCTODURUS, town on the Drance, occupied by the Verigri.

ODENATHUS, prince of Palymra, who drove Sapor out of Syria after the defeat of Valerian by the Persians in 260 A.D.

ODESSUS, Greek town of Thracia, on the Pontus Euxinus, founded by the Milesians in the time of Astyages, King of Media (594-559 B.C.).

ODIUS, leader of the Halizones, slain by Agamemnon before Troy.

ODOACER, leader of the barbarians who overthrew the Western empire in 467 A.D.

ODOMANTICE, district of N.E. Macedonia occupied by the Thracian tribe of the Odomanti.

ODRYSAE, after the Persian wars Teres, King of the Odrysae, overcome several other Thracian tribes, extending his influence to the Black Sea. His son, Sitalces, who succeeded him, became ruler of nearly the whole of Thrace.

ODRYSSES, tributary of the Rhyndacus, in Mysia.

ODYSSEY, epic poem by Homer, relating the adventures and wanderings of Odysseus (Ulysses) after the conquest of Troy.

OEA, town on the island of Aegina.

OEANTHE, town of the Locri Ozolae, near the mouth of the Crissaean Gulf.

OEBALUS, King of Sparta, father of Tyndareus.

OEBARES, (a) Groom of Darius Hystaspis, who gained the Persian throne for his master, after the murder of Smerdis. (b) Son of Megabazus, represented Darius Hystaspis, in Dascyleum, in Bithynia.

OEDIPUS, in Greek Legend, son of Laius, King of Thebes, and Jocasta. An oracle having declared that Laius would perish at the hands of a son born of Jocasta, Oedipus was exposed, at birth, on the mountains, with his feet pierced. He was discovered by shepherds. After he reached manhood he met Laius, and killed him not knowing who he was. Oedipus delivered Thebes from the Sphinx, and as a reward received his own mother in marriage. A plague then ravaged the land, and an oracle declared that this would continue until the slayer of Laius was found. Oedipus set himself to discover the murderer, learning the truth from the prophet Tiresias. Jocasta hanged herself, and Oedipus put out his own eyes.

OENANTHE, mother of Agathocles, the notorious minister of Ptolemy Philopator, and of Agathoclea, through whom she gained influence with the king. After the accession of Epiphanes, her family was delivered to the multitude, who tore them to pieces.

OENEON, maritime town of the Locri Ozolae, E. of Naupactus.

OENEUS, King of Pleuron and Calydon in Aetolia; grandfather of Diomedes.

OENIADAE, ancient town of Arcanania near the mouth of the Achelous.

OENOBARAS, tributary of the Orontes, in Syria.

OENOPHYTA, town in Boeotia, between Tanagra and Oropus, where the Athenians gained a victory over the Boeotians in 456 B.C.

OENOPIDES, distinguished mathematician and astronomer, who gained his knowledge from Egyptian priests. He is said to have discovered the quadrature of the meniscus.

OENOTRIDES, two islands of the Tyrrhene Sea, opposite the mouth of the Helos.

OENUS, town or a river of the same name, rising on the frontier of Arcadia, and flowing into the Eurotas, famous for wine.

OENUSSAE, name of two groups of islands, one lying off Messenia, and the other between Chios and the coast of Asia Minor.

OEOLYCUS, son of Theras of Sparta, and brother of Aegeus.

OESALCES, brother of Gala, King of the Numidian tribe of the Massylians, whom he succeeded.

OESTRYMNIDES INSULAE, group of islands in the Sinus Oestrymnicus, rich in tin and copper.

OESYMA, where lived a colony of Thrasians, between Stryman and the Nestus.

OETA, pile of rugged mountain in S. Thessaly.

OETYLUS, ancient town of Laconia, S. of Thalama.

OEUM, mountain fortress in E. Locris, above Opus, was destroyed by an earthquake.

OFELLA, Q. LUCRETIUS, deserted the Marian party and went over to Sulla, by whom he was made commander of the army sent to blockade Praeneste, in 82 B.C. He became a candidate for the consulship, though he had been neither quaestor nor praetor, thus acting in defiance of one of Sulla's laws, who ordered him to be put to death.

OGYRIS,island in the Erythraean Sea (Indian Ocean), off Carmania, supposed burial-place of King Erythras.

OILEUS, son of Hodoedocus and Laonome, was King of the Locrians, who married Eriopus. He was father of Ajax, and is mentioned among the Argonauts.

OLARION INSULA, island in the Sinus Aquitanicus, off the W. coast of Gallia.

OLBA, ancient city of Cicilia, between the Lamus and the Cydnus, which became see of a bishop.

OLBIA, Greek colony founded about 645 B.C., near the mouth of the Hypanis, which became a grain emporium.

OLBIUS, river in N. Arcadia, also known as Aroanius.

OLCADES, ancient people of Hispania Tarraconensis, N. of Carthago Nova, of which Hannibal transplanted some to Africa.

OLCINIUM, ancient town of Illyria, S.W. of Scodra.

OLD TESTAMENT, name given to the collection of books which form the first part of the Bible, and give an account of the history and religion of the Jewish people. There are 3 well-defined stages in the growth of the O.T. (1) The earliest canon, which was formed about 440 B.C., contained the Pentateuch, or rather the Hexateuch—for the Book of Joshua was included. It contains the Law of God, on which the whole national life was centered. (2) About 200 years later the first edition of the O.T. was expanded by the addition of the prophetical writings, among which were included the historical books known as Samuel and Kings. (3) During the last two centuries B.C., various other additions were made, known as "The Writings," including Job, the Psalter, the Minor Prophets, Proverbs, Ecclesiastes, Chronicles, etc. The process of enlarging the canon continued in Alexandria, where a fourth addition was made, consisting of the books now in the Apocrypha.

OLENIA RUPES, the rock mentioned in the Iliad, said by Strabo to be the summit of Mt. Scollis in Achaia.

OLENNIUS, a chief centurion, in command of the Frisii, who by harshness caused revolt in 28 B.C.

OLIARUS, one of the Cyclades, in the Aegaean, W. of Paros, first colonized by the Phoenicians, famous for its grotto.

OLINA, river in W. Gallia Lugdunensis, flowing through the territory of the Viducasses.

OLISIPO, town in Lusitania, a Roman municipium, and famous for swift horses.

OLIVES, MT. OF, (OLIVET), Mt. about 2,700 ft. high, E. of Jerusalem. Its chief associations are with the life of Jesus.

OLLIUS, T., father of Poppaea Sabina; put to death in the days of Tiberius.

OLMIUS, river flowing from Helicon, which unites with the Permessus near Haliartus, and empties into Lake Copais.

OLOPHYXUS, Macedonian town, on the peninsula of Mt. Athos.

OLYBRIUS, ANICIUS, Roman emperor 472 A.D., who died after reigning three months and thirteen days; he was succeeded by Glycerius.

OLYMPIA, small plain of Peloponnese, in ancient times the scene of the Olympic games, a great athletic festival, held from the earliest times by the Greeks, in honour of Zeus. The games lasted for five days, and took place every four years; a period of four years being called an Olympiad. There was a record of victors from 776 B.C., but the games were regularly held long before that date. They were abolished in 394 A.D. The center of the festival was the precinct consecrated to Zeus and known as the Altis, an enclosure 750 ft. by 550 ft. Outside stood the palaestra or wrestling ground, the stadium or racing track, the hippodrome where the chariot racing took place, and the gymnasium.

OLYMPIAS, fierce, ambitious Epirote princess, wife of Philip II of Macedon, and mother of Alexander the Great: she died in 316 B.C.

OLYMPIUM, temple of Olympian Zeus.

OLYMPUS, name of several mountains, or mountain ranges, in ancient Greece, the best known forming the boundary between Macedonia and Thessaly, the highest peak of which is 9,796 ft. On its snow-capped summit the ancient Greeks placed the home of the Gods, whence Olympus came to be used as a synonym for heaven, and later for the sky. Other mountains of the same name were in Asia Minor and Cyprus.

OLYNTHUS, important city of Chalcidice, at the head of the Toronaic Gulf. The district originally belonged to a Thracian people, the Bottiaei, but was given over to Greek colonists at the Persian invasion. It was under Athens in the 5th cent., but regained its independence during the invasion by Brasidas, in 424 B.C. It became head of a great confederacy, its power exciting the jealousy of Sparta. After war (383-379), Olynthus was forced to join the Spartan confederacy. Philip of Macedon found the city his most powerful rival. The Athenians formed an alliance with Olynthus, but gave no active aid, though Demosthenes tried hard to induce them to oppose Philip before he grew too strong. After a long siege the city was captured by treachery in 347 B.C., razed to the ground and the people sold as slaves.

OMANA, port on the N.E. coast of Arabia Felix. Also, the name of a port and town in E. Carmania, a trading center between India, Persia, and Arabia.

OMBI, last but one of the great cities of Upper Egypt, on the E. bank of the Nile, in the Ombites Nomes, and famous as a chief seat of crocodile worship.

OMPHALION, a slave who became a painter, and was afterwards a disciple of Nicias, son of Nicomedes. He decorated the walls of the temple of Messene.

ONATAS, Greek artist and statuary of the 5th cent. B.C., contemporary with Polygnotus, Ageladas, and Hegias.

ONCHESMUS, coastal town of Epirus in Chaonia.

ONCHESTUS, ancient town of Boeotia, S. of Lake Copais, near Haliartus, with a famous grove and temple of Neptune. Also, the name of a river in Thessaly.

ONESICRITUS, Greek historian who accompanied Alexander on his Asian campaigns, and wrote their history. He acted as chief pilot of Alexander's fleet constructed on the Hydaspes.

ONESIMUS, Christian convert, who was a slave who ran away from Philemon of Colossae and made his way to Rome. There he met S. Paul, who converted him and sent him back with the *Epistle to Philemon.*

ONOBA, coastal town of the Turdetani in Hispania Baetica, on the estuary of the Luxia. There was another city of the name near Corduba.

ONOMACLES, Athenian general, sent with Phrynichus and Scironides, in 412 B.C., to besiege Miletus, and was repelled by the Peloponnesian fleet. He was afterwards ordered to attack Chios.

ONOMACRITUS, a Greek writer who compiled a collection of ancient oracles, about 500 B.C., but was expelled on the discovery that he had made an interpolation.

ONOMARCHUS, Phocian general in the Sacred War, who was defeated by Philip in Thessaly.

ONOMASTUS, confidential officer to Philip V, whose instrument he was in many acts of cruelty and oppression.

ONOSANDER, wrote a famous book on military tactics, probably about 50 A.D. The work is extant.

ONUPHIS, chief town of the Nomos Onuphites in the Egyptian delta.

OPHELESTES, Trojan warrior, slain by Teucer. Another of the name was a Paeonian warrior who was slain by Achilles.

OPHELION, Athenian comic poet, about 380 B.C.

OPHELLAS, one of Alexander's generals, after whose death he joined Ptolemy, and was responsible for the conquest of Cyrene in 322 B.C., which he held on behalf of Ptolemy, but later seized power for himself, and governed Cyrene as an independent state. He formed an alliance with Agathocles in 308 B.C., and marched on Carthage, but was treacherously waylaid by Agathocles, and killed.

OPHELTIUS, Trojan warrior, slain by Euryalus. Also a Grecian warrior of that name, was slain by Hector.

OPHILIUS, AURELIUS, a freedman who taught philosophy, rhetoric, and grammar at Rome, who flourished about 90 B.C.

OPHIODES, island of the Arabicus Sinus, very rich in topaz.

OPHIR, land famed in O.T. times for its gold, which was brought to Palestine by Solomon's ships, and by Hiram, King of Tyre. Its locality is uncertain, but S.E. Arabia is the most likely region.

OPIMIUS, (a) Q., consul in 154 B.C. (b) L., son of the above, praetor in 125 B.C., and consul in 121 B.C.; a violent opponent of C. Gracchus.

OPITES, Greek warrior, slain by Hector in the Trojan War.

OPPIANICUS, (a) Statius Albius Opp., accused by A. Cluentius, of having attempted to bring about his death by poisoning; was condemned, in 74 B.C. (b) son of the above, accused Cluentius of three acts of poisoning, in 66 B.C. (c) C. Opp., brother of (a); said to have been poisoned by him.

OPPIANUS, author of two Greek hexameter poems still extant entitled *Halieutica* and *Cynegetica*. These poems were in fact written by two different persons of this name. One, a native of Anazarba or Corycus, in Cilicia, wrote *Halieutica*. He flourished about A.D. 206. The other was born at Apamea or Pella, in Syria, and flourished about A.D. 180.

ORBILIUS PUPILLUS, Roman grammarian, mentor of Horace, born at Beneventum, settled in Rome at the age of 50 in 63 B.C. He lived to be nearly a centenarian.

ORBITANIUM, city of Samnium, N.W. of Beneventum.

ORCADES INSULAE, (Orkney and Shetlands), islands off the N. coast of Britain, first discovered by the Romans when Agricola sailed round the N. of Britain.

ORCHOMENUS, ancient Greek city in Boeotia; a great continental and maritime power in prehistoric times, was superseded by Thebes. Also, the name of an ancient town of Arcadia.

ORDOVICES, people of Britain, occupying the N. part of what is now Wales.

ORESTAE, people in the N. of Epirus, at first independent, but later subject to the Macedonians: they were declared free by the Romans in their war with Philip.

ORESTES, in *Greek Legend,* son of Agamemnon and Clytaemnestra. When his father was murdered, Orestes was saved by his sister Electra, who sent him to Phocis, where he became a friend of Pylades, the King's son. Having slain his father's murderers, he was pursued by the Furies, until his acquittal by the court of the Areopagus, at Athens. Another legend says he went for purification, with Pylades, to the country of the Tauri, to fetch a statue of the goddess Artemis, returning with his sister Iphigenia, to Argos, where Orestes reigned over his father's kingdom at Mycenae. There were three more of the name (a) Regent of Italy during the reign of his infant son Romulus Augustulus, 475-6 A.D. (b) L. Aurelius Orestes, consul, in 126 B.C. (c) Cn. Aufidius Orestes, consul in 71 B.C.

ORETANI, powerful people of S.W. Hispania Tarraconensis, with their chief town at Castulo.

ORFIUS, M., Roman eques of the municipium of Atella; tribune of the soldiers in Caesar's army.

ORICUM, important Greek town on the coast of Illyria, founded by Euboeans.

ORIGENES, (ORIGEN), Greek father of the Church, was born at Alexandria, son of Leonidas, a Christian martyr, he taught in the catechetical school, was imprisoned during the Decian persecution in 250 A.D., and died at Caesarea or Tyre. He was a voluminous and learned writer, who wrote the first textual criticism of the Bible, and many commentaries.

ORINE, island of the Sinus Arabicus, off the Aethiopian coast.

ORION, in *Greek Mythology,* a famous giant and hunter. Falling in love with Merope, daughter of Oenopion, King of Chios, he obtained from her father the promise of her hand, provided he cleared the island of wild animals. This task he accomplished, but Oenopion made him drunk and put out his eyes. Having recovered his sight by following the advice of an oracle, Orion took vengeance. He was killed either by the arrows of Artemis or the bite of a scorpion. After his death he was placed among the stars, and Orion is the subject of the earliest star myth.

ORIUS, son of Mycale, the Thessalian sorceress, one of the Lapithae, slain by Gryneus at the wedding of Pirithous.

ORMINIUS MONS, range of mountains in the N.W. of Bithynia, terminating in Promontorium Posidium, on the coast.

ORNEAE, ancient town of Argolis, originally independent, was subdued by the Argives in the Peloponnesian War.

ORNYTUS, Arcadian hero, who led an army from Teuthis to join the Greeks against Troy, but during the stay in Aulis he quarrelled with Agamemnon, and led his forces back.—Another of the name was a Tyrrhenian, who was companion to Aeneas in Italy, and was slain by Camilla.

OROBIAE, coastal town of Euboea, with an oracle of Apollo.

OROBII, Gallic people in Gallia Transpadana.

OROETES, satrap of Sardis who decoyed Polycrates, and put him to death in 522 B.C., he himself was put to death by Darius on suspicion of his aim to set up an independent kingdom.

ORONTES, greatest river in Syria, having two sources, one in the Antilibanus, the other in the Libanus, flowing into the sea at the foot of Mt. Pieria.—Also the name of a mountain on the S. of the Caspian: and a people of Assyria.

OROSIUS, PAULUS, Spanish cleric who fled to Africa before the Vandals in A.D. 414. He became S. Augustine's disciple. He wrote *Historiae,* a history of the world to 417 which work was apologetic in tone.

ORPHEUS, in *Greek Mythology,* son of the muse Calliope, was famed for his skill with the lyre, bestowed upon him by Apollo. He accompanied the Argonauts in their expedition to the Black

Sea, and lulled to sleep the dragon which guarded the Golden Fleece. On his return he settled in Thrace, and there his wife, Eurydice, died of a serpent bite. Her memory remained with him, and he consistently rejected the advances of the Thracian women, who in revenge tore him to pieces. The muses set his lyre among the stars.

ORPHIDIUS BENIGNUS, legate of the Emperor Otho, who was slain in the battle of Bedriacum, against the army of Vitellius, in 69 A.D.

ORSABARIS, daughter of Mithridates the Great, who was taken prisoner by Pompey, and paraded in his triumph in 61 B.C.

ORTHE, a place in the Thessalian district of Perrhaebia, thought by Strabo to be the Acropolis of Phalanna.

ORTONA, a port of the Frentani, on the road from Aternum to Histonium.

ORXINES, wealthy Persian noble, descendant of Cyrus, led a section of the troops at Gaugamela, and became satrap of Persis. He was charged with misdemeanor, probably sacrilege, and was crucified by Alexander.

OSCI, very ancient tribe of Italy, occupying the center of the peninsula, from whence they had driven the Siculi. They were sometimes known as Opici.

OSIRIS, Egyptian deity, originally the local god of Bursiris, whose worship developed during the Old Kingdom at Abydos, where he was traditionally interred. From being considered a virtuous benefactor, whence Egypt obtained her law and agriculture, he became, by assimilation with Ra, a sun-god. He was also identified with other gods. The son of earth and sky, he was brother and husband of Isis and father of Horus. He was god of resurrection and eternal life, and judge of the dead. As lord of the underworld Osiris appears with a mummified body, wearing a plumed crown, and associated with ideas concerning the after-life.

OSISMII, a people of Gallia Lugdunensis.

OSSA, mountain of Greece, in Thessaly, E. of the Peneus, and with its neighbouring height, Pelion, q.v., is separated from Olympus by the valley of Tempe.

OSTIA, ancient port of central Italy, was the port of Rome, standing on the S. arm of the Tiber. Its harbour became a naval station, and imported much wheat.

OSTRACINA, city of Lower Egypt, E. of the Nile, on the road from Rhinocorura to Pelusium, which was destitute of water.

OSTRACISM, political practice introduced by Cleisthenes at Athens in 508 B.C., and later employed in other Greek states. Once a year every citizen had the privilege of writing on an ostrakon (oyster-shell) the name of any statesman whom he thought it would be desirable to exile. If 6,000 votes were cast against any statesman, ostracism took effect. Miltiades, Themistocles, Aristides, and Alcibiades, suffered ostracism, but the latter abolished the practice.

OSTROGOTHS, eastern branch of the Gothic people, who remained on the Dnieper when the Visigoths moved W. in the 3rd cent.

OTACILIUS CRASSUS, T., Roman general, was praetor in 217 B.C., and later propraetor in Sicily, where he died in 211 B.C. —Another of the name was one of Pompey's officers, with command of Lissus in Illyria.

OTACILIUS PILITUS, L., Roman rhetorician who opened a school there in 81 B.C. Originally a slave, he wrote a history of Pompey, and his father.

OTHO, MARCUS SALVIUS, (A.D. 32-69) Roman Emperor. He joined Galba in the rising against Nero, but later formed the conspiracy which resulted in Galba's murder. Otho was proclaimed emperor Jan. 15, 69, but in the same month Vitellius was also proclaimed by the legions in Germany. The rival forces met at Bedriacum, where Otho was defeated, and put an end to his own life, April 16, 69.

OTHRYONEUS, an ally of Priam, and suitor for the hand of Cassandra, Priam's daughter. He was slain by Idomeneus.

OTREUS, King of Phrygia, who was aided by Priam against the Amazons.

OTRIS, town of Babylonia, above the marshes of the Euphrates, S. of Babylon.

OVIDIUS NASO, P., (OVID), Roman poet, born March 20th, 43 B.C., at Sulmo, in the country of the Paeligni. He was intended for the legal profession, and studied at Rome under the most famous rhetoricians, but soon gave up the law for poetry. In 9 A.D., he was suddenly exiled to Tomi, on the Euxine. Unable to obtain remission of his sentence, he died there. His extant poems (all except *Metamorphoses,* written in hexameters) may be divided into three classes:—1. Erotic, including *Heroides,* a collection of fictitious love letters. 2. Mythological. 3. Poems of exile: *Tristia,* and *Epistulae ex Ponto.*

OXATHRES, youngest son of Darius II, by Parysatis, and brother of Artaxerxes Mnemon. — Another of the name was brother of Darius Codomannus.

OXUS, river rising in the mountains which form the N. boundary of India, and flowing into the Sea of Aral.

OXYARTES, a Bactrian, father of Roxana, wife of Alexander the Great, was one of the leaders who accompanied Bessus into Sogdiana.

OXYNTAS, son of Jugurtha, led captive with his father before the triumphal car of Marius, in 104 B.C.

OXYRHYNCHUS, ancient city of Upper Egypt, near Bahnasa. The oxyrhynchus fish was venerated in the vicinity. Many papyri have been discovered here.

OZENE, capital of Larica, in India intra Gangem, in the days of Ptolemy. It exported onyxes, myrrh, and fine cotton stuff. It was the seat of a prince entitled Tiascanus.

OZOGARDANA, city of Mesopotamia, on the Euphrates.

P

PACARIUS DECIMUS, procurator of Corsica in 69 A.D., was put to death by the inhabitants.

PACCIUS, physician who made much money from a medicinal prescription concocted by himself, which he kept secret. On his death he left it to the Emperor Tiberius, who ordered a copy to be placed in public libraries. Paccius flourished at the beginning of the Christian era. He had been pupil of Philonides.

PACHES, Athenian general who reduced Lesbos and took Mytilene, during the Peloponnesian War.

PACIANUS, Bishop of Barcelona, famous for eloquence: he wrote against the Novatians. He flourished about 370 A.D.

PACIDII, name of two of Pompey's generals in Africa under Metullus Scipio.

PACTOLUS, famous river of Lydia, noted for its golden sands, which became proverbial. It rose on the N. side of Mt. Tmolus, flowing past Sardis into the Hermus.

PACULLA, MINIA, woman of Campania, largely responsible for the introduction of Bacchus worship into Rome in 186 B.C.

PACUVIUS, M., tragic poet of Rome, born at Brundisium, about 220 B.C., to which place he returned as an old man, dying there in his ninetieth year, in 130 B.C.

PADUS, (Po) chief river of Italy, identified by Roman writers with the fabulous Eridanus, from which amber was obtained.

PAEAN, (healing), the title of the physician to the Olympian gods. The name was later used for a hymn sung in honour of Apollo, who was also called Paean. It was sung at all solemn festivals of the god, at the cessation of a plague, and by Greek troops previous to an engagement.

PAEONES, a people of Teucrian origin, occupying parts of

Macedonia and Thrace.

PAEONIUS, of Ephesus, an architect who with Demetrius completed the temple of Diana at Ephesus, which had been started by Chersiphron. Another of the name was a statuary flourishing about 435 B.C.

PAEOPLAE, a Paeonian people, who, having been subdued by the Persians, were transplanted to Phrygia by Darius in 513 B.C., but returned in 500 B.C., with the assistance of Aristagoras.

PAESTUM or POSEIDONIA, ancient town of Lucania whose origin is obscure, but the place was at some early time occupied by a Greek colony, which gave it the name of Poseidonia, or the city of Poseidon. The Romans are said to have sent a colony to Paestum, after the war against Pyrrhus. The city assisted the Romans against Hannibal.

PAETUS, a common last name in Roman gentes, given to those with a cast in the eye.

PAETUS, AELIUS P., plebeian aedile in 204 B.C., praetor in 203 B.C., magister equitum in 202 B.C., and consul in 201 B.C. He became censor with P. Scipio Africanus in 199 B.C. After becoming auger, he died during a plague in 174 B.C.—Paetus, Aelius Sex., brother of the above, was curule aedile in 200 B.C., consul in 198 B.C., and censor with Cn. Cethegus in 193 B.C.

PAETUS, P. AUTRONIUS, consul with P. Cornelius Sulla in 65 B.C.; he took part in the Catilinarian conspiracy in 63 B.C., and was brought to trial, condemned, and exiled to Epirus.

PAETUS, C. CAESENNIUS, was consul in 61 A.D., and in 61 A.D., was sent to aid Domitius Corbulo in Armenia. He was defeated and forced to sue for peace on dishonourable terms. He became governor of Syria under Vespasian.

PAGAE, a colony from Megara; the town had a good harbour at the E. end of the Alcyonian Sea.

PAGASAE, town on the coast of Magnesia, was port of Iolcos, and later of Pherae, famous as the shipyard when Jason built his Argo.

PAGASUS, Trojan warrior, slain by Camilla in Italy, was companion of Aeneas.

PAGRAE, Syrian city, between Antioch and Alexandria, where the battle between Alexander Balas and Demetrius Nicator was fought in 145 B.C.

PALAEOGRAPHY, study of ancient handwriting, often used to decide problems of date by examination of styles, and to determine the genuineness of documents.

PALAEOLITHIC, term used to describe the older phase of the pre-historic stone-age civilization, before metals were in use.

PALAESTE, town of Epirus, S. of the Acroceraunian Mountains, where Caesar landed to carry on war against Pompey.

PALAESTINA, (Palestine, The Holy Land), country of Asia whose boundaries have varied at different periods. After being under Egypt for several centuries, it fell to the Philistines, about 1100 B.C. The Hebrews, fused with the Canaanites, drove out the Philistines, and under David Palestine enjoyed great prosperity. From the 9th to the 6th cent. B.C., Assyria and Babylonia won, lost, and rewon control of the country. From the 6th to the 4th cent. B.C., Persia controlled the provinces of Babylon, including Palestine, set the Babylonian exiles free, and allowed them to return and rebuild the Temple, and Jerusalem. Alexander the Great conquered the Persian empire (333 B.C., onwards), and in the division of the empire, after his death, Palestine fell to Egypt, and the Ptolemies, who fought the Seleucids across the prostrate body of Palestine. As these powers were weakened by the blows of Rome, the Jews rose in revolt. Led by the Maccabean family, in 168 B.C., the Jews won freedom in 143 B.C. In 70 A.D., Jerusalem was almost completely destroyed after a long siege, and through 6 centuries the Roman Empire held Palestine with a gradually relaxing grasp, and in 635 A.D., the fall of Damascus yielded Palestine to Mohammedan rule.

PALAMEDES, son of Nauplius and Clymene, was a Greek hero at Troy, who detected the feigned madness of Ulysses by putting his infant son before him as he was ploughing.

PALE, one of four cities of Cephallenia.

PALES, in *Roman Mythology,* deity whose care was flocks and shepherds, with a festival on 21st of April, which was birthday of the city of Rome. This divinity is described by some as a male, and by others as being a female.

PALFURIUS SURA, one of the delators under Domitian, who had been expelled from the Senate by Vespasian, after which he studied Stoic philosophy and became celebrated for eloquence.

PALICE, city of Sicily, founded by Ducetius, near the celebrated lakes and temple of the Palici, q.v.

PALICI, Sicilian gods, sons of Zeus and Thalia. Their sanctuary was an asylum for runaway slaves.

PALINURUM, cape on the W. coast of Lucania, named after Aeneas' pilot, Palinurus, who was murdered on this coast.

PALIURUS, African town, on the borders of Cyrenaica and Marmarica.

PALLA, city on the S.E. coast of Corsica, at the end of the Roman road running along the E. coast.

PALLACOPAS, a canal, running from the Euphrates westward to the Arabian desert.

PALLADIUM, in *Greek Legend,* a statue of Pallas Athena, which fell from heaven, and was kept at Troy, which could not be taken while the statue remained there. Just before the fall of Troy it was taken away by Odysseus and Diomedes, who had entered the city in disguise.

PALLADIUS, (a) of Methone, rhetorician in the time of Constantine. (b) Bishop of Helenopolis, 400 A.D. (c) Greek medical writer, after Galen: was surnamed Iatrosophista. (d) P. Rutilius Taurus Aemilianus, author of the farmer's calendar entitled *De Re Rustica,* written fairly early in the Christian era.

PALLANTIA, chief city of the Vaccaei, in N. Hispania Tarraconensis.

PALLANTIUM, ancient town of Arcadia, probably founded by Pallas, son of Lycaon, from which place Evander is supposed to have come.

PALLAS, favourite freedman of the Emperor Claudius, who with Narcissus, administered affairs of empire. Nero deprived Pallas of all offices, and dismissed him in 56, and had him poisoned in 63.

PALMA, Roman colony on the S.W. coast of the Balearis Major.

PALMYRA, city of Syria, standing 150 m. N.E. of Damascus, first called Tadmor, was founded by Solomon. Under the Roman empire it became a great trading center. The city was surrounded by walls in the days of Justinian, and was intersected by a street with a quadruple colonnade, and a triumphal arch. There are ruins of sepulchral towers, and a temple of the sun.

PALMYS, warrior from Ascania, who aided the Trojans against the Greeks.

PAMMENES, famous Theban general, politically allied with Epaminondas. When Philip was sent to Thebes as a hostage he was under the charge of Pammenes.—Another of the name was an Athenian rhetorician, contemporary with Cicero.

PAMPHILA, female historian, living in the time of Nero.

PAMPHYLIA, province of Asia Minor, at first colonized by Greeks, and afterwards included in the Persian empire, then that of the Seleucids, and fell to Rome in 189 B.C.

PAN, in *Greek Mythology,* the god of shepherds, generally regarded as son of Hermes, and especially associated with Arcadia, he had the horns and legs of a goat, was the inventor of the flute, or shepherd's pipe, which he made from reeds. The sudden appearance of Pan to travellers caused terror, hence the name "panic."

PANACHAICUS MONS, mountain in Achaia, rising behind Patrae, to 6,300 ft.

PANAENUS, Athenian painter of repute, was nephew of Phidias, whom he assisted in painting the temple of Zeus at Olympia. He flourished about 448 B.C.

PANAETIUS, famous Stoic philosopher, was born in Rhodes, studied under Crates at Pergamum, then at Athens under Diogenes of Babylon, and Antipater of Tarsus. He later went to Rome, where he succeeded Antipater as head of the Stoic school.

PANDARUS, son of Lyacon, who had charge of the inhabitants of Zelea, on Mt. Ida, in the Trojan War. He was a noted archer, and was afterwards honoured as a hero.

PANDATARIA, island to which Julia, daughter of Augustus was banished, situated in the Tyrrhenian Sea, off Campania.

PANDION, (a) King of Athens, and father of Procne and Philomena. (b) King of Athens, was expelled by Metionidae, and went to Megara, of which he became king.

PANDORA, in *Greek Mythology*, the first woman on earth. She married Epimetheus, and in his house was a box he had been forbidden to open, but Pandora, overcome by curiosity, opened the box, thereby letting out all the evils that afflict mankind. She was able to shut the box however, in time to prevent the escape of hope.

PANEUM, cave of a mountain at the S. end of the range of Antilibanus, whence the Jordan rises. The Greek name signifies "Pan's abode."

PANGAEUM, mountain range of Macedonia, famous for its gold and silver mines, also roses.

PANNONIA, important Roman province, between the Danube and the Alps. Trajan divided it into two parts, Pannonia Superior and Pannonia Inferior.

PANOPES, follower of Aeneas, in his voyage to Italy.

PANOPEUS, ancient town in Phocis, near the border of Boeotia, founded by Panopeus, son of Phocus.

PANOPION URBINIUS, was proscribed by the triumvirs, in 43 B.C., but saved by a slave, who assumed his master's clothes, and sending him through another door, as soldiers entered the villa, entered his master's bed and allowed himself to be killed.

PANSA, C. VIBIUS, friend and partisan of Caesar, and tribune of the plebs in 51 B.C., appointed to the government of Cisalpine Gaul, in 46 B.C., and subsequently consul with Hirtius, in 43 B.C.

PANTAENUS, teacher of Clemens of Alexandria, was a Stoic, and conducted a mission to India. He was master of the cate-chetical school at Alexandria c. 181 A.D.

PANTHEON, temple in the Campus Martius at Rome, built by Agrippa, in 27 B.C., but the present edifice was built by Hadrian between 120-130 A.D. It is now a Christian place of worship. The main structural parts consist of a rotunda, and a dome, the total height and diameter of the building amount-ing to 142 ft. 6 ins. A portico of Corinthian columns sup-ports a massive pediment, surmounted by another partly screen-ing the dome, which is constructed of solid concrete and lighted at the summit. The interior is lined with marble. It was con-secrated in 609. It was originally supposed to be sacred to all the gods, but Cassius states it was dedicated to Mars and Venus.

PANTHOEDAS, a Spartan, sent by the ephors, in 403 B.C., against Clearchus, who had gone to Byzantium against orders. He was killed in battle, in 377 B.C., while fighting against Pelo-pidas.

PANTIAS, sculptor of Chios, of the school of Sicyon.

PANTICAPAEUM, town in the Tauric Chersonesus, founded by the Milesians, about 541 B.C., became the residence of the Greek kings of the Bosporus. New walls were built here by Justinian. It had an excellent harbour.

PAPHLAGONIA, district on the N. side of Asia Minor, be-tween Bithynia and Pontus.

PAPHOS, two towns on the W. coast of Cyprus, Old and New Paphos. The old city was chief seat of the worship of Venus, and was of Phoenician origin. In Roman times New Paphos was capital of one of the four districts into which Cyprus was divided.

PAPIAS, Bishop of Hierapolis, in Phrygia, and an ecclesiastical writer of the 2nd cent., contemporary with Polycarp. Irenaeus speaks of him as "a hearer of John, and an ancient man." Euse-bius speaks highly of Papias in one place, but in another dis-paragingly. He wrote a work in five books, *Explanations of the Lord's Discourses.*

PAPINIANUS, AEMILIUS, famous Roman jurist, who came

to York with Septimus Severus, where the emperor died in 211 A.D., leaving his two sons to the care of Papinianus. Caracalla dismissed Papinianus, and later had him put to death.

PAPREMIS, city of Lower Egypt, sacred to the god Ares (identified by the Greeks with Mars).

PARAETONIUM, important town on the N. coast of Africa, near Cape Artos, with a harbour, and a stronghold; it was a famous seat of the worship of Isis. Justinian restored it.

PARAGON SINUS, gulf of the Indicus Oceanus, on the coast of Gedrosia.

PARALIA, district of Attica, around the promontory of Sunium, inhabited by the Paralii.

PARIS, also called Alexander, in *Greek Legend,* son of Priam and Hecuba. The goddess of strife having thrown a golden apple inscribed "for the fairest" among the guests at the nuptials of Peleus and Thetis, this was claimed by Hera, Athena, and Aphrodite. Zeus ordered them to submit to the judgment of Paris. Paris gave the apple to Aphrodite, who caused Helen, wife of Menelaus of Sparta, to fall in love with Paris. He carried her off to Troy, so provoking the Trojan War.

PARIUM, city of Mysia, on the Propontis, founded by a colony from Miletus. It was made a Roman colony under Augustus, and named Colonia Pariana Julia Augusta. It was a seat of Cupid, Bacchus, and Apollo worship.

PARMA, town in Gallia Cispadana, originally a city of the Boii, but made a Roman colony in 183 B.C.

PARMENIDES, famous Greek philosopher, born at Elea in Italy. He came to Athens with Zeno, where he met Socrates, then quite young, probably in about 448 B.C.

PARMENION, general of Philip and Alexander; in the latter's invasion of Asia, he was second in command.

PARMYS, daughter of Smerdis, son of Cyrus; she married Darius Hystaspis, and became mother of Ariomardos.

PARNASSUS, mountain range of Greece, in Phocis, whose highest peak is 8,069 ft. Parnassus was sacred to Apollo and the

Muses, also to Dionysus. Above Delphi is the famous Castalian spring.

PAROREATAE, most ancient inhabitants of the mountains in Triphylia, who were driven out by the Minyae.

PAROS, one of the larger Cyclades in the Aegaean Sea, colonized by Cretans, but later peopled by Ionians. It was famous for its white marble, which was esteemed by sculptors. The *Parian Marble,* an inscription recording a chronological account of Greek history from 1581-263 B.C., was discovered here. The poet Archilochus was born at Paros.

PARRHASIUS, son and pupil of Evenor, was born at Ephesus, but became a citizen of Athens. He raised the art of painting to great perfection. Claiming to be descended from Apollo, he carried his arrogance so far as to dedicate his own portrait in a temple as Mercury, and thus receive adorations: he wore a purple robe and golden garland. Parrhasius flourished about 400 B.C.

PARTHENIUS, grammarian and poet, who taught Virgil Greek. He was a voluminous writer of poems but only one of his prose works exists, containing thirty-six short love stories. Parthenius lived in the 1st cent. B.C.

PARTHENON, (Virgin's chamber), temple of Athena, on the Acropolis, at Athens. It is in plan a parallelogram, divided into two main parts. There were eight exterior columns at either end, and seventeen on each side. The portico at each end included an inner line of six columns. Its chief glory was the sculpture by Phidias and his school. It was built under the administration of Pericles, being dedicated in 438 B.C.

PARTHIA, country of ancient Asia, S.E. of the Caspian, adjoining Media, and forming part of the old Persian or Archaemenid empire. When this empire was overthrown by Alexander it was included in the Dominion of the Seleucid Kings of Syria. About 250 B.C., it became an independent kingdom under Arcases I. It increased in the succeeding centuries, and under Mithridates I became the Parthian empire, reaching from the Euphrates to beyond the Indus, with its capital at Ctesiphon.

PASARGADAE, one of the three chief tribes of ancient Persia, the others being the Maspii, and the Maraphii. It was from this tribe that the royal house was recruited.

PASEAS, father of Abantidas, the Sicyonian tyrant, who made himself tyrant after his son's death, and was slain by Nicocles.

PASSARON, town of Epirus, destroyed by the Romans in 168 B.C. It was the capital of the ancient Molossian kings.

PASSION, Christian term for the sufferings and Crucifixion of Jesus. From early times it was a custom in the Church to recite the story of the Passion as told in the Gospels, the narrative portion being sung by a tenor, while individual speeches were allotted to other voices, the answers of the crowd being sung by a chorus.

PASSOVER, ancient Jewish feast, instituted at the Exodus, and so named from the passing over by the destroying angel of the thresholds of the Israelites when all the first-born of Egypt were slain. The feast is celebrated from Nisan 15-22, and is also called the Feast of Unleavened Bread.

PATARA, a chief sea-port city of Lycia, E. of the estuary of the Xanthus, early colonized by Dorians from Crete. There was an oracle of Apollo here. The city was restored and enlarged by Ptolemy Philadelphus, who named it Arsinoe, but the old name persisted.

PATARBEMIS, a principal officer of Apries, King of Egypt.

PATAVIUM, ancient town of the Veneti in N. Italy, between Mutina and Altinum. Under the Romans it became the most important city of N. Italy. It was plundered by Attila, and later destroyed by Agilolf, King of the Langobards. The historian Livy was born here.

PATERCULUS, C. VELLEIUS, Roman historian, born about 20 years before the Christian era.

PATMOS or PATIMA, island of the Aegaean, and one of the Sporades group, on the S.E. side of the sea. It is famous as the place of banishment of S. John the Apostle.

PATRAE, one of the twelve cities of Achaia, W. of Rhium, founded by Eumelus, and first called Aroe.

PATRICII, (Patricians), members of the ruling order in ancient Rome, as opposed to the plebs. As descendants of the original citizens, they had the monopoly of the priestly offices, and the exclusive right of interpreting the law. The senators were almost invariably patricians.

PATUMUS, Egyptian city, in the Arabian desert, near Bubastis, built by the Israelites while in captivity, and called Pithom in the O.T.

PAUL, THE APOSTLE, born at Tarsus, in Cilicia, about the same time that Jesus was born in Judaea; his name then being Saul. He was a Jew of the Dispersion, who learned tent making and was sent to Jerusalem to be a Rabbi. He became one of the first opponents of the Christian religion, heading a persecution to repress it, but on the way to Damascus, where he was going to hunt out the Christians, he was converted by a vision. Paul spent three years in Arabia, thinking over his experience. He then went to Jerusalem, but the disciples were afraid of the persecutor turned Apostle until Barnabas won for him their confidence. The opposition of the Jews was too strong, so he went to Tarsus, spending some years evangelizing his native province. Then, in company with Barnabas, he was sent forth on his first missionary journey round Cilicia. On his second missionary journey he evangelized the cities of Greece, Athens among them. The third journey went over the same ground, but its principal center was Ephesus. On arriving at Jerusalem at the end of it, he was arrested at the instance of the Jews, appealed to Caesar, and was sent to Rome for trial. He was beheaded under Nero.

PAULINUS, GAIUS SUETONIUS, Roman general, was appointed governor of Britain in 59 A.D., and in 61 subdued Anglesey. He was called south to quell the Iceni, who had rebelled under their queen, Boudicca (q.v.), gaining a decisive victory over them near London. The following year he was recalled to Rome.—Another Paulinus became first bishop of York.

PAULUS, (a) of Samosata, heresiarch of the 3rd cent., bishop of Antioch about 260 A.D., deposed in 269. (b) Silentiarius, chief secretary to the emperor Julian. (c) Julius, distinguished Roman jurist in the reign of S. Severus, was exiled by Elagabalus, but recalled by A. Severus. He was a voluminous writer on Roman law.

PAUSANIAS, Greek traveller and geographer. Probably a native of Lydia, he travelled extensively in Greece, recording the results of his journeys in a work of ten volumes, *The Itinerary of Greece.* He wrote about the middle of the 2nd cent. Also the name of two kings of Sparta, the former victor at battle of Plataea 479 B.C.

PAUSIAS, Greek painter, contemporary with Aristides, and a pupil of Pamphilus.

PAUSICAE, a people of the Persian empire, living between the Oxus and Jaxartes, and being classed under the 11th division.

PAUSIRAS, satrap of Egypt.

PEDANIUS, T., first centurion of the principes, distinguished for bravery in the second Punic War.—Also, Pedanius Secundus, was praefectus urbi in the time of Nero. He was killed by a slave.

PEDASA, ancient city of Caria, which Alexander assigned to Halicarnassus.

PEDIUS, Q., great nephew of C. Julius Caesar, named as one of his heirs. He was consul with Octavius in 43 B.C., in which year he died.

PEDNELISSUS, city of Pisidia, forming an independent state, but was frequently at war with Selge.

PEGASUS, in *Greek Mythology,* the winged horse which sprang from the blood of Medusa, the Gorgon, when her head was struck off by Perseus. Pegasus created Hippocrene, the spring of the Muses, with a kick of his hoof.

PELAGIUS, British theologian, traveller, and a student of early literature, who held that sin is not transmitted from Adam, but that each child born into the world is morally clean, and that it is possible for him not to sin. Also, that for all his good deeds he accumulates merit with God. He was anathematized as a heretic in 417 A.D.

PELARGE, daughter of Potneus, and wife of Isthmiades, who introduced Cabiri-worship into Boeotia, and becoming herself an object of worship.

PELASGI, the most ancient inhabitants of Greece, as far as the knowledge of the Greeks themselves extended. Greek traditions represent the Pelasgic race as spread widely over almost all parts of Greece, and its islands. The W. coast of Asia Minor was also inhabited by the Pelasgi; and they were also spread widely over S. Italy.

PELEUS, in *Greek Legend,* King of the Myrmidons in Thessaly, and father of Achilles. His wedding with Thetis, a sea-deity, daughter of Nereus, was of great magnificence, all the gods being invited, except Eris, goddess of Discord.

PELIAS, in *Greek Legend,* King of Iolcus, the throne of which he had seized from Aeson. When Jason came to claim it, Pelias sent him in search of the Golden Fleece, hoping he would perish.

PELION, mountain range of ancient Greece, in the Thessalian district of Magnesia, S.E. of Mt. Ossa. It is famous in Greek mythology as the scene of the conflict between the gods of Olympus and the giants, who are said to have piled Pelion and Ossa on Olympus, to reach the sky.

PELLA, Macedonian town which Philip made his capital. It was birthplace of Alexander the Great.—Also, Pella was the name of a city, E. of Jordan, to which the Christians fled before the Romans captured Jerusalem.

PELOPIDAS, Theban general, son of Hippoclus; he took a leading part in expelling the Spartans from Thebes, in 379 B.C.

PELOPONNESUS, the south portion of ancient Greece, divided into 7 states, Achaea, Corinthia, Elis, Argolis, Messenia, Laconia, and Arcadia. The Peloponnesian War between Sparta and Athens was carried on from 431-404 B.C. The apparent cause was the quarrel between Corcyra and Corinth, in which Athens supported the former, and Sparta the latter. In reality it was a struggle between the democratic Ionians of Athens, the islands, and maritime towns, and the oligarchical, continental, Dorians, represented by Sparta.

PELOPS, in *Greek Legend,* son of Tantalus, King of Phrygia, who being expelled from his native country went to Pisa, where he became a suitor of Hippodamia, daughter of King Oenomaus. The conditions of winning were that he should enter for a chariot race with her father, in which unsuccessful competitors were put to death. Pelops won the race by inducing Myrtilus, the King's charioteer, to remove the lynch-pin from his master's chariot-wheel.

PELTAE, ancient city of Asia Minor, in N. Phrygia.

PENATES, household gods of the ancient Romans, at one time distinct from, but afterwards identified with, the Lares.

PENELOPE, in *Greek Legend,* wife of Odysseus, q.v., the long absence of her husband caused a number of suitors to come to the royal palace at Ithaca, where, in spite of her refusals, they lived riotously. She promised to make up her mind as soon as she had finished a garment, of which she secretly unwove each night as much as she had woven in the day.

PENTATEUCH, term used by Christian scholars, from the time of Tertullian to indicate the first five books of the O.T. Some modern scholars contend that Joshua, the sixth book, should be included, making it a Hexateuch.

PENTELICUS MONS, mountain of Attica, famous for its marble.

PENTHILIDAE, a noble family of Mytilene in Lesbos, descendants of Penthilus, who led a colony to Lesbos.

PENTRI, important tribe in Samnium, who were subdued by the Romans with the other Samnite tribes, and were the only tribe to remain faithful, when the rest revolted to Hannibal in the second Punic War.

PEOR, mountain of Palestine, mentioned in the O.T., was probably a summit of the mountains called Abarim.

PERDICCAS, (a) Founder of the Macedonian monarchy, who was succeeded by his son Argaeus. (b) King of Macedonia from about 454-413 B.C. (c) One of Alexander's generals.

PERGA, ancient city of Pamphylia, N.E. of Attalia, was a seat of Diana-worship.

PERGAMUM or PERGAMUS, ancient city of Mysia, in Asia Minor. The kingdom established by Philetaerus in 280 B.C., reached its zenith in 190 B.C., under Eumenes II, who was tactful enough to identify himself with the Romans, receiving from them most of W. and central Asia Minor. Eumenes founded an important library, and erected many buildings and sculptures. In 133 B.C., Attalus III, the last king, died, the kingdom passing to the Romans.

PERGUS, Sicilian lake, near the walls of Enna, on the bank of which Proserpine was said to have been gathering flowers, when carried off by Pluto.

PERIANDER, one of the Seven Sages, was son of Cypselus, tyrant of Corinth, whom he succeeded in 625 B.C. He died 585 B.C.

PERICLES, Athenian statesman, making his appearance in public life in 469 B.C., and six years later, in conjunction with his colleague Ephialtes, brought about the important reform of restricting the powers of the aristocratic Areopagus, q.v. The murder of Ephialtes in 461 B.C., left him without a rival in his party. In 443 B.C., the exile of the conservative leader, Thucydides, left him without rival in the state, in which he remained supreme till his death in 429. Pericles regarded the state as existing in the interests of all, not a class. He made Athens free, and the first state in the Grecian world, but did not give her the organization which would fit her for the position he had won for her. He saw that the true policy for Athens, was to seek naval supremacy. The age of Pericles was most brilliant in the history of Greece.

PERICTIONE, daughter of Critias, and mother of Plato.

PERILLUS, a sculptor who executed the bronze bull of the tyrant Phalaris, q.v.

PERINTHUS, town of Thrace, founded by the Samians, about 559 B.C., on the Propontis, 22 m. W. of Selymbria.

PERISADII, a people of Illyria, established near the silver mines of Damastion.

PERPERENA, was consul in 130 B.C., when he defeated Aristonicus in Asia, taking him prisoner.—Another of the name, grandson of the above, joined the Marians in the civil war, and became praetor.

PERSEPHONE or PROSERPINE, in *Greek Mythology*, daughter of Zeus and Demeter, the goddess of agriculture. While gathering flowers she was carried off by Pluto, god of the underworld, and thereafter spent six months in the underworld, and six months with her mother. The rape of Persephone is symbolic of the process of agriculture.

PERSEPOLIS, capital of the ancient Persian empire. It was situated 35 m. N.E. of the modern Shiraz. The palaces and public buildings were built on a terrace of masonry, some distance from the city proper, and were approached by elaborate stairways. The great hall alone covered 2½ acres.

PERSEUS, in *Greek Legend*, son of Zeus and Danaë. Polydectes, King of Seriphus, wishing to marry Danae, got rid of Perseus by sending him to Libya to secure the head of Medusa the Gorgon. With the aid of Athena, Perseus succeeded, and on his return passed through Aethiopia, where he saved Andromeda from a sea-monster and made her his wife. Arriving at Seriphus, and finding that Polydectes had been treating his mother unkindly, he turned the King and his whole court into stone by showing them the Gorgon's head. Perseus is regarded as the founder of the city of Mycenae.

PERSIS, (rarely Persia), country of Asia. In ancient times Persia included the whole of the tableland enclosed S. by the Arabian Sea, E. by the Indus Valley, W. by the Persian Gulf and Mesopotamia, and N. by the depression between the Caspian and Aral Seas. Its total area was nearly a million sq. miles. The first inhabitants in historical times seem to have been of Sumerian stock, but on the fall of the Assyrian empire an Aryan people, the Medes, became heirs of its political power, and to a great extent its civilization. Media became a powerful empire under Cyaxares (died 584 B.C.). His son, Astyages, was attacked by Cyrus, and in 550 B.C., the empire passed to the kindred

Aryan people of Persia. Darius, a usurper, reduced the Greek cities of Thrace and Macedonia, and refounded the Persian empire. The rise of Macedonia under Philip and Alexander brought a temporary fall of Persia. At the death of Alexander, what was modern Persia, was ruled by the Seleucids, descendants of one of his generals. The Parthians produced the Arsacid dynasty c. 249 B.C. The Parthian power was superseded by the Sassanian dynasty which ruled the land until 651.

PERSIAN ART, ancient Persian art developed from Babylonian and Assyrian art. The sun-dried brick of the Assyrians was discarded for stone, though their peculiar raised palaces were repeated in Persia, and the columnar feature, seen in the remains of the palace of Cyrus at Pasagardae, was borrowed from the Medes.

PERSIUS, FLACCUS AULUS, Roman satiric poet, born at Volaterrae, in Etruria, Dec. 4, 34 A.D., who studied Stoic philosophy in Rome under Cornutus, and died Nov. 24, 62 A.D. He left six Satires, displaying original genius, in spite of their obscure style.

PERUSIA, ancient city of Etruria, between Lake Trasimenus and the Tiber.

PESSINUS, city of Asia Minor, in the S.W. of Galatia, a chief seat of the worship of Cybele Agdistis. The city became capital of Galatia Salutaris under Constantine.

PETER, one of the twelve Apostles, was son of Jonas, and, in partnership with his brother Andrew, a fisher on the lake of Galilee. Originally named Simon, he received the name of Cephas or Peter from Jesus, who, with reference to the meaning of the name, declared that on this rock he would build his Church. He preached the first sermon after Pentecost, and was first to admit a Gentile to the Church. He is believed to have preached throughout Asia Minor, to have gone to Rome, and to have suffered crucifixion, probably under Nero, 68 A.D.

PETER, EPISTLES OF, two books of the N.T. attributed to S. Peter. Several works have survived which were ascribed to the Apostle, but were not his. The claim for the first epistle may be accepted, and we may conclude that it was written from Rome before 64 A.D. It is addressed to the Christians of Asia Minor, encouraging them to face persecution. It is possible that the second epistle was written by a disciple of Peter in his master's name.

PETOSIRIS, Egyptian priest, who with King Nechepsos, is said to have founded astrology.

PETRA, a name given to a number of cities which were built on rocks. The best known was capital of the Nabataeans, who in Assyrian and Babylonian invasions took refuge there. They used the valley as a burial place and treasure store, which was raided in 312 B.C., by Macedonians, and later by Pompey.

PETRINES, a general of the Persians, at the beginning of their war with Alexander, who fell at the battle of Granicus.

PETRONIUS ARBITER, G., Roman writer, who passed his days in sleep, and his nights in business or pleasure, but was an able administrator. He aroused the jealousy of Tigellinus, and anticipated his fate, by opening his veins in a warm bath. He was author of a work called *Satyricon,* which describes the adventures of a Greek freedman in Italy.

PHACUSA, capital of the Nomos Arabia, in Lower Egypt, where the canal commenced which ran from the Nile to the Arabian Gulf.

PHAEAX, Athenian orator, contemporary with Nicias and Alcibiades.

PHAEDIMA, daughter of Otanes, was one of the wives of Cambyses, and of the magician Smerdis, and through her the false Smerdis, q.v., was exposed.

PHAEDRA, in *Greek Mythology,* daughter of Minos, King of Crete, and wife of Theseus, King of Athens. She took her own life because the passion she had conceived for her step-son, Hippolytus, was not returned.

PHAEDRUS, Latin writer of the Augustan age, appears to have been a native of Thrace, whence he was brought to Rome as a slave. He is said to have been emancipated by Augustus Caesar. His works, exclusive of 32 fables considered spurious, consist of 95 fables, written in iambic verse, and in 5 books.

PHAESTUS, ancient city of Crete, S.W. of Candia, occupied from Neolithic to Venetian times. Excavation has discovered a palace of c. 1800 B.C., with an earlier one beneath it.

PHAETHON, in *Greek Mythology*, son of Helios, the sun god. Attempting to drive his father's chariot across the skies, he was too weak to control the spirited horses, with the result that he came so near to earth that some of it was burned, the parched condition of the Sahara being attributed to this.

PHALANX, tactical formation of infantry introduced by Philip of Macedon, and perfected by Alexander. The Macedonian spearmen, armed with very long spears, were arranged many ranks deep, so that many spears projected beyond the front line. The charge was made in this formation. Alexander's victories were largely due to this method. The ruse was checkmated by the Roman legionaries by giving it no opportunity to charge, by luring it on to broken ground, then breaking it up with missiles.

PHALARIS, tyrant of Agrigentum in Sicily. Eusebius places his accession to power in 570 B.C. He is said to have reigned 16 years, when he was deposed and put to death. He was infamous for cruelty, burning his victims in a bull of bronze, in order to have the pleasure of hearing their cries. He is said to have been burned in his own bull.

PHALERUM, most easterly of three harbours at Piraeus, port of Athens.

PHALINUS, a Zacynthian, who after the battle of Cunaxa, in 401 B.C., accompanied the Persian heralds sent to the army of the 10,000, to require them to lay down their arms; he returned unsuccessful from Clearchus.

PHANIAS, peripatetic philosopher, disciple of Aristotle, and friend of Theophrastus, flourishing about 336 B.C.

PHANOCLES, Greek elegiac poet, living about the time of Alexander.

PHANOSTHENES, an Adrian instructed by Athens to command four ships in 407 B.C., and go to Andros to succeed Conon at that base. Falling in with two Thurian galleys he captured both, with their crews.

PHARAOH, name given by the Hebrews to an Egyptian dynasty, and equivalent in meaning to the Roman "Caesar." It was either derived from *Pa Ra,* the sun, the chief title of all ancient Egyptian Kings; or the popular nomenclature, *Phouro,* "the King." The Pharaohs mentioned in the Bible are difficult to identify. The King who patronized Joseph may have been Oristesen or Sesertesen I, of the XIIth dynasty; he whose tyranny led to the Hebrew Exodus, Menephthes, son of Rameses II.

PHARISEES, religious party among the Jews, springing from the Chasidim during the Maccabean wars, and originally the patriots of the nation, who insisted on the permanent separateness of Jews and Gentiles, and the unchanging authority of the Mosaic Law. As champions of Jewish nationalism they were opposed to the Sadducees and Herodians.

PHARNACES, King of Pontus, son of Mithridates IV, whom he succeeded in 190 B.C.

PHAROS, W. extremity of the city of Alexandria, formerly an island, was connected with the city by a causeway. There stood the ancient Pharos, or lighthouse, one of the seven wonders of the world, built under Ptolemy II, about 260 B.C.

PHARSALUS, town in the district of Pharsalia, Thessaly, near the river Enipeus, scene of much fighting in the war between Rome and Macedonia, 197 B.C. The battle of Pharsalus was fought on Aug. 9, 48 B.C., on this territory, between Caesar with 22,000 men, and Pompey with twice the number. This was the decisive battle of the civil war.

PHEIDIAS, sculptor of ancient Greece, son of Charmides, was born at Athens. He was employed on the famous statue of Athena Parthenos, superintending the decoration under Pericles. He was later accused of misappropriation of treasure entrusted to him, and either died in prison, or fled to Elis.

PHERECRATES, of Athens, poet of the Old Comedy, contemporary with Plato and Aristophanes.

PHIDIAS, *see* Pheidias.

PHIDIPPIDES, was sent to Sparta by the Athenians, in 490 B.C., to ask for aid against the Persians, and arrived the second day, having covered 150 m.

PHIDON, King of Argos, was the son of Aristodamidas, who in 668 B.C., deprived the Eleans of their presidency of the Olympic games.

PHILADELPHIA, (an ancient city of Lydia, Asia Minor, founded by Attalus Philadelphus, King of Pergamum, about 150 B.C. (b) Rabbath-Ammon of the Old Testament and (c) a city of Egypt.

PHILAE, small island in the Nile near Assuan, noted for its temples.

PHILEMON, friend and disciple of S. Paul, to whom the Apostle addressed one of the epistles belonging to the group known as the epistles of the captivity. It is concerned with a runaway slave of his, who had become one of S. Paul's converts. The slave, Onesimus, had wronged his master and been unprofitable, and S. Paul sends him back and pleads forgiveness. The epistle may have been written about 60-62 A.D.

PHILEMON, in *Greek Legend,* the name of an aged man who, with his wife Baucis, received Zeus and Hermes when they visited the earth and no one else entertained them.—Philemon was also the name of an Athenian poet of the New Comedy. He was son of Damon and a native of Soli in Cilicia. He was a great favourite with the Athenians, and often conquered his rivals in dramatic contests.

PHILIP, one of the Apostles, born at Bethsaida, who estimated the cost of feeding the hungry multitude that had come some distance to hear Jesus.—Another Philip was one of the seven deacons selected by the apostles to relieve them of the work of caring for the poor.

PHILIPPI, city of ancient Macedonia, founded by Philip of Macedon, on a spur of Mt. Pangaeus. S. Paul founded one of the first Christian churches here. It was the scene of two battles, fought in 42 B.C., between the forces of Brutus and Cassius, and those of Octavian. In the second engagement Brutus was defeated, his army annihilated, while he took his own life. The result made Octavian and Antony masters of the Roman world.

PHILIPPIANS, EPISTLE TO, one of S. Paul's epistles belonging to the group known as the epistles of the captivity. It is addressed from prison to the Church at Philippi, which was founded by S. Paul on his second missionary journey. Since the imprisonment was probably in Rome rather than Caesarea, the epistle may have been written in 63 A.D. It is a personal letter expressing S. Paul's thanks for gifts and friendly acts, and his great joy in the Gospel, and asking the Philippians to rejoice with him.

PHILIPPICS, speeches of Demosthenes, so-called because their aim was to warn his country against the plans cherished by Philip of Macedon, for the overthrow of Greek independence.

PHILIPPUS (Philip), Philip II, King of Macedonia, younger son of King Amyntas, was brought up at Thebes, where he studied military science under Epaminondas. He was recalled to Macedonia in 364 B.C., to act as regent for his nephew Amyntas. Seizing the throne he set about to bring the army under discipline, and to organize it as an efficient instrument of war. Philip invented the Macedonian phalanx (which see), adding to it the cavalry organization which gave overwhelming superiority over Greek tactics. Athens united with Thebes to oppose him but was decisively defeated at Chaeronea, in 338 B.C., and at the congress of the Greek states Philip was elected captain-general, in 337 B.C. Philip was father of Alexander the Great. Philip's reign was from 382-336 B.C.—Philip V, King of Macedonia, was son of Demetrius II. In 215 B.C., he concluded an alliance with Hannibal in consequence of which the Romans formed a combination against him in 211 B.C., which kept Philip busy fighting until 205 B.C. The war was renewed by the Romans in 200 B.C., and in 197 Philip was overthrown.

PHILIPPUS, MARCUS JULIUS, Roman emperor from 244-49 A.D. He commanded the army led by Gordian III against the Persians, and incited a mutiny; Gordian was murdered and Philippus declared his successor; he concluded an unfavourable peace with the Persians. He was slain at Verona.

PHILISCUS, Athenian poet of Middle comedy, flourishing about 400 B.C.—P. of Miletus, a rhetorician, and disciple of Isocrates.—P. of Aegina, cynic philosopher, disciple of Diogenes.

PHILISCUS, was sent in 368 B.C., to Greece by Ariobarzanes to effect a reconciliation between the Thebans and Lacedaemonians, but did not fully succeed. Returning to Asia, he made himself master of a number of Greek states. He was murdered at Lampsacus by Thersagoras and Execestus.

PHILISTINES, an ancient people living along the coast of Palestine, who appear to have come originally from Crete and the Anatolian coast, establishing themselves in five cities in Palestine:—Gaza, Ashkelon, Ashdod, Gath and Ekron. They remained independent until the time of Tiglath-Pileser, in 734 B.C., who started to subdue them. In 701 B.C., Sennacherib overcame them.

PHILO, a leader of Academic Scepticism, founder of the fourth academy. He was born at Larissa, and became disciple of Clitomachus.

PHILO THE JEW, was born at Alexandria. He was sent to Rome in 39 A.D., as envoy to Caligula. Of his writings the most important works deal with the books of Moses, and are generally cited under different titles.

PHILOCTETES, son of Poeas and Demonassa, was the most famous archer in the Trojan War.

PHILODEMUS, of Gadara, in Palestine, was an Epicurean philosopher, and epigrammatic poet, contemporary with Cicero.

PHILOLAUS, Pythagorean philosopher, contemporary with Socrates.

PHILOMELIDES, a King of Lesbos, was in the habit of compelling his guests to wrestle with him: he was overcome by Ulysses.

PHILONIDES, Athenian poet of the Old Comedy.

PHILOPOEMEN, of Megalopolis who distinguished himself at the battle of Sellasia, in 221 B.C. He became general of the Achaean League eight times. In 183 B.C., he was carried by

Messenian troops to Messene, where he was made to take poison. He was one of the few great men Greece produced in the decline of her independence.

PHILOTAS, friend of Alexander the Great, accused in 330 B.C., of being involved in a plot against the King's life. Confession was dragged from him by torture and he was stoned to death. There was no proof of his guilt.

PHOCION, Athenian general and statesman, contemporary with Demosthenes. His first appearance in history is at the battle of Naxos, in 376 B.C. Phocion attended the school of Plato and, later, that of Xenocrates. Phocion often led Athenian armies with success. He was put to death in 317 B.C.

PHOCIS, a country in Central Greece, divided into two by the range of Parnassus. In the Persian invasion Xerxes ravaged the country at the instigation of the Thessalians, who were their enemies. The great even in the history of Phocis, was the Sacred War, which ended in the ruin of the Phocians. The Delphic oracle was situated in Phocis.

PHOENICIA, ancient territory on the W. coast of the Mediterranean, N. of Palestine, between the range of Lebanon and the sea. Its length did not exceed 200 m.; its breadth averaging about 15 m. The fame of the Phoenicians rests on their supremacy as navigators. In the 5th cent. B.C., this pre-eminence was still undisputed after 1000 years. They alone had passed out of the Mediterranean, coasted along Spain and France, established a trade with the "tin islands," the Scilly Isles, and Cornwall, and possibly penetrated the Baltic. Phoenician ships in the Egyptian service actually circumnavigated Africa about 610 B.C. Phoenicia never formed a united nation with a common government: it was a group of city states, among the most important of which were Tyre and Sidon. In the 11th cent. B.C., Tyre had become the leading state. Hiram, King of Tyre, was an ally of David and Solomon, during the brief period of Hebrew consolidation and expansion. After being subjugated by Assyria and Babylonia, Phoenicia formed for 200 years an autonomous province, in one of the satrapies of the Persian empire. After Alexander had routed Darius at Issus, in 333 B.C., the cities of Phoenicia, except Tyre, broke from Persia and submitted to Macedonia. Then came the siege. Tyre had defied Nebuchadnezzar for 13 years: now it defied Alexander. With the fall of Tyre in 332 B.C., the separate history of Phoenicia ends.

PHOENIX, in *Greek Legend,* King of Dolopes. He was tutor to Achilles, whom he accompanied to the Trojan War: also he took part in the hunt for the Calydonian boar.

PHOENIX, mythical bird of the Egyptians, sacred to the sungod, supposed to appear at Heliopolis once in every five hundred years and build a pyre, on which it was burnt, a new bird arising from the ashes.

PHORMION, commanded the Athenian fleet in the Peloponnesian War, and won two victories in 429 B.C.

PHRAORTES, King of Media, killed at the siege of Nineveh. He reigned from 656-634 B.C.

PHRYGIA, ancient country of Asia Minor, covering much the same ground as modern Anatolia. It was peopled by the Phryges, warlike people of Aryan descent. The earlier inhabitants, displaced by the Phryges about 1200 B.C., appear to have been of the same mixed race as the Hittites. There was a powerful Phrygian monarchy, commencing at an unknown date, and remaining until the beginning of the 7th cent. B.C., when it was overthrown. The Lydians then ruled it, and later the Persians, and eventually it became part of the Roman empire.

PHRYNICUS, early Athenian tragic poet, the disciple of Thespis. Another of this name was a poet of the Old Comedy, flourishing about 429 B.C.; while a third of the name was a Greek sophist and grammarian, in the days of Aurelius and Commodus.

PHRYNNIS, famous dithyrambic poet, born at Mytilene, he flourished in Athens about 445 B.C.

PHRYNON, an Athenian, famous for strength and courage, who commanded the Athenian forces in their struggle with the Mytileneans for possession of Sigeum.

PHTHIOTIS, district of S.E. Thessaly inhabited by the Achaeans.

PHYLACE, (a) town of Thessaly, birthplace of Protesilaus.

(b) Town in Arcadia on the frontiers of Tegea and Laconia.

(c) Town of Epirus in Molossia.

PHYLARCHUS, Greek historian, contemporary with Aratus. His principal work was in 28 books, covering the 52 years from the expedition of Pyrrhus to Peloponnesus in 272 B.C., to the death of Cleomenes, in 220 B.C.

PHYLLIDAS, a Theban secretary to the Polemarchs who held office under the protection of Sparta.

PICENTIA, town in S. Campania whose inhabitants were compelled by the Romans, because they had revolted to Hannibal, to leave their town for the neighbouring villages.

PICENUM, narrow strip of land on the W. coast of the Adriatic, in Central Italy, which was the 5th region in the division of Italy by Augustus.

PICTI, (Picts), name of a people formerly living in N. Scotland. They were divided into two nations, the Northern Picts, between Pentland Firth and the Grampians; the Southern Picts, between the Grampians and the Firth of Forth. From the 3rd cent. A.D., the Picts were harassing foes of the Roman occupation, and were never completely subdued. SS. Ninian and Columba laboured to convert them to Christianity. King Oswald of Northumbria held temporary sway over Pictland in the 7th cent. Their royal succession was unique, in that rule passed to brothers, or the son of a sister.

PICTONES, people of Gallia Aquitanica, whose chief town was Limonum.

PICUS, (Woodpecker) in *Roman Legend,* a prophetic divinity. The story is founded on the idea that the woodpecker is a prophetic bird, sacred to Mars. Pomona was beloved by him, and when Circe's love for him was not returned, she changed him into a woodpecker.

PILATE, (Pontius Pilatus), Roman procurator of Judaea from 26-36 A.D. His rule was oppressive and unacceptable to the Jews. The N.T. accounts of the trial of Jesus before him credit him with a sense of justice and a desire to save him. Pilate was called to Rome to answer charges, was banished to Gaul, where he took his own life. The Copts aver that he died a Christian martyr, and the Ethiopic Church includes him in the canon, with a festival on June 25. His wife, Claudia Procula, is a saint in the calendar of the Greek Church.

PINDARUS (PINDAR), Greek lyric poet, born near Thebes, of a noble Dorian family. The family traditions were musical and Pindar is said to have excelled on the lute. His first poetic composition was a choral ode, written at the age of 20 to commemorate the victory of a Thessalian youth at the Pythian games. He rapidly rose to fame, receiving commissions to write choral songs for special occasions from all parts of the Greek world, from democracies such as Athens, and from tyrants such as Hiero of Syracuse. He came to be regarded as the great national lyric poet, and after his death his memory was held in the utmost veneration. His Odes are divided into four books according to the victories celebrated at the Olympian, Pythian, Nemean, and Isthmian games. Nearly all his other work is lost. He lived from about 522-443 B.C.

PINDUS, mountain range of N. Greece, part of the backbone which runs N. to S. The name was confined to the part of the range which separates Thessaly and Epirus.

PINTIA, town of the Vaccaei, in Hispania Tarraconensis, on the road from Asturica to Caesaraugusta.

PIRAEUS or PIRAEEUS, sea-port of Greece, being the port of Athens, on the Saronic Gulf, 6 m. S.W. of Athens, owed its foundation to Themistocles and Pericles. It was destroyed by Sulla in 86 B.C., and not rebuilt until after the establishment of the modern kingdom of Greece.

PIRITHOUS, in *Greek Mythology,* King of the Lapithae in Thessaly, and son of Zeus and Dia, who invaded Attica, but when opposed by Theseus conceived a warm admiration for the Athenian King. When Pirithous was celebrating his nuptials with Hippodamia, the drunken Centaur Eurytion carried her off, which caused the famous fight between the Centaurs and Lapithae, in which the Centaurs suffered defeat. Hippodamia afterwards died. Pirithous and Theseus each determined to marry a daughter of Zeus. Pirithous resolved to carry off Persephone. Theseus would not desert his friend in the enterprise.

The two went to the underworld, were seized by Pluto and fastened to a rock. Hercules delivered Theseus, but Pirithous remained in torment.

PISA, ancient city of Etruria, was founded about 6th cent. B.C., and like other Etruscan cities, in due time fell to Rome. It preserved its own municipal privileges, and political freedom. It received favours from the emperors, but on the decline of the Roman power was not able to defend itself against the invasions of the Northmen.

PISGAH, Mt. summit in Moab, from which Moses was allowed to view the land of Gilead.

PISIDIA, ancient district of S. Asia Minor; mountainous, with wild and warlike inhabitants who kept independence against all successive rulers of Asia Minor until reduced by Rome.

PISISTRATUS, son of Hippocrates. His mother was cousin to the mother of Solon. He became tyrant of Athens in 560 B.C. He died in 527 B.C.

PISO, CALPURNIUS, name of a distinguished plebeian family. (a) was taken prisoner at Cannae, 216 B.C. He became praetei urbanus 211, and later commanded as propraetei in Etruria 210. (b) Son of above, was praetor in 186, and received Further Spain as his province. He became consul in 180. (c) was praetor in 154 and became consul in 146 when he was sent to Carthage to conduct war against it. (d) Son of the above, was consul in 112 with M. Livius Drusus. In 107 he was legatus to the consul L. Cassius Longinus. (e) Son of the above who never rose to office. (f) Son of the above and a debauchee first mentioned in 59 when brought to trial by P. Clodius for plundering a province. (g) Son of above, consul in 15, and later obtained the province of Pamphylia. There were several others of the same name.

PITTACUS, one of the so-called Seven Wise Men of Greece, born at Mitylene, in Lesbos, about 652 B.C. With the help of the brothers of Alcaeus, he delivered his island from the tyranny of Melanchrus, in 612 B.C., and when the Mityleneans were involved in a war with the Athenians Pittacus gained the victory over Phrynon in 606 B.C. The popular party at Mitylene elected Pittacus to the office of aesymnetes to defend the constitution. He administered with prudence and success. In 580 B.C., he retired, dying in 570 B.C., aged 82. He wrote many elegies.

PLACENTIA, Roman colony, founded at the same time as Cremona in Cisalpine Gaul, in 219 B.C., was destroyed by the Gauls in 200, and rebuilt by the Romans to become a place of importance.

PLACIA, ancient Pelasgian settlement in Mysia, early destroyed.

PLANCUS, (a) L. Munatius, nominated by Julius Caesar as governor of Transalpine Gaul for 44 B.C. (b) T. Munatius Bursa, brother of the above, and tribune of the plebs in 52 B.C. (c) Cn. Munatius, another brother, praetor in 43 B.C. (d) L. Plautius, still another brother, adopted by L. Plautius, included in the proscription of the triumvirs in 42, was put to death.

PLATAEA, ancient city of Boeotia. Leaving the Theban league, Plataea became an ally of Athens, and sent 1000 men to the battle of Marathon. In the second Persian War, Xerxes destroyed the city at the instigation of Thebes, in 480 B.C. The Persian army fought the allied Greeks under Pausanias of Sparta before Plataea in 479 B.C., and was almost annihilated. This victory, following that of Salamis, decided the struggle between East and West.

PLATO, (427-347 B.C.) Greek philosopher, born at Athens, or in the island of Aegina, of distinguished parents, spent most of his life in Athens immersed in philosophy. He travelled and was captured and sold as a slave at Aegina. After the trial and death of Socrates, in 399 B.C., he devoted himself to the mission of his martyred teacher, the record of which is written in the collection of Dialogues that have come to us. Of the 35 treatises, some 24 are probably by his hand. Plato set himself to understand Hellenic society with the object of indicating reforms. He formulated a system of philosophy based on contemporary experience, designed to state the principles of life and conduct. The note of his conclusions is idealistic, and the question of

Platonism depends on an understanding of the "ideas." His great dictum was "what is wholly real is wholly knowable, and what is utterly nonexistent is completely unknowable," which answers to the modern assertion of "the unity of the intelligible world with itself and the mind that knows it." In ethics and politics Plato was the first thinker to offer a satisfying account of the principles that form and govern conduct and character; but his morality is far from being intellectual in the sense of abstract. "Justice" is the virtue of the good citizen, and his idea of the good is to be realized in the life of the commonwealth. He shows in the Republic that it is in the larger life of the justly organized state of society, that the good life of the individual finds expression. Here is the embodiment, even if imperfectly attained, of the idea of the good, which for Plato solves the riddle of the universe.

PLAUTIUS, AULUS, Roman soldier, was governor of Pannonia, and, in 43 A.D., was ordered to lead the British expedition by Claudius. Recalled in 47 A.D., he received an ovation.

PLAUTUS, TITUS MACCIUS, Roman comic poet, born at Sarsina, in Umbria about 251 B.C. In his spare time he wrote comedies which proved so successful that he devoted the rest of his life to playwriting. Of his 130 comedies only 21 have been preserved, and are adaptations from Demophilus, Diphilus, Menander, and Philemon. The pungent wit, the rapidity of the action, and the shrewd knowledge of human nature displayed, have made the comedies popular down to modern times. Plautius died in 184 B.C.

PLEMINIUS, Q., propraetor and legatus of Scipio Africanus, sent in 205 B.C., against Locri, in S. Italy, which was held by the Carthaginians. He captured the town, and remained as governor. His cruelty was such that he was recalled and imprisoned in 204 B.C., but died before his trial.

PLEURON, ancient city of Aetolia, originally peopled by the Curetes, but abandoned when Demetrius Poliorcetes laid waste the area. A new city was built to the west.

PLINIUS (PLINY), (a) Gaius Plinius Secundus, called Pliny the Elder, to distinguish him from his nephew. He was born in

23 A.D., and in 67 was appointed procurator in Spain. His last official appointment was as admiral of the fleet at Misenum, when he was killed at the eruption of Vesusius. He wrote, among other works, a Natural History, in 37 books, reading more than 2000 volumes for information. (b) Gaius Plinius Caecilius Secundus, called the Younger to distinguish him from his uncle. He was born at Novum Comum in 61 A.D., and was adopted by his uncle who educated him. He started as a pleader in the courts and developed a successful public career. His correspondence is of great interest but the *Letters*, published in 9 books were obviously written for publication.   Perhaps Pliny the Younger's most important letter is that sent by him to Trajan, concerning the Christians.

PLISTOANAX, eldest son of Pausanias, was King of Sparta from 485-408 B.C., but from 445-426 B.C., he was an exile. He was recalled on the instruction of the Delphic oracle.

PLOTINA, POMPEIA, the Emperor Trajan's wife, who persuaded him to adopt Hadrian, in whose reign she died. Hadrian mourned her nine days, and erected a temple in her honour.

PLOTINUS, most famous writer and teacher of the Neo-Platonic school at Alexandria, was born at Lycopolis in Egypt, in 204 A.D. He studied at Alexandria under Ammonius, founder of the Eclectic School. He joined Gordian's army in 248 A.D., when the emperor was marching against the Parthians, and on the death of the emperor went to Antioch and thence to Rome, where he taught for many years. In his 50th year, at the request of Porphyrius, he committed his lectures to writing. He died in 274 A.D., in Campania. His work consists of 54 books, which Porphyrius distributed into 6 Enneads. Plotinus treated the most obscure subjects, such as *On the Essence of the Soul, On the Unity of the Good,* etc.

PLUTARCHUS (PLUTARCH), Greek biographer and philosopher, born at Chaeronea, in Boeotia about 48 A.D., and appears to have spent much of his time in Rome. His fame rests almost entirely on his *Parallel Lives,* a collection of biographies of notable men (with the exception of 4) in pairs, one Greek, and the other Roman. The resemblance is often slight. They are historically important, much of the matter being taken from authorities now lost. He died in 122 A.D.

PLUTO, Roman name for the god of the underworld, more commonly known to the Greeks as Hades. He is regarded as a stern ruler of the lower regions, but as a beneficent deity who distributes to mankind the fruits of the earth, both mineral and grain. He had as wife Persephone. He is not to be confused with Plutus, god of wealth.

POLA, ancient town on the W. coast of Istria, founded by the Colchians, and subsequently a Roman colony.

POLEMON, son of Zenon, the orator of Laodicea, was King of Pontus and the Bosporus, who accompanied Antony on his expedition against the Parthians, in 36 B.C.

POLLIO, C. ASINIUS, Roman orator, poet, and historian, born at Rome, in 76 B.C., who fought on Caesar's side in the civil war. Finally he united his forces with those of Octavian, Antony, and Lepidus. He was chosen by Antony to settle the veterans in the lands which had been assigned to them in the Transpadane Gaul. Pollio was consul in 40 B.C. In 39 B.C., Antony went to Greece, and Pollio, as his legate, overcame the Parthini, taking the Dalmatian town of Salonae. Pollio died in 5 A.D., aged 80.

POLLUX, in *Greek Mythology,* twin brother of Castor. *Also,* Pollux, Julius, scholar and rhetorician of 2nd cent. A.D.

POLYBIUS, Greek historian, born in Megalopolis, in Arcadia, about 210 B.C., was deported to Italy after the conquest of Macedonia, and was received into the house of Aemilius Paulus, with whose son, the younger Scipio, he formed a lifelong friendship. He returned to Greece in 146 B.C., and when the inevitable defeat took place Polybius set himself to secure the best terms for his fellow countrymen. He succeeded so well that statues were erected to his honour in a number of Greek cities. He wrote a history of Rome in 40 books, but only the first 5 remain.

POLYCARPUS (POLYCARP), Apostolic father, born about 69 A.D., is said to have become a Christian about 80 A.D., and to have been consecrated Bishop of Smyrna, by S. John, about 96 A.D. He wrote an epistle to the Philippians, and, about 155 A.D., went to Rome to discuss matters of church observance with

Anicetus, the pope. After his return he was caught up in a persecution of the Christians and burnt at the stake in 155 A.D.

POLYCLITUS, Greek sculptor, flourished about 452-412 B.C., one of the greatest artists of his age. His *Doryphorus* (spearsman), of which there are copies at Rome, Florence, Naples, and Berlin, was, according to Pliny, the last word in perfect sculpture. Among his other works was the famous chryselephantine statue of Hera, once in the temple at Argos.

POLYDORUS, son of Priam, slain by Achilles.

POLYGNOTUS, one of the most famous Greek painters of the 5th cent. B.C.

POLYPHEMUS, in *Greek Mythology*, a Cyclops, son of Poseidon and Thoosa, lived on the coast of Trinacria, where he was a shepherd. In their wanderings, Odysseus and his companions sought refuge in his cave. Polyphemus killed and ate some of Odysseus' companions, and when the giant slept Odysseus destroyed the sight of his one eye, thus escaping with the remainder of his comrades.

POLYSPERCHON, a Macedonian officer of Alexander the Great, who Antipater, (on his deathbed), appointed to succeed him.

POLYSTRATUS, philosopher of the Epicurean school, and its head after Hermarchus.

POMPEIA, name of a plebeian gens, the most important member of which was Gnaeus Pompeius (106-48 B.C.). Known as Pompey the Great, he was born on Sept. 30, 106 B.C. When Sulla came to Italy in 84 B.C., Pompey led a strong force to support him. After Sulla's death Pompey remained leader of the senatorial party, commanding their armies in Spain. In 67 B.C., he suppressed the pirates in the Mediterranean, and in 66 overcame Mithridates, q.v., so bringing the whole of the West under Roman sway.

POMPEII, ancient city of Italy, partly destroyed by an earthquake in 63 A.D., was hastily rebuilt, though many buildings were still in ruins when it was completely destroyed by the great eruption of Vesuvius, Aug. 24, 79 A.D.

POMPILIUS ANDRONICUS, a Syrian who taught rhetoric

at Rome, about 50 B.C.

PONTIFEX, member of the most important college of priests in ancient Rome, charged with the maintenance of the law, inasmuch as it was connected with religion, and the supervision of the calendar.

PONTIUS, GAVIUS, Samnite general who defeated the Romans in a mountain pass near Caudium in 321 B.C. Thirty years later Pontius was defeated by Fabius Gurges and put to death.

PONTUS, ancient district of Asia Minor, along the Euxine. It was a monarchy about 400 B.C., being strong and independent until Mithridates was defeated by Pompey, in 63 B.C. Part of it became a Roman province, the remainder surviving under a native ruler until 64 B.C., when this too was taken in by Rome.

POPULONIA, ancient town of Etruria, founded by the Corsicans: it was not one of the twelve Etruscan cities but carried on commerce through its sea-port. It was destroyed by Sulla in the civil war.

PORPHYRIUS (PORPHYRY), Greek philosopher of the Neo-Platonic school, antagonist against Christianity, originally called Malchus. He studied under Origen at Caesarea, and under Apollonius and Longinus at Athens, settling in Rome in his thirtieth year where he became a disciple of Plotinus. After six years his mind became unsettled and he voyaged to Sicily where he wrote against Christianity. Returning to Rome he continued to teach until his death in 305 A.D., or 306.

PORSENA or PORSENNA LARS, King of Clusium in Etruria, who was said to have led his army against Rome to restore Tarquin. An attempt to storm the city was defeated by Horatius Cocles q.v.

POSEIDON, in *Greek Mythology,* son of Cronus and Rhea, was god of the sea. For conspiring against Zeus he had to labour for Laomedon, King of Troy, for whom he constructed the famous walls. When he claimed the promised reward, Laomedon refused, in consequence Poseidon sent a sea-monster which ravished the country, exacting a tribute of maidens, until it was slain by Hercules. His wife was Amphitrite. The Romans identified him with Neptunus.

POSIDONIUS, Stoic philosopher who studied at Athens and taught at Rhodes; he was born in Syria about 135 B.C. Cicero was his pupil. In 51 B.C., he went to Rome and died soon after.

POSTUMUS, emperor of Gaul from 258-267 A.D.: in the latter year he was killed by his soldiers.

POTIDAEA, town of a colony of Corinthians in Macedonia, which became tributary to Athens. Its revolt in 432 B.C., was a contributory cause of the Peloponnesian War. It fell to the Athenians in 429 B.C. It was destroyed by Philip in 356 B.C.

PRAEFECT, title held by various officials, appointed by authority and not chosen by the people, in the Roman constitution. Such were the praefectus urbi, or deputy governor of the city; the military and naval praefects; and the praefect of Egypt.

PRAENESTE, ancient city of Latium, 22 m. E. of Rome, bordering on the country of the Aequi, believed to have been founded by Caeculus, son of Vulcan. It was a favourite resort, having a temple of Fortune, famed for its oracle.

PRAETOR, second in dignity among the Roman magistrates, the consuls being first. The duties of the praetor urbanus were legal, but there were praetores militares charged with the administration of provinces. The praetors were preceded by lictors. The Praetorian Guard were the household troops of the Roman Empire.

PRATINAS, tragic poet of Athens, contemporary with Aeschylus.

PRAXITELES, Greek sculptor of Athens, whose only authentic work is the group of Hermes and Dionysus, discovered among the ruins of Olympia.

PRIAMIDES, title of the sons of Priam.

PRIAMUS (PRIAM), in *Greek Mythology,* King of Troy, son of Laomedon and father of Hector, Paris, Polyxena, Cassandra, and many more, he having been credited with 50 sons and daughters. He was the only one of the sons of Laomedon that was spared when Hercules came to take vengeance for being cheated out of his reward for saving Hesione from the sea-monster. At the fall of Troy, Priam was killed by Neoptolemus, son of Achilles.

PRIAPUS, in *Greek Mythology,* god of the productive powers of nature, and patron of gardens. He was son of Dionysus and Aphrodite. The chief seat of his worship was at Lampsacus on the Hellespont.

PRIENE, one of the twelve Ionian cities on the coast of Asia Minor. Bias, one of the Seven Sages, was born here.

PRIMUS, M. ANTONIUS, Roman general who was victorious over the Vitellian army at Bedriacum, in 69 A.D.

PRISCUS, HELVIDIUS, son-in-law of Thrasea, devoted to liberty and virtue; put to death by Vespasian.

PROBUS, MARCUS AURELIUS, Roman emperor from 276 to 282 A.D., was born in Pannonia, and became Aurelian's most distinguished general. On the death of Tacitus he was proclaimed emperor by the armies of the east, where he was in chief command. He proved an excellent ruler, defeating the Germans, and restoring order in Egypt and Gaul. As he was preparing for an expedition against Persia he was murdered.

PROCLUS, famous teacher of the Neo-Platonic School, born at Byzantium in 412 A.D.; he died in 485 A.D.

PROCOPIUS, Roman emperor of the East from 365 to 366 A.D., was born in Cilicia, and a kinsman of Julian the Apostate, who made him joint commander of the army in Mesopotamia. On the accession of Valens in 364, Procopius finding his life in danger, fled to Constantinople, and, favoured by popular discontent, was proclaimed emperor, but was later beheaded.

PROCRUSTES, (the stretcher), in *Greek Legend,* the nickname of Polypemon, a robber of Attica, killed by Theseus. He boasted that he had a bed which fitted everyone and made good his boast by stretching the limbs of his victims who were too short, cutting them off in the case of those who were too long. He has become proverbial to illustrate attempts to make all conform to one standard.

PROETUS, in *Greek Legend,* twin brother of Acrisius, who after a struggle obtained part of his kingdom of Argolis. His three daughters were driven mad by Dionysus or Hera. Perseus, to avenge Acrisius, turned Proetus into stone.

PROMETHEUS, in *Greek Mythology,* first a god of fire, and later a Titan. He stole fire from heaven for the use of mortals, and for so doing was chained by Zeus to a rock in Scythia. Every day an eagle consumed his liver, which grew again in the night. He had to suffer this torture till he was rescued by Hercules, who killed the eagle and released him.

PROPERTIUS, SEXTUS, Roman elegiac poet, born about 49 B.C., at Asisium. He was educated and continued to live in Rome, where he enjoyed the patronage of Maecenas and Augustus, and was a friend of Ovid and Virgil. Most of his earlier poems deal with his relations with his mistress Cynthia; his latter poems deal chiefly with Roman history and legend.

PROPRAETOR, Roman governor of a province.

PROTAGORAS, Greek philosopher and sophist was born in 490 B.C., at Abdera in Thrace. He taught in Sicily and later at Athens. He had to flee Athens on a charge of atheism. He was drowned at sea in 415 B.C. He was the first to study and write on grammar.

PROTEUS, in *Greek Mythology*, "an old man of the sea," who tended the flocks (seals) of Poseidon, rising at mid-day from the deep, to sleep on shore, surrounded by sea-monsters. His favourite residence was either Pharos or Karpathos. To obtain his prophecies, it was needful to surprise him during sleep, and hold him until he had exhausted all his powers of transformation.

PROTOGENES, Greek painter, born at Caunus, but resident at Rhodes. He flourished about 332-300 B.C.

PROVERBS, O.T. book belonging to a class of Hebrew literature called Wisdom Literature. The full title is *The Proverbs of Solomon, son of David, King of Israel*. The book is a collection of wise sayings and proverbs, and apparently not the work of a single writer. The divisions have been described as 1. A group of discourses on wisdom and wise conduct. 2. A collection of aphorisms in couplet form. 3. Two collections of aphoristic quatrains. 4. A collection of aphoristic couplets. 5. A collection of discourses of various characters.

PRUDENTIUS, AURELIUS CLEMENS, Christian poet, born at Caesaraugusta, in 348 A.D. He practiced as an advocate, held several provincial appointments, and lived for some time at the court of Honorius. Losing the imperial favour, he retired to a monastery, and wrote religious poems. His chief works in hexameters and lyrics, are *Cathemerinon,* prayers for daily use; *Peristephanon,* acts of Martyrs; *Hamartigenia,* the origin of evil. Prudentius died in 410 A.D.

PSALMS, O.T. book; a collection of 150 poems, divided, in the Hebrew Bible, into 5 smaller books. 1. Pss. 1-41; 2. Pss. 42-72; 3. Pss. 73-89; 4. Pss. 90-106; 5. Pss. 107-150. According to Jewish tradition the fivefold division was intended to correspond to the fivefold division of The Law. Each of the first four books ends with a doxology, while the last psalm of the 5th division serves as such. In the Hebrew Bible, and in the Septuagint, all but 24 bear titles, or superscriptions which make statements about the authorship, or occasion of composition, or give musical directions.

PSAMMENTIUS, King of Egypt, was conquered by Cambyses. He succeeded Amasis in 526 B.C., and reigned only six months.

PSAMMIS, King of Egypt, 601-595 A.D., successor of Necho.

PSAMMITICHUS or PSAMMETICHUS, Greek form of Psametik, King of Egypt, founder of the Saitic dynasty, reigned from 671-617 B.C. He was originally one of the 12 Kings who obtained an independent sovereignty in the confusion following the death of Setho. He built the south propylaea of the temple of Hephaestus at Memphis, and an elaborate aula with a portico around it, for the habitation of Apis, in front of the temple.

PSYCHE, in *Classical Mythology,* a maiden so beautiful that she aroused the envy of Venus, who sent Cupid to inspire her with love for the meanest of men. Cupid fell in love with her beauty, but left her owing to the machinations of her jealous sisters. Psyche then set out to look for Cupid, and after long wandering was united to her lover.

PTAH, Egyptian deity, local god of Memphis, in the first dynasty, was the divine artificer, creating all things from the Nile mud.

PTOLEMY, or Claudius Ptolemaeus. Egyptian astronomer and geographer, who flourished 127-51 A.D. The dates of his birth and death are not known. He conducted his observations at

Alexandria during the reigns of Hadrian and Antoninus Pius. His doctrines were incorporated in 13 books, written about 140 A.D., called *Almagest* by the Arabs. The Ptolemaic system is the theory expounded by Ptolemy to account for the movements of heavenly bodies. He supposed that the sun, moon, and stars revolved in circles about the earth. Beyond the latter, and beyond the fire and water which it supported, was the ether. The zones of the heavens were in and beyond the ether, each zone a transparent spherical shell. Each shell, or sphere, had its own heavenly body which, revolving with it, moved round the earth. —As a geographer, he was equally celebrated. His *Geographike Syntaxis* was the first attempt to place geography on a scientific basis. He laid down the latitude and longitude of places, and constructed maps of the known inhabited world on a mathematical basis in a manner far in advance of his time.

PTOLEMY (PTOLEMAEUS), name of several Kings of Egypt. Ptolemy I Soter, was a favourite general of Alexander, at whose death in 323 B.C., he became satrap of Egypt, and in 305 B.C., assumed the kingly title, thus inaugurating the Ptolemaic dynasty, which lasted until 30 B.C. Soter founded Ptolemais in Upper Egypt, as rival to Thebes; he built the Serapeum, and planned the famous library and museum, in 285 B.C., he abdicated, dying two years later. Ptolemy II Philadelphus, succeeded his father in 285 B.C. He opened a canal from the Nile to the Red Sea, and founded the port of Berenice. Ptolemy III Euergetes, succeeded Philadelphus in 246 B.C., and by marrying Berenice, daughter of Ptolemy Soter's stepson Magas, added Cyrenaica to the Kingdom of Egypt. The remaining Ptolemies were not so important. Ptolemy IV Philopator, dying in 205 B.C., was succeeded by his son Ptolemy V Epiphanes. Then came Ptolemy VI Philometor. The legitimate line came to an end with Ptolemy X, in 80 B.C. Ptolemy XII and XIII were both brothers of Cleopatra and associated with her in the government. Ptolemy XIV was her son, and Ptolemy XV, last of the dynasty, who died in 40 A.D., was her grandson.

PUBLICANI, (Publicans), in ancient Rome, farmers of taxes and revenue.

PUNIC WARS, series of wars between the Romans and Carthaginians or Poeni, for mastery of the W. Mediterranean. In the first Punic War, 264-241 B.C., the center of the struggle was Sicily, the largest portion of which was in the hands of the Carthaginians. In the end the Romans prevailed. In the 2nd Punic War, 218-201 B.C., the scene of the first fighting was Spain, but in 218 B.C. Hannibal led an army first across the Pyrenees and then across the Alps, descended into the valley of the Po, and won victories at Lake Trasimenus, 217, and Cannae, 216, but was checked by Quintus Fabius Maximus, surnamed Cunctator. Hasdrubal, brother of Hannibal, made his way from Spain to Italy, with reinforcements, but was defeated and slain at Metaurus. Scipio with a Roman army then landed in Africa in 204. Hannibal was recalled the following year, but at Zama in 202 his army was completely defeated. The Carthaginians lost Spain by the peace terms concluded shortly after. The 3rd Punic War 149-146 B.C., provoked by Rome, ended in the fall of Carthage in 146. The city was razed and the territory of Carthage became the Roman province of Africa.

PUPIENUS MAXIMUS, MARCUS CLODIUS, Roman emperor, 238 A.D. When the tyrant Maximinus had been declared a public enemy by the Senate, Pupienus was called to the throne, together with Balbinus as joint ruler. They could not agree, and their authority was defied, both being murdered in a revolt of the praetorian guard.

PYGMALION, in *Greek Mythology*, King of Cyprus, who made a statue in ivory of a beautiful maiden, and was so charmed with his handiwork that he fell in love with the statue and prayed to Aphrodite to give it life. His request being granted he married the maiden and had a son by her called Paphus.

PYLON (gateway), huge temple portal in ancient Egypt, developed at Thebes, during the XVIIIth dynasty; there was a monolithic lintel, corniced on lofty jambs, flanked by two truncated pyramidal towers with sculptured hieroglyphs. The approach was between royal statues, and a pair of obelisks.

PYLOS, town in ancient Greece, S.W. of Messenia, with a fine harbour.

PYRAMID, stone structure on a polygonal, or square base with triangular sides, sloping to a point. They originated in early dynastic Egypt, and are gigantic tombs, each of a single interment. The design developed from the mastaba-tomb, a transitional form being the step-pyramid at Sakkara.

PYRAMUS, in *Babylonian Legend,* a youth who loved a maiden named Thisbe. The two agreed to meet by the tomb of Ninus and flee together. Thisbe, arriving first, was frightened away by a lion. Pyramus, thinking she had fallen victim to the lion, killed himself. Thisbe, returning to find Pyramus dead, killed herself. The story is told in Ovid's *Metamorphoses,* and is made use of in *A Midsummer Night's Dream.*

PYRRHO, founder of the Sceptical School of philosophy, born at Elis, in Peloponnesus, about 360 B.C. He died in 270 B.C.

PYRRHUS, King of Epirus, who succeeded his father in 306 B.C., and was driven into exile in 301 B.C., but regained the throne. In 281 B.C., the people of Tarentum, in S. Italy, then at war with Rome, appealed to Pyrrhus for assistance. The Romans were defeated at Heraclea, 280 B.C., and at Asculum, 279 B.C., but at such cost that "Pyrrhic victory" has passed into a proverb. An invitation from the Sicilian Greeks for help against the Carthaginians took Pyrrhus to Sicily in 278 B.C. The campaign was at first successful, but in 276 B.C., he returned to Tarentum. His last battle with the Romans was at Beneventum in 275 B.C., resulting in a defeat. Later he attacked Argos, having failed to take Sparta, but was killed by a tile thrown by a woman. *Pyrrhus* is also an alternative name for Neoptolemus, q.v.

PYTHAGORAS, Greek philosopher, born about 582 B.C., at Samos. He went to Crotona, in Italy, about 529 B.C., where he founded a school semi-religious and semi-philosophical. His followers underwent training in gymnastics, mathematics and music, were vegetarians, and believed in immortality and transmigration of the soul. The philosopher found the first principle of the universe in number. He is regarded as founder of Geometry, and discoverer of the musical octave. The 47th proposition of Euclid is attributed to him.

PYTHEAS, of Massilia, in Gaul, Greek navigator in the time of Alexander the Great or a little later. He is reputed to have visited Britain and Thule, and he also coasted along the whole of Europe from Gades to the Tanais.

PYTHON, in *Greek Mythology,* the serpent born of the mud left by the flood which inundated the world in the time of Deucalion. It was slain by Apollo.

Q

QARQAR, here the Kings of Hamath and Damascus, with the assistance of twelve subject princes, were able to meet Shalmaneser in 853 B.C., with a force of 63,000 foot soldiers, 2,000 light cavalry, 4,000 chariots, and 1,000 camels. The battle caused them heavy losses but resulted in the abandonment of Shalmaneser's campaign.

QAWE or QUE, name by which Cilicia was known to the Assyrians from the time of Shalmaneser III onwards; a name for which no explanation has yet been found.

QUADI, a people of the Suevic race, living in S.E. Germany, who in the reign of Tiberius were put under the protection of Rome. In the days of Marcus Aurelius they allied themselves to the Marcomanni, and other tribes and took part in the long war against the Roman Empire. Marcus Aurelius defeated them in 174. We hear no more of the tribe after the 4th cent.

QUADRANS, a Roman copper coin, the fourth part of the as.

QUADRATUS, Christian apologist, and Apostolic Father, who spent his early days in Asia Minor, afterwards becoming Bishop of Athens. He presented the Apology to Hadrian, in 126 A.D.

QUADRATUS, ASINUS, Roman historian living in the middle of the 3rd cent., who wrote two books in the Greek language. One a history of Rome in 15 books, in Ionic dialect, and the other a history of Parthia.

QUADRATUS, FANNIUS, an envious Roman poet who tried to deprecate the works of Horace.

QUADRATUS, L. NINNIUS, tribune of the plebs in 58 B.C., who opposed the measures of his colleague, P. Clodius against Cicero.

QUADRIFONS, a name of Janus, given because after the defeat of the Faliscans a statue of Janus was found having four foreheads. A temple of Janus Quadrifons was built in the Forum, having four gates.

QUADRIGA, in Greek and Roman times, a two-wheeled car, drawn by four horses abreast.

QUADRIGARIUS, Q. CLAUDIUS, Roman historian of the last century B.C., whose work in many books, covered the period from the destruction of Rome by the Gauls to the death of Sulla. Livy drew freely from his work, figments of which have survived.

QUAESTOR, name common to two distinct classes of officers in Rome, who were only distinguished from each other by different attributes: the name of one class was *Quaestores Parricidii;* and of the other *Quaestores Classici.* The origin of the former was traced by some writers to the earliest period of Roman history. Their function was prosecution in capital charges. The latter had the superintendence of the public treasury, and are said to have been instituted by Valerius Publicola, who gave the right of electing them to the people.

QUARIATES, people of Gallia Narbonensis.

QUE, *see* Qawe.

QUERCUS, the Latin word for an Oak Tree, which is of frequent occurrence in the Roman writers.

QUIES, Roman goddess of tranquillity, with a sanctuary on the Via Lavicana, and another outside the Porta Collina.

QUINQUEREME, an ancient ship with five sets of rowers.

QUINTIA, name of a patrician family at Rome, many of whose members held high office during the republican days.

QUINTIANUS AFRANIUS, a senator of dissolute character, who was ridiculed by Nero, and in revenge took part in Piso's conspiracy against the emperor. On the discovery of the conspiracy, he had already committed suicide.

QUINTILIANUS, was born in 40 A.D., at Calagurris in Spain, and educated at Rome. He was most famous of Roman rhetoricians, and is well-known as the author of *The Institutes of Oratory.*

QUINTILLUS, Q. AURELIUS, brother of M. Aurelius Claudius, the emperor. He was called to the throne by his soldiers at Aquileia, in 270 A.D. But the troops at Sirmium, where Claudius had died, proclaimed Aurelius emperor. Quintillus took his own life.

QUINTUS, well-known physician of Rome at the beginning of the 2nd cent. He was forced to leave Rome on account of jealous slander on the part of his less distinguished colleagues. He died about 148 A.D.

QUINTUS, T. CAPITOLINUS BARBATUS, a distinguished general in the early republican days, who more than once acted as mediator between the patricians and plebeians, and was 6 times consul between 471-439 B.C.

QUINTUS CALABER, (sometimes Smyrnaeus), was a Greek poet of the 4th cent., who wrote an epic poem, taking Homer as a model, on the Trojan War.

QUIRINAL, one of the hills of Rome.

QUIRINALIA, a festival in honour of Quirinus, held on Feb. 17.

QUIRINUS, an Italic god, afterwards identified with Romulus.

QUIRINUS, P. SULPICIUS, born in Lanuvium, who was consul in 12 B.C. He was appointed by Augustus in 1 B.C., to instruct his grandson G. Caesar, then in Armenia. Later he became governor of Syria. He died 21 A.D.

QUIRITES, a name given to the populace of Rome as distinguished from the soldiery.

QUIZA, town in N. Africa, W. of Arsenaria, was a Roman municipium.

R

RA or RE, Egyptian sun god, was represented as a solar disc crossing the sky in a bark. Assimilated to Horus of Edfu, he became hawk-headed. From the 5th dynasty every king bore a Ra-name.

RAAMESES or RAAMSES, treasure city, built by the Israelites, in Lower Egypt, during the oppression of Pharaoh.

RABATHMOBA, ancient capital of the Moabites, on the E. side of the Dead Sea, S. of the Arnon.

RABBATAMANA, ancient capital of the Ammonites, in Peraea, N.E. of the Dead Sea. Under its later name of Philadelphia it continued to flourish for a long period.

RABBI or RABBIN, Jewish expounder or doctor of the law.

RABIRIUS, senator, charged by T. Labienus, in 63 B.C., of killing the tribune L. Appuleius Saturninus. He was defended by Cicero.

RACHEL, in the O.T., daughter of Laban, sister of Leah, wife of Jacob, and mother of Joseph and Benjamin. She died giving birth to Benjamin, and the Jewish captives of Nebuchadnezzar passed her tomb on the way to exile.

RACILIUS, L., a close friend of Cicero and Lentulus Spinther, was tribune of the plebs in 56 B.C. He was of Caesar's party in the civil war and fought with his army in Spain in 48 B.C. He was put to death for conspiracy by Longinus.

RAETIA, *see* RHAETIA.

RAMA, (same as Arimathaea), town of Judaea, N. of Jerusalem, in the mountains of Ephraim.

RAMBACIA, capital of the Oritae, on the Gedrosian coast, was colonized by Alexander.

RAMESES, (or Ramessu), name of two kings of Egypt, of the

344

XIXth, and of nine of the XXth dynasty. Rameses II, the Great, supposed to be the Pharaoh of the Oppression, reigned about 1300 B.C. He was frequently at war with the Hittites but in the 21st year of his reign he made a treaty with them. The tablet on which this was recorded was discovered at Boghazköi in 1907. He was a noted builder, a half of the temples remaining date from his reign. Rameses III, (called Rhampsinitus) by Herodotus, was virtual founder of the XXth dynasty. He reigned about 1200 B.C. The British Museum has a papyrus, 133 ft. long and the longest extant, recording his military successes and opulent temple-gifts.

RAPHIA, coastal town of S.W. Palestine, beyond Gaza. It was destroyed at some period, being rebuilt by Gabinius. It was here that Ptolemy Philopator gained a decisive victory over Antiochus the Great.

RAPO, a Rutilian warrior in the army of Turnus, who slew Parthenius.

RATIARIA, headquarters of a Roman Legion in Moesia Superior, on the Danube, and station of a Roman fleet.

RATOMAGUS, capital of the Vellocasses in Gallia Lugdunensis.

RAVENNA, town of Gallia Cisalpina, on the Bedesis, built in the marshes, capable of being reached in only one direction by land. It was founded by the Thessalians, and passed to the Umbrians. Augustus made it one of the two chief stations of the fleet. When the barbarians threatened the empire, the emperors of the West removed to Ravenna. At the fall of the W., Theodoric made it his capital. After the overthrow of the Gothic dominion it became residence of the exarchs.

REATE, ancient city of the Sabines in Central Italy, probably founded by the Pelasgians.

REGILLUS LACUS, lake, on whose banks the Romans gained their victory over the Latins in 498 B.C.

REGINUM, headquarters of a Roman legion, on the Danube, having a fortress.

REGULUS, (a) M. Atilius Regulus, consul in 267 B.C., and in 256 B.C., with Manlius Vulso Longus. They defeated the Carthaginian fleet, and landed in Africa where they were successful. Manlius returned to Rome with part of the army, while Regulus remained with the rest. The Carthaginian generals retired to the mountains, where they were defeated by Regulus, who overran the country without opposition. The Carthaginians sued for peace, but the terms offered not being acceptable the Carthaginians continued the war. Xanthippus, a Lacedaemonian was placed at the head of their army, defeated the Romans, taking Regulus prisoner, in 255 B.C. After the defeat of the Carthaginians by the proconsul Metellis, they sent to Rome to sue for peace, allowing Regulus to accompany the mission on his parole to return if their proposals were not accepted. Regulus advised the senate to refuse the proposals, and returned to Carthage where he was allegedly tortured and put to death. When the news reached Rome the senate is said to have delivered Hamilcar and Bostar, two Carthaginian prisoners, to Regulus' family, who tortured them to death. (b) C. Regulus Serranus, was consul in 257 B.C., and defeated the Carthaginian fleet, and gained possession of Lipara and Melite. With L. Manlius Vulso he was also consul in 250 B.C.

REGULUS, M. AQUILIUS, an informer in the days of Nero. Under Domitian he became an instrument of that tyrant's cruelty.

REHOBOAM, Jewish King, son and successor of Solomon. His treatment of the tribes led to a revolt of all except Judah and Benjamin, and a division of the kingdom. During his reign Judah was conquered by Shishak, founder of the XXIInd dynasty of Egypt.

REII APOLLINARES, Roman colony, E. of the Druentia, in Gallia Narbonensis.

REMI, people of Gallia Belgica, bounded S. by the Nervii, on the S.E. by the Veromandui, on the E. by the Suessiones and Bellovaci, and on the W. by the Nervii; they joined Caesar when the other Belgae made war against him in 57 B.C. The Axona flowed through their territory, and their chief town was Duro-cortorum.

REMUS, *see* ROMULUS.

REPENTINUS, CALPURNIUS, centurion of the Roman army in Germany, put to death on account of his loyalty to Galba, in 69 A.D.

REVELATION, BOOK OF, book of the N.T. belonging to a special type of literature known as Apocalyptic. It stands in the same class as the Book of Daniel and the many Jewish Apocalypses which appeared in the period between the O.T. and N.T.

REX, MARCIUS, (a) Q., praetor in 144 B.C., who built an aqueduct. (b) Q., was consul in 118 B.C., when he founded the colony of Narbo Martius in Gaul. (c) Q., consul in 68 B.C., pro-consul in Cilicia 67 B.C.

RHA, a large river of Asia rising N. of Sarmatia, in two arms, Rha Occidentalis and Rha Orientalis; the Rha was first men-tioned by Ptolemy.

RHADAMANTHUS, in *Greek Mythology*, son of Zeus and Europa, and brother of Minos, King of Crete. On account of the uprightness of his life he was made a judge of the dead, with Minos and Aeacus.

RHAETIA or RAETIA, province of the Roman empire, S. of the Danube, corresponding roughly to the greater part of the Tirol with the adjoining Carisons.

RHACOTIS, village of Lower Egypt, afterwards incorporated into the city of Alexandria.

RHAGAE, most important city of Media, S.E. of the present day Tehran. It was destroyed by earthquake and restored by Seleucus Nicator, when it was renamed Europus. It was de-stroyed again in the Parthian wars, and rebuilt by Arsaces, who called it Arsacia.

RHAMNUS, a demus in Attica possessing a famous temple of Nemesis, with a colossal statue of the goddess, executed by Agoracritus, disciple of Phidias.

RHAMPHIAS, a Lacedaemonian, father of Clearchus, one of three ambassadors sent to Athens in 432 B.C., with the final demand of Sparta for the independence of all Greek states. The demand was refused and the Peloponnesian war followed.

RHAMPSINITUS, ancient King of Egypt, successor to Proteus, who was in turn succeeded by Cheops. Said to be immensely wealthy he had a treasury built of stone. He belonged to the XXth dynasty.

RHAPTA, most southerly sea-port known to the ancients, was capital of the district of Barbaria, on the E. coast of Africa, on the river Rhaptus.

RHATHINES, a Persian commander sent by Pharnabazus to assist the Bithynians in opposing the passage of the Cyrean Greeks under Xenophon through Bithynia, in 400 B.C.

RHEA, in *Greek Mythology,* daughter of Uranus and Ge. She was wife of Cronus, and mother of Zeus, Demeter, Hera, Poseidon, and Pluto. Rhea was originally a Cretan divinity but early became identified with the Phrygian goddess of nature and fertility, Cybele. She is represented as wearing a mural crown, with lions drawing her chariot or sitting by her throne.

RHEGIUM or REGIUM, Greek town on the coast of Bruttium, in S. Italy, on the Fretum Siculum (Straits of Messina). Its history is connected with that of Sicily and the Greek colonies of S. Italy. Under the Romans, and in the time of Strabo it was one of the few Greek towns which preserved their language and customs. In ancient times it was one of the most renowned cities of Magna Graecia, and was celebrated for its wines. Agathocles, Hippias, and Hipparchus were born here.

RHEGMA, a lagoon formed by the Cydnus, in Cilicia, at its mouth, which served as a harbour for the city of Tarsus.

RHENUS, (Rhine), in ancient times this river, in length about 850 m., formed the boundary between Gaul and Germany. Caesar was the first Roman general to cross the Rhine. He built a bridge of boats for this purpose, probably near Andernach.

RHIANUS, of Crete, Alexandrian poet and grammarian who was flourishing in 222 B.C.

RHIPAEI MONTES, a name applied by the Greek poets, apparently quite indiscriminately to all mountains in N. Europe and Asia.

RHODUS, (Rhodes), most easterly island of the Aegaean, off the S. coast of Caria. The island was probably called Rhodus from its cultivation of roses. Its three chief towns, together with Cnidus and Halicarnassus, in Asia, and the island of Cos, formed the Doric hexapolis. It first acquired political importance when the three towns, in 408 B.C., built a new city called Rhodes, which became capital of the island. Rhodes lost its independence, in the days of Alexander, regaining it after his death. Its maritime code was adopted by the Romans, and through them, by modern European states.

RHOEMETALCES, King of Thrace, brother of Cotys, and uncle and guardian of Rhascuporis, at whose death in 13 B.C., he was expelled from Thrace.—Another of the name was nephew of the above: he received a portion of the Thracian kingdom.

RHOESACES, a Persian, who deduced his lineage from one of the seven chiefs who overthrew the government of the Magi, was satrap of Ionia and Lydia about 350 B.C., and was associated with the Theban Lacrates in the war against Egypt. He was slain by Alexander at Granicus.

RHOXOLANI, warlike people of European Sarmatia, on the coast of Palus Maeotis, and supposed ancestors of the Russians.

RIMMON, Syrian deity, worshipped at Damascus. His temple probably contained the altar which Ahaz reproduced at Jerusalem. He is identified with the Babylonian god of thunder, Ramman, and the Assyrian Adad.

ROMA, (Rome), capital of Italy and the world, was on the L. bank of the Tiber on the N.W. confines of Latium, 16 m. from the sea. The traditional date of its foundation is 753 B.C. The nucleus of the city was the Palatine hill. There were other settlements on the surrounding hills, these being fused into one about the middle of the 6th cent. B.C., when the Cloaca Maxima was constructed, and the adoption of the Forum as a market place made possible. To this period belongs the building of the earliest city walls, which enclosed the seven hills, Palatine, Capitol, Aventine, Caelian, Esquiline, Viminal, and Quirinal. Augustus completed what Julius had begun, and displayed much activity in other directions, so that his boast that he found Rome of brick and left it of marble is justified. He raised three groups of public buildings in the Campus Martius, restored 82 temples, built others, and constructed the first public baths. His successors constructed a splendid palace on the Palatine hill, while Nero occupied the whole district between the Palatine and Esquiline with his enormous Golden house. Vespasian built the first permanent amphitheatre, added a new forum, and rebuilt the temple of Jupiter on the Capitol. To Domitian is mainly due the construction of a still more magnificent residence on the Palatine, also the beginning of a new forum, which was finished by Nerva. Trajan completed the series of imperial fora and brought another aqueduct to Rome, also he constructed enormous public baths. Hadrian erected an immense villa for himself near Tivoli, and built the temple of Venus, the Pantheon (in its present form), and his own mausoleum, which became the Castle of S. Angelo, the fortress of the popes. Marcus Aurelius raised a column on which his campaigns were recorded. Septimus Severus restored the temple of Vesta, the house of the Vestals, and restored other buildings. His son, Caracalla, built huge thermae on the Via Appia. In 283 a fire gave Diocletian the opportunity for further restoration, and he also constructed famous baths. Maxentius built the greater part of the Basilica in the Forum which Constantius completed. In republican times the Romans mainly employed Etruscans or Greeks as builders, but by the last century of the republic a flourishing school of portrait sculpture had arisen. Busts are extant of Caesar, Pompey, and Cicero. Pasitales founded a school which practiced adaptation of Greek types. Under Augustus Greek influence was still dominant. The *Ara Pacis Augustae,* 13 to 9 B.C., celebrating the emperor's pacification of the West, heralded a series of triumphal arches which reached its zenith under the Flavian emperors, when the Arch of Titus was built. Technical accomplishments declined under Trajan, but a new form was developed in the "continuous" spiral relief such as those on the columns of Trajan and Antoninus, representing imperial conquests. Decadence soon set in. The Arch of Trajan suffers from overcrowding, and the bird's-eye reliefs from the Arch of Septimus Severus lack proportion and perspective. Portrait sculpture continued to flourish, the busts of Caracalla, and that of Philip the Arabian showing frank and intimate characterization. The handicrafts, gem cutting, silver and brass work, and die-cutting for coins, flourished under the early empire, and frescoes reached a high level.

ROMAN EMPIRE, the generally accepted date for the foundation of Rome is 753 B.C. Incessant warfare marked its early stages. The Etruscans held the right bank of the Tiber, while raiders occupied the mountains in all directions. The Latins, dwelling on the plains were akin to the Romans. First Rome was a member of a confederation of Latin-speaking communities, of which she formed the principal defensive outpost. When Rome became a republic the first great move towards empire was gaining control of the League of Latin Cities, which had been accomplished by 338 B.C., at about the same period that control of the Greek cities of Campania had been obtained, and then followed the subjugation of the Etruscans. By the beginning of the 3rd cent. B.C., Rome controlled the entire peninsula. Her greatest early struggle was with Carthage but after three great campaigns Carthage was completely destroyed. Next Macedonia was reduced and annexed, and in 133 B.C., the last King of Pergamum left his dominions to Rome, who made them the Roman province of Asia. The first bids to conquer Gaul followed. The late history of the republic is a story filled with the struggles for control of the Roman polity between military leaders—the Scipios, Marius, Sulla, Pompey, Julius Caesar, and Mark Antony—then the republic ended. The imperial system rose from a great scene of bloodshed, both in Italy and outside. Augustus' victory at Actium in 31 B.C., raised him to undisputed power. As first Roman emperor he did not aspire to extension of empire though there were many wars with the barbarians on the boundaries of Roman territory. Augustus established the Pax Romana (Roman Peace) within the empire. The provinces were well governed and Italy flourished. The termination of his line with the death of Nero, in 68 A.D., made little difference. The Julian-

Claudian line was succeeded by the nominees of the eastern armies. After Vespasian and Nerva came soldier emperors of renown, Trajan and Hadrian, and the Antonines, who proved the best rulers of the imperial period. Marcus Aurelius was followed by a weak and cruel son, Commodus, and after his assassination in 180 A.D., military chosen emperors followed until in 270 A.D., Aurelian found a tottering empire. With the great emperor Diocletian a new era opened. He revived the imperial institutions for administrative purposes, and devided the empire into East and West. Rome lost its pre-eminence in 330 A.D., when Constantine the Great changed the capital to Constantinopolis (Byzantium). After his death his three sons divided the empire. Then through a succession of emperors continuous wars were waged, and by the first quarter of the 5th cent., the Goths had overrun Italy and Gaul, and the Vandals and Germans were in Spain. In 410 Rome was sacked by Alaric, and was plundered by the Vandals in 455. The Great Roman Empire was followed by the medieval empire, the Holy Roman Empire, and by the Byzantine Empire.

ROMAN LAW, a system of civil law which grew up in the Roman state from the time of the kings until it was codified by Justinian, and which remains the basis of a great deal of European jurisprudence, while many of its principles are common to English law. Roman law, in its early form, was represented in the Twelve Tables set forth in 450 B.C. The following are the chief sources of Roman law: 1. Imperial decisions. 2. Equity of the Praetors and Curule Aediles. 3. Opinions of the juriconsults, to whom the best part of Roman law may be ascribed. Institutes and Pandects of Justinian were formulated in 533-4 A.D.

ROMANS, EPISTLE TO THE, one of the four principal letters of S. Paul, which seems to have been written from Corinth near the end of his third missionary journey, being intended to prepare the way for a visit to the Christians in Rome. It explains the universal character of the Gospel, and the leading ideas of Christian doctrine. It must have been written about 58 A.D., to a community of both Jews and Gentiles.

ROMULEA, an ancient city of the Hirpini, in Samnium, early destroyed by the Romans.

ROMULUS, the legendary founder of Rome, represented as a son of Mars by a daughter of Numitor, son of the last King of Alba Longa. When her twin sons Romulus and Remus were born, mother and children were cast into the river by order of Amulius, brother of Numitor. The children drifting ashore were suckled by a she-wolf. When grown up they slew the usurper Amulius and reinstated their mother's father Numitor. Then they proceeded to found a city on the Palatine hill. Romulus was taken up to heaven in a chariot by Mars, and thereafter worshipped by the Romans as a god under the name Quirinus.

ROSCIANUM, name of a fortress on the E. coast of Bruttium, between Thurii and Paternum.

ROSCIUS, QUINTUS GALLUS, Roman comic actor, born as a slave at Solonium, near Lanuvium, who reached a proverbial perfection in his art. He obtained the patronage of Sulla and was a friend of Cicero. He died in 62 B.C.

ROSETTA, town in Egypt, on an arm of the Nile delta, was an important harbour. The Rosetta Stone is an inscribed black basalt slab, discovered by one of Napoleon's officers in 1799, being acquired by Gt. Britain at the capitulation of Alexandria in 1801. It reached the British Museum in 1802. It bears an inscription in three versions, hieroglyphic, demotic, and Greek, thus furnishing the key to hieroglyphic writing.

ROSTRUM, in ancient Rome, only in the plural form, rostra, was used to indicate the tribunal or platform in the Forum. Magistrates addressed assemblies from it. It was so called from its being decorated with the beaks or rams (rostra) of ships captured in battle.

ROXANA, daughter of Oxyartes, a Bactrian, was captured by Alexander when he captured "The Rock" (a hill-fort) in 327 B.C. She captivated him and he married her. Soon after his death she bore a son, Alexander Aegus, who was admitted to a share of the nominal sovereignty with Arrhidaeus, under the regency of Perdiccas.

RUBICO (Rubicon), in *Ancient Geography,* a stream forming the boundary between Italy and Cisalpine Gaul. Its crossing by Julius Caesar in 49 B.C., began the civil war. The phrase to cross the Rubicon is tantamount to burning one's boats.

RUBRIUS, tribune of the plebs with C. Gracchus.

RUFUS EPHESIUS, Greek physician in the reign of Trajan, was born at Ephesus. He wrote medical books.

RUGII, a powerful people of Germany living on the Baltic coast between the Viadus and the Vistula.

RUTENI, a people of Gallia Aquitanica, with their chief town at Segodunum. They had silver mines and cultivated flax.

RUTILIA, mother of C. Cotta, the orator, who went with her son into exile in 91 B.C., remaining with him until his return.

RUTILIUS RUFUS, P., Roman statesman and orator, was military tribune under Scipio in the Numantine War, praetor in 111 B.C., consul in 105 B.C., and legatus in 95 B.C., under Q. Mucius Scaevola, proconsul of Asia.

RUTULI, ancient people of Italy, occupying a narrow strip on the coast of Latium, S. of the Tiber.

RUTUPAE, (Richborough, England), a harbour town of the Cantii in S.E. Britain, noted for oysters.

S

SABA, (Sheba of the Bible), capital of the Sabaei people in Arabia Felix, by tradition the residence of the Queen of Sheba who went to Jerusalem to hear the wisdom of Solomon.

SABAEI, ancient people of S.W. Arabia, speaking a S. Semitic dialect. The Sabaeans were agriculturists, and carried on caravan trade and worked mines. They controlled a gold and spice trade, and took toll of early commerce with India and E. Africa.

SABAOTH, a Hebrew word, signifying armies of hosts.

SABATE, town on the road from Cosa to Rome.

SABATINI, a people of Campania.

SABATRA, town of Lycaonia, noted for scarcity of water, which was there an article of commerce.

SABAZIUS, Phrygian and Thracian god, whose cult was popular in Italy during the imperial days.

SABBATH, in the Jewish religion, the seventh day of the week, kept sacred by worship and a cessation of work. In the oldest parts of the Mosaic Law, rest on the seventh day is enjoined. According to Mosaic Law, the Sabbatical Year was every seventh year, during which the land was to lie fallow; spontaneous growth was to be shared; and, with certain exceptions, debts were to be remitted.

SABELLIUS, heresiarch of the middle 3rd cent., who was an African Bishop or presbyter, living in the Pentapolis of Cyrenaica, who held there was only one person in the Godhead, viz., The Father; that Jesus was a man with a certain energy proceeding from God, or a portion of the Divine Nature. They conceived the Holy Spirit to be merely a divine energy, or emanation from God. He was opposed by Dionysius of Alexandria.

SABINA, wife of Hadrian, whom she married about 100 A.D.

SABINI, a very ancient and powerful people of central Italy, noted for their love of freedom. The Sabines formed one of the elements of which the Roman people was composed.

SABINUS, (a) brother of Vespasian, who governed Moesia in the days of Claudius. (b) a distinguished jurist in the days of Tiberius.

SABIS, large river of Gallia Belgica, emptying into the Mosa. —Sabis was also the name of a stream on the coast of Carmania.

SABISM, an ancient religion prevailing to a great extent in Arabia and Mesopotamia, not to be confounded with the Sabaei, as it was not their religion. The two words are quite distinct, and are written differently in the Semitic languages. The religion was traditionally derived from Tsabi, son or brother of Enoch. According to the Arabic writers it was the same as the religion of the ancient Chaldaeans, and seems to have been one of the earliest and simplest forms of idolatry.

SABURA, commander of Juba's forces in Africa who defeated Caesar's general, C. Curio, in 49 B.C., and was later destroyed with all his army by P. Sittius, in 46 B.C.

SACADAS, established the second great school of music at Sparta; he gained musical prizes in connection with the Pythian games in 590, 586, and 582 B.C.

SACAE, Scythian nomad tribe, excelling as archers. They became tributary to the Persian empire, whose army they greatly strengthened.

SACRATIVIR, M., of Capua, a Roman eques, who was killed fighting at Caesar's side at the battle of Dyrrachium, in 48 B.C.

SACROVIR, JULIUS, and JULIUS FLORUS, two chieftains of Gaul who in 21 A.D., in the reign of Tiberius, excited a revolt among the Gauls: they were both defeated and took their own lives.

SADALES, son of Cotys, King of Thrace, was sent to the assistance of Pompey against Caesar, in 48 B.C. Together with Scipio, he defeated L. Cassius Longinus, one of Caesar's legates.

After Pharsalia he was pardoned by Caesar. When he died in 42 B.C., he left his dominions to the Romans.

SADDUCEES, Jewish religious party, named after Zadok, the high priest, formed about 200 B.C., as the party of priestly aristocracy. They denied resurrection from the dead, and the existence of angels and spirits. They paid great attention to the letter of the Law. They disappeared after the final destruction of the Temple.

SADYATTES, King of Lydia, from 629 to 617 B.C.

SAGALASSUS, strong city of Pisidia, S.E. of Apamea Cibotus.

SAGARTII, a nomad tribe of Persis, later found in Media, and the mountain passes of Zagros.

SAGUNTUM, town in Hispania Tarraconensis, S. of the Iberus, founded by Greeks from Zacynthus; it formed an alliance with the Romans, and its siege by Hannibal, in 219 B.C., was the immediate cause of the second Punic War.

SAIS, great city of the Egyptian Delta, capital of Lower Egypt and burial place of the Pharaohs; and here was the tomb of Osiris. It was the center of the worship of the goddess Neith.

SALAMIS, island of the W. coast of Attica, famous for the naval battle fought between the Greeks and Persians, in 480 B.C. To bring the Persians to action, Themistocles sent a messenger saying that the Greeks were withdrawing and advising them to blockade the entrances to the bay of Eleusis, and so cut off their retreat. This the Persians did, having 1,000 ships against 360. After a prolonged battle the Persians were defeated. —Another Salamis was a town in Cyprus.

SALASSI, powerful people of Gallia Transpadana, occupying the valley of the Duria at the foot of the Alps, whose passes they defended so obstinately that the Romans found it difficult to subdue them.

SALEM, city of the Jebusites, of which in the days of Abraham, Melchizedek was King. It has been identified with Jerusalem.

SALERNUM, ancient town of Campania, became a Roman

colony, in 194 B.C.

SALIENUS, T., Roman centurion of Caesar's army in Africa, who in 46 B.C., induced the two Titti to surrender their ship to C. Virgilius, the Pompeian leader. He was dismissed in disgrace.

SALINATOR, M. LIVIUS, was consul with L. Aemilius Paulus, in 219 B.C. They waged war against the Illyrians.

SALLUSTIUS, Praefectus Praetorio under Julian, and was his friend. Although a pagan he dissuaded the emperor from persecuting the Christians.

SALLUSTIUS CRISPUS, C., Roman historian, born at Amiternum, in 86 B.C.; was quaestor about 59 B.C., and tribune of the plebs in 52 B.C., the year in which Milo killed Clodius. In 50 B.C., he was expelled by the senate, but was made quaestor the following year by Caesar, whom he joined in the civil war. He narrowly escaped death in a mutiny of some of Caesar's troops in Campania. He fought with Caesar in his African war, in 46 B.C., and was left as governor of Numidia. He died in 36 B.C. His main works were, *Bellum Catilinae, Bellum Jugurthinum,* and the *Historiarum Libri quinque.*

SALMYDESSUS, town of Thrace, on the Euxine, S. of Cape Thynias.

SALOME, sister of Herod the Great, assassinated for plotting against his sons and the daughter of Herodias, who to please her mother, danced before Herod, and as a reward was granted the head of John Baptist.—Salome was also the name of the sister of Mary, the mother of Jesus.

SALONA, capital of Dalmatia, was strongly fortified by the Romans, and later became a Roman colony. Diocletian was born near Salona, and after his abdication he returned to the neighbourhood, where he lived till his death.

SALONIA, CORNELIA, wife of Gallienus, who saw her husband killed before Milan in 268 A.D. She was mother of Saloninus.

SALSULAE FONS, fountain near the Sordice Lacus, in Gallia Narbonensis, S. of Narbo.

SALUS, Roman goddess, the personification of health, prosperity, and public welfare.

SALVIANUS, distinguished Christian writer of the 5th cent., born near Treves. The latter part of his life was passed as presbyter of the church at Marseilles. Some of his works remain, viz., *Adversus Avaritiam Libri IV., ad Ecclesiam Catholicam, De Providentia S. de Gubernatione Dei et de Justo Dei praesentique Judicio Libri, Epistolae IX.*

SALVIUS, sometimes called Polemius, author of a sacred calendar, drawn up in 448 A.D., which is entitled Laterculus S. Index Dierum Festorum, including pagan as well as Christian festivals, is believed to have been Bishop of Martigny.

SALYES, most famous of the Ligurian tribes, living on the S. coast of Gaul, between the Rhone and the Maritime Alps. They were subdued by the Romans in 123 B.C., after a prolonged struggle. The Roman consul Sextius founded among them the colony of Aquae Sextiae.

SAMARIA, province in central Palestine, was colonized by the remnants of the tribes of Ephraim and Manasseh, and a number of Assyrian immigrants. The city of Samaria was founded about 920 B.C., by Omri, who transferred the seat of government to it from Shechem. It was destroyed by Sargon, and rebuilt by Herod the Great, who named it Sebaste.

SAMARITANS, THE, after the fall of Samaria, in 721 B.C., Sargon deported many of its people, replacing them with captives from Babylon, Syria, and Arabia. These, and later colonists, mingled with the old Hebrew population that remained, and the new mixed race that grew up were known as the Samaritans. The foreign colonists decided to worship Jehovah, the God of the land, but they blended His worship with their own cults. This syncretism offended the Jews, and accounts for the strife between the Jews and Samaritans.

SAMBUS, Indian prince, whose kingdom bordered on Pattalene. When Alexander entered India, Sambus immediately submitted to him, and was allowed to keep his kingdom.

SAMNITES, ancient nation, or confederacy of nations in Central Italy, who made a brave struggle against Rome. They occupied country on both sides of the central ridge of the Apennines, bounded N. by the Peligni and Marrucini, and by the Adriatic; on the E. by Apulia and Lucania; on the S. by the Campanians; and on the W. by Latium Novum, and the country of the Marsi. They were originally a colony of the Sabini, which migrated to the banks of the Vulturnus and the Tamarus, and thence spread. They were an agricultural and pastoral people and as their numbers increased beyond the means of subsistence they sent forth colonies. War broke out between the Romans and Samnites in 343 B.C., continuing on and off for 53 years. The civil war gave them hopes of recovering independence, but they were defeated by Sulla before the gates of Rome in 82. Their towns were sacked, the people enslaved, and their place taken by Roman colonists.

SAMOS, island of the Aegaen, in the section known as the Icarian Sea, off Ionia. In the time of Cyrus, King of Persia, Polycrates was tyrant of Samos; he was put to death by a Persian satrap, the Persians taking possession of the island. It recovered independence after the Persian defeat at Mycale, in 479 B.C. From this time its history belongs to the general history of the Greek states of Western Asia. It finally became subject to Rome in 84 B.C.

SAMOTHRACE, a small island opposite the mouth of the Hebrus in Thrace, N.E. of Lesbos. It was chiefly celebrated for the worship of the Cabiri. It was originally inhabited by the Pelasgians, from whom the people learned the religious mysteries which they solemnized. The Samothracians fought on the side of Xerxes at the battle of Salamis.

SAMUEL, first prophet of Israel, and last of the Judges, born at Ramah, in answer to the prayers of his mother Hannah, was dedicated to the service of God from birth, and taken to Eli the priest to serve him as boy attendant. The misconduct of Samuel's sons, who were expected to succeed to the judgeship, led to a popular demand for a king, and Saul was chosen. Samuel was often brought into conflict with him, and later he anointed the youth David, who after took refuge with him from the king's anger. In his later days he seems to have conducted a school of the prophets, and he had a house of his own at Ramah, where he was buried.

SAMUEL, THE BOOKS OF, in the Septuagint these two books are called the First and Second Books of Kingdoms, and in the Vulgate the First and Second Books of Kings. The contents fall into five sections: 1. Eli and Samuel. 2. Samuel and Saul. 3. Saul and David. 4. David. 5. An appendix. The period covered is from about 1070 to 970 B.C. The only ancient source mentioned is the Book of Jashar.

SANA, town on the W. coast of Pallene, S. of Potidaea, a colony of Andros.

SANHEDRIN, supreme senate of the Jews, established shortly before the time of Antiochus the Great. It was made up of persons of the upper classes, 71 in number, who met under the presidency of the high priest. It acted as the supreme court of justice, with jurisdiction over Jews of all countries, and was allowed considerable freedom of action by both Greeks and Romans.

SANNYRION, Athenian comic poet belonging to late Old Comedy, or early Middle Comedy. He flourished from 407 B.C., onwards.

SANSKRIT, ancient sacred language of the Hindus, in which all their literature was written. Its most ancient form is found in the Vedas, parts of which go back to about 2000 B.C. The Sanskrit of the Vedas, differed from classical Sanskrit as the Greek of Homer from classical Greek. About the 4th cent. B.C., the renowned grammarian Panini stereotyped the rules of grammar and syntax.

SANTA SCALA, stairway belonging to the Lateran palace in Rome; twenty-eight marble steps, said to have been ascended by Jesus when he was in the house of Pilate at Jerusalem. They are protected with wood, and are only ascended on the knees.

SAPPHO, Greek poetess who lived at Mitylene, and with her contemporary Alcaeus was one of the greatest of the Aeolic group of poets and leader of a literary society of women. She flourished about 580 B.C.

SARAH, a Hebrew word meaning "princess," and the name of Abraham's wife.

SARDANAPALUS, legendary Assyrian king. According to Ctesias, Diodorus, and other writers, he was an effeminate voluptuary who reigned in the 9th cent. B.C. Besieged in Nineveh by Arbaces, a Median satrap, for two years, he caused himself, his wives, and treasure to be burned on a funeral pyre, 400 ft. high. The name and date are reminiscent of Ashurdaninpal, the rebellious son of Shalmaneser III, about 825.

SARDICA, city of Moesia Superior, on a plain watered by the Oescus. Near here the emperor Maxamian was born; it was also famous for a church council held here.

SARDINIA, a large island in the Mediterranean. Iolaus is said to have led a Greek colony into Sardinia, and to have founded Olbia on the N.E. coast. The island became well-known to the Greeks. Nura, afterwards one of its chief towns, is particularly noticed in the Roman period. The first Carthaginian expedition to Sardinia, was led by Machaeus, or Malchus, or Melech. About 490 B.C., Hasdrubal and Hamilcar, sons of Mago, gained a footing in the S. part of the island, and built or colonized Caralis and Sulcis. The lower districts were permanently in possession of the Carthaginians until the first Punic War. A disagreement between the Carthaginians and the Sards resulted in the conquest of the greater part of the island by the Romans, who incorporated it, with Corsica, into a Roman province, under a praetor, about 228 B.C. After the outbreak of the second Punic War, the Sards, weary of their Roman masters, applied to Carthage for aid, but the Romans quickly crushed the revolt. About 178 B.C., Sardinia, again in a state of revolt, was made a consular province, and an army was sent which completely defeated the insurgents. The people returned to their allegiance, and a double tribute was imposed upon them. Later Gaius Gracchus suppressed another revolt. During the civil wars Sardinia shared the calamities of the other Roman provinces, following alternately the fortunes of Marius or Sulla, of Caesar or Pompey.

The island remained quiet during the period of the empire, being used by the Romans as a granary and a penal settlement. It was conquered by Genseric, King of the Vandals, and after the overthrow of the Vandal Kingdom by Belisarius, it was annexed to the prefecture of Africa, and governed by an officer styled Duke.

SARDIS, capital of the old Kingdom of Lydia. It was captured by the Persians in 546 B.C., and figured later in the Ionian revolt. After Alexander the Great took it in 334 B.C., it became a Greek city of importance. It was seat of one of the earliest Christian Bishoprics, and was one of the seven churches of Asia addressed in the Apocalypse. The city was destroyed by Tamerlane, in the 15th cent.

SAREPTA, city of Phoenicia, S. of Sidon, to whose district it belonged. It is called Zarepath in the O.T. and known as the scene of two of Elijah's miracles.

SARGON, King of Assyria from 722 to 705 B.C. After the capture of Samaria he deported the inhabitants. He overthrew Hamath in 720 B.C.; Carchemish in 717; Ashdod in 711 B.C.; and Mita and Merodach-Baladan of Babylon in 709 B.C. His son Sennacherib succeeded him.—Another of the name was King of Akkad, Babylonia. The Neo-Babylonian tradition which dates him c. 3,800 B.C., is regarded today as 1,000 years too early.

SARMATIA, name given by the Romans to all the country in Europe and Asia between the Vistula and the Caspian. It was bounded by the S. by the Euxine and Mt. Caucasus, and was divided by the Tanais into Sarmatia Europaca, and Sarmatia Asiatica. The people were usually called Sauromatae.

SARMATICAE PORTAE, the central pass of the Caucasus.

SARMENTUS, a runaway slave, who had been employed by Maecenas as a scribe.

SARMIZEGETHUSA, town which was the residence of the Kings of Dacia, was on the River Sargetia. It became a Roman colony named Colonia Ulpia Trajana Augusta.

SARON, (Sharon of the O.T.), beautiful plain of Palestine, between Joppa and Caesarea, noted for its fertility and flowers.

SASERNA, was the name of two writers on agriculture, living between the days of Cato and Varro.—It was also the name of two brothers who served under Julius Caesar in the African War in 46 B.C.

SASSANIDAE, name of a Persian dynasty which ruled from 226-651 A.D. Within 100 years of the destruction of the Persian Empire by Alexander the Great, a new empire, called Parthian, under a dynasty called Arsacidae, was set up in the regions E. of the Euphrates. This dynasty ruled until 226 A.D., when it was overthrown by a chief of true Persian blood, Babegan or Ardashir.

SATASPES, son of the Persian, Teaspes, sentenced by Xerxes to be impaled for offering violence to the daughter of Zopyrus. The punishment was remitted on condition of his circumnavigating Africa. This he failed to accomplish and the original sentence was carried out.

SATRAP, a viceroy or governor of an ancient Persian province.

SATURNALIA, the annual festival of Saturn in Rome, kept under the republic on Dec. 19th, was extended by Augustus to three days, and afterwards to a week. Schools and courts of law were closed, and no public business transacted. Slaves enjoyed temporary liberty and were waited on by their masters.

SATURNINUS, L. APPULEIUS, Roman demagogue, was quaestor, 104 B.C., and tribune of the plebs for the first time, 103. During his first tribunate he introduced *lex frumentaria.* He allied himself with Marius, and gained great popularity. He was candidate for the tribunate for the second time in 100, obtaining it by the murder of his rival. He now brought forward an agrarian law which led to the banishment of Metellus Numidicus. Saturninus put ofrward other popular measures. In the following year he was made tribune for the third time. At this period there was rivalry for the consulship between Glaucia and Memmius and as the latter was likely to be elected, Saturninus and Glaucia hired assassins who murdered him. The Senate declared Saturninus and his associates public enemies, and ordered the consuls to put them down by force. Marius was unwilling to act against his friends but had no alternative. Driven from the

Forum, Saturninus, Glaucia and the quaestor Saufeius took refuge in the Capitol. Here their water supply was cut off and unable to hold out any longer, they surrendered to Marius who placed them in the Curia Hostilia but the mob tore off the tiles of the Senate-house and pelted them till they died.

SATURNUS, (Saturn), in *Classical Mythology,* the god of agriculture. He was legendary ancient King of Latium, whose reign, being a time of great happiness and prosperity, was the so-called Golden Age. Saturn was later identified with the Greek Cronus.

SATYRI, (Satyrs), in *Greek Mythology,* minor nature deities, chiefly found in attendance on Bacchus. Of repellent appearance, they had pointed goat's ears, horns, and a tail, and were addicted to drunkenness and licentiousness. The Roman poets sometimes confused them with the fauns.

SAUL, first King of Israel, died about 1010 B.C. He was son of Kish, a Benjamite. He delivered Jabesh-Gilead from Nahash, King of Ammon, and was anointed King at Gilgal. He defeated the Philistines at Gibeah, and crushed the Amalekites, but disobeying the order to destroy them utterly, Samuel told him he was rejected of Jehovah. Later he was overthrown by the Philistines at Gilboa, where his sons were killed, and he fell upon his sword.

SAXONES, (Saxons), Teutonic people, whose territory varied; the name signifies swordsmen. Ptolemy states that they inhabited Slesvig, and three islands off its W. coast. In 286 A.D., they appear as pirates in the N. Sea and English Channel, and by 350 they had crossed the Elbe, extending their sway almost to the Rhine. In the 5th cent. they had settlements at Bayeux, and the mouth of the Loire, and were associated with the Angles and Jutes in the conquest of Britain.

SCAEA PORTA, a famous gate of Troy, on the W., towards the sea. Laomedon was buried near it.

SCAEVOLA, family of he Mucian clan at ancient Rome. (a) Gaius Mucius Scaevola, who is said to have won the name Scaevola ('left-handed') by his attempt to murder Porsena, in which he lost his right hand. (b) Quintus Mucius Scaevola, known as the augur, was praetor and governor of Asia in 121 B.C., and consul in 117. He lived to about 88 B.C. Cicero was his pupil in law. (c) Quintus Mucius Scaevola, son of (b) was consul in 95 B.C. He rose to be *pontifex maximus* but was murdered in 82 B.C., after being proscribed by the Marians. He was famed for eloquence, equity and knowledge of the law.

SCANTILLA, MANLIA, wife of Didius Julianus, whom she urged to buy the empire when set up for sale: she was known as Augusta during her husband's brief reign.

SCAPULA QUINTIUS, T., a Roman officer who passed over into Spain with Cn. Pompeius, and took an active part against Caesar: he fought at the battle of Munda in 45 B.C., and after the battle fled to Corduba, where he took his own life.

SCAPULA, P. OSTORIUS, succeeded Aulus Plautius as governor of Britain in 50 A.D. It was he who captured Caractacus, King of the Silures, and sent him in chains to Rome.

SCATO, VETTIUS, an Italian general in the Marsic War in 90 B.C., who defeated L. Julius Caesar and P. Rutilius Lupus, in two successive battles.

SCAURUS, (a) M. Aemilius, was born in 163 B.C., became curule aedile in 123 B.C., and consul in 115 B.C., when he made war successfully against the Alpine tribes. He headed an embassy to Jugurtha in 112 B.C., and in 11I B.C., went with L. Calpurnius Bestia to the war against Jugurtha. They both took bribes from the Numidian King to obtain a favourable peace. Scaurus was censor with M. Livius Drusus in 109 B.C. He was elected consul a second time in 107 B.C. He died about 89 B.C. (b) M. Aemilius, son of the above, who served under Pompey as quaestor in the third Mithridatic War, later commanding an army in the east. He became curule aedile in 58 B.C., and praetor in 56 B.C. He was condemned in 52 B.C., under Pompey's new law against *ambitus* (canvassing for a public office). (c) M. Aemilius, son of the above, went with Sex. Pompey into Asia. (d) Mamercus Aemilius, son of the above, was an orator and poet. He was accused of treason under Tiberius, in 34 A.D., and took his own life.

SCIPIO, PUBLIUS CORNELIUS, Roman general. When Italy was invaded by Hannibal, Scipio endeavoured to check his progress, but was defeated at the battle of Ticinus, in 218 B.C. He then went to Spain, with his brother Gnaeus, where they kept the Carthaginians so much engaged that they were unable to send reinforcements to Hannibal. The brothers were defeated by Hasdrubal in 211 B.C.

SCIPIO, PUBLIUS CORNELIUS, known as Scipio Africanus Major, was a Roman general who at the outbreak of the second Punic War in 218 B.C., fought in the Roman armies, and so distinguished himself that in 210 B.C., he was chosen by popular accord to command in Spain, where in three years he destroyed the Carthaginian power. On his return in 206 B.C., he urged a direct attack on Carthage. He was made consul in 205 B.C., when he organized forces and led them to Africa, destroying the forces of Syphax, the ally of the Carthaginians, and in 202 B.C., met Hannibal, annihilating his army at the Battle of Zama. For this he was awarded the title of Africanus.—His brother Lucius Cornelius, also a Roman general, defeated Antiochus at Magnesia, in 190 B.C., gaining the name Asiaticus.

SCIPIO, PUBLIUS CORNELIUS AEMILIANUS, known as Scipio Africanus Minor, Roman general and statesman. At the outbreak of the third Punic War in 149 B.C., he first served in a subordinate capacity, but after his consulship in 147 B.C., was made governor of Africa, and reduced Carthage in 146 B.C. In 134 B.C., he became governor of Spain, and ended the war there by taking Numantia, in 133 B.C. After the death of Tiberius Gracchus, Scipio was prominent in the opposition to the commissioners appointed to carry out Gracchus' agrarian reforms. For this he became unpopular, and one morning was found dead.

SCIRADIUM, headland on the N. side of Salamis, on which was built a temple of Minerva.

SCIRITIS, mountainous district of N. Laconia, on the borders of Arcadia. Its people formed a division of the Lacedaemonian army.

SCIRRI, a people in the N. of European Sarmatia, E. of the Vistula, who later merged with the Huns.

SCODRA, important town of Illyricum, on the Barbana, was strongly fortified. Gentius, King of Illyricum, lived here.

SCOLOTI, native name of the Scythians.

SCOLUS, an early town of Boeotia, between Thebes and Aphidnae.

SCOPAS, a leading Aetolian at the outbreak of Philip's war with the Achaeans, in 220 B.C. After the war he went with Philip to Alexandria. Ptolemy V gave him command of the army against Antiochus the Great, in which ventures he was not successful.—Scopas was also the name of a sculptor and architect who built the temple of Athena at Tega, in Arcadia, about 395 B.C., and executed bas-reliefs on the Mausoleum at Halicarnassus.

SCOTI, (Scots), mentioned with the Picti (Picts) by later Roman historians as chief tribes of the Caledonians, living in S. Scotland and Ireland.

SCOTUSSA, very ancient town of Thessaly, where Flaminius gained the famous victory over Philip in 197 B.C.

SCRIBE, term used in the Bible for a writer or secretary but particularly for the official copyists and expounders of the Mosaic Law. Their most important function was to give counsel and advice in points of difficulty or doubt in the observance of the Law. They were closely connected with the Pharisees, the religious teachers of the nation.

SCRIBONIA, wife of Octavianus, who became the emperor Augustus.

SCULPTURE, the palaeolithic cave-dwellers first carved in the round, then in relief, the animals they hunted, about 10,000 B.C. Later they carved the human form, their only equipment being chipped flints. For several thousand years the neolithic peoples developed no sculpture until the Egyptians made figures in terra-cotta, ivory, and stone. Marble was common in Greece and was a superb medium for carving. The Persian invasion involved much destruction, and the Greeks had to rebuild their temples. The land blossomed with art. Myron wrought his famous athletes, of which Discobolus is most famous. Polyclitus moulded his great bronzes, of which the Doryphorus was held

by the ancients to give the right proportions of the male figure.
Pericles gave to Phidias the oversight of the many sculptors
who were called to build the Parthenon. The keynote of the 5th
cent. B.C., was serenity and calm, free from emotion. Later,
sculpture developed a meditative vision. Of this age the most
famous sculpture is the Winged Nike of Samothrace, in which
the triumphant swing of the body is revealed through the flutter
of windswept draperies. Like the Apollo Belvedere, which we
only know in a bronze copy, it is of the school of Scopas. When
Alexander conquered Athens, Greek art passed to Alexandria,
Rhodes, and Pergamum, and thereafter developed towards expressing tragedy, pathos, and pity. The Dying Gaul of the
Pergamene school was of the period 240-238 B.C., and the Laocoon group of about 150 B.C. Later we find Gothic and Classic
meeting in Italy in the feverish, restless age of the Renaissance.

SCYLLA, in *Greek Mythology,* a sea-monster on the Straits of
Messina at the narrowest part. Opposite was the whirlpool
Charybdis. Scylla had twelve feet, and six heads, snatching sailors from the decks of ships that passed too near. Ships in avoiding Scylla risked being swallowed in the whirlpool of Charybdis.

SCYLLIAS, famous diver of Scione, in Macedonia. When
Xerxes' fleet was wrecked off Mt. Pelion Scyllias recovered much
of the treasure.

SCYROS, island of the Aegaean, E. of Eurobia; one of the
Sporades.

SCYTHIA, name given in ancient times to a region N. and
N.E. of the Euxine. Its boundaries varied from age to age, and
the term came to be applied to any barbarian region. The Scythians, who appeared in the 7th cent. B.C., gave their name to the
country, but were absorbed among the Cimmerians. From the
middle of the 4th cent. B.C., the power of the Scythians declined
before the Samaritans, new invaders from the east, and by the
first cent. B.C., the name Scythia had ceased to have any political
significance. The early Scythians were nomadic, but gradually
agriculture was developed together with some Greek culture.
Then religion was infiltrated by central Asian Shamanism.

SCYTHOPOLIS, (Bethshean of the O.T.), important city of Palestine, S.E. of Galilee, on a hill in the Jordan valley.

SEBOSUS, STATIUS, geographer mentioned by Pliny.

SEGALLAUNI, people of Gallia Narbonensis, whose chief town was Valentia.

SEGESTA, (formerly Egesta), ancient Greek City in Sicily on Mt. Varvaro.

SEJANUS, LUCIUS AELIUS, a Roman courtier, favourite of Tiberius; executed in 31 A.D., for plot to seize imperial power.

SELEMNUS, river of Achaia, emptying near Cape Rhium.

SELENE, in *Greek Mythology,* goddess of the moon, daughter of Hyperion, and sister of Helios, the sun god, and Eos, goddess of the dawn. She made her journey across the heavens in a chariot drawn by two white horses. She became identified with Artemis.

SELEUCIA, ancient city of Asia, was situated on the Tigris, on the frontiers of Babylonia and Assyria. It was built by Seleucus I, King of Syria, between 312-302 B.C., becoming a great city, but was later eclipsed by Ctesiphon. After its capture by Severus, in 198 A.D., it fell into decay.

SELEUCID, name of the Macedonian dynasty which ruled Syria and other parts of W. Asia from 312 B.C., until the Roman annexation in 65 B.C. It was founded by Seleucus Nicator, one of Alexander's generals, who in the partition of the empire acquired Syria, Mesopotamia, and territories E. of the Euphrates. He was succeeded by his son Antiochus I., Soter (280-262 B.C.). Seleucus II (246-226 B.C.) lost territory to Ptolemy III of Egypt, to Arsaces of Parthia, and to the King of Pergamum. These territories were mostly recovered by Antiochus III the Great (223-187 B.C.). The ablest of his successors was his son Antiochus IV Epiphanes. The dynasty ended with Antiochus XIII, who was deposed by Pompey in 65 B.C., when Syria became a Roman province.

SELINUS, town in Sicily founded by Dorians from Megara Hyblaea, was sacked by the Carthaginians in 409 B.C., and destroyed by them in 250 B.C.

SEMECHONITIS, (Waters of Meron in the O.T.), lake in N. Palestine, formed by the Jordan.

SEMELE, in *Greek Mythology,* daughter of Cadmus, King of Thebes, beloved by Zeus. Hera persuaded her to ask of Zeus, that he should appear before her in all his glory. In the lightning which was the symbol of his majesty, Semele was consumed, after giving birth to a son by him, the god Bacchus of Dionysus.

SEMIRAMIS, mythical Assyrian queen, daughter of a Syrian youth and the Syrian fish-goddess, Derceto; she married Onnes, one of the generals of Ninus, and, having heroically taken part in the siege of Bactra, won the King's attention. Her husband then took his own life, and Semiramis married Ninus, whom she succeeded. She ruled for 42 years, conquering many nations, and founding Babylon. She resigned her crown to her son.

SENATE, in Rome, originally a council of patres, or heads of families, chosen by the King, to advise on public matters. With the establishment of the republic the senate became the most powerful factor in the new constitution under which Rome was developed from a city state into a world-empire. The number of Senators varied from 300 in early times to 1,000 in the days of Julius Caesar. Augustus fixed the number at 600. Under the empire the senate became a law-making body, and supreme judicial authority.

SENECA, LUCIUS ANNAEAUS, known as Seneca the Younger was born at Corduba about 4 B.C. He became tutor to Nero, after whose accession he continued in close association with him. Then he fell into disfavour, and in 65 A.D., was charged with conspiracy and compelled to take his own life. Many of his works have been preserved, including nine tragedies which influenced 16th cent. drama. His father, Seneca the Elder, was a noted rhetorician.

SENNACHERIB, King of Assyria from 705 to 680 B.C., was son of Sargon II. He fought against Elam, Cilicia, Phoenicia, and Palestine. Although his siege of Hezekiah in Jerusalem was raised, he laid waste Judah. He built Cicilian Tarsus in 698 B.C., and destroyed Babylon in 689 B.C. Nineveh owed much of its greatness to Sennacherib's improvements. He was succeeded by his son Esarhaddon.

SENONES, a strong people of Gallia Lugdunensis living on the upper course of the Sequana. A number of them crossed the Alps about 400 B.C., to settle in Italy, the N. of which was already occupied by other Celtic tribes. The Senones penetrated further south, settling between the Utis and the Aesis on the Adriatic coast, after expelling the Umbrians. They marched against Rome and took the city in 390 B.C., after which they engaged in constant hostilities with the Romans until they were completely subdued by the consul Dolabella in 283 B.C.

SENTIUS AUGURINUS, epigrammatic poet in the days of Pliny the Younger.

SEPINUM, a city of the Samnites which became a Roman colony in the reign of Nero.

SEPTUAGINT, Greek version of the Old Testament, commonly referred to as LXX. It was so called from a tradition preserved by Philo, Josephus, and in the so-called letter of Aristeas to Philocrates, that the translation of the Law was made by 70 or 72 translators.

SEQUANI, a Celtic people who in the days of Caesar occupied modern Franche-Comté and most of Alsace.

SERAPHIM, in Hebrew Scriptures, angelic spirits attendant upon Jehovah and guardians of His sanctuary.

SERAPIS, Greco-Egyptian deity. Ptolemy I Soter introduced a Greek Hades-image into Alexandria. This was Serapis for whose worship he built the Serapeum. The new cult gained prompt recognition in Egypt, and soon spread through the Greco-Roman world. The most famous temple was at Alexandria.

SERTORIUS, QUINTUS, was born in Nursia, in the country of the Sabines. He started as an orator at Rome but turned to military affairs distinguishing himself in the campaign of Marius against the Cimbri and Teutones. He was sent to Spain as tribune under the praetor Didius. On his return to Rome the Marsic war broke out. He was made quaestor of Gallia Circumpadana, and commissioned to levy troops. On his again returning to Rome he was a candidate for the tribuneship of the people but was defeated by Sulla. He now joined the party of Cinna and Marius, and after the latter had been driven from Italy, Cinna and he raised fresh troops and held against their opponents. When Marius returned from Africa, in 87 B.C., and took vengeance upon his enemies Sertorius showed moderation. He was appointed proconsul of Spain in 83 B.C., went to his province where he gained Spanish good-will. He prepared to oppose Sulla who was sending a force against him, but was unable to prevent the passage of a Roman army across the Pyrenees, and leaving Spain, cruised the Mediterranean, and made a descent on Africa. Again he landed in Spain at the mouth of the Guadalquivir, and was invited by the Lusitani, to command their forces. Sulla was now dead. The Lusitanians and the Romans in that part declared for Sertorius, who was successful against the Roman forces sent against him. He was joined by Perperna and many of the Marian party, and he reduced the Roman commander Metellus Pius to such extremities, that the senate sent Cn. Pompeius, in 76 B.C., with a large force to his support. Sertorius maintained himself in Spain against all power of the Senate until 72 B.C., when he was treacherously murdered by his own adherents, at the head of whom was Perperna.

SERVIUS TULLIUS, sixth legendary King of Rome who reigned from 578 to 534 B.C. He is reputed founder of the so-called Servian constitution, which was military and formed the basis of a new assembly, *comitia centuriata,* in which the power of wealth predominated. Servius made an alliance with the Latins, brought the seven hills within the city, surrounding the whole with a ditch and rampart.

SESOSTRIS, one of the early Kings of Egypt, third of the XIIth dynasty of Manetho, and the successor of Moeris. He reigned about 1500 B.C. His reign is represented as a succession of conquests, beginning with an expedition into Arabia and followed by an expedition into the countries W. of Egypt. On his accession he divided Egypt into 36 nomes or districts, and raised an enormous army for the conquest of the world. He subdued the Ethiopians, and sent a fleet to India, and penetrated as far as the Ganges, and to the eastern shores of Asia. He returned and carried his victorious arms to the Tanais (the Don), leaving monuments of his conquests. After 9 years of victory he returned where he narrowly escaped being burnt in his tent by his brother. Two of his children perished in the flames. To record his own and his wife's escape he erected colossal statues in Memphis. He spent the rest of his reign adorning Egypt. The last of his great works were two obelisks of hard stone, 120 cubits high, on which he recorded the greatness of his power. Towards the end of his life he became blind and took his own life.

SESTERCE, ancient Roman coin at first equal to 2½ asses, and later to four asses, or just over 2d in English money. It was at first a small silver coin, but under the empire was of copper.

SESTUS, town of Thrace founded by the Aeolians, was for some time in Persian hands, but was recaptured by the Greeks in 478 B.C., after a siege. Later it formed part of the Athenian empire.

SESUVII, a people of Gallia Celtica, occupying part of the department of de l'Orne and of that of Calvados: Seez.

SET, Egyptian deity, was originally a predynastic tribal god at Kom Ombo, he came to represent the powers of darkness, and was portrayed as a grotesque animal. He was rehabilitated in the XIXth dynasty, whose two monarchs Seti bore his name; he was identified with the Greek Typhon.

SEVEN CHURCHES OF ASIA, name given to the seven chief churches in Asia Minor which were presided over by Bishops in Apostolic days. They were Ephesus, Smyrna, Pergamos, Thyatira, Sardis, Philadelphia, and Laodicea.

SEVEN WONDERS OF THE WORLD, in ancient times, the Hanging Gardens of Babylon, the Pyramids of Egypt, the Temple of Diana at Ephesus, the Statue of Jupiter, by Phidias, at Athens, the Colossus of Rhodes, the mausoleum built by Artemisia at Halicarnassus, and the Pharos (lighthouse) at Alexandria.

SEVERUS, MARCUS AURELIUS ALEXANDER, was son of Julia Mammaea. He was born in Phoenicia, in 208 A.D., and was brought to Rome at an early age. On the death of Elagabalus he became emperor in 222 A.D. In the course of a mutiny among his troops he and his mother were killed, at Sicilia in Gaul, in 235 A.D.

SEVERUS, FLAVIUS VALERIUS, became Roman emperor from 306-7 A.D., and was sent against Maxentius, who had assumed the imperial title at Rome. At Ravenna he surrendered and was taken prisoner to Rome, putting an end to his own life in 307.

SEVERUS, LIBIUS, Roman emperor from 461-65 A.D.

SEVERUS, LUCIUS SEPTIMIUS, Roman emperor from 193-211 A.D., was born near Leptis Magna, in Africa, in 146 A.D. He commanded the legions in Pannonia when the emperor Pertinax was murdered, and was then proclaimed emperor. He disposed of rival claimants, and then turned his attention to the Parthians. He captured Babylon, Seleucia and Ctesiphon, the Parthian capital. His eastern victories are recorded on the arch at Rome which bears his name. The end of his reign was occupied with campaigns in Britain from 208 A.D. He is said to have rebuilt the wall between the Forth and Clyde. He died at York in 211 A.D.

SEXTIUS, P., quaestor in 63 B.C., and tribune of the plebs in 57 B.C. He kept armed servants to oppose P. Clodius, and in 56 B.C., he was accused of acts of violence while tribune. Cicero defended him and was acquitted, largely through Pompey's influence. In the civil war he at first supported Pompey but later joined Caesar.

SEXTUS EMPIRICUS, philosopher and physician, contemporary with Galen. Three of his works remain.

SEXTUS, of Chaeronea, Plutarch's sister's son, a Stoic philosopher who instructed the emperor Antoninus.

SHEBA, ancient kingdom in the S. part of Arabia Felix, famous for gold, frankincense, spices, and precious stones. Its people were known as Sabaeans. Abyssinian tradition dates its royal house from Solomon and the Queen of Sheba, but it is doubtful whether Solomon's visitor came from the Arabian Sheba, or from the Ethiopian Sheba.

SHEKEL, name of a Hebrew weight or coin. As a weight it equalled 225-253 grs. or 10 dwts. Troy. 50 shekels went to a maneh, and 60 manehs to a talent. As a coin the silver shekel was worth about 2s. 8d., and the gold shekel about £2. The silver shekel was 13/16 in. in diameter.

SHIBBOLETH, password of the Gileadites under Jepthah during their war with the Ephraimites, who pronounced the word "sibboleth," so betraying their identity.

SHILOH, town in Ephraim, between Bethel and Shechem, about 19 m. from Jerusalem. The Ark of the Covenant rested here.

SIBAE, an uncultured people in the N.W. of India, who clothed themselves in skins and carried clubs. The soldiers of Alexander regarded them as descendants of Hercules, probably in jest.

SIBYL, in *Classical Legend*, the term used for a number of prophetesses inspired by Apollo. The Cumaean Sibyl offered to sell Tarquin the Proud nine prophetic books, on his refusing she burnt three, then another three, finally selling him the other three. The extant Sibylline Oracles were mostly written between 200 B.C., and 300 A.D., being Jewish and Christian predictions, partly Messianic.

SICILIA (Sicily), island in the Mediterranean. When the Phoenicians began to colonize Sicily, about 1000 B.C., they found the E. portion occupied by the Siceli, and parts of the N.W. by the Elymi. The first Greek colony was founded in 735 B.C., but after a long series of wars with Carthage, Sicily became a Roman province in 210 B.C. The island was ruled by the Goths until Belisarius conquered it in 535, when it became part of the Eastern Empire.

SICYON, Greek city, in the N.E. Peloponnese, between Corinth and Achaea, on the Asopus, and 2 m. from the coast. In the 7th and 6th cents. B.C., it became prominent on account of its famous pottery, wood carving, and bronze work. It was the home of classical Greek painting.

SIDON, city of Phoenicia, famous for purple dyes and glass. It was taken by Sennacherib in 701 B.C., and as H.Q. of the Phoenician navy, contributed the best ships to Xerxes' expedition against Greece. In 351 B.C., it was destroyed. It became a free city under the Romans.

SIDONIUS APOLLINARIS, was born at Lugdunum about 341 A.D. He married the daughter of the emperor Avitus, and became a senator. At the downfall of the emperor he retired, but reappeared in 467 as ambassador from the Arverni to Anthemius. He gained favour of that prince by a panegyric. His extant works are some poems and nine books of epistles.

SIGA, sea-port of Mauretania Caesariensis.

SIGEUM, the N.W. headland of the Troad, of Asia Minor, site of the Grecian camp and fleet during the Trojan war.

SILA SILVA, the great forest on the Apennines, in Bruttium, celebrated for its yield of pitch.

SILANUS, JUNIUS, (a) M., praetor in 212 B.C., was killed in battle against the Boii in 196 B.C., (b) M., consul in 109 B.C. (c) D., was consul in 62 B.C., with Licinius Murena. (d) M., was legatus to Caesar in Gaul, in 53 B.C. He was made consul in 25 B.C.

SILENUS, in *Greek Mythology,* companion of Dionysus, son of Hermes, or some say Pan. He is represented as an old man, stout and cheerful, bearing a wine-skin, and always drunken. He was endowed with prophetic powers.

SILICIUS, P., one of the judges appointed to try the conspirators against the life of Caesar in 43 B.C., according to the *Lex Pedia.* He voted for the acquittal of Brutus, and was afterwards proscribed by the triumvirs.

SILIUS ITALICUS, T., Roman poet born about A.D. 25. His great work was the heroic poem in seventeen books entitled *Punica,* which is extant in its entirety.

SILO, Q. POMPAEDIUS, leader of the Marsi in the Social War, who was killed in battle against Q. Metellus Pius, in 88 B.C., when the war ended.

SILOAM, rock-hewn reservoir outside the wall of Jerusalem. About 700 B.C. Hezekiah cut a 1,700 ft. conduit, to convey the Gihon waters from their source, in what is now the Virgin's fountain, to the Pool of Siloam.

SILPIA, city of Hispania Baetica, N. of the Baetis.

SILURES, Celtic people, once occupying a great part of S. Wales. They stubbornly resisted the Romans, only being subdued about 80 A.D. Their capital Venta Silurum, was made a centre of Roman civilization, with walls, baths etc.

SILVANUS, Latin divinity of commons, rough ground and

forests, he was in addition protector of field boundaries.

SIMEON, name of one of the tribes of Israel, and its traditional ancestor. He was second son of Jacob and Leah, and was born at Haran, in Mesopotamia, and with Levi, took part in a feud with Shechem, resulting in the dispersion of the two tribes. The remnant of Simeon settled S. of Judah, with which tribe they became absorbed.

SIMMIAS, the first disciple of Philolaus, the Pythagorean philosopher, who became friend and disciple of Socrates, at whose death he was present. Another Simmias was a poet and grammarian of Rhodes who flourished about 300 B.C.

SIMONIDES, Greek lyric poet, born on the Ionian island of Ceos. He spent most of his life at Athens, in Thessaly, and at the court of the tyrant Hiero in Sicily, where he died. He was born about 556 B.C., and died in 468 B.C.

SIMPLICIUS, one of the last of the Neo-Platonists, was born in Cilicia, and was a disciple of Ammonius and Damascius.

SINAE, people inhabiting the most eastern part of Asia, of whom nothing was known until the days of Ptolemy.

SINAI, peninsula at the head of the Red Sea, between the gulfs of Suez and Akaba. It is a wild mountainous region, shut in on the N. by desert. The Mt. Sinai of the O. T. is generally regarded as the same as Gebel Catherina, which has two peaks, Horeb and Gebel Musa, or mountain of Moses. Gebel Musa is reckoned the scene of the Hebrew law-giving.

SINGARA, fortified Roman colony in Mesopotamia, S. of Nisibis, at the foot of Mt. Singaras. It was scene of the defeat of Constantius by Sapor, through which the city was lost to the Romans.

SINGIDUNUM, H.Q. of a Roman legion in Moesia Superior, at the junction of the Danube and Savus.

SINON, in *Greek Mythology,* a relative of Odysseus, distinguished for cunning, he allowed himself to be taken prisoner by the Trojans and persuaded them to drag the wooden horse into the city, and in the dead of the night he opened the side of the horse and let out the band of armed men concealed in it.

SINOPE, Greek colony on the Euxine, on the N. coast of Asia

Minor. It was destroyed in the invasion of Asia by the Cimmerians, and restored by a new colony from Miletus, in 632 B.C., and became chief center of commerce on the Euxine. It was birthplace and home of Mithridates the Great, and native city of Diogenes, Diphilus, and Baton.

SINTICA, district of Macedonia occupied by the Sinti, with its chief town Heraclea Sintica.

SIPHNUS, island in the Aegaean, one of the Cyclades, originally called Merope. It was colonized by Ionians from Athens. There were gold and silver mines, and the Siphnians were regarded as the wealthiest of the islanders. They placed a tenth of the produce of the mines in a treasury of Delphi. Their riches exposed them to pillage. In the days of Polycrates a party of Samian exiles invaded them, compelling them to pay 100 talents.

SIPONTUM, ancient town of Apulia, on the S. slope of Mt. Garganus, said to have been founded by Diomedes. It was colonized by the Romans, and became commercially important.

SIRENES, (Sirens), in *Classical Mythology,* sea-nymphs who by the attraction of song lured to their ruin those who listened. According to the Odyssey the sirens lived on an island near the straits of Messina. In art they are represented as birds with women's faces.

SIRMIUM, city of Pannonia Inferior, on the Savus, founded by the Taurisci. Sirmium became capital of Pannonia under the Romans, and their H.Q. in their wars against the Dacians. The emperor Probus was born here.

SISAMNES, a Persian judge under Cambyses, who had him put to death for allowing himself to be bribed to an unjust decision. He had him flayed and his skin fixed to the judicial bench. He was followed by his son Otanes, who was enjoined ever to keep his father's fate in mind.

SISAPON, town of Hispania Baetica, N. of Corduba, famous for its silver mines.

SISCIA, town of Pannonia Superior, strongly fortified, but captured by Tiberius, who probably made it a colony. It was later colonized by Septimius Severus.

SISTRUM, ancient Egyptian metal rattle, often a bronze horseshoe-shaped frame, pierced for three or four loose rods, and sometimes adorned with jingling rings. The handle often bore an image of Hathor. Women worshippers held it, particularly in late Isis ritual.

SISYGAMBIS, mother of the last king of Persia, Darius Codmannus, who was captured, after the battle of Issus, in 333 B.C., by Alexander, who treated her with every consideration. Sisygambis became attached to her conqueror and felt his death keenly. Eventually she took her own life saddened by misfortunes.

SISYPHUS, in *Greek Legend,* King Corinth, notable for deceit and rapacity. After death he was compelled perpetually to push a huge stone uphill, which as soon as the summit was reached rolled back again.

SITACE, great city of Babylonia, not far from the Tigris, and inside the Median wall.

SITHON, King of Thrace, and father of Pallene.

SLAVERY, economic institution consisting in the utilisation of forced labour without pay. The civilization of the ancient world was based on the institution of slavery and without this economic foundation neither Athenian culture nor the Roman imperial system could have existed. Christianity did not forbid slavery, but commended manumission, a practice which profoundly modified the population of S. Europe.

SMERDIS, son of Cyrus, was put to death by order of Cambyses, his brother. Patizithes, a Magian, had been left in charge of the palace of Cambyses, and taking advantage of the likeness of his own brother to Smerdis, proclaimed him king. Cambyses heard of this in Syria, but was killed by an accidental wound. The Persians acknowledged the false king, and he reigned 7 months without opposition. Phaedima discovered the deception and told her father, Otanes, who with six noble Persians entered the palace and killed the bogus Smerdis and his brother, in 521 B.C.

SMERDOMENES, son of Otanes, and a general who had command of the land forces of Xerxes in his Greek invasion.

SMYRNA, one of the most ancient Greek cities of Asia Minor, on the N.E. side of the Hermaean Gulf. Originally an Aeolian colony, it was seized by Ionians from Colophon. It was known to the Greeks as "Old Smyrna," and disputed the honour with six other cities of being birthplace of Homer. A grotto near the town was shown, in which it was said he composed his poems. The city was destroyed by the Lydian King Sadyattes but was rebuilt 400 years later by Antigonus and Lysimachus. The new Smyrna became one of the richest cities of Asia, continuing as such under the Romans. Christianity was early established, and Polycarp is said to have been its first Bishop, and to have suffered martyrdom here. It was seat of one of the "Seven Churches." The city often suffered earthquakes, by one of which it was reduced to ruins, but it was restored by M. Aurelius. During the period of the Eastern empire it experienced several severe vicissitudes.

SOANES, a people of the Caucasus, with a King capable of putting 200,000 soldiers into the field. They were also known as Suani and Suanocolchi.

SOCRATES, Greek philosopher, son of Sophroniscus and Phaenarete, was born about 470 B.C., and is reputed to have learned the hereditary craft of a sculptor. He married Xanthippe, by whom he had three sons. His wife was said to have been a shrew. We are dependent on the dialogues of Plato for our knowledge of Socrates. He was thickset and ugly. Socrates rapidly became notable in Athens. About 435 B.C., his friend Chaerephon asked the Delphic oracle whether any man was wiser than he, and received a negative answer. Socrates took this to mean that he alone was conscious of his own ignorance, and that his mission was to convince others of the same truth about themselves. This mission he carried out to the end of his life. In 432 B.C., war with Sparta broke out, and Socrates served with distinction. In 399 B.C., after the restoration of democracy, he was arraigned for corrupting youth and introducing new divinities in place of those recognized by the state. The real ground of prosecution seems to have been political, as he was held responsible for the anti-democratic careers of such as Alcibiades and Critias, who had been members of his circle. The death penalty was only voted by 280-220. A month later he drank hemlock in prison, having refused the offers of his friends to contrive an escape. His last hours were spent in discussing the immortality of the soul.

SODOM, city of Palestine, near the Dead Sea; a so-called city of the plain. It is associated with Gomorrah as a place of unusual wickedness. After Lot had been warned to leave, the cities were destroyed.

SOEMIS, JULIA, daughter of Julia Maesa, and mother of Elagabalus. The praetorians killed her on March 11, 222 A.D.

SOLIDUS, Roman gold coin struck to replace the aureus, which became a standard in the Eastern Empire.

SOLOMON, third King of Israel, younger son of David, by Bath-Sheba. Solomon waged few wars, but made alliances, marrying a daughter of Pharaoh, perhaps the last of the Tanite dynasty. He also married a daughter of Hiram, King of Tyre, and other foreign princesses. His relations with Phoenicia and Egypt enabled him to share in the trade with Ophir and other distant countries. He accumulated great wealth which made his reign proverbial for splendour. He employed forced labour for his great buildings at Jerusalem. He was renowned for wisdom as a judge and writer of songs and proverbs. Solomon died about 937 B.C.

SOLON, born about 638 B.C., was an Athenian statesman and law giver. He was of noble birth and attained such eminence as a gnomic poet that he was reckoned among the Seven Sages. As Athens was suffering from great distress from an economic and political crisis, Solon was elected archon in 594 B.C., with full power to amend the laws. He cancelled existing debts, forbade enslavement for debt, and limited the rate of interest. He repealed most of Draco's legislation, and gave Athens a new constitution. To stop clan divisions and feuds, the citizens were divided into four classes, according to wealth. Soon after the overthrow of his constitution by Peisistratus, Solon died about 558 B.C., at the age of 80.

SOMNUS, god of Sleep, a brother of Death, and son of Night.

SOPHISTS, a class of teachers in Greece, first prominent in the 5th cent. B.C. They represented an intellectual movement which reflected the altered social, political, and religious conditions of Greek life. Early sophists were Protagoras of Abdera, the first to ask a fee for teaching, and Gorgias of Leontini. Later sophists were advanced freethinkers; like Critias the tyrant. Later generations of Sophists, by their greed for money, and their attacks on family life, and all social, religious, and political institutions, drew upon them the odium of the people. They were the first to pay attention to style, rhythm, and rhetoric as an art.

SOPHOCLES, son of Sophilus, was born at Colonus, near Athens, in 495 B.C. At fifteen years of age, on account of his beauty, he was selected to lead the chorus which danced round the trophies in Salamis and sang the hymn of victory. His first tragedy was produced in 468 B.C. Aeschylus was the great dramatist of Athens at this time, but his young rival, contending with him for the prize, gained the victory. Sophocles was active in his art from 468-440 B.C., when he produced his *Antigone*, his 32nd drama, and gained the prize. He was appointed commander in the war against the aristocrats of Samos, who after being expelled by the Athenians, had returned, trying to induce the Samnians to revolt. Sophocles and Pericles were colleagues in this campaign. Whether after this expedition, which ended in 439 B.C., he took any further part in public affairs is not certain. His life seems to have been passed in the glorious career of a successful dramatist. His first wife was Nicostrata, by whom he had a son Iophon. His second wife was Theoris, by whom he also had a son, Ariston. Sophocles died in 406 B.C.

SOPHONISBA, daughter of Hasdrubal, the Carthaginian general, who betrothed her Masinissa, prince of Numidia, but later, anxious to gain over Syphax, the rival prince of Numidia, to Carthaginian alliance, gave her in marriage to that prince. After Syphax had been defeated by Masinissa, Sophonisba fell into the hands of the conqueror, who for her beauty, determined to marry her himself. The marriage took place without delay, but Scipio, afraid she might exercise some influence over Masinissa which she had previously done over Syphax, refused to ratify the agreement, insisting on the surrender of the princess. Unable to resist, the Numidian King spared her the humiliation of captivity by sending her poison, which she drank without hesitation.

SOPHRON, of Syracuse, the leading writer of the mime, a variety of Dorian comedy. He flourished from about 460 to 420 B.C.

SOPHUS, P. SEMPRONIUS, tribune of the plebs in 310 B.C., and consul in 304 B.C., was one of the earliest jurists.

SORDICE, lake in Gallia Narbonensis, formed by the Sordis, at the foot of the Pyrenees.

SOSICLES, a Corinthian deputy to the congress which had in consideration the restoration of Hippias to the tyranny of Athens. His opposition induced the allies to abandon the project.

SOSIGENES, a peripatetic philosopher, and the astronomer employed by Julius Caesar to superintend the correction of the calendar in 46 B.C.

SOSTHENES, Macedonian officer, who had supreme direction of affairs during the period of confusion which followed the invasion of the Gauls, whom he defeated. Chronologers include him among the Kings of Macedonia, but it is questionable whether he assumed the royal style.

SOSTRATUS, name of several Greek artists who are often taken for one another. (a) A statuary in bronze, disciple of Pythagoras of Rhegium: he flourished about 424 B.C.—(b) of Chios, flourished about 400 B.C.; Pantias was his pupil.—(c) Statuary in bronze, contemporary with Lysippus.—(d) Son of Dexiphanes, was a great architect, in the days of Alexander the Great.—(e) An engraver of gems.

SOSUS, of Pergamus, a very famous worker in mosaic.

SOTHIS, Greek form of the ancient Egyptian name of Sirius, the dog-star. Its rising with the sun on July 20, when the Nile inundation commenced, gave it importance in the Egyptian calendar.

SOUS, one of the earliest Kings of Sparta, was son of Procles, whom he succeeded, and father of Eurypon, from whom the Proclid Kings were styled Eurypontidae.

SOZOMENUS, HERMIAS, (SOZOMEN), church historian of the 5th cent., was born in Palestine, and was educated in a monastery. After studying law at Berytus, he went to Constantinople, where he practiced as an advocate, and also wrote, in Greek, his *Church History*, in nine books, covering the period 323-439 A.D.

SPAIN, *see* HISPANIA.

SPARTA, city and Kingdom of Greece, in Laconia, and sometimes called Lacedaemon. It was founded about 1100 B.C. Its jurisdiction was extended over the surrounding country, and it became head of the Greek states. It had two Kings but the real power rested with a council, and officials called Ephors. The Spartan system was directed to one end, i.e., military efficiency. The Spartans were bred to be soldiers, were contemptuous of the amenities of life, of pain, and of death. The system was attributed to Lycurgus, the lawgiver. With the prestige won by Athens in the Persian wars, the rivalry between Sparta and Athens for leadership in the Hellenic world began in 431 B.C. After ten years fighting the matter remained unsettled, and war was temporarily suspended. Athens weakened her power by a disastrous expedition to Sicily, and, in 412 B.C., Sparta renewed hostilities. With the annihilation of the Athenian fleet at Aegospotami, by Lysander, in 405 B.C., Sparta achieved a decisive victory. For a quarter of a century Sparta was dictator of Greece, but in 379 B.C., Thebes revolted against her domination, and Spartan ascendancy never recovered from the great Theban victory at Leuctra in 371 B.C.

SPARTACUS, Thracian soldier who led the insurgents in the Third Servile War in Rome. He started as a shepherd, and was taken prisoner by the Romans and trained as a gladiator in the school at Capua, from which in 73 B.C., he escaped with 70 others to the crater of Vesuvius. He raised an army of runaway gladiators and other slaves, estimated as 100,000 men, devastating Italy from end to end. In 71 B.C., he was defeated and killed.

SPES, the personification of Hope, as worshipped at Rome, her most ancient temple being built in 354 B.C., by the consul Atilius Calatinus. The Greeks worshipped the personification of Hope, under the name Elpis.

SPEUSIPPUS, the philosopher, was born at Athens, and was son of Eurymedon and Potone, a sister of Plato. He followed

Plato as head of the Academy, which seat he only occupied for eight years, 347-339 B.C., dying, as he did, of a lingering illness. All his writings are lost.

SPHAERUS, Stoic philosopher, disciple of Zeno, and later of Cleanthes, living at Alexandria during the days of the first two Ptolemies. He also taught at Lacedaemon. He was noted for the accuracy of his definitions. None of his works are extant.

SPHINX, hybrid creature of Egyptian and Greek art and mythology. In Egypt the Sphinxes are colossal images, with a human head and breast, and the body of a lion lying down. The largest is at Gizeh. From Egypt the figure passed to Assyria, where it appears with a bearded male head on cylinders. The female Sphinx, lying down, and winged, is first found in the palace of Esarhaddon (7th cent. B.C.). Sphinxes have also been found in Phoenicia. In Asia Minor, an ancient wingless female Sphinx stands on the sacred road near Miletus. Sphinxes of the Greek type (female heads with bodies of winged lions) are represented as sitting on each side of two doorways in an ancient frieze, discovered at Xanthus in Lycia. In the early art of Cyprus such types are not uncommon. In *Greek Mythology,* the most famous Sphinx was that of Thebes in Boeotia. She was daughter of Orthus and Chimaera, and dwelt on a rocky mountain called Phicium. The Muses taught her a riddle and the Thebans had to guess it. When they failed she devoured them. The riddle was: What is that which is four-footed, three-footed, and two-footed. Oedipus guessed correctly that it was man; for a child crawls on hands and feet, the adult walks upright, and the old man supports himself with a stick. Then the Sphinx threw herself down from the mountain.

SPINA, a very ancient town in Gallia Cispadana, in the country of the Lingones, founded by the Greeks.

SPORADES, islands "scattered" (as the name implies) about the Greek Archipelago, are distinguished from the Cyclades, which are grouped around Delos, and from the islands attached to the mainland of Europe.

STADIUM, Greek measure of length equal to about 582-5 feet. This was the distance of a short race at Olympia, the name came to be used first of the race, and then of the building in which racing and other contests took place. The stadium at Olympia was rectangular, but most others had a semicircular end.

STAGIRUS or STAGIRA, birthplace of Aristotle, in Macedonia.

STASINUS, a Greek epic poet.

STATIRA, wife of Artaxerxes II, who was poisoned by the King's mother, Parysatis.—Another of the name was sister and wife of Darius III; taken prisoner by Alexander after the battle of Issus, in 333 B.C., she was treated with respect. She was accounted the most beautiful woman of her time.

STATIUS, PUBLIUS PAPINIUS, Roman poet, living from about 45 to 96 A.D. The poet's father was the Orbilius of his time, and taught at Naples and Rome. Juvenal speaks of the public enthusiasm which attended the recitation of Statius' *Thebais,* when the benches "were breaking" with applause.

STELA or STELE, upright slab bearing sculptural designs or inscriptions. Many examples pertain to ancient Egypt, but stelas are also found in Greece and Asia. One engraved with a charter of Nebuchadnezzar I, King of Babylon, about 1120 B.C., is preserved in the British Museum.

STENTOR, in *Greek Mythology,* herald of the Greeks in the Trojan War. He was famous for the loudness of his voice, said to equal that of thirty men.

STENYCLERUS, town in N. Messenia, residence of the Dorian Kings.

STEPHANUS BYZANTIUS, author of a geographical dictionary called *Ethnica,* of which, apart from fragments, we possess only the epitome by Hermolaus. Even in its imperfect form it is valuable for references to ancient writers which it preserves.

STESICHORUS, of Himera, famous Greek poet, contemporary with Pittacus, Phalaris, and Sappho. He died in 552 B.C., aged 80. The works we possess may be divided under the following heads: 1. Mythical Poems. 2. Hymns and Paeans. 3. Erotic Poems. 4. The pastoral poem, *Daphnis.* 5. Fables. 6. Elegies. The poet's dialect was Dorian.

STESICLES, was sent with 600 peltastae, by the Athenians to aid the Corcyreans against the Lacedaemonians under Mnasippus, in 373 B.C., which aid proved effective.

STHENELAIDAS, Spartan ephor, who urged declaration of war against Athens in the council of the Spartans and their allies before the Peloponnesian War.

STICHIUS, an Athenian leader in the Trojan War, who was killed by Hector.

STILICHO, FLAVIUS, Roman soldier and statesman. A Vandal by birth, he became a notable commander under Theodosius I, on whose death in 395 A.D., he virtually ruled the West. Guardian of Honorius, he defeated Alaric, King of the Visigoths, at Pollentia in 403 A.D., and conquered the invading army of Radagaisus at Faesulae in 405 A.D. He was murdered in 408 A.D.

STILO, L. AELIUS PRAECONINUS, famous Roman grammarian, and one of the teachers of Varro and Cicero.

STILPO, celebrated philosopher, who taught at Megara.

STOBAEYS, JOANNES, was born in Stobi, in Macedonia. We know nothing of his personal history. In the course of his reading he noted down the most interesting passages around the year A.D. 500. We are indebted to him for a proportion of the fragments that remain of the lost works of poets.

STOICISM, philosophical system, founded at Athens by Zeno of Citium, about 300 B.C. The system divided philosophy into logic, physics, and ethics. Logic supplies the means of acquiring true knowledge. All knowledge comes from sensual perceptions, which are only true if they carry conviction. Physics teaches the laws of the universe. There are two principles of things—passive matter—and active God. God is the universal intelligence. Man's soul is partly divine, but perishable. Ethics provides rules for practical conduct. Virtue consists in living according to nature in rational action. Pleasure is rather an evil than a good. Suicide was allowable.

STONE AGE, term denoting the phase of human culture before the use of metals. The European stone age is divisible into eolithic, palaeolithic, and neolithic. The oldest is attested by implements revealing traces of artificial fabrication. Of the palaeolithic phase the Chellian and Acheulian form the lower, the Mousterian the middle, the Aurignacian, Solutrian, and Magdalenian the upper division. In the new stone age many edged tools were made of stone.

STONEHENGE, prehistoric stone monument, possibly connected with the worship of the sun, and partly a sepulchral monument, is on Salisbury Plain, W.N.W. of Amesbury, Wiltshire. It comprised integrally two concentric stone rows, on a horseshoe plan, surrounded by two concentric stone circles. Now much damaged, it stands inside a circular earthwork, 300 ft. across, opening towards the N.E. into an embanked avenue 200 ft. long. At the summer solstice the open part of the horseshoe faces sunrise.

STRABO, Greek geographer, born in Amasia, Pontus, about 63 B.C. He travelled widely, settling in Rome in 29 B.C., where he died in 19 A.D. His two great works were 1. *Historical Memoirs*, in 46 books, a continuation of Polybius from 146 B.C., to the death of Caesar, of which we possess fragments. 2. *Geographica*, in 17 books, nearly all of which we possess.

STRATON, tutor of Ptolemy Philadelphus, was son of Arcesilaus of Lampsacus. He was head of the Peripatetic school, in 288 B.C., in succession to Theophrastus. He presided for 18 years, being followed by Lycon.

STRATONICE, daughter of Demetrius Poliorcetes and Phila; she married Seleucus, King of Syria in 300 B.C., when she was 17 years old.

STRIGIL, a flesh-scraper, used in the Roman baths, and by athletes after exercise.

STRONGYLION, famous Greek statuary, who flourished at the end of the 5th cent. B.C.

STROPHADES INSULAE, two islands in the Ionian, off Messenia.

STROPHIUS, King of Phocis, son of Crissus and Antiphatia.

STRYMON, Macedonian river marking the boundary between Thrace and Macedonia until the time of Philip. It was notable for the large numbers of cranes on its banks.

STYX, in *Greek Mythology*, river of Hades, abode of the dead. Its waters were poisonous.

SUBLICIUS PONS, the oldest bridge in Rome. It was a wooden bridge, and when it was periodically washed away by floods was always rebuilt of wood. Ancus Marcius is said to have been responsible for its inception.

SUEBI, a powerful people of Germany or, rather, the collective name of a number of German tribes, grouped on account of their migratory mode of life, and spoken of in opposition to the more settled tribes.

SUESSA POMETIA, ancient town of the Volsci in Latium, taken by Tarquinius Priscus.

SUETONIUS TRANQUILLUS, G., Roman writer, and private secretary to the emperor Hadrian. His *Lives of the Twelve Caesars,* published in 120 A.D., is the only one of his many writings which has come to us intact. The Lives have no particular literary merit but give full information about the emperors of the 1st cent.

SULLA, LUCIUS CORNELIUS, Roman soldier and statesman, born of noble parents, in 138 B.C. He defeated Marius and Mithridates, King of Pontus, and was appointed dictator. He revolutionized the constitution, making the senate supreme, and reforming the judiciary and executive. At the height of his power he abandoned all his high offices, in 79 A.D., and retired to a life of profligacy. He was intellectually in advance of any of his countrymen, a master of war and statecraft, completely self-reliant, but completely devoid of morality.

SUSA, (Shushan of the O.T.), ancient city of Persia, capital of the old province of Susiana. It stood on the Choaspes, and was the winter residence of the Persian Kings. Its ruins include what is known as the tomb of Daniel, and the Acropolis. Excavation has discovered the remains of the palace built by Darius.

SUSIANA, a chief province of the ancient Persian empire, roughly corresponding to *Khuzistan.*

SYMPLEGADES, two islands near the entrance to the Hellespont, reputed to close together and crush ships trying to pass between them. The Argo was the first ship to pass through unscathed; after this the rocks became fixed.

SYRACUSE, seaport of Sicily, founded in 734 B.C., became the chief Greek colony in the island. Dionysius the tyrant, after 405 B.C., extended the authority of the city over E. Sicily, and S. Italy. After a siege from 214-212 B.C., the Romans captured and sacked the city. Its ruins include Greek fortifications and a theatre, Doric temples, a Roman amphitheatre, Roman houses, and Christian catacombs.

SYRIA, to the ancients Syria was the coastland of the E. Mediterranean between the Taurus and Egypt. About 2000 B.C., Syria formed a part of Amram. It was subject to Egypt from about 1530 B.C., till about 1250 B.C., when the growing power of Assyria began to make itself felt. In the 6th cent. B.C., Assyria subjugated the whole land, which, however, passed to Babylon in the 7th cent. Persia overran it in 538 B.C., and held it till Alexander the Great took it 200 years later. In 64 B.C., it became a Roman province, and remained under Rome and under the Byzantine empire until 634 A.D.

SYRTES, the two gulfs in the east half of the north coast of Africa, Syrtis Major, and Syrtis Minor.

SYRTICA REGIO, part of the N. coast of Africa, between the two Syrtes. It was a narrow strip interspersed with salt marshes. It was occupied by Libyan tribes. Under the Romans it was part of the province of Africa.

SYRUS, PUBLILIUS, (*not* Publius), a slave in Rome before the fall of the republic, who was a famous mimographer. A collection of many lines from his mimes, has passed to us under the title *Publii Syri Sententiae.*

T

TABAE, (a) City of Persis, between Ecbatana and Persepolis, in the district of Paraetacene. (b) City of Caria near the borders of Phrygia. (c) An inland town of Sicily.

TABAL, (Tubal in the Bible), a Hittite city-state, probably chief of a confederacy including the city-states Tuwana, Tunna, Hupisna, Shinukhtu, and Ishtunda, about the 12th cent. B.C.

TABALIC, a name given by Forrer to Hieroglyphic Hittite, because the district where most inscriptions in this unnamed language have been found, bore the name of Tabal, q.v.

TABARNA, that is, Great King, a style given to themselves by the Kings of the Hittites, belonging to the Old Kingdom.

TABOR, mountain of Galilee, traditional scene of the Transfiguration.

TABURNUS, mountain partly in Campania, and partly in Samnium. The S. side was fertile, and famous for olives.

TACAPE, city of N. Africa, in the Regio Syrtica. It belonged to Byzacena under the Romans, but it was later raised to a colony. A little to the W. were warm mineral springs called Aquae Tacapitanae.

TACFARINAS, a Numidian in the time of Tiberius, who had served among the Roman auxiliaries. He collected a body of Freebooters and became leader of the Musulamii. For a long period he defied Roman arms but was overcome and killed in battle by Dolabella in 24 A.D.

TACHOMPSO, city of Aethiopia, immediately above Egypt, on an island in the river.

TACHOS, King of Egypt, immediately following Acoris. He asked Chabrias of Athens to command his fleet, and Agesilaus to command his armies. Both came to Egypt, but the latter was

392

angry in having only mercenaries under his charge. So when Nectanabis claimed the Egyptian crown to be his, Agesilaus deserted, assisting Nectanabis, who became King in 361 B.C.

TACITUS, MARCUS CLAUDIUS, Roman emperor, was consul in 273, and at the age of 70 was elected emperor, after the murder of Aurelian. He tried to restore the power of the senate, and curb extravagance. After reigning from only Sept. 275 to April 276, he became victim of a conspiracy, and was followed by Probus.

TACITUS, CORNELIUS, Roman historian, born about 55 A.D. He first wrote a dialogue on oratory. He produced the *Agricola* and the *Germania,* when about 40. The *Germania* gave the first full account of manners and customs of the people occupying central Europe at the beginning of the Christian era. His great work was his history of the Roman empire from the accession of Tiberius. Only half of the 30 books have come down to us, but they give the author's views concerning Tiberius, Claudius, Nero, and the events of 69 A.D., when there were three emperors in one year. The firm belief that the early Roman empire was a mass of iniquity and corruption is due more to Tacitus than to any other writer.

TAENARUM, a headland of Laconia, the S. point of Peloponnesus.

TAGES, mysterious Etruscan boy with the wisdom of an old man. When Tarchon was ploughing near Tarquinii, Tages rose out of the ground, being son of Genius Jovialis, and grandson of Jupiter. When he spoke to Tarchon, he shrieked with fear, and other Etruscans came to his aid, and in a short time all the people were gathered round him. Tages instructed them in the art of haruspices, dying immediately after. The Etruscans recorded what he had said, and so came into being the books of Tages, reputed to be twelve in number.

TAGUS, an important river of Spain, rising in the territory of the Celtiberians, flowing westward, and emptying into the Atlantic. The town of Olisippo (Lisbon) stood at its mouth. Ancient writers mention its gold sand and precious stones.

TALAURA, fortress, residence of Mithridates the Great, in Pontus.

TALION, THE LAW OF, in ancient Hittite civilization, the law of "an eye for an eye and a tooth for a tooth."

TALTHYBIADAE, Spartan family, tracing their descent from Talthybius, holding the hereditary office of herald.

TAMASSUS, town of central Cyprus, near the famous plain, *ager Tamaseus,* sacred to Venus.

TAMESIS, (Thames), river of Britain, flowing into the sea on the eastern coast, on which stood Londinium, (London). Caesar crossed the Thames near Cowey Stakes. Large stakes have been found at this spot, supposed to be those fixed in the river by Cassivellaunus to retard Caesar's crossing.

TAMMLIS or TAMMUZ, Phoenician god of the sun. Half the year he spends with the goddess of the underworld, and half with Astarte, goddess of the heavens. He is equivalent to the Greek Adonis.

TAMNA, large city in the S.W. of Arabia Felix, and the capital of the Catabani, maintaining a caravan traffic, in the products of Arabia, with Gaza.

TANAGRA, town of ancient Greece, in Boeotia, near the frontier of Attica, best-known for the terra-cotta statuettes made there.

TANIS, (Zoan of the O.T.). Very ancient city of Lower Egypt, in the E. part of the Delta, was one of the capitals of Lower Egypt under the early Kings. It is said to have been the residence of the court in the days of Moses.

TANTALUS, in *Greek Mythology,* son of Zeus, and father of Pelops. He was a favourite of the gods, but betrayed confidence by divulging the secrets of Zeus. So he was condemned to stand in Hades with water all round him and rich fruits over his head. Both water and fruits receded when he tried to reach them.

TAPHIAE INSULAE, several small islands in the Ionian Sea between Arcarnania and Leucadia. Homer mentions them as haunts of notorious pirates.

TAPROBANE, (Ceylon), great island in the Indian Ocean off the S. of India. The Greeks first knew of it through Onesicritus in the days of Alexander. An embassy was sent by it to Rome in the days of Claudius.

TARBELLI, a powerful people in Gallia Aquitanica. Their country between the sea and the Pyrenees was sandy and barren, but contained gold and other minerals. Their chief town was Aquae Tarbellicae.

TARENTUM, a famous Greek city of S. Italy. It was a Spartan colony founded at the close of the 8th cent. B.C., to relieve the parent state. The Greeks were not the first settlers, and the name of Taras may be older than the colony. It was a fertile district, famous for olives and sheep, and with a magnificent harbour. It grew in power and wealth and extended its domain inland. Even a great defeat by the natives, in 473 B.C., did not break its prosperity, but led to a change of government from aristocracy to democracy. In the 4th cent. B.C., Tarentum was the first city of Great Greece. In the latter half of the century Tarentum was at war with the Lucanians and only held its ground with the aid of Spartan and Epiroti condottieri. In 281 B.C., they were at war with Rome, and in 272 B.C., came the surrender of the city. Tarentum retained nominal liberty as an ally of Rome. It suffered severely in the second Punic War, when taken by Hannibal, in 212 B.C., and retaken and plundered by Fabius, in 209 B.C. After this it fell into decay, but revived after receiving a colony in 123 B.C. It remained a considerable seaport, and its purple, second only to that of Tyre, was still valued. At the fall of the West it was held from time to time by Goths, Lombards, and Saracens.

TARICHEA, strongly fortified town on the Lake of Tiberias, in Palestine, whose population caused Rome much trouble during the Jewish war.

TARPEIA, in ancient *Roman Legend,* daughter of Spurius Tarpeius, governor of the citadel on the Capitoline Hill. Bribed by the besieging Sabines, she betrayed the garrison by opening a gate. As the Sabines entered they crushed the traitress to death with their shields. Her unhappy memory was perpetuated in the name of the cliff on the Capitoline Hill, the Tarpeian rock from which traitors were hurled to death.

TARQUINII, Etrurian city where Demaratus, father of Tarquinius Priscus lived. It was made a Roman colony and a municipium.

TARQUINIUS PRISCUS, LUCIUS, fifth legendary King of ancient Rome, who reigned from 616-578 B.C. He had been exiled from Corinth and came to Rome, finding favour with King Ancus Martius. He was elected King when Ancus died and proved a vigorous ruler. He was murdered by Ancus Martius' sons.

TARQUINIUS SUPERBUS, LUCIUS, Seventh, and last, of the legendary Kings of Rome, who reigned from 534-510 B.C. He was an able monarch but tyrannical. His son Sextus Tarquinius violated Lucretia, which caused a revolt, and Tarquin and his family were banished from Rome, and finally defeated at Lake Regillus, in 496 B.C.

TARRACO, ancient town on the E. coast of Spain, on a high rock, between the river Iberus and the Pyrenees, founded by the Massilians. It was H.Q. of the brothers Scipio in their campaigns against the Carthaginians, in the second Punic War.

TARSHISH, Biblical name of an unidentified Phoenician mart, probably the classical Tartessus, q.v.

TARSUS, ancient city in the fertile plain of Cilicia, on the river Cydnus, whose cool swift waters were the pride of the city, and bore traffic to and from the port of Rhegma. In the days of Xenophon Tarsus was already great, and residence of the vassal King of Cilicia. Its civilization at this period was mainly Semitic. Coins of Tarsus of the Persian period bore Aramaic inscriptions. The deities of the town, known in later times as Heracles, Perseus, Apollo, and Athena, seem to have been akin to those of the Phoenicians and Syrians. The Semitic influence was very ancient, the Assyrians having invaded Cilicia in the 9th cent. B.C., at which date Tarsus is mentioned as Tarzi. After Tarsus was Hellenized the citizens learned to boast that they were Argives sprung from the companions of Triptolemus, and the town became seat of a famous school of philosophy, which sent out teachers as far as Rome itself. More than one philosopher, notably Athenodorus (teacher of Augustus) and Nestor, held the chief magistracy of the city. Tarsus made rapid progress after Cilicia became Roman; in 66 B.C. It was capital of a rich province, and received freedom from Antony, and from Augustus the dignity of a metropolis. The inhabitants were vain and effeminate, and their sensuous Eastern religion had more attraction for them than the philosophy of Porch. S. Paul quotes the inscription on the statue of Sardanapalus at Anchiale, a nearby city, "let us eat and drink, for tomorrow we die." The emperor Tacitus died at Tarsus, and Julian was buried there. The city was deserted and lay waste during the frontier wars of Greeks and Arabs in the first century of Islam.

TARTARUS, in *Greek Mythology*, the prison, or place of punishment in Hades, surrounded by a brass wall, and steeped in impenetrable darkness.

TARTESSUS, ancient town of Spain, and a chief settlement of the Phoenicians, probably the Tarshish (q.v.) of Scripture. Its exact location is in doubt but it was probably situated at the mouth of the Baetis. The whole country west of Gibraltar was called Tartessis.

TATIANUS, (Tatian), one of the earliest Christian apologists. By birth an Assyrian, he received a Greek education, and travelled the Roman empire as a wandering teacher. He reached Rome in 150 A.D., where he came across an Old Testament, at the same time coming into closer contact with Christians. He became a convert, and soon after wrote his *Oratio ad Graecos*, which gained him great repute. Tatian later came into close relation with the famous apologist Justin. He himself established a school. He developed heretical views, but in spite of this his *Diatessaron*, held its ground in the Syrian churches, and was even in ecclesiastical use for two centuries.

TATTA, the great salt lake of central Asia Minor, source of the salt supply to all the adjacent country.

TAULANTII, a people of Illyria, often referred to by Greek and Roman writers. Glaucias was their King in the days of

Alexander the Great.

TAUNUS, German mountain range, not far from the confluence of the Rhine and Moenus.

TAURENTUM, stronghold near Massilia, on the S. coast of Gaul.

TAURI, a savage tribe of European Sarmatia. They inhabited the peninsula Chersonesus Taurica, and sacrificed strangers to a goddess identified with Artemis.

TAURINI, a people living on the upper reaches of the Po, near the foot of the Alps. Taurasia, their most important town, was colonized by Augustus, under the name Augusta Taurinorum.

TAURISCI, a race of Celts in Noricum, called Norici by the Romans.

TAURUS, the great chain of mountains which runs through Asia, being the southern margin of the great tableland of Central Asia.

TEATE, chief town of the Marrucini, on the road between Aternum and Corfinium.

TECTAEUS and ANGELION, these early Greek statuaries are always mentioned together. They taught Callon of Aegina, and flourished about 550 B.C.

TEGEA, a chief city of Arcadia, said to have been founded by Tegeates, son of Lycaon. The people were of four tribes— the Clareotis, Hippothoetis, Apolloniatis, and Athaneatis. The city offered a stubborn resistance to Lacedaemon, on more than one occasion defeating its ambitious neighbour. About 560 B.C., the Lacedaemonians found the bones of Orestes in Tegea and took them to Sparta, and thenceforth Spartan valour, backed by this powerful fetish, proved too much for the merely carnal weapons of Tegea. The Tegeatae sent 3,000 men to the battle of Plataea. They were faithful to Sparta in the Peloponnesian War, but after Leuctra, joined the Arcadians. In the wars of the Achaean League, Tegea was captured by Cleomenes, King of Sparta, and Antigonas, King of Macedonia.

TELAMON, in *Greek Legend,* brother of Peleus, and father of Ajax. He took part in the hunt for the Calydonian boar, and accompanied the Argonauts.

TELEGONUS, in *Greek Mythology,* son of Odysseus by the enchantress Circe. When he reached manhood Circe sent him to find his father, and, being shipwrecked on the coast of Ithaca, he began to ravish the country. Odysseus and his son Telemachus went to meet the stranger, who, not knowing him, killed his father.

TELEMACHUS, in *Greek Mythology,* son of Odysseus and Penelope. He was a baby when his father went to take part in the Trojan War. After twenty years Telemachus set out to find him, visiting Nestor at Pylos, and Menelaus at Sparta. On returning home he found that his father had arrived.

TELEPHUS, in *Greek Legend,* son of Hercules, who became King of Mysia, married Laodice, daughter of Priam, and was wounded by Achilles. The oracle pronounced that the wound could only be healed by the man who inflicted it, and that the aid of Telephus was necessary for the taking of Troy, so Achilles healed his wound.

TELESIA, town in Samnium, taken by Hannibal in the second Punic War, and afterwards recaptured by the Romans. Augustus colonized it with veterans. Pontius, who fought against Sulla, was born here.

TELESILLA, the lyric poetess of Argos, who flourished about 510 B.C. She took up arms and led her countrywomen in the war between Argos and Sparta; in memory of which her statue was set up in the temple of Aphrodite.

TELESINUS, C. LUCIUS, was consul with Suetonius Paulinus in 66 A.D. Domitian banished him because of his love of philosophy.

TELESTAS, a celebrated poet of the later Athenian dithyramb, who was flourishing in 398 B.C.

TELEUTIAS, a Spartan, was the brother on the mother's side to Agesilaus II, by whose influence he was given command of the fleet, in the war of the Lacedaemonians against Corinth, in 393 B.C. Later he went as general against the Olynthians and was slain.

TELO MARTIUS, a seaport of Gallia Narbonensis, on the Mediterranean.

TELOS, small island in the Carpathian, one of the Sporades, off Caria.

TEMPE, a valley in Thessaly, between Mts. Olympus and Ossa, about 6 m. long, watered by the Peneus, was associated with the worship of Apollo, and was an important pass of N. Greece.

TEN COMMANDMENTS, THE, term in use for the Decalogue, or code of 10 laws, given through Moses to the Israelites. They formed part of the Jewish law, and were adopted by the Christian Church.

TENCTERI, a German people, living on the Rhine, south of the land occupied by the Usipetes, with whom their name is often associated. Both tribes crossed the Rhine to settle in Gaul, but were defeated by Caesar. The Tencteri later joined the league of the Cherusci.

TENEA, town in the interior of Corinthia, supposed to have been colonized by some Trojan captives brought from Tenedos by the Greeks. The town submitted to the Romans without resistance, thus escaping the destruction that overwhelmed Corinth.

TENEDOS, an island of the Aegaean, N. of Delos, fifteen miles in length, with a town of the same name, and a temple of Neptune. Its wine was greatly cherished.

TENTYRA, city of Upper Egypt on the W. bank of the Nile with temples of Athor, Isis, and Typhon. Its populace are said to have been crocodile haters.

TEOS, Ionian city of Asia Minor, on the coast, birthplace of Anacreon and Hecataeus. In the days of the Roman emperors it had two harbours, and a temple of Bacchus.

TEREDON, Babylonian city on the west of the Tigris, was a great center of trade with Arabia.

TERENTIA, wife of Cicero, by whom he had a son and a daughter. On Cicero being banished in 58 B.C., she tried to cheer her husband with cheerful letters, and exerted herself on his behalf among his influential friends. During the civil war, Cicero became offended with her and divorced her. Terentia is said to have lived until she was 103.

TERENTIUS AFER, P., (TERENCE), Roman comic poet. He devoted himself to translating Greek drama into Latin. His first play, *Andria,* was produced in 166 B.C., and was an instant success, procuring for him admission to a brilliant literary group. *Hecyra* followed in 165 B.C., *Heauton Timoroumenos* in 163 B.C., *Eunuchus* and *Phormio,* both in 161 B.C., and *Adelphi* in 160 B.C. He is supposed to have died of grief at the loss at sea of his translations of Menander in 159 B.C.

TERENTIANUS MAURUS, Roman poet of the latter part of the 1st cent., under Nerva and Trajan, was born in Africa.

TEREUS, son of Ares, King of the Thracians in Daulis. Pandion called in the assistance of Tereus against an enemy and gave him Procne, his daughter, in marriage. Tereus hid her in the country that he might marry her sister Philomela, whom he told Procne was dead. At the same time he cut out Philomela's tongue. Philomela, learning the truth, made it known to her sister by a few words which she wove into a peplus. They fled pursued by Tereus with an axe, and when overtaken the sisters prayed to be changed into birds. Procne became a nightingale, Philomela a swallow, and Tereus a hoopoe.

TERIBAZUS, a Persian in high favour with Artaxerxes II. At the time of the retreat of the Ten Thousand in 401 B.C., T. was satrap of W. Armenia. Later he assisted the Lacedaemonians in 392 B.C.

TERIOLIS, a stronghold in Raetia, which gave its name to the country of the Tyrol.

TERMANTIA, town of the Arevaci in Hispania Tarraconensis, whose people frequently resisted the Romans, who in consequence made them abandon the town and build a new one, not so well placed strategically, in 98 B.C.

TERMERA, Dorian city in Caria, which under the Romans was a free city.

TERMINUS, in *Roman Mythology,* a deity presiding over boundaries and frontiers. When boundaries were fixed, sacrifices were made, and trenches dug, into which the bodies of the animals were put. A fire of pine branches was then kindled in the trench, and a stone, or emblem of Terminus was set up over the ashes.

TERPANDER, father of Greek music and lyric poetry. He was born at Lesbos, and flourished between 700 and 650 B.C.

TERRASIDIUS, T., one of Caesar's officers in Gaul, who was sent to the Unelli to obtain corn in 57 B.C., but was made prisoner by them.

TERTULLIANUS, Q. SEPTIMUS FLORENS, (TERTULLIAN), theologian, son of a Roman centurion, was born at Carthage, well educated, and probably became an advocate. He became a Christian about 190 A.D., was ordained priest, and devoted his life to the defence of the Faith. About 202 he adopted the Montanist heresy, and became leader of the sect in Africa. His *Apologeticus* is the most important of his many works.

TETA, C. TREBATUS, Roman jurist, and friend of Cicero, who recommended him to Julius Caesar when he was proconsul of Gaul. He followed Caesar in the civil war.

TETRAPOLIS, union of four cities of states, e.g., the Attic Tetrapolis, made up of Oenoe, Marathon, Probalinthus, and Tricorythus, founded by Xuthus.

TETRARCH, ruler of a fourth part of a region. Later the term was applied to minor rulers. Herod Antipas, to whom Jesus was sent, was tetrarch of Galilee.

TETRICUS, C. PESUVIUS, one of the Thirty Tyrants, last pretender to rule Gaul during its separation from the empire.

TEUTA, wife of Argon, King of Illyria, who assumed power on her husband's death in 231 B.C.

TEUTOBURGIENSIS SALTUS, range of hills in Germany, famous for the defeat of Varus and three legions by the Germans led by Arminius, in 9 A.D.

TEUTOMATUS, son of Ollovicon, King of the Nitiobriges, who joined Vercingetorix with a body of cavalry. Being suddenly attacked by Caesar's soldiers while in his tent he with difficulty escaped half naked from the camp.

TEUTON, name denoting a group of peoples, of the Caucasian, or white race, whose languages constitute the Teutonic sub-family of Indo-European speech. The word Teutonic, used by late Roman writers as synonymous with Germanic, is preferred in modern English because Germanic is liable to confusion with German, which has a narrower implication. It is derived from the tribal name of the Teutones, q.v., who probably lived in or near Jutland in the 2nd cent., B.C.

TEUTONES, powerful people of Germany, who invaded Gaul with the Cimbri, towards the end of the 2nd cent. B.C.

THABOR, *see* Tabor.

THAIS, Athenian courtesan, said to have accompanied Alexander on his Eastern campaigns, and to have persuaded him, in a drunken mood, to set fire to the old palace of the Persians at Persepolis, as a reprisal for the destruction of Athens by Xerxes.

THALA, large city of Numidia, connected by a road with Tacape on the Syrtis Minor.

THALASSIUS, Roman senator in the days of Romulus. When a beautiful maiden was carried off for him, during the rape of the Sabine women, the persons conducting her protected her by saying "for Thalassius."

THALES, Ionic philosopher, one of the seven wise men of ancient Greece, was born in Miletus, Asia Minor, in 640 B.C. He was said to be of Phoenician descent, and was the first recorded man to suggest a scientific, as opposed to a mythological explanation of the universe. He held that water was the all-pervading principle of the universe, and that material substances were variants of water. Also, he held that the universe is a living creature. Thales is regarded as the pioneer in the sciences of geometry and astronomy among the Greeks.

THALIA, in *Greek Mythology,* one of the nine Muses, whose care was pastoral poetry and comedy.

THALNA, M. JUVENTIUS, tribune of the plebs in 170 B.C., praetor in 167 B.C., and consul in 163 B.C.

THALPIUS, son of Eurytus, and one of Helen's suitors, and so compelled to fight against Troy. He led the Epei, in ten ships.

THAMYDENI, people of Felix Arabia, living on the Arabian Gulf.

THASOS, island in the N. of the Aegaean, off Thrace, colonized at an early date by Phoenicians, probably attracted by its gold mines. They founded a Temple of Hercules. Thasos, is said to have been leader of the Phoenicians, and in 720 B.C. (?) the island received a Greek colony from Paros. After the capture of Miletus, in 494 B.C., Histiaeus laid siege to Thasos. The attack failed, but warned by the danger, the Thasians built ships and strengthened their fortifications. This excited the suspicions of Persia and Darius compelled them to surrender their ships, and pull down their walls. After the defeat of Xerxes the Thasians joined the Greek confederacy, but later, on account of a dispute about mines, they revolted. The Athenians defeated them at sea, and after a siege of over two years took their capital, made them pay an indemnity, and an annual contribution, and resign their possessions on the mainland. In 411 B.C., Thasos again revolted, and received a Lacedaemonian governor. In 407 B.C., the partisans of Lacedaemon were expelled, and the Athenians, under Thrasybulus, were admitted. After the battle of Aegospotami, in 405 B.C., Thasos again fell into the hands of the Lacedaemonians, but the Athenians must have recovered it, for it formed one of the subjects of dispute between them and Philip of Macedonia. Thasos submitted to Philip, but received its freedom at the hands of the Romans after the battle of Cynoscephalae, in 197 B.C., and was still a free state in the days of Pliny.

THEATRUM, in the earliest days of Greek drama the theatre was merely the open place where the altar of Dionysus was set up, round which the chorus revolved and was addressed by a single actor from a wagon. The first great stone theatre was begun in 500 B.C., within the Lenaeum, or enclosure sacred to Dionysus at Athens. It was an immense semicircular excavation in the side of the hill. Round the concavity seats for 30,000 rose tier over tier, the whole topped by a balustraded portico. The lowest seats were used by the priests and high officials, as being nearest the orchestra, on the other side of which was the great permanent stage. Similar theatres were erected throughout Greece and there are remains of others in Asia Minor. The three great Roman theatres were on the Greek model.

THEBAE, (Thebes), ancient capital of Upper Egypt, built on both banks of the Nile, 450 m. upstream from Cairo, and a varying region N. and S. was called the Thebaid. In the Bible it is No-Amon. Of prehistoric foundation, it provided the XIth and XIIth dynasty Kings, and after the Hyksos expulsion flourished again under the Empire. It was reputed to have had a hundred gates, and its monuments include funerary temples, richly appointed rock-hewn tombs, and two great terraced temples.

THEBAE, (Thebes), city of ancient Greece, which from early times was most prominent in Boeotia. In legendary days it was associated with the names of Dionysus, Hercules, and Cadmus. When the Peloponnesian War started in 431 B.C., Thebes was in alliance with Sparta. In 379 B.C., the Thebans ejected their Spartan masters, and joined the struggle for independence, and Epaminondas led her troops to victory over Sparta at Leuctra in 371 B.C. Though Thebes could not maintain her supremacy, she joined with Athens in resisting Philip, but the allies were beaten at Chaeronea, in 338 B.C. After Philip's death she revolted against Alexander, bringing upon herself final destruction in 336 B.C.

THEBE, city of Mysia, destroyed by Achilles, said to have been the birthplace of Andromache and Chryseis.

THELXINOE, one of the earlier Muses.

THEMIS, in *Greek Mythology*, daughter of Uranus and Ge, the wife of Zeus before Hera. Among her children by Zeus were the three Horae and the Fates. She was personification of law and order, and presided over the oracle at Delphi before Apollo.

THEMISON, famous Greek physician, founder of the Methodici (a medical sect).

THEMISTOCLES, Athenian statesman, who realizing the capacity of Athens for maritime development, foresaw that imperial ascendancy would follow naval supremacy. He procured the exile of Aristides, the conservative leader, in 483 B.C., thus securing the direction of Athenian policy. When the Persians invaded the Greek peninsula in 480 B.C., the fleet was smashed at Salamis by the Greek fleet under Themistocles. In 479 B.C., his diplomacy compelled Sparta to advance to the protection of Attica and fight against the Persians at Plataea. He refortified the Piraeus before Sparta could prevent it, and this time Athenian naval supremacy was assured. In 471 B.C., he was charged with peculation, and expelled. In exile he was accused of treasonable intrigues with Persia. In Athens it was believed that he took poison through despair at the failure of his schemes. He died in 449 B.C.

THEOCRITUS, Greek poet, born at Syracuse. For many years he lived at the court of Ptolemy Philadelphus in Alexandria. A crude poetry in Dorian dialect had been characteristic of the shepherds and rustics of Sicily, but Theocritus was first to raise it to the dignity of literary form. His poems are full of exquisite passages. The 30 poems we possess, known as *Idylls* are reputed to be his. Our own Milton and Spenser were close imitators of his.

THEODORICUS, (Theodoric), King of the Ostrogoths, known as Theodoric the Great, was born in Pannonia. His father was Theodemir, who sent him at an early age as a hostage to Constantinople. When he succeeded his father in 473 A.D., he received the support of Zeno, the East Roman emperor, who gave his sanction for him to attack Odoacer in Italy. The murder of Odoacer left Theodoric master of Italy, which he ruled as Zeno's viceregent, but actually as an independent ruler. Italy was at peace during the 33 years in which he held sway. He died in 526 A.D., and was buried in Ravenna.

THEODOSIUS, name of Eastern Roman emperors. Theodosius I, born in Spain, was son of Theodosius, one of Valentinian's generals. He served in Britain under his father, and in Moesia, where he defeated the Sarmatians in 374 A.D. In 379 A.D., Gratian called him to the Eastern throne, after the defeat of the Romans by the Goths at Adrianople. He proved equal to the emergency and by 382 A.D., had cleared the Balkans of Goths. His reign was marked by the complete triumph of orthodox Christianity. Theodosius and Gratian were much influenced by S. Ambrose, and pagan and heretical worship were prohibited. Theodosius used unnecessary violence to crush a riot in Thessalonica, thereby displeasing S. Ambrose, who made him do penance. Theodosius died in Milan, in 395 A.D. Theodosius II followed his father Arcadius when only seven years old, being under the guardianship of his sister Pulcheria. His name is chiefly associated with the code of laws known as *Codex Theodosianus*.

THEODOTA, Athenian courtesan who having attached herself to Alcibiades, performed his funeral rites after his murder.

THEOGNIS, Greek elegiac poet, born at Megara, in Attica. The 1,400 verses of his poetry contain a bitter attack on bad citizenship and upon democrats, who are contrasted with the good aristocrats. He addresses most of his poems to Cyrnus, a young Megarian noble. He lived about 540-508 B.C.

THEON, name of two mathematicians who have often been confused. Theon the Elder was of Smyrna and lived in the days of Trajan and Hadrian. Theon the Younger was of Alexandria and is best known as an astronomer and geometer, who lived in the days of Theodosius the Elder.

THEOPHRASTUS, successor of Aristotle in the Peripatetic school was born at Eresus, in Lesbos, about 370 B.C. Originally called Tyrtamus, Aristotle gave him the name of Theophrastus on account of his eloquence. He received his introduction to philosophy from Leucippus, and went to Athens, and became a member of the Platonic circle. After the death of Plato he attached himself to Aristotle. He was friend of Callisthenes, fellow pupil of Alexander. Aristotle made Theophrastus guardian of his children, and designated him as his philosophic successor at the Lyceum when he removed to Chalcis. Aristotle left his library to Theophrastus, who presided over the Peripatetic school for 35 years, and died in 288 B.C.

THEOPOMPUS, of Chios, famous historian and rhetorician, was born about 378 B.C., and spent his early years in Athens with his exiled father. He became pupil of Isocrates, making rapid progress in rhetoric. At first he composed epideictic speeches in which he gained a prize given by Artemisia, in honour of her husband. His teacher advised him to become an historian. Through the influence of Alexander he was restored to Chios about 333 B.C., and became a bold leader of the aristocratical party in his native town. When Alexander died he was again expelled, taking refuge with Ptolemy in Egypt.

THERA, island in the Aegaean, chief of the Sporades; in *Greek Legend,* it was connected with the story of the Argonauts. Cadmus is supposed to have founded a Phoenician colony there. Later a colony from Sparta was led to Thera. An event which gave importance to Thera was the planting of its colony of Cyrene, on the N. coast of Africa, by Battus in 631 B.C., in accordance with a command of the Delphic oracle.

THERAMENES, an Athenian who played an important part in Athenian affairs at the close of the Peloponnesian War, and the revolution which followed. He was one of the conspirators who, in 411 B.C., abolished the democracy of Athens and substituted the Four Hundred.

THERMOPYLAE, pass in Greece, leading into Thessaly, affording the only passage for an army from N. to S. Greece. A heroic effort was made to hold it in 480 B.C., against the Persians by a Greek force of about 1,000 men, under Leonidas, King of Sparta. As a result of treachery, the Persians took the Greeks in the rear, who were all killed.

THERSITES, in *Greek Legend,* the ugliest man in the Greek army before Troy, represented as a man of the people who delighted in disputing with his superiors.

THESEUS, in *Greek Legend,* great hero of Attica and Athens, unacknowledged son of Aegeus, King of Athens, he was reared at Troezen by Aethra, his mother, who gave him his father's sword and sent him to Athens. Acknowledged by Aegeus as his son and successor, he killed the bull of Marathon, went to Crete and, assisted by Ariadne, killed the Minotaur. On his father's death, he succeeded him. He led an expedition against the Amazons, married Hippolyte, their queen, by whom he had his son Hippolytus. Failing to carry off Persephone from Hades as a wife for Pirithous, Theseus was confined in Hades until rescued by Hercules. On his return to Athens he found that Helen's brothers, Castor and Pollux, had recovered their sister. Theseus retired to Scyros, where he was murdered by Lycomedes. His bones were brought to Athens in 469 B.C., and a temple built to receive them.

THESPIS, father of Greek tragedy, was born at Icaria, in Attica. In order to give the Dionysian chorus some rest, Thespis introduced an actor into these shows, devising a linen mask so that the actor might sustain more than one character. He invented the prologue and dialogue of Greek drama, while by placing the actor upon a table so that he might be on an equal elevation with the chorus ranged upon the steps of the altar of Bacchus, he introduced the earliest form of stage.

THESPROTI, people of Epirus, occupying Thesprotia, which stretched along the coast from the Ambracian Gulf to the Thyamis.

THESSALIA, the largest district of Greece, bounded N. by the Cambunians, W. by Mt. Pindus, E. by the Aegaean, and S. by the Maliac Gulf. It was a vast plain enclosed by mountains, only broken by the valley of Tempe. The plain was watered by the Peneus.

THESSALONIANS, EPISTLES TO THE, Two of the epistles of S. Paul, usually grouped by themselves as being the earliest of his writings. S. Paul visited Thessalonica on his second missionary journey, making many converts, but Jewish opposition caused his hasty withdrawal to Beroea. He later sent Timothy to Thessalonica, and on his return the Apostle wrote from Corinth the First Epistle to the Thessalonians. The Second Epistle was written from the same place, not long after the first, which it closely resembles, both belonging to the year 52 or 53 A.D.

THESSALONICA, first called Therma, was an ancient city of Macedonia. The Athenians captured it just before the Peloponnesian War (432 B.C.). Cassander made it an important city.

THESTIUS, son of Ares and Demonice, was King of Pluron, and father of Idas, Lynceus, Althaea, Hypermestra, and Leda.

THETIS, in *Greek Mythology,* one of the Nereids, and wife of Peleus, and mother of Achilles.

THISBE, in *Babylonian Legend,* heroine of the love tragedy of Pyramus and Thisbe.

THOMAS, one of the twelve Apostles. He showed courage in calling on the other Apostles to follow Jesus into Judaea, and although he doubted the Resurrection without ocular evidence, yet, when that was granted, he made a confession of faith. He is supposed to have preached in Parthia and to have been buried at Edessa. Later stories make him founder of the Church in India.

THOTH, Egyptian divinity, the name signifying measurer. As divine scribe Thoth recorded the result of the weighing of souls in the Underworld.

THOTHMES, name of four Egyptian Kings of the XVIIIth dynasty. Thothmes I, son of Amenhotep I, reigned from about 1539-1489 B.C. He was the first great Egyptian military commander. In his Syrian campaigns he carried arms as far as the Euphrates. His son, Thothmes II, reigned from about 1514-1501 B.C., together with his half-sister Hatshepsut. Thothmes III appears to have become co-regent with his aunt and step-mother Hatshepsut about 1501 B.C., reigning alone after her death for 32 years. His territory stretched from Armenia to the Sudan. He was possibly the Pharaoh of the Oppression. Thothmes IV, son of Amenhotep II, reigned from about 1447-1438 B.C.

THRACIA, (Thrace), in *Ancient Geography,* a country in the E. of the modern Balkan peninsula. Its boundaries were, roughly speaking, the Danube on the N., the Euxine on the E., the Aegaean and Propontis on the S., and Macedonia on the W. The chief rivers were the Strymon and Hebrus.

THRASYBULUS, Athenian statesman and general, who assisted in the overthrow of the tyranny of the Four Hundred in 411 B.C. When the new oligarchy of the Thirty Tyrants was set up by the Spartans, after Athens had been taken in 404 B.C., he suffered banishment. With the assistance of the Thebans, he re-established the democracy at Athens in 403 B.C. He was killed while commanding the Athenian fleet in the Aegaean.

THUCYDIDES, Greek historian, who wrote the history of the Peloponnesian War in eight books, taking the story to 411 B.C., though the war did not end until 404 B.C. His work is accurate and impartial. His love for Athens did not blind him to her defects and errors, and he holds the balance equally between her and her enemies. He also endeavours to show the underlying causes of the events described. He puts speeches into the mouths of prominent men on both sides, such as the funeral oration delivered by Pericles on the Athenians who died in the first year of the war. The account of the expedition to Sicily was regarded by Macaulay to be the finest prose composition in the world.—Another of the name was an Athenian statesman, who after the death of Cimon became leader of the aristocratic party.

THULE, in *Ancient Geography*, a remote island in the northern seas, often referred to as Ultima Thule. It has been identified with the Orkneys, Shetlands, Iceland, and Norway. It is first mentioned by the ancient voyager Pytheas of Marseilles, q.v.

THURII, Greek city in Lucania, founded in 443 B.C., to replace the ancient Sybaris.

THYAMIS, river of Epirus, being the boundary between Thesprotia and Cestryna.

THYATIRA, large city of N. Lydia, near Mysia, on the Lycus, and a Macedonian colony, said to have been built by Seleucus Nicator. It was famous for its purple dye. It was an early seat of Christianity being mentioned in the Apocalypse as one of the Seven Churches of Asia.

THYMBRA, city of the Troad, N. of Ilium Vetus, with a famous temple of Apollo.

THYMIA, stronghold in S. Sicyonia, on the borders of Phliasia.

THYNI, a people of Thrace, originally dwelling near Salmydessus, but later moving to Bithynia.

THYREA, chief town of Cynuria, for possession of which the battle was fought between the 300 Spartans and 300 Argives.

TIBERIAS, town of Palestine, founded by Herod Antipas, was chief town of ancient Galilee, and famous for its school of Jewish teachers.

TIBERIS, (Tiber), river of central Italy, known as Albula in early times, and said to have been renamed after Tiberinus, King of Alba, who was drowned in the river, and, as a river-god, was its patron. Rising in the Tuscan Apennines it empties into the Tyrrhenian Sea, after flowing 245 m. The alluvium of its waters has caused it to be called the Yellow Tiber. Rome, of course, stood on this river.

TIBERIUS, Roman emperor from 14 to 37 A.D., was born in 42 B.C., and was son of Tiberius Claudius Nero and Livia Drusilla. In 2 B.C., Augustus, having married Livia Drusilla in 38 B.C., adopted his step-son as his heir, and Tiberius succeeded in 14 A.D. He displayed great ability in guarding the frontiers, but in character he was morose and bitter. He retired to Capreae in 26 A.D., Sejanus being given almost a free hand in the government, which he used to institute a reign of terror. In 31 A.D., Tiberius, realizing his treasonable designs put him to death, but the terror continued. Tiberius lived a dreadful life at Capreae, and was murdered in 37 A.D.—Another of the name was an emperor of the East from 578 to 582 A.D.

TIBULLUS, ALBIUS, Roman poet, whose four books of Elegies have come down to us. The poems have great delicacy of treatment and depth of emotion. He was born in 53 B.C., and died in 18 B.C.

TIBUR, ancient town of Latium, N.W. of Rome, on the left bank of the Anio. Said to have been founded by the Siculi, it passed to the Aborigines and Pelasgi. Later it was a chief town of the Latin league, becoming subject to Rome in 338 B.C. The emperor Hadrian had a villa here. Zenobia and Horace also lived here (now called Tivoli).

TIGELLINUS, (C. OFONIUS), son of man living in Agrigentum, was the most odious of all Nero's favourites. When Otho came to power Tigellinus was ordered to end his own life.

TIGLATH-PILESER, there were four Assyrian Kings of this name. The first reigned about 1100 B.C., and extended the Assyrian power into Armenia, Cappadocia, and Lebanon. He also rebuilt Asshur. The fourth King of this name reigned from 745 to 727 B.C. He subdued N. Syria, and held court at Damascus, which was attended by Ahaz of Jerusalem.

TIGRANES, name of several Kings of ancient Armenia. Tigranes the Great, who lived from 121-55 B.C., succeeded his father, Artavasdes II in 95 B.C. His father-in-law, Mithridates the Great, King of Pontus, assisted him in ruling W. Asia, from Pamphylia to the Caspian. He was defeated by the Romans, under Lucullus, in 69 and 68 B.C., and was made subject by Pompey in 66 B.C.

TIGRIS, the shorter of two large rivers, rising in Armenia and running to the Persian Gulf. The Tigris rises from two principal sources. After the junction of the eastern and western branches the river pursues a winding course for 800 m. passing through Mosul and Baghdad, to the point of union with the Euphrates at Kurna, whence it becomes known as the Shatt-al-Arab.

TIGURINI, a clan of the Helvetii, who, with the Cimbri, invaded the country of the Allobroges in Gaul, where they defeated L. Cassius Longinus, the consul, in 107 B.C.

TIMAEUS, the historian, was son of Andromachus, tyrant of Tauromenium. He was born about 356 B.C. Agathocles banished him from Sicily, and he went to Athens where he remained for fifty years.—Another of this name was a Pythagorean philosopher.

TIMOLEON, Greek soldier, liberator of Sicily, was born in Corinth, about 411 B.C. He freed Syracuse from Dionysus, and the Carthaginians, re-establishing the democracy. He succeeded in expelling most of the tyrants from the Greek cities in Sicily. He probably died in 337 B.C.

TIMON, Athenian misanthrope of the 5th cent. B.C., who was so disgusted with his friends' conduct, when he lost his wealth, that he shut himself in a tower, seeing no one but Alcibiades.

TIMOTHEUS, (a) Athenian general from 378-356 B.C. (b) Poet and musician, 446-357 B.C. (c) A statuary and sculptor of the Attic school in the days of Scopas.

TIMOTHY, S. Paul's companion, was son of a gentile father and Jewish mother. He went to Europe with S. Paul, being with him at Athens and Corinth. He shared S. Paul's imprisonment at Rome. He was later consecrated Bishop of Ephesus.

TIMOTHY, EPISTLES TO, two N.T. epistles, ascribed to S. Paul, and belonging, with "Titus" to the Pastoral Epistles. They probably contain genuine fragments of S. Paul's writings, but seem to have been written in the name of the Apostle, rather than by him.

TIRESIAS, in *Greek Legend,* a soothsayer of Thebes. Athena, having been asked to restore his sight, he having been blind from childhood, gave him the gift of prophecy.

TIRIDATES, name of several Parthian and Armenian Kings (a) King of Parthia, 32 B.C. (b) Grandson of Phraates IV, made King of Parthia by Tiberius, in 35 A.D. (c) Brother of Vologaeses I, who made him King of Armenia in the 3rd Cent. A.D.

TIRYNS, ancient Greek city in Peloponnesus, its massive walls were said to have been built by Proetus, King of Argos, by masons from Lycia, called the Cyclopes, hence "Cyclopean" architecture. Tiryns was destroyed by Argos, in 468 B.C.

TISSAPHERNES, was satrap of Lower Asia in 414 B.C., and supported the Spartans in the Peloponnesian War, but gave no practical aid, because it did not suit his policy that either side should gain supremacy, but rather that they should wear one another down. Cyrus, however, arriving in 407 B.C., gave the Lacedaemonians effectual aid. At Cunaxa, in 401 B.C., Tissaphernes was one of four who led the armies of Artaxerxes, and his section of the forces was the only one not to be routed by the Greeks. When the 10,000 retreated, Tissaphernes undertook to lead them to safety, but treacherously arrested their generals. As a reward the King gave him wide authority in W. Asia, which led to war with Sparta, in which Tissaphernes was unsuccessful. He was put to death at the instigation of Parysatis, mother of Cyrus, in 395 B.C.

TITANES, (Titans), in *Greek Mythology*, a family of giants, the offsprings of Uranus and Ge, were 12 or 13 in number, the best known being Oceanus, Hyperian, Cronus, Rhea, and Themis. The Titans rose against their father, influenced by their mother, and made Cronus ruler of the universe in his place. When Zeus became chief of the gods the Titans refused to acknowledge him and carried out a struggle with him.

TITANUS, JULIUS, Roman writer, father of the rhetorician of that name.

TITHONUS, in *Greek Mythology*, son of Laomedon, King of Troy, by a nymph; he asked Eos to give him immortality, which request was granted, but he omitted to ask for perpetual youth. He asked the goddess to revoke her gift, upon which she turned him into a grasshopper.

TITHRAUSTES, successor to Tissaphernes, q.v., in his satrapy.

TITORMUS, a herdsman of Aetolia, famous for strength.

TITUS, companion of S. Paul; of Greek birth, he is first mentioned as going with the Apostle to Jerusalem. We find him, on three occasions, working in Corinth. S. Paul addressed a short epistle to him. He was with S. Paul in his second imprisonment.

TITUS, FLAVIUS SABINUS VESPASIANUS, Roman emperor from 79 to 81 A.D.; he was eldest son of Vespasian, and had been military tribune in Britain and Germany. He captured Jerusalem, in 70 A.D., thus ending the Jewish war, which event is commemorated by his arch at Rome. He proved to be most popular of the emperors. His death took place at his Sabine villa in 81 A.D.

TITYUS, in *Greek Mythology*, the giant who attempted to violate Artemis, for which he was killed by Apollo, her brother. (some say by Zeus). He was consigned to Tartarus, where he lay on the ground with two vultures perpetually tearing his liver.

TLOS, interior city of Lycia, between Mt. Massicytus and Cibyra.

TOBIAS, character in the Biblical book of Tobit. The name is Hebrew, and signifies "God is good."

TOBIT, book of the O.T. Apocrypha, probably written by an Egyptian Jew in the 3rd cent. B.C. It deals with the Jew, Tobit, who with Anna his wife, and Tobias his son, had been carried to Nineveh by Shalmaneser.

TOGA, the usual outer garment of men in ancient Rome, in form a woollen cloak with pointed ends 12 or 15 feet long, worn over the tunic, and wrapped round the body. It could not be worn by slaves or foreigners, and remained the official robe until the 5th cent.

TOLETUM, capital of the Carpetani in Hispania Tarraconensis, said to have been founded by the Jews, after Nebuchadnezzar had captured Jerusalem.

TOLOSA, capital of the Tectosages, in Gallia Narbonensis, near the borders of Aquitania (modern Toulouse).

TOLUMNIUS, an augur among the Rutulians, renowned for bravery.

TOLUMNIUS, LAR, King of the Veientes, who was killed in single combat with Cornelius Cossus.

TOPETH, equivalent to the Hebrew Sheol, and the Greek Gehenna and Hades. It is applied in the Bible to the valley of Hinnon, where idolatrous worship was carried out. Later the refuse of Jerusalem, and the bodies of dead animals and criminals, were burned here.

TOXANDRI, a people of Gallia Belgica, living on the right bank of the Scaldis.

TRACHALUS, GALERIUS, with Silius Italicus, Trachalus was consul in 68 A.D.

TRACHONITIS, district of N. Palestine, beyond the Jordan, between Antilibanus and the Arabian mountains.

TRADUCTA, town of Hispania Baetica, founded by the Romans, who placed there the people of Zelas, a town in Africa, in addition to some of their own colonists.

TRAJANUS, MARCUS ULPIUS, (TRAJAN), a Spaniard of Italica, who won rapid distinction in the Roman army and commanded the forces on the Rhine when Nerva chose him as his colleague and successor. Nerva adopted him in 97 A.D. In 98 he became emperor on the death of Nerva. His character and talent fitted him for administration, and he set himself to extend Roman dominion. From 101-105 he subjected the Dacians, and later he led an expedition east, but after capturing the Parthian capital was forced to retreat. He died in 117 A.D., at Selinus in Cilicia. Trajan's Pillar in Rome was raised to record his deeds.

TRALLES, trading center of Asia Minor; under the Seleucidae the town was known as Antiochia, also Seleucia. It was peopled by Greeks and Carians.

TRANIPSAE, a people of Thrace, mentioned in connection with the Melanditae and Thyni, by Seuthes.

TREBONIUS, C., was to the fore during the latter days of the republic. As tribune of the plebs in 55 B.C., he proposed Lex Trebonia, by which Pompey received the two Spains, Crassus Syria, and Caesar the Gauls and Illyricum for a further period of five years. He was appointed Caesar's legate in Gaul, and in 48 became city praetor, and the following year succeeded Q. Cassius Longinus as pro-praetor of Farther Spain. In 45 he was raised to the consulship by Caesar, who promised him the province of Asia. In spite of this Trebonius was a mover in the conspiracy to assassinate Caesar, and after the murder in 44 he went as pro-consul to Asia. His end came when Dolabella surprised the town of Smyrna, where Trebonius was living, and slew him in bed.

TREVERI, a people of Gallia Belgica, allies of the Romans, and noted for the quality of their cavalry. Their country stretched from the Rhine to Remi. Augustus made their chief town a colony, calling it Augusta Treverorum. It became capital of Belgica Prima, and after the division of the empire in 292 A.D., into four, it became residence of the Caesar of Britain, Gaul, and Spain.

TRIBUNE, title of various military and civil officers of Rome. The military tribunes were originally commanders of the tribes. Six were appointed for each legion. More important were the tribunes of the plebs. When Rome became a republic, the plebeians shared in the comitia centuriata, or assembly, but magistracies were confined to patricians. In 494 B.C., the plebeians won the right to appoint two tribunes authorized to protect them against arbitrary action by the magistrates: later they were represented by five, and then ten. In 278 B.C., the comitia tributa, became an independent legislative body, while the tribunes had power of introducing legislation, and of imposing a veto upon the enactment of new laws.

TRINOBANTES, a tribe of Britain, whose territory approximated to Essex.

TRIPOLIS, confederacy of three cities, or a district containing three cities.

TRIPTOLEMUS, in *Greek Mythology*, son of Celeus, King of Eleusis. Demeter gave him a chariot with winged dragons with which to visit the whole world and give corn-seed to man.

TRIREME, an ancient galley—especially a war-galley—with three sets of rowers.

TRITAEA, one of the twelve cities of Achaia.—Also the name of a town in Phocis, on the borders of Locris.

TRITANTAECHMES, son of Artabanus, and cousin of Xerxes, and a commander of Persian infantry when the barbarians invaded Greece in 480 B.C.—It was also the name of a Persian satrap of Babylon.

TRITON, in *Greek Mythology*, a minor sea-deity, son of Poseidon.

TRIUMPH, in ancient Rome, a solemn procession in honour of a victorious general.

TRIUMVIR, in ancient Rome, one of a commission of three, charged with some specific duty, such as repairing temples, coining money, or founding colonies. The most famous Triumvirate was that of Octavian, Antony, and Lepidus in 43 B.C. This was known as the Second Triumvirate, to distinguish it from a private combination of Caesar, Pompey, and Crassus in 60.

TROAS, (TROY), scene of Trojan War, when the Greeks, led by Agamemnon and Menelaus, fought to recover Helen, from Paris, son of Priam, who had eloped with her. It is immortalised in Homer's Iliad. There had been nine different settlements in Troy, it has been stated, but there were probably even more, and the history of the town covers about 3,500 years. The Mycenaean settlement dates from 1,500-1,000 B.C., and was the period of Troy's greatest splendour.

TROEZEN, capital of Troezenia, a district in S.E. Argolis, on the Saronic Gulf, was a very ancient city, long dependent on the Kings of Argos, but in the historic period seems to have been independent. The Troezenians distinguished themselves when the Persians entered Attica, by the kindness with which they received the Athenian refugees.

TROGLODYTAE, name given by Greek geographers to cave dwellers.

TROGUS, POMPEIUS, Roman historian, in the time of Augustus, from whose *Historiae Philippicae*, Justinus took his *Historiarum Philippicarum*.

TUBERO, AELIUS, (a) Q., son-in-law of L. Aemilius Paulus. (b) Q., son of the above, called the Stoic, was praetor in 118. (c) L., served under Pompey in Greece. He was a friend of Cicero. (d) Q., son of the above, was a jurist.

TULLIUS, see Servius T.

TULLUS HOSTILIUS, third of the seven legendary Kings of Rome, was reputed to have reigned from 670 to 640 B.C. He was warlike, conquered and destroyed Alba, and deported its people to Rome.

TUMULUS, burial or memorial mound, particularly one distinguished by form, size, or association, such as the grave, 100 ft. across, of Patrochus at Troy; the mound, 30 ft. high, raised to Athenian warriors at Marathon, in 490 B.C.; The Lydian tomb near Sardis, 200 ft. high of Alyattes II, in 560 B.C., etc.

TURDETANI, a people of Hispania Baetica, living on both sides of the Baetis.

TUSCULUM, city of Latium, among the Alban hills, 15 m. S.E. of Rome. The city became an ally of Rome in 497 B.C. Towards the end of the Roman period Tusculum was made a municipium, and was a favourite country residence of wealthy Romans.

TUTANKHAMEN, Egyptian King of the XVIIIth dynasty, who reigned from 1358-1353 B.C. He was only a youth when he succeeded Akhenaton. He re-established Thebes as capital, and restored the old religion. He was buried in the Valley of the Kings. His tomb has been excavated.

TYANA, a city of Asia Minor, in S. Cappadocia, native place of Apollonius.

TYMPHAEI, a people of Tymphaea, in Epirus.

TYNDAREUS, in *Greek Mythology*, King of Sparta. His wife Leda was mother of Castor and Pollux, by Zeus.

TYPHON or TYPHOGUS, in Greek mythology, a monstrous, fire-breathing giant with 100 heads. He was son of Ge, and was father of the three-headed dog Cerberus, the Chimaera and other monsters. Having revolted against Zeus, he was slain with a thunderbolt, buried under Mt. Etna, and seems to have personified earthquakes and volcanoes.

TYRANNION, nickname for Theophrastus, the Greek grammarian, who Lucullus took prisoner and deported to Rome in 72 B.C. He was given to Murena who manumitted him.

TYRTAEUS, son of Archembrotus, of Aphidnae in Attica. During the second Messenian War the Spartans were commanded by an oracle to take a leader from among the Athenians and they chose Tyrtaeus. Later writers say Tyrtaeus was a lame school-master whom the Athenians, when approached by the Lacedaemonians, purposely sent as the most inefficient leader. They little thought that the poetry of Tyrtaeus would achieve victory. His poems exercised an influence on the Spartans, making them peaceful at home and courageous in the field. He seems to have flourished down to 668 B.C. His work was in elegiac metre, except his war songs.

TYRUS, (Tyre), important city of the ancient world, on the coast of Phoenicia, 20 m. from Sidon. It was colonized by Sidonians; Hiram, its King in the days of Solomon, was also King of Sidon. Shalmaneser, of Assyria, besieged Tyre for five years without success, and Nebuchadnezzar besieged it for thirteen years. When the Greeks came into contact with Tyre its old site had been abandoned and a new city built on an island half a mile from the shore. In 332 B.C., the Tyrians withstood Alexander, who besieged the city seven months, constructing a mole to the mainland. After its capture by Alexander, Tyre never regained its former prosperity.

U

UBII, a German people who first occupied a part of the right bank of the Rhine, but were deported to the other bank by Agrippa, in 37 B.C. This was in accordance with their wishes, as they were anxious to escape attacks from the Suevi. They afterwards called themselves Agrippenses.

UCALEGON, is mentioned as an elder at Troy. His house was destroyed by fire at the fall of the city.

UCUBIS, town near Corduba, in Hispania Baetica.

UDA, center of the worship of the goddess Hebat (or Hepit) and her husband Teshub, in Hittite Anatolia.

UFENS, river of Latium, emptying into the Amasenus.

UFFUGUM, town of Bruttium, lying between Rhegium and Scyllacium.

UGERNUM, town of Gallia Narbonensis. It was here that Avitus was proclaimed emperor. It was situated between Nemausus and Aquae Sextiae.

ULIA, town on the road from Gades to Corduba, in Hispania Baetica, situated on a hill, was a Roman municipium.

ULIARUS, an island in the Aquitanian Gulf, off the W. coast of Gaul.

ULLIKUMMI, THE SONG OF, ancient Hittite, long epic in three tablets.

ULPIANUS, DOMITIUS, Roman jurist, was of Tyrian ancestry, but the time and place of his birth are not known. He first appears in public life as assessor in the *auditorium* of Papinian, and a member of the council of Septimius Severus; under Caracalla he was master of the requests. Elagabalus deprived him of his functions, banishing him from Rome, but on Alexander's accession in 222, he was reinstated, finally to become chief advisor to the emperor and praefectus praetorio. His curtailment

422

of the privileges granted to the praetorian guard by Elagabalus provoked their enmity, and he more than once narrowly escaped their vengeance. Ultimately he was murdered in the palace, in 228, in the course of a riot between the soldiers and the mob. Ulpian's period of literary activity extended from c. 211 to 222 A.D. His works include, *Ad Sabinum*, *Ad Edictum*, *Domitii Ulpiani Fragmenta*, *Institutiones*, etc.

ULPIANUS, of Antioch, was a sophist in the days of Constantine the Great, and writer of several rhetorical works.

ULTOR, a surname of Mars, signifying "the avenger." Augustus built a temple to Mars Ultor in the Forum at Rome, after he had revenged Julius Caesar's death.

ULUBRAE, town of Latium in the vicinity of the Pontine Marshes.

ULYSSES, ULYXES, or ULIXES, called ODYSSEUS by the Greeks, was the hero of Homer's "Odyssey," and son of Laertes and Anticlea, King of Ithaca, husband of Penelope, and father of Telemachus. His story, as related by Homer, has been much extended and modified by later poets and mythographers. In Homer he is represented as the model of a prudent warrior, as a man of great experience and acuteness, always ready to devise means of avoiding, or escaping from difficulties, as superior to all men in eloquence and intelligence, in wisdom equal to the gods, and in adversity courageous. Later poets, and sometimes Greek tragedians, depict him in a different light as cunning, false, and mean. When the Greek chiefs had resolved upon their expedition against Troy, Agamemnon went to Ithaca to invite Ulysses to join them, but it was not without difficulty that he was induced to assist. He joined the other Greek chiefs in the port of Aulis, with twelve ships. During the war against Troy, he took a prominent part, sometimes as a gallant warrior, and sometimes as a bold and cunning spy or emissary. After the destruction of the city his wanderings and sufferings began, which form the interesting story of the "Odyssey," from the fifth book included. The story ends with his return to Ithaca, the destruction of the suitors who had been eating up his substance, and the acknowledgment of their true King by the Ithacan people.

UMBRENUS, P., an accomplice of Catiline, was a freedman who had been a negotiator in Gaul, and so was used to gain over the ambassadors of the Allobroges to agree with the designs of the conspirators.

UMBRI, OMBIRI, O'MBRICI, were one of the oldest peoples of Italy. They appear to have been living at a very remote period in the highlands of the central Apennines, whence they descended into the valleys of the Tiber and the Nar. They spread also beyond the Apennines, to the coast of the Adriatic. Sarsina, on the Sapis, and Sentinum, were towns of the Umbri, N. of the Apennines. They came into collision with the Etruscans, who took many towns from them. They afterwards joined the Etruscans against Rome, and about 307 B.C., they acknowledged Roman supremacy. Umbria, under the Roman republic, was a division of Italy proper, extending from Ocriculum to Ariminum and Pisaurum. The Rubicon formed its boundary towards Cisalpine Gaul.

UMBRICIUS, a diviner who predicted to Galba, shortly before his death, that a plot threatened him.

UMBRO, a magician of the country of the Marsi, who aided Turnus against the Trojans, but was slain in battle. He was brother of Angitia, the nymph.

UMBRO, river of Etruria, emptying into the Tyrrhene Sea.

UNELLI, people of the N. coast of Gaul, on a headland opposite Britain.

UPELLURI, an Atlas figure of ancient Hittite mythology.

UPIS, (a) Surname of Diana, as the goddess assisting women in child-birth. (b) A mythical being, reared by Diana, and a nymph in her train.

UR, (Edessa), Sumerian city, on the Euphrates, 140 m. S.E. of Babylon. In about 3100 B.C., Mes-anni-padda founded the first dynasty of Ur, which lasted five generations. Under the Sargonids, Ur remained the center for the worship of the moon-god Nannar. About 2450 B.C., Ur-Nammu (Ur-Engur) founded the third dynasty, and then followed the period of Ur's greatest prosperity. The city was practically rebuilt on a magnificent scale, the Ziggurat, or staged tower, being one of the most striking remains in Iraq. Abraham lived at Ur between 2000 and 1900 B.C., the region being mentioned in the Bible as Ur of the Chaldees. About 1900 B.C., Hammurabi of Babylon conquered Ur, but it long retained its religious importance. Later Kings of Babylon repaired the temples, Nebuchadnezzar being busy in the work of restoration about 600 B.C. By 300 B.C., the city was in ruins. Valuable archaeological discoveries have been made on the site.

URANIA, (a) One of the Muses. (b) Daughter of Oceanus and Tethys. (c) A surname of Venus.

URANUS, in *Greek Mythology*, the first King of the gods, was son of Ge, the Earth, and by her became father of Oceanus, Hyperion, Themis, Cronus, and others. These children he confined in Tartarus, and eventually they rose in revolt against him.

URARTU, ancient Hittite name for the district of Ararat.

URBINUM HORTENSE, Umbrian town, and a municipium.

URBINUM METAURENSE, Umbrian town on the Metaurus.

URCI, town in Hispania Tarraconensis, on the coast, belonging to the Bastetani.

URCINIUM, town on the W. coast of Corsica.

URGO, or GORGON, island off the coast of Etruria.

URHI-TESHUB, succeeded his father King Muwatallis, about 1282 B.C., in ancient Hittite history.

URIA, a town of Calabria, the ancient capital of Iapygia, founded by the Cretans.

URIM AND THUMMIM, a mysterious kind of ornament worn in the habit of the Jewish high priest, which was consulted as an oracle on occasions of importance.

URIUM, town in Apulia, from which the Sinus Urias was named.

URSHU, SIEGE OF, probably occurred during a campaign by Mursilis I, in ancient Hittite history.

URSO, city of Hispania Baetica, the last to be held by the partisans of Pompey in Spain.

URSUS, dissuaded Domitian from killing his wife Domitia.

USCANA, town in Illyria, on a tributary of the Aous.

USIPETES, a German people, who were driven across the Rhine by the Suevi, where they were defeated by Caesar and compelled to return, being received by the Sigambri who let them live on the N. bank of the Lippe.

USPE, capital of the Siraceni, of Sarmatia Asiatica.

USTICA, valley near the Sabine villa of Horace.

UTICA, greatest city of ancient Africa, after Carthage, was a Phoenician colony older than Carthage. Utica maintained comparative independence. It was a coastal town on the N. of the Carthaginian Gulf. In the Third Punic War, Utica took part with the Romans against Carthage, and after received most of the Carthaginian territory. It became renowned as the scene of the last stand made by the Pompeian party against Caesar, and of the self-sacrifice of the younger Cato.

UTUS, river in Moesia, being a tributary of the Danube, joining it at the town Utus.

UXAMA, town of the Arevaci, in Hispania Tarraconensis, W. of Numantia.

UXANTIS, island off the N.W. coast of Gaul.

UXELLODUNUM, town of the Cadurci, in Gallia Aquitanica.

UXENTUM, town in Calabria, N.W. of the Iapygian headland.

UXII, a strong people of predatory habits, having their fortifications in Mt. Parachoathras.

UZZIAH, King of Judah, son of Amaziah, whom he succeeded when 16 years old, and is said to have reigned 52 years. Uzziah restored Elath, and when he became a leper his son Jotham acted as his representative.

V

VACCA, city of Zeugitana, in N. Africa, bordering on Numidia, was a great trading center between Hippo, Utica, and Carthage. Metellus destroyed it in the Jugurthine war, but it was restored and colonized by the Romans.

VACCAEI, a people of Hispania Tarraconensis, living E. of the Cantabri, W. of the Celtiberi, and N. of the Vettones. Their most important towns were Pallantia and Intercatia.

VACCUS, M. VITRUVIUS, general of the Fundani and Privernates in their revolt against the Romans in 330 B.C.

VACUNA, a Sabine divinity, identical with Victoria, with an ancient sanctuary near Horace's villa at Tibur, and another at Rome.

VADA, (a) A stronghold of the Batavi in Gallia Belgica, E. of Batavodurum. (b) Vada Sabbatia, town of Liguria, was the harbour of Sabbata. (c) Vada Volaterrana, coastal town of Etruria.

VADICASSII, people of Gallia Belgica.

VADIMONIS LACUS, circular lake in Etruria, with floating islands, described by Pliny the Younger. It was scene of the defeat of the Etruscans in two battles, one by the dictator Papirius Cursor in 309 B.C., and the other in 283 B.C., when the allied armies of the Etruscans and Gauls were crushed by the consul Cornelius Dolabella. The waters of the lake were sulphurous.

VAGEDRUSA, stream in Sicily, between Gela and Camarina.

VAGIENNI, tribe of Liguria, with a town known as Augusta Vagiennorum.

VALA, C. NUMONIUS, friend of Horace.

VALENS, FLAVIUS, Roman emperor of the East, younger brother of Valentinian I, who assigned to Valens the government

427

of the Eastern provinces. He reigned from 364-378 A.D. His reign was marked by fighting with the Persians and Goths. Valens allowed the Goths to settle in Thrace, but at Adrianople, in 378 A.D., the Romans were defeated, and Valens disappeared. The Arian heresy raged in his reign, and the emperor persecuted orthodox Christians.

VALENS, ABURNUS, a jurist of the Sabinian school, who flourished under Antoninus Pius.

VALENS, FABIUS, a general of the Emperor Vitellius who in 69 A.D., marched through Gaul, joined the forces of Caecina, and defeated Otho at the battle of Bedriacum, which secured Vitellius the sovereignty of Italy, for which Valens and Caecina received consulships.

VALENTIA, capital of the Edetani, on the Turia, between Carthago Nova and Castulo, founded by Junius Brutus.—Also the name of two other towns, one on the Rhone, in Gallia Narbonensis, the other a town in Sardinia.

VALENTINIANUS, (Valentinian), Name of three Roman emperors. Valentinian I, was born at Pannonia, rising to high rank in the army. On his election as emperor by the soldiers, he associated his brother Valens with himself in the government. The rebellion of Procopius in 366 A.D., was crushed. Fighting against the Alamanni on the Rhine frontier kept Valentinian in Gaul for a great part of his reign, which was from 364-375 A.D. He ruled with ability, and endeavoured to alleviate the condition of his subjects. He died in 375 A.D. Valentinian II became joint emperor in 383 A.D., when still a child. His uneventful reign ended with his murder in 392 A.D. Valentinian III succeeded Honorius in 425 A.D., and reigned until he was killed in 455 A.D.

VALERIA, (a) This woman advised the Roman matrons to ask Veturia, the mother of Coriolanus, to go to his camp in order to deprecate his resentment. (b) Sulla's last wife, who had a daughter soon after his death. (c) Galeria Valeria, daughter of Diocletian and Prisca.

VALERIANUS, (Valerian), Roman emperor, whose full name was Publius Licinius Valerianus. He was senator and censor in

251 A.D., and was sent by Gallus against the upstart emperor Aemilianus on the Danube. However, both Gallus and Aemilianus were murdered, and Valerian, who was proclaimed emperor in Rhaetia, was acknowledged by the senate. He was a good soldier and administrator. He deputed his son Gallienus to rule the West, and after defeating the Goths, in 257 A.D., he captured Antioch from the invading Persians, and pursued Shapur I, their King, to the Euphrates, but was captured near Edessa, in 260 A.D., and spent the remainder of his life in captivity.

VALERIUS FLACCUS, GAIUS, Roman poet, one of the fifteen officials to whom the keeping of the Sibylline books was entrusted. He wrote the *Argonautica,* being an account of the voyage of the Argonauts.

VALERIUS MAXIMUS, gathered a collection of historical anecdotes under the title *Factorum ac dictorum memorabilium Libri IX.* He lived in the days of Tiberius, to whom he dedicated the work.

VALERIUS VOLUSUS MAXIMUS, M., was dictator in 494 B.C. He was popular and induced the people to enlist for the Sabine and Aequian wars, by a promise that when the enemy had been defeated, the condition of the debtors should be alleviated. The Sabines were defeated, but being unable to fulfill his promise, he resigned.

VALGIUS, (a) Father-in-law of Rullus, who proposed the agrarian law during the consulship of Cicero. (b) Son of a senator who deserted the Pompeian party in the Spanish War, in 45 B.C., going over to Caesar. (c) C. Valgius Hippianus, son of Q. Hippius, who was adopted by C. Valgius.

VALGIUS, RUFUS, C., Roman poet, contemporary with Virgil and Horace.

VANDALI, (Vandals), Teutonic people of the E. Germanic stock, who having moved from the shores of the Baltic to the middle Danube, migrated W. At the beginning of the 5th cent., they poured into Gaul, and in 409 reached Spain. They were soon followed by the Visigoths, who destroyed half of them, and confined the rest in the district known as Andalusia. In about 428 they left Spain for N. Africa, where they established a powerful dominion, and held sway for a century. Gaiseric carried out the conquest between 429 and 439, and sacked Rome in 455. Their pirate fleet terrorized the Mediterranean, but in 533 Justinian sent Belisarius against them, and the race was blotted out.

VANGIONES, a German people, living on the Rhine.

VANNIC or KHALDIAN, language of the ancient Kingdom of Urartu, and a direct descendant of the Hurrian language.

VARDAEI, an Illyrico-Dalmatian nation, whom Pliny calls *populatores quondam Italiae.*

VARDULI, a people of Hispania Tarraconensis, dwelling W. of the Vascones.

VARENUS, L., centurion in Caesar's army, who with T. Pulfio, distinguished himself in a daring act of bravery, when the camp of Q. Cicero was besieged by C. Julius Nervii, in 54 B.C.

VARGUNTEIUS, a senator, who was one of Catiline's conspirators, undertook, with C. Cornelius, to murder Cicero, in 63 B.C., but Fulvia discovered their plan. He was brought to trial, but found no one to defend him.

VARIA, town of the Berones in Hispania Tarraconensis, on the Iberus.

VARINI, a people of Germany, dwelling N. of the Langobardi.

VARIUS RUFUS, L., Roman poet, friend of Virgil and Horace. By the latter he is placed in the front rank of epic poets. Together with Plotius Tucca he revised Virgil's *Aeneid.* He flourished in Augustan days.

VARRO, CINGONIUS, Roman senator in the time of Nero, who supported the claims of Nymphidius to the throne after Caesar's death, and was put to death by Galba.

VARRO, MARCUS TERENTIUS,   was born at Rome, in 116 B.C.; he was taught by L. Aelius, and later by Antiochus, an Academic philosopher. In 67 B.C., he commanded a division of the fleet of Pompeius in his war against the pirates. He held W. Spain for Pompeius during the civil war. After his colleagues had surrendered he did so near Corduba. Being set free he returned to Pompeius at Dyrrachium. After the defeat of Pompeius Varro retired from public life, and when Caesar came to Rome was reconciled with the dictator, who put him in charge of the libraries. He was one of the most learned of men and he left many literary works. Of his *De Lingua Latina*, originally in 24 books, only six remain in a mutilated condition.

VARUNA, an Indo-Aryan deity, worshipped also by the rulers of Mitanni.

VARUS, ALFENUS, Roman jurist, was born at Cremona, where he worked as a barber or cobbler. Coming to Rome he became pupil of Servius Sulpicius and attained to the consulship.

VARUS, PUBLIUS QUINTILIUS, a Roman general who was appointed to chief command in Germany, and by his administration roused the Germans to revolt. Under Arminius the Germans caught the Romans in the swamps of the Teutoburger Wald; three legions were annihilated, and Varus took his own life. He died in 9 A.D.

VARUS, river in Gallia Narbonensis, forming the boundary between it and Italy.

VASATES, a people of Gallia Aquitanica, with a chief town, Cossium.

VASCONES, a people on the N. coast of Hispania Tarraconensis, with the two principal towns of Pompelon and Calagurris. They had a reputation for divination.

VASIO, a town of the Vocontii, in Gallia Narbonensis.

VATINIUS, was quaestor in 63 B.C., and tribune in 59 B.C. Caesar was then consul with Bibulus, and Vatinius, who was a political adventurer, sold his services to him. In 56 B.C., he gave evidence against Milo and Sestius, both friends of Cicero, who made a violent attack on the politician's character. Vatinius became praetor in 55 B.C., and the next year was accused by C. Licinius Calvus of having gained office by bribery. Cicero defended him, to please Caesar. In 47 B.C., Vatinius was consul, and became proconsul of Illyricum in 45 B.C. He sided with Caesar in the civil war.—Another of the same name was a dissolute public informer in the days of Nero.

VECTIS, (Isle of Wight), island off the S. coast of Britain. The Romans heard of it from the Massilians before their conquest of Britain. In those days, at low tide, the Britons brought tin in wagons to the island from the mainland for sale to the Massilians. The island was taken by Vespasian.

VEGETIUS, FLAVIUS RENATUS, compiler of a treatise on the art of war, dedicated to Valentinian II. His sources were Cato, Cornelius Celsus, Frontinus, Paternus, and the imperial constitutions of Augustus, Trajan, and Hadrian.

VEIANIUS, famous gladiator in the days of Horace, who retired to the country, after dedicating his arms in the temple of Hercules at Fundi, in Latium.

VEII, very ancient city of Etruria, on the Cremera, twelve miles from Rome. Its people were at war with Rome for nearly four centuries.

VELAUNI, people of Gallia Aquitanica, originally subject to the Arverni, but later independent.

VELEDA, a virgin with prophetic gifts, of the Bructerian people.

VELINUS, river, rising in the central Apennines, and emptying into the Nar.

VELITRAE, ancient town of the Volscians in Latium, which joined the Latin league. It was colonized by the Romans but often revolted. Augustus was born here.

VELIUS LONGUS, Latin grammarian, author of the treatise *de Orthographia.*

VELLAUNODUNUM, town of the Senones in Gallia Lugdunensis.

VELLEIUS, C., Roman senator, introduced by Cicero as one of the supporters of the Epicurean philosophy, in his *De Natura Deorum.*

VELLOCASSES, people of Gallia Lugdunensis, dwelling N.W. of the Parisii, with a chief town, Ratomagus.

VENAFRUM, town in N. Samnium, famous for olives.

VENEDI, people of European Sarmatia, occupying the Baltic coast, E. of the Vistula.

VENERIS PORTUS, coastal town of the Indigetes, in Hispania Tarraconensis, near the frontier of Gaul.

VENETIA, district of N. Italy, the tenth Regio of Italy in the days of Augustus. The Veneti formed an early alliance with Rome. On the conquest of the Cisalpine Gauls, the Veneti were included under the Roman dominion and enjoyed prosperity until the Marcomannic wars in the days of Aurelius. Later they were devastated by the barbarians.—A district of N.W. Gallia Lugdunensis also bore this name.

VENILIA, a nymph, daughter of Pilumnus, sister of Amata, and mother of Turnus and Juturna, by Daunus.

VENNONES, a people of Raetia, living in the Alps.

VENTA, (Winchester), chief town of the Belgae in Britain.

VENTIDIUS, BASSUS P., Roman general, born at Picenum, was taken prisoner by Pompeius Strabo in the Social war, in 89 B.C., and taken to Rome. When he grew up he became a job-master of mules, but Caesar employed him in Gaul in the civil war. After Caesar's death Ventidius attached himself to Antony, and became consul in 43 B.C. He was sent to Asia in 39 B.C., where he defeated the Parthians and Labienus. He was awarded a triumph in 38 B.C.

VENULUS, Latin chieftain, sent by Turnus to Diomedes to persuade him to lend aid against Aeneas and the Trojans. He was captured by Tarchon.

VENUS, in *Roman Mythology,* originally the goddess of gardens, and later identified with the Greek Aphrodite, goddess of love. All myths relating to Aphrodite were also attributed to Venus. As wife of Mars, and mother of Aeneas, the legendary founder of the race, Venus became one of the major deities of the Romans.

VENUSIA, ancient town of Apulia, S. of the Aufidus, near Mt. Vultur. It was birthplace of Horace.

VERAGRI, people of Gallia Belgica.

VERANIUS, Q., was appointed by Tiberius Caesar as governor of Cappadocia when it became a Roman province in 18 A.D.

VERCELLAE, chief town of the Libici in Gallia Cisalpina, became a Roman municipium.

VERCINGETORIX, famous chieftain of the Arverni, who fought against Caesar, in 52 B.C. He fell into Caesar's hands on the capture of Alesia, and was taken to Rome to adorn the triumph in 45 B.C., after which he was put to death.

VEROLAMIUM or VERULAMIUM, (near St. Albans, England), capital of the Catuellani, and probable residence of King Cassivellaunus. It was conquered by Caesar, and made a Roman municipium. It was destroyed under Boadicca, but was rebuilt.

VERONA, town of Gallia Cisalpina, one of the most prosperous towns of N. Italy under the empire. Catullus was born here, and probably the elder Pliny.

VERRES, GAIUS, Roman governor. His government of Sicily from 73-71 B.C., was so extortionate that the inhabitants had him prosecuted at the end of his term of office. Cicero's speech at the trial in 70 B.C., made his reputation as the most promising forensic orator of his time. The defender Hortensius, gave up his brief in face of such overwhelming evidence against Verres.

VERUS, LUCIUS, Roman emperor who reigned as colleague of Marcus Aurelius from 161-169 A.D. In 162 A.D., he attacked the Parthians, but left the campaign to his generals, while he reveled in debauchery. In 164 A.D., he went to Ephesus, where he married Lucilla, daughter of his adoptive father, Antoninus Pius. In 166 A.D., he and Marcus Aurelius solemnized a triumph over the Parthians. Soon after Rome was visited by a pestilence and the Marcomanni and the Quadi invaded the empire from the north. After the hostilities the emperors returned to Rome, but on his way Verus was seized with apoplexy at Altinum, where he died in 169 A.D.

VESPASIANUS, TITUS FLAVIUS SABINUS, (VESPASIAN), Roman emperor from 69-79 A.D. He was a man of obscure family who rose to high military commands in Germany and Britain, and was in charge of the war against the Jews during the confusion which followed the death of Nero in 68 A.D. He was proclaimed emperor by his soldiers in 69 A.D. His general Primus defeated the forces of the reigning emperor Vitellius, in Italy, and Vespasian came to Rome in 70 A.D., leaving his son Titus to continue the war against the Jews. He devoted himself largely to setting in order the finances of the empire, and built many public buildings.

VESTA, in *Roman Mythology*, Italian goddess of the hearth, later identified by the Romans with the Greek goddess Hestia. The worship of Vesta was a recognition of the extreme importance of fire in primitive communities. A temple, the Atrium Vestae, was maintained in her honour in the Forum. According to tradition, this sacred fire was brought from Troy by Aeneas. There were six priestesses, called Vestal Virgins, in attendance at her temple. At six years of age they were either offered by their parents, or chosen by lot from families selected by the Pontifex Maximus. Service lasted for thirty years, after which they were free to return to civil life. During their service they were vowed to chastity, and breaking this vow, they could be buried alive by the Pontifex Maximus. Their chief duty was the maintenance of the sacred fire. They were abolished in 394 A.D.

VESTINI, a Sabellian people of Central Italy, conquered by the Romans in 328 B.C. They joined the allies in the Marsic war and were defeated by Pompeius Strabo in 89. They were celebrated for a particular kind of cheese.

VESUVIUS, volcanic mountain in Campania, S. E. of Neapolis. No records of any eruption are extant before the Christian era, but ancient writers were aware of its volcanic nature. It first gave symptoms of agitation in an earthquake in A.D. 63. The first great eruption occurred in A.D. 79 on Aug. 24, overwhelming Stabiae, Herculaneum and Pompeii. Pliny the elder lost his life in this eruption.

VETRANIO, was in command of the legions in Illyria and Pannonia when Constans was treacherously murdered and his throne seized by Magnentius.

VETTIUS, L., Roman eques, in the pay of Cicero, in 63 B.C., who he kept informed regarding the Catilinian conspiracy.

VETTONES, a people of Lusitania, living E. of the Lusitani, and W. of the Carpetani.

VETULONIA, ancient city of Etruria, one of the twelve cities of the Etruscan confederation.

VEXILLUM, a standard of the legion's cavalry under the republic. Under the emperors the term was applied to the standard of a troop of auxiliary cavalry, and from the days of Constantine to a cavalry force itself.

VIADUS, river of Germany, emptying into the Baltic.

VIBO, Roman name of Hipponium, a Greek town on the S.W. coast of Bruttium, said to have been founded by the Locri Epizephyrii.

VICTOR, SEX. AURELIUS, a Latin writer who attracted the attention of Julian, who appointed him prince governor of a division of Pannonia. Under Theodosius he became city praefect.

VICTORIA, in *Roman Mythology*, the personification of victory, who in later times had three or four sanctuaries in Rome.

VICTORINUS, one of the Thirty Tyrants, who was murdered at Agrippina by one of his officers, in 268 A.D.—Also the name of a Latin rhetorician who taught S. Jerome.

VIDRUS, a stream of Germania, between the Amisia and the Rhenus.

VIDUCASSES, a small people, being a section of the Amorici, in Gallia Lugdenensis.

VINDALUM, town of the Cavares, in Gallia Narbonensis, at the junction of the Rhone and the Sulgas.

VINDELICIA, Roman province, S. of the Danube, originally part of the province of Raetia. It was conquered in the reign of Augustus by Tiberius.

VINDEX, C. JULIUS, was propraetor of Gallia Celtica in the days of Nero, and the first governor to disown Nero's authority in 68 A.D.

VINDICIANUS, famous physician in the days of Valentinian.

VINDICIUS, a slave who laid information to the consuls, about the conspiracy to restore the Tarquins, thereby gaining liberty and franchise.

VINDOBONA, town in Pannonia, on the Danube, which had been a Celtic town, but was later made a Roman municipium. It was chief station of the Roman fleet on the Danube, and H.Q. of a legion. Marcus Aurelius died here, in 180 A.D. (the modern Vienna).

VIPSANIA AGRIPPINA, daughter of M. Vipsanius Agrippa by Pomponia, was given in marriage by Augustus to Tiberius, by whom she bore Drusus.

VIRGILIUS or VERGILIUS MARO, P., (VIRGIL), Roman poet, born Oct. 75, 70 B.C., at Pietole, near Mantua, son of a small landowner. He was educated at Cremona, Milan, and Naples, where he learned Greek, and Rome where he studied rhetoric and philosophy. After the battle of Philippi his father's estate was made over to the veterans who had fought for Octavian against Brutus and Cassius. On the advice of his friend, Asinius Pollio, Virgil went to Rome and made personal appeal to Octavian. The result is not clear, but if Virgil did not finally recover his property, he received compensation in the form of an estate in Campania. His visits to Rome secured him the patronage of Maecenas, and the friendship of Horace. Relieved from financial anxiety by the generosity of Maecenas, he was able to devote himself to literary work. From 37 on his life was spent alternately in Rome and Naples. He visited Greece in 19 B.C., the year of his death. He was buried at Naples. The poems universally recognized as his are 1. Ten Eclogues or Bucolics, written 42-37 B.C. 2. The Georgics (37-30). 3. The Aeneid, an epic in 12 books. Imitated from Homer—the first 6 based on the Odyssey, the last 6 on the Iliad—its purpose was the glorification of the Julian house represented by Augustus. the reputed founder of which was Ascanius, the son of Aeneas.

VIRGINIA, heroine of ancient *Roman Legend*, daughter of Lucius Virginius, the centurion, her beauty inflamed the decemvir Appius Claudius, who suborned one of his supporters to claim her as his slave, and when the case came before him declared her to be the man's property. Thereupon her father seized a knife and killed his daughter. A popular revolution broke out over the tyrannical decemvirs, and Appius Claudius committed suicide.

VIRGINIUS RUFUS, was consul in 63 A.D., and governor of Upper Germany in 68 A.D.

VIRIATHUS, a Lusitanian shepherd who became a robber. He had escaped the massacre by Galba, in 150 B.C., and collected a force which defeated one Roman army after another. In 141 B.C., the proconsul Fabius Servilianus made peace with him to save his army. Later Servilius Caepio renewed the war and procured the murder of Viriathus by bribing some of his friends.

VIRIDOMARUS, tribal chieftain whom Caesar raised to high honour, but he joined the Gauls in their revolt, in 52 B.C.

VIROCONIUM or URICONIUM, (Wroxeter, Eng.), Roman military center and town.

VISTULA, river boundary between Germany and Sarmatia, emptying into the Baltic.

VITELLIUS, AULUS, Roman emperor from Jan. 2 to Dec. 22, 69 A.D. He was commanding the Roman legions in Lower Germany when the news of Galba's accession reached him. All the Roman troops in Germany refused to accept him, and Vitellius was proclaimed emperor at Cologne. Vitellius reached Rome in July and gave himself up to gluttony. The legions in Illyricum declared Vespasian as emperor, and, advancing into Italy, entered Rome, and slew Vitellius.

VITRUVIUS POLLIO, MARCUS, Roman author and architect who flourished 16 B.C. He was a N. Italian and was probably employed by Julius Caesar as a military engineer in the African war, in 46 B.C., and worked as an architect under Augustus, to whom he dedicated *On Architecture,* his work in 10 books.

VOCONTII, a strong people of Gallia Narbonensis, in the S.E. of Dauphine and a part of Provence. The Romans allowed them to retain their own code of laws.

VOLATERRAE, one of the twelve cities of the Etruscan Confederation.

VOLCAE, a Celtic people of Gallia Narbonensis, consisting of two tribes, the Tectosages and the Volcae Arecomici.

VOLSCI, ancient people of Latium on the Liris. The Romans conquered them in 338 B.C.

VOLSINII, ancient city of the Etruscan Confederation, whose people carried on war with the Romans in 392, 311, 294, and 280 B.C., when they were finally conquered. Their city was destroyed and its inhabitants shifted to a site on the plain, in an exposed military position.

VOLTURCIUS, T., a Catilinian conspirator who turned informer.

VOPISCUS, FLAVIUS, Roman historian, born at Syracuse, who flourished about 300 A.D.

VULCANUS, (Vulcan), in *Roman Mythology,* ancient Italian deity, the god of fire. He was identified with the Greek Hephaestus.

X

XANTHICLES, an Achaean. The Greek mercenaries of Cyrus, elected to have him for their general in place of Socrates. He was later charged and fined for a deficiency in the cargos of the ships which took the troops from Trapezus.

XANTHIPPUS, son of Ariphon, and father of Pericles, who impeached Miltiades, in 490 B.C., on his return from Paros. He followed Themistocles in commanding the Athenian fleet. He also led the Athenians at the battle of Mycale. There were two others of this name, one the elder of Pericles' two legitimate sons, and the other, a Lacedaemonian, who led the Carthaginians against Regulus.

XANTHO, daughter of Oceanus and Tethys, a nymph in the train of Cyrene.

XANTHUS, son of Phaenops, brother of Thoon, a warrior of the Trojan army, killed by Diomedes.

XANTHUS, lyric poet, flourished about 650 B.C.

XANTHUS, Lydian historian, flourished about 480 B.C.

XANTHUS, most important river in Lycia, rising in Mt. Taurus, and emptying into the Mediterranean to the W. of Patara.

XANTHUS, chief city of ancient Lycia, in Asia Minor, on a river of the same name. The Persians besieged it in 546 B.C. It was destroyed by the Romans in 42 B.C.

XANTIPPE or XANTHIPPE, wife of Socrates, who is said to have made his home life wretched by her quarrelsome disposition and shrewish tongue.

XENARCHUS, (a) Son of Sophron, and a writer of mimes, flourished c. 399-389 B.C. (b) Athenian comic poet of Middle Comedy, at the time of Alexander. (c) Of Seleucia, was a Peripatetic philosopher and grammarian, in the days of Strabo.

XENIADES, a Corinthian who became master of Diogenes, when he was sold as a slave, by the pirates.

XENIAS, a Parrhasian, who commanded the mercenaries in the army of Cyrus the younger. Another of the name was a very wealthy Elean, who became proxenus of Sparta. In 400 B.C., during the war between Sparta and Elis, Xenias and his partisans attempted to overthrow their opponents, and subject their country to the Spartans, but they were defeated and exiled by Thrasidaeus, leader of the democracy.

XENIPPA, a city of Sogdiana.

XENOCLES, an Athenian tragic poet, contemporary with Aristophanes. He gained the victory over Euripides in 415 B.C.— Another of the name was an Athenian architect who had charge of the erection of the temple of Ceres, at Eleusis, in the days of Pericles.

XENOCRATES, a philosopher born in Chalcedon, in 396 B.C. He read with Aeschines the Socratic, and later attached himself to Plato, with whom he went to Syracuse.—Another of the name was a physician of Aphrodisias in Cilicia, who lived in the first century A.D.

XENOCRITUS, of Locri Epizephyrii, in Lower Italy, was a musician and Lyric poet, and a leader of the second school of Dorian music.

XENOPHANES, philosopher, born at Colophon, who flourished about 540-500 B.C. He was also a poet. He was regarded in antiquity as founder of the Eleatic doctrine of the oneness of the universe. *Zen'ə f ən 430? - 355 B.C.*

XENOPHON, Greek writer and general, born at Athens. He joined the expedition of Cyrus the Younger against Artaxerxes. On the death of Cyrus at Cunaxa the command devolved on Xenophon, who led his 10,000 fellow countrymen back to the coast. He preserved the story in his *Anabasis*. His chief work after the *Anabasis* is the *Hellenica*, a history of Greece. *Memorabilia* was written to vindicate Socrates, whose pupil he had been. Xenophon also wrote treatises on domestic economy, hunting, etc.

XENOPHON, the Ephesian, wrote a romance, *Ephesiaca.* He is probably the oldest writer of Greek romance.

XERXES, King of Persia from 485-465 B.C.; on the death of his father Darius, his first task was to quell a revolt which had broken out in Egypt. In 480 B.C., he went with his army from Sardis in Asia Minor, to conquer Greece. The Hellespont was crossed by a bridge of boats, and a canal was cut through Mt. Athos. His army, after a repulse at Thermopylae, reached Athens, but his fleet was defeated at Salamis. Xerxes returned with the bulk of his army, but was murdered in 465 B.C., by Artabanus, commander of his bodyguard.

XERXES, the only legitimate son of Artaxerxes I, who succeeded his father as King of Persia in 425 B.C., but was murdered after two months by his half-brother Sogdianus, who became King.

XIPHONIA, headland on the E. coast of Sicily.

XOIS, (sometimes Chois), ancient city of Lower Egypt, N. of Leontopolis, on an island of the Nile, seat at one period of a dynasty of Egyptian Kings. It seems to have perished under the Roman Empire.

XUTHUS, son of Hellen by the nymph Orseis. He was King of Peloponnesus, and husband of Creusa.

XYLINE, town of Pisidia, between Termessus and Corbasa.

XYNIA, or XYNIAE, town of Thessaly, E. of a lake of the same name.

XYPETE, a demus of Attica belonging to the Cecropis.

Z

ZABABA, Sumerian war god.

ZABDICENE, district in Mesopotamia, containing the city of Zabda, or Bezabda.

ZABE, the S. part of Numidia, up to the edge of the Great Desert, was known by this name, under the later Roman emperors.

ZABUS, a river of Assyria, known to the Macedonians as Caprus.

ZACYNTHUS, an island, off the coast of Elis, in the Ionian Sea, noted for its pitch wells. It was early populated by Greeks, and is said to have taken its name from Zacynthus, son of Dardanus, who colonized the island from Psophis, in Arcadia. It was later colonized by Achaeans from Peloponnesus, and still later was subject to Macedonia, and then passed to Roman hands.

ZADRACARTA, a city and royal residence of Hyrcania, at the foot of the main pass of Mt. Coronus.

ZAGREUS, one of the surnames of Dionysus, said to have been begotten by Zeus, who appeared as a dragon, of Persephone, before Pluto bore her away. The Titans tore him to pieces, and Athena took his heart to Zeus.

ZAGROS or ZAGRUS, the mountain range, being the S.E. continuation of the Taurus. The name was more particularly applied to the central part of the range.

ZAITHA, town on the E. bank of the Euphrates, in Mesopotamia. It was here that the soldiers erected a monument to the emperor Gordian, who had been murdered.

ZAKIR, an Aramean who gained control of the Hittite city of Hamath in about 800 B.C.

ZALEUCUS, a famous lawgiver of the Epizephyrian Locrians;

the period of his legislation has been assigned to 660 B.C. His was the first set of written laws possessed by the Greeks. The laws were austere, but well observed. The loss of the eyes was the penalty for adultery. It is said that the son of Zaleucus, becoming liable to this penalty, his father gave one eye, that his son should not be blind. To enter the senate house under arms entailed the death penalty. In a sudden emergency in war time Zaleucus broke his own law, when this was pointed out to him, he fell on his own sword, that he might vindicate the law.

ZALMOXIS, according to the current Greek story Zalmoxis was a Getan, and slave to Pythagoras, who had manumitted him. He acquired both wealth and knowledge, and travelled widely. He returned to his own people, the Getae, introducing civilization and religious reforms.

ZALPA, a city of the Hittites.

ZAMA REGIA, city in the Roman province of Numidia, five days' march W. of Carthage. It was scene of the defeat of Hannibal by the younger Scipio, in 202 B.C., which engagement ended the second Punic War.

ZAPAORTENE, city in S.E. Parthia, among the mountains of the Zapaorteni.

ZARADUS, river of N. India, rising beyond the Himalaya, and emptying into the Hyphasis.

ZARANGAE, a people of N. Drangiana, probably a section of the Drangae.

ZARATHUSTRA, founder of the religion of ancient Persia and the Parsees, known as Zoroaster, q.v.

ZARAX, central part of the mountains running along the E. coast of Laconia.—Also the name of a coastal town of Laconia.

ZARIASPIS, an earlier name of the river Bactrus. People dwelling along its banks were known as Zariaspae.

ZECHARIAH, minor Hebrew prophet, who functioned from the 2nd to the 4th year of Darius Hystaspis.

ZEDEKIAH, last King of Judah, youngest son of Josiah. He was raised to the throne by Nebuchadnezzar, when Jehoiachin was led captive to Babylon. He was 21 when he became King, and he reigned for 11 troublous years. Against the word of Jeremiah he joined an intrigue against the King of Babylon. His eyes were put out, and he spent the remainder of his life a prisoner at Babylon.

ZELA, city of S. Pontus, near to an ancient temple of Anaitis, and other Persian deities. It was at Zela that Valerius Triarius was defeated by Mithridates. It was also the scene of the battle in which Julius Caesar defeated Pharnaces, and from which he sent the famous message, *Veni: Vidi: Vici.*

ZELARCHUS, a market inspector of the Greek mercenaries of Cyrus who was attacked by the soldiers while at Trapezus: he escaped by sea.

ZELIA, ancient city of Mysia, on the Aesepus, H.Q. of the Persian army at the time of Alexander's invasion.

ZEND-AVESTA, the sacred books of the Parsees. More correctly the name should be Avesta and Zend, Law and Commentary. Written originally in Zend, a language allied to Sanskrit, translated into Pahlavi, about the 3rd cent. A.D., and later into Parsee, what exists is regarded as a fragment. The work is attributed in part to Zoroaster, q.v.

ZENO, Greek philosopher, born in 490 B.C., lived at Elea in Italy. He was friend and associate of Parmenides, and is chiefly remembered as author of the famous paradoxes of Achilles and the Tortoise and the Arrow.—Another Zeno, born about 340 B.C., was also a Greek philosopher, and founder of the Stoic school, and known as Zeno of Citium, a town in Cyprus. In succession an adherent of the Cynic, Megarian, and Academic schools, in about 310 B.C., he founded a new system and school at Athens. He opened his school in the Stoa Poikile, and was president for 56 years.

ZENO, Roman emperor of the East, from 426-491 A.D.

ZENOBIA, queen of Palmyra from 267-272 A.D., was famous for her beauty and strength of character. Her husband was

Odenathus, and after his murder she became regent for her son, Vaballath. While Claudius II was repelling the Goths, she occupied Egypt, in 270 A.D., and after the defeat of Aurelian she proclaimed her son Augustus. Aurelian defeated her at Emesa, and took Palmyra, in 273 A.D. Zenobia was made prisoner and spent her remaining life in retirement at Tibur.

ZENOBIA, city of Chalybonitis, in Syria, founded by Zenobia.

ZENOBIUS, author of a collection of proverbs in Greek. He lived at Rome in the days of Hadrian.

ZENODORUS, Greek artist who produced an enormous statue of Nero, setting it up in front of the Golden House. It was 110 ft. high. Vespasian rededicated it as a statue of the Sun.

ZENODOTUS, (a) Of Ephesus, was a grammarian, and first superintendent of the great library at Alexandria. He flourished about 208 B.C. (b) Of Alexandria, another grammarian, who lived later than Aristarchus.

ZEPHANIAH, minor Hebrew prophet, in the days of King Josiah, was son of Cushi, and probably of the royal house.

ZEPHYRIUM, the name of a number of promontories of the ancient world.

ZEPHYRUS, in *Greek Mythology*, personification of the west wind, was son of Eos, the Dawn, and was regarded as beneficent to sailors.

ZERNA, a city of Dacia, which became a Roman colony.

ZERYNTHUS, town of Thrace, with a temple of Apollo, and a grotto of Hecate.

ZETES and CALAIS, sons of Boreas and Orithyia, known as the Boreadae, were among the Argonauts, and are said to have been winged.

ZEUGIS, the N. district of Africa Propria.

ZEUGMA, city of Syria, built by Seleucus Nicator, on the Euphrates.

ZEUS, in *Greek Mythology*, the supreme god, identified by the Romans with Jupiter. A god of the weather, particularly thunder and rain, he was associated with Thessaly, especially Mt. Olympus. His chief shrine and oracle were at Dodona, where the oak was sacred to him. He was son of Cronus and Rhea; he dethroned his father, and overthrew the Titans and Gigantes. His chief wife is Hera, and Athena and Apollo are among his many children.

ZEUXIDAMUS, King of Sparta, being tenth of the Eurypontidae.—Another of the name was son of Leotychides, King of Sparta.

ZEUXIS, famous Greek painter who flourished about 424-400 B.C.

ZIGGURAT, temple-tower, built in diminishing stages, in Babylonia and Assyria. The word signifies a high place. The external ascent, usually spiral, was sometimes an upright stairway.

ZIKLAG, town in S.W. Palestine, belonging to the Philistines. It was given to David, by King Achish, for a residence during his banishment from the court of Saul.

ZILLA, ancient Punic city in Mauretania Tingitana, which was a Roman colony after the time of Augustus, when it became known as Julia Constantia.

ZIOBETIS, a river in Parthia, which after flowing for a short distance disappears underground, when it reappears it flows until it joins the Ridagnus.

ZOAR, city on the S.E. of the Dead Sea, belonging to the Moabites, and afterwards the Arabs. It was smallest of the "cities of the plain" in the days of Abraham. It was saved at Lot's intercession when Sodom and Gomorrah were destroyed.

ZOETIUM, a town in Arcadia, N. of Megalopolis.

ZOILUS, was born at Amphipolis. He was a grammarian who flourished in the days of Philip of Macedon. He was notorious as a captious and malignant critic.

ZONE, a town in Thrace, where Orpheus is reputed to have sung.

ZOROASTER or ZARATHUSTRA, founder of the old Persian religion, who figures as an historical person in the oldest portion of the Zend-Avesta, q.v. He is believed to have been born in N.W. Persia, about 660 B.C.

ZORZINES, King of the Siraci, in Sarmatia Asiatica.

ZOSIMUS, the learned freedman of the younger Pliny.

ZOSIMUS, Greek historian, who held public office at Constantinople in the first half of the 5th cent. His *History* is mainly a compilation from previous authors, and consists of six books.

ZOSTER, headland on the W. coast of Attica, with altars of Leto, Artemis and Apollo.

ZYGANTES, a people of Libya, of somewhat uncertain location. They probably dwelt either on the W. side of Lake Triton, or on the coast of Marmarica.

APPENDIX

TABLE OF THE KINGS

HITTITE KINGS

Name	Yrs.	Reigned Ms.	B.C.
PITKHANAS	?		
ANITTAS	?		

Old Kingdom

TUDHALIYAS I	30		1740-1710
PU-SARRUMAS	30		1710-1680
LABARNAS I	30		1680-1650
LABARNAS II	30		1650-1620
MURSILIS I	30		1620-1590
HANTILIS	30		1590-1560
ZIDANTAS I	10		1560-1550
AMMUNAS	20		1550-1530
HUZZIYAS I	5		1530-1525
TELIPINUS	25		1525-1500
ALLUWAMNAS	10		1500-1490
HANTILIS II	?		1490-1480
ZIDANTAS II	?		1480-1470
HUZZIYAS II	?		1470-1460

Empire

TUDHALIYAS II	20		1460-1440
ARNUWANDAS I	20		1440-1420
HATTUSILIS II	20		1420-1400
TUDHALIYAS III	15		1400-1385
ARNUWANDAS II	10		1385-1375

449

Name	Yrs.	*Reigned* Ms.	B.C.
SUPPILULIUMAS	40		1375-1335
ARNUWANDAS III	1		1335-1334
MURSILUS II	28		1334-1306
MUWATALLIS	24		1306-1282
URHI-TESHUB	7		1282-1275
HATTUSILIS III	25		1275-1250
TUDHALIYAS IV	30		1250-1220
ARNUWANDAS IV	?		1220-
SUPPILULIUMAS II	?		

(This table practically corresponds with that to be found in "THE HITTITES" by Dr. O. R. Gurney, 1952).

KINGS OF LYDIA

Name	Yrs.	*Reigned* Ms.	B.C.
GYGES	38		716-678
ARDYS	49		678-629
SADYATTES	12		629-617
ALYATTES	57		617-560
CROESUS	14		560-546

KINGS OF MEDIA

Name	Yrs.	*Reigned* Ms.	B.C.
DEIOCES	53		709-656
PHRAORTES	22		656-634
CYAXARES	40		634-594
ASTYAGES	35		594-559

KINGS OF EGYPT

Name	Yrs.	*Reigned* Ms.	B.C.
PSAMMETICHUS	54		671-617
NECO	16		617-601
PSAMMIS	6		601-595

Name	Yrs.	Reigned Ms.	B.C.
APRIES	25		595-570
AMASIS	44		570-526
PSAMMENITUS	-	6	526-525

(See also later kings of Egypt).

KINGS OF PERSIA

	Yrs.	Ms.	B.C.
CYRUS	30		559-529
CAMBYSES	7	-5	529-522
SMERDIS		-7	522-522
DARIUS I. *Hystaspis*	36		521-485
XERXES I	20		485-465
ARTABANUS		-7	465-465
ARTAXERXES I. *Longimanus*	40		465-425
XERXES II		-2	425-425
SOGDIANUS		-7	425-425
DARIUS II. *Nothus*	19		424-405
ARTAXERXES II. *Mnemon*	46		405-359
OCHUS	21		359-338
ARSES	2		338-336
DARIUS III. *Codomannus*	4	-11	336-331

KINGS OF SPARTA

(The earlier generations are legendary rather than historic).

Aristodemus

Elder, or Agid line

Name	Yrs.	Reigned Ms.	B.C.
EURYSTHENES			
AGIS I			
ECHESTRATUS			
LABOTAS			
DORYSSUS			
AGESILAUS I			
ARCHELAUS			

Name	Yrs.	Reigned Ms.	B.C.
TELECLUS			
ALCAMENES			
POLYDORUS			
EURYCRATES			
ANAXANDER			
EURYCRATIDES			
LEON			
ANAXANDRIDES I			520
CLEOMENES	29		520-491
LEONIDAS	11		491-480
PLISTARCHUS	22		480-458
PLISTOANAX	50		458-408
PAUSANIAS	14		408-394
AGESIPOLIS I	14		394-380
CLEOMBROTUS I	9		380-371
AGESIPOLIS II	1		371-370
CLEOMENES II	61		370-309
AREUS I	44		309-265
ACROTATUS	1		265-264
AREUS II	8		264-256
LEONIDAS II			
CLEOMBROTUS II			
LEONIDAS *again*			
CLEOMENES III	16		236-220
AGESIPOLIS III			

Younger, or Eurypontid line

PROCLES
SOUS
EURYPON
PRYTANIS
EUNOMUS
POLYDECTES
CHARILAUS
NICANDAR

		Reigned	
Name	*Yrs.*	*Ms.*	*B.C.*
THEOPOMPUS			
ZEUXIDAMUS			
ANAXIDAMUS			
ARCHIDAMUS I			
AGESICLES			
ARISTON			
DEMARATUS			
LEOTYCHIDES	22		491-469
ARCHIDAMUS II	42		469-427
AGIS II	29		427-398
AGESILAUS II	37		398-361
ARCHIDAMUS III	23		361-338
AGIS III	8		338-330
EUDAMIDAS I			
ARCHIDAMUS IV			
EUDAMIDAS II			
AGIS IV	4		244-240
EURYDAMIDAS			
ARCHIDAMUS V			

KINGS OF MACEDONIA

PERDICCAS I			
ARGAEUS			
PHILLIPUS I			
AEROPUS			
ALCETAS			
AMYNTAS I			
ALEXANDER I			
PERDICCAS II			
ARCHELAUS	14		413-399
ORESTES and AEROPUS	5		399-394
PAUSANIAS	1		394-393
AMYNTAS II	24		393-369
ALEXANDER II	2		369-367
PTOLEMAEUS *Alorites*	3		367-364

		Reigned	
Name	*Yrs.*	*Ms.*	*B.C.*
PERDICCAS III	5		364-359
PHILIPPUS II	23		359-336
ALEXANDER III,			
the Great	13		336-323
PHILIPPUS III, Aridaeus	7		323-316
OLYMPIAS	1		316-315
CASSANDER	19		315-296
PHILIPPUS IV	1		296-295
DEMETRIUS Poliorcetes	7		294-287
PYRRHUS		-7	287-286
LYSIMACHUS	5	-6	286-280
PTOLEMAEUS Ceraunus			
MELEAGER			
ANTIPATER			
SOSTHENES	3		280-277
PTOLEMAEUS			
ALEXANDER			
PYRRHUS again			
ANTIGONUS Gonatus	44		283-239
DEMETRIUS II	10		239-229
ANTIGONAS Doson	9		229-220
PHILIPPUS V	42		220-178
PERSEUS	11		178-167

KINGS OF SYRIA

SELEUCUS I, Nicator	32	312-280
ANTIOCHUS I, Soter	19	280-261
ANTIOCHUS II, Theos	15	261-246
SELEUCUS II, Callinicus	20	246-226
SELEUCUS III, Ceraunus	3	226-223
ANTIOCHUS III, the Great	36	223-187
SELEUCUS IV, Philopator	12	187-175
ANTIOCHUS IV, Epiphanes	11	175-164
ANTIOCHUS V, Eupator	2	164-162
DEMETRIUS I, Soter	12	162-150

	Name	Yrs.	*Reigned* Ms.	B.C.

Name	Yrs.	Ms.	B.C.
ALEXANDER *Bala*	5		150-146
DEMETRIUS II, *Nicator* ⎫			
ANTIOCHUS VI ⎬			146-137
TRYPHO ⎭			
ANTIOCHUS VII, *Sidetes*	9		137-128
DEMETRIUS II, *again*	3		128-125
ANTIOCHUS VIII, *Grypus* ⎫			
ANTIOCHUS IX, *Cyzicenus* ⎭			125- 95
SELEUCUS VI ⎫			
ANTIOCHUS X, *Eusebes* ⎪			
PHILIPPUS ⎪			
DEMETRIUS III, *Eucaerus* ⎬			95- 83
ANTIOCHUS XI, *Epiphanes* ⎪			
ANTIOCHUS XII, *Dionysus* ⎭			
TIGRANES, *King of Armenia*	14		83- 69
ANTIOCHUS XIII, *Asiaticus*	4		67- 65

LATER KINGS OF EGYPT

Name			Yrs.	B.C.
PTOLEMAEUS	I,	*Soter*	38	323-285
"	II,	*Philadelphus*	36	285-247
"	III,	*Evergetes*	25	247-222
"	IV,	*Philopator*	17	222-205
"	V,	*Epiphanes*	24	205-181
"	VI,	*Philometor*	35	181-146
"	VII,	*Evergetes II*	29	146-117
"	VIII,	*Soter II*	36	117- 81
"	IX,	*Alexander I*		
CLEOPATRA				
PTOLEMAEUS	X,	*Alexander II*		81- 80
"	XI,	*Dionysus*	29	80- 51
CLEOPATRA			21	51- 30
PTOLEMAEUS	XII			
"	XIII			

KINGS OF PERGAMUS

Name	Yrs.	Reigned Ms.	B.C.
PHILETAERUS	17		280-263
EUMENES I	22		263-241
ATTALUS I	44		241-197
EUMENES II	38		197-159
ATTALUS II, *Philadelphus*	21		159-138
ATTALUS III, *Philometor*	5		138-133

KINGS OF BITHYNIA

Name	Yrs.	Reigned Ms.	B.C.
ZIPOETES			
NICOMEDES	28		278-250
ZIELAS	22		250-228
PRUSIAS I	48		228-180
PRUSIAS II	31		180-149
NICOMEDES II, *Epiphanes*	58		149- 91
NICOMEDES III, *Philopator*	17		91- 74

KINGS OF PONTUS

Name	Yrs.	Reigned Ms.	B.C.
ARIOBARZANES I			
MITHRIDATES I			
ARIOBARZANES II	26		363-337
MITHRIDATES II	35		337-302
MITHRIDATES III	36		302-266
ARIOBARZANES III	26		266-240
MITHRIDATES IV	50		240-190
PHARNACES I	34		190-156
MITHRIDATES V, *Evergetes*	36		156-120
MITHRIDATES VI, *Eupator*	57		120- 63
PHARNACES II	16		63- 47

KINGS OF CAPPADOCIA

Name	Yrs.	*Reigned* Ms.	B.C.
DATAMES			
ARIAMNES I			
ARIARATHES I			
ARIARATHES II	7		315-308
ARIAMNES II			
ARIARATHES III			
ARIARATHES IV	58		220-162
ARIARATHES V	32		162-130
ARIARATHES VI	34		130- 96
ARIOBARZANES I	30		93- 63
ARIOBARZANES II	21		63- 42
ARIARATHES VII	6		42- 36
			A.D.
ARCHELAUS	50		36- 15

KINGS OF ROME

ROMULUS	38		753-715
NUMA POMPILIUS	42		715-673
TULLUS HOSTILIUS	32		673-641
ANCUS MARCIUS	24		641-616
L. TARQUINIUS PRISCUS	38		616-578
SERVIUS TULLIUS	44		578-534
L. TARQUINIUS SUPERBUS	25		534-510

ROMAN EMPERORS

AUGUSTUS		14
TIBERIUS	23	14- 37
CALIGULA	4	37- 41
CLAUDIUS	13	41- 54
NERO	14	54- 68
GALBA		68- 69
OTHO		69- 69
VITELLIUS		69- 69
VESPASIAN	10	69- 79

457

Name	Yrs.	Reigned Ms.	B.C.
TITUS	2		79- 81
DOMITIAN	15		81- 96
NERVA	2		96- 98
TRAJAN	18		98-117
HADRIAN	21		117-138
ANTONINUS PIUS	23		138-161
M. AURELIUS ⎫	19		161-180
L. VERUS ⎭	8		161-169
COMMODUS	12		180-192
PERTINAX			193-193
SEPTIMUS SEVERUS	18		193-211
CARACALLA ⎫	6		211-217
GETA ⎭	1		211-212
MACRINUS	1		217-218
ELAGABALUS	4		216-222
ALEXANDER SEVERUS	13		222-235
MAXIMINUS	3		235-238
GORDIANUS I ⎫ GORDIANUS II ⎭			238-238
PUPIENUS MAXIMUS ⎫ BALBINUS ⎭			238-238
GORDIANUS III	6		238-244
PHILIPPUS	5		244-249
DECIUS	2		249-251
TREBONIANUS GALLUS	3		251-254
AEMILIANUS			253-253
VALERIAN ⎫	7		253-260
GALLIENUS ⎭	15		253-268
CLAUDIUS II	2		268-270
AURELIAN	5		270-275
TACITUS	1		275-276
FLORIANUS			276-276
PROBUS	6		276-282
CARUS	1		282-283

ROMAN EMPERORS—(*Continued*)

Name	*Yrs.*	Reigned *Ms.*	*B.C.*
CARINUS NUMERIANUS	1		283-284
DIOCLETIAN	21		284-305
MAXIMIAN	19		286-306
CONSTANTIUS I, *Chlorus*	1		305-306
GALERIUS	6		305-311
CONSTANTINE I, *the Great*	31		306-337
LICINIUS	16		307-323
CONSTANTINE II	3		337-340
CONSTANTIUS II	24		337-361
CONSTANS I	13		337-350
JULIAN	2		361-363
JOVIAN	1		363-364

(At this period comes Eastern and Western Emperors).

THE MOST IMPORTANT LATIN WRITERS

APPULEIUS
AULUS GELLIUS
CAESAR
CATO THE CENSOR
CATULLUS
CLAUDIAN
CICERO
ENNIUS
GAIUS
HORACE
HORTENSIUS
JUVENAL
LIVY
LUCAN
LUCRETIUS
MARCUS AURELIUS
MARTIAL

PERSIUS
PETRONIUS
PLAUTUS
PLINY THE ELDER
PLINY THE YOUNGER
PROPERTIUS
QUINTILIAN
SALLUST
SALVIUS JULIANUS
SENECA THE ELDER
SENECA THE YOUNGER
SUETONIUS
TACITUS
TERENCE
TIBULLUS
TREBONIAN
ULPIAN

OVID
PAPINIAN
PATERCULUS
PAULUS

VARRO
VIRGIL
VITRUVIUS

GREEK WRITERS AND ARTISTS

ACHILLES TATIUS
AESCHINES
AESCHYLUS
ALCAEUS
ALCMAN
ANACREON
ANDOCIDES
APELLES
APOLLONIUS RHODUS
ARCHILOCHUS
ARISTOPHANES
ARRIAN
ATHENAEUS
BACCHYLIDES
BRYGUS
CALLICRATES
CALLIMACHUS
CHARITON
DEMOSTHENES
DIOGENES LAERTIUS
EPICTETUS
EUPHRONIUS
EURIPIDES
EXECIAS
HELIDORUS
HERODOTUS
HESIOD
HOMER
ICTINUS
ISAEUS
ISOCRATES

LEONIDAS
LONGUS
LUCIAN
LYCIAS
LYSIPPUS
MELEAGER
MENANDER
MICON
MYRON
PANAEUS
PAUSANIAS
PHIDIAS
PINDAR
PLUTARCH
POLYBIUS
POLYCLETUS
POLYGNOTUS
PRAXITELES
PROCOPIUS
PYTHIUS
SAPPHO
SCOPAS
SIMONIDES
SOPHOCLES
STRABO
THEOCRITUS
THUCYDIDES
TYRTAEUS
XENOPHON
ZEUXIS

For dates and descriptions see under proper headings.

PHILOSOPHERS

AENESIDEMUS
ALCMAEON OF CROTON
AMMONIUS SACCAS
ANAXAGORAS
ANAXIMANDER
ANAXIMENES
ANNICERIS
ANTISTHENES
APOLLODORUS
ARCESILAUS
ARCHYTAS
ARISTIPPUS
ARISTOTLE
ARISTOXENUS
CARNEADES
CLITOMACHUS
CRANTOR
CRATES
DEMETRIUS OF
    PHALERUM
DEMOCRITUS
DIOGENES
EMPEDOCLES
EPICTETUS
EPICURUS
EUCLID OF MEGARA
EUDEMUS
GORGIAS
HEGESIAS
HETRODORUS

HERACLITUS
HERMARCHUS
HIPPIAS
IAMBLICHUS
LEUCIPPUS
MARCUS AURELIUS
MELISSUS
MENEDEMUS
PANAETUS
PARMENIDES
PHILOLAUS
PLATO
PLOTINUS
POLYSTRATUS
PORPHYRY
POSIDONIUS
PROCLUS
PRODICUS
PROTAGORAS
PYRRHO
SENECA
SOCRATES
SPEUSIPPUS
STILPO
THEODORUS
THEOPHRASTUS
XENOCRATES
XENOPHANES
ZENO
ZENO OF ELEA

For dates and description see under appropriate headings.

BIBLIOGRAPHY
General

Bailey, C., *The Legacy of Rome.*
Livingstone, Sir R. W., *The Legacy of Greece.*
Sandys, Sir J. E., *Companion to Latin Studies.*
Stobart, J. C., *The Grandeur that was Rome.*
Stobart, J. C., *The Glory that was Greece.*
Whibley, L., *Companion to Greek Studies.*

THE HITTITES
General

Baikie, J., *The Amarna Age.*
Cavaignac, E., *Les Hittites.*
Drower, M. S., *"Hittites" Article in latest Chambers Ency.*
Garstang, J., *The Land of the Hittites.*
Goetze, A., *Das Hethiter-Reich.*
Hogarth, D. G., *Hittite Civilization.*
Mercer, S. A. B., *The Tell-El-Amarna Tablets.*
Sayce, A. H., *The Hittites. The Story of a Forgotten Empire.*
Wright, W., *The Empire of the Hittites.*
Historical and Chronological Problems
Albright, W. F., *New Light on the History of Western Asia in the Second Millennium B.C.*
Hardy, R. S., *The Old Hittite Kingdom.*
Sayce, A. H., *What Happened After the Death of Tut'-ankhamun?*

The Battle of Kadesh
Breasted, J. H., *The Battle of Kadesh.*
Burne, A. H., *Some Notes on the Battle of Kadesh.*

Neo-Hittite Kingdoms
Hogarth, D. G., *The Hittites of Syria.*
Smith, S., *The Greek Trade at Al Mina.*

462

Karatepe

Bossert, H. T., *Found At Last: a Bi-lingual Key to the Previously Undecipherable Hittite Hieroglyphic Inscriptions.*

Religion

Albright, W. F., *The Anatolian Goddess Kubada.*
Garstang, J., *The Sun-goddess of Arinna.*
Gaster, T., *Thespis.*
Pettazzoni, R., *Confession of Sins in the Hittite Religion.*
Strong, H. A., and Garstang, J., *The Syrian Goddess.*

Law

Sturtevant, E. H., *Selections from the Code.*
Walther, A., *The Origin and History of Hebrew Law.*

THE ANCIENT WORLD
History

Bury, J. B., *History of Greece.*
Cary, M., *History of Rome to the Reign of Constantine.*
Cary, M., *Geographical Background of Greek and Roman History.*
Cochrane, C. N., *Christianity and Classical Culture.*
Frank, T., *An Economic Survey of Ancient Rome.*
Glotz, G., *The Aegaean Civilization.*
Heitland, W. E., *The Roman Republic.*
Nilsson, M. P., *Imperial Rome.*
Rostovtzeff, M., *A History of the Ancient World.*
Tarn, W. W., *Hellenistic Civilization.*
Zimmern, A. E., *The Greek Commonwealth.*

Art

Anderson, W. J., *The Architecture of Ancient Greece.*
Buschor, E., *Greek Vase Painting.*
Gardner, E. A., *The Art of Greece.*
Gardner, P., *New Chapters in Greek Art.*
Lawrence, A. W., *Later Greek Sculpture.*
Robertson, D. S., *Greek and Roman Architecture.*
Sachs, C., *The Rise of Music in the Ancient World.*
Strong, E., *Art in Ancient Rome.*

Swindler, M. H., *Ancient Painting.*
Walters, H. B., *The Art of the Romans.*

Literature

Atkins, J. W. H., *Literary Criticism in Antiquity.*
Bowra, C. M., *Greek Lyric Poetry.*
Harvey, Sir P., *Oxford Companion to Classical Literature.*
Mackail, J. W., *History of Latin Literature.*
Murray, G., *History of Ancient Greek Literature.*
Pickard-Canbridge, A. W., *Dithyramb, Tragedy and Comedy.*
Rose, H. J., *Handbook of Greek Literature.*
Sandys, Sir J. E., *History of Classical Scholarship.*
Sikes, E. E., *Roman Poetry.*

Philosophy

Barker, E., *Greek Political Theory.*
Benn, A. W., *The Greek Philosophers.*
Burnet, J., *Early Greek Philosophy.*
Gomperz, T., *Greek Thinkers.*
Jaeger, W., *Theology of the Early Greek Philosophers.*
Zeller, E., *History of Greek Philosophy.*

Religion

Altheim, F., *History of Roman Religion.*
Cook, A. B., *Zeus, A Study in Ancient Religion.*
Cumont, F., *Oriental Religions in Roman Paganism.*
Farnell, L. R., *The Cults of the Greek States.*
Glover, T. R., *Conflict of Religions in the Early Roman Empire.*
Guthrie, W. K. C., *The Greeks and Their Gods.*
Nilsson, M. P., *Minoan-Mycenean Religion.*
Rose, H. J., *Handbook in Greek Mythology.*

Science

Brock, A. J., *Greek Medicine.*
Heath, Sir T. L., *History of Greek Mathematics.*
Heitland, W. E., *Agricola.*
Tozer, H. F., *History of Ancient Geography.*

464

Naval and Military

Cheesman, G. L., *The Auxilia of the Roman Army.*
Clark, F. W., *Influence of Sea Power on the History of the Roman Republic.*
Parker, H. M. D., *The Roman Legions.*
Rose, H. J., *The Mediterranean in the Ancient World.*
Stan, C. G., *The Roman Imperial Navy.*
Tarn, W. W., *Hellenistic Military and Naval Developments.*
Torr, C., *Ancient Ships.*

Law

Bonner, R. J., and Smith, G., *The Administration of Justice from Homer to Aristotle.*
Buckland, W. W., *Textbook of Roman Law.*
Jolowicz, H. F., *Historical Introduction to the Study of Roman Law.*
Phillipson, C., *International Law and Custom of Ancient Greece and Rome.*
Strachan-Davidson, J. L., *Problems of the Roman Criminal Law.*